ART AND LITERATURE UNDER THE BOLSHEVIKS
Volume One

ART AND LITERATURE UNDER THE BOLSHEVIKS

Volume One: The Crisis of Renewal 1917–1924

Brandon Taylor

PLUTO  PRESS

London • Concord, Mass

First published in 1991 by Pluto Press
345 Archway Road, London, N6 5AA
and 141 Old Bedford Road,
Concord, MA 01742, USA

British Library Cataloguing-in-Publication Data
Taylor, Brandon
    Art and Literature under the Bolsheviks.
    Volume one: the crisis of renewal 1917–1924.
    1. Soviet Union. Arts, history
    I. Title
    700'.947

        ISBN   0-7453-0293-9   Vol I
        ISBN   0-7453-0556-3   Vol II

Library of Congress Cataloging-in-Publication Data
Taylor, Brandon
    Art and literature under the Bolsheviks / Brandon Taylor.
        p. cm.
    Includes bibliographical references and index.
    Contents: Contents: v. 1. The crisis of renewal 1917–1924 –
v. 2. Authority and revolution 1924–1932.
    ISBN 0-7453-0293-9
    1. Arts, Soviet. 2. Socialist realism in art–Soviet Union. 3. Arts,
Modern–20th century–Soviet Union. 4. Art and state–Soviet Union.
I. Title.
NX556.A1T39 1991
700'.947'09041–dc20   90-28332
                                                                  CIP

Designed by Ray Addicott

Typeset by Archetype, Stow-on-the-Wold

Printed and bound in the UK

Contents

List of Illustrations

In Memory
of my Father
VERNON TAYLOR

Introduction

Thus the new times are born, in the din of toil, in eyes glazed and dying with fatigue... Do you know how to cook soup out of a hatchet? We shall teach you this magic chemistry.

from Sergey Bobrov, *The Revolt of the Misanthropes*, 1922[1]

1. V. Zavalishin, *Early Soviet Writers*, Atlantic Books, New York, 1958, p 89.

This is the first of two volumes about art and the Bolshevik Party in the Soviet Union in the years between the October Revolution of 1917 and the Decree 'On the Reconstruction of Artistic and Literary Organisations' of April 1932; that is, between one of the most dramatic upheavals in modern political history and a moment, almost fifteen years later, when a small yet far-reaching administrative change brought one momentous period to a close and simultaneously marked the beginning of another. But the purpose of the story that I attempt to tell in these pages is to re-connect the cultural events and aspirations of the period to the economic and ideological patterns of the time. The central proposition of these books is that the history of the art of this period is well nigh indistinguishable from the history of the political party that nurtured and cajoled it. The visual arts and literature are our central concern; yet we shall be interested in music, the theatre and, to a lesser extent, in architecture, town planning and film.

It is surprising that such a history has never been written before. No doubt the traditional institutional cleavage between art history and political history is partly responsible; though the full explanation is certain to be more complex. As things stand, much in Soviet culture in the period immediately following the Revolution is almost impossible to recognise, and Soviet visual art, particularly, has been badly misrepresented in Western scholarship. In keeping with the principles of 'modernism' generally, painting and sculpture in Russia in the 1920s have been depicted as playing a largely autonomous role in relation to the vicissitudes of the Soviet state; in effect a history of 'works' by 'individuals' which more or less successfully conformed to the prospectus of modernist culture as it developed in very different conditions in the West.

Such misrepresentations have their own aetiology. Because of the circumstances of the Civil War in Russia in 1918–20, fanned by the attempts of British and French forces to foment counter-revolution on

Soviet soil, little accurate information about the arts became available to the rest of the world during that period and the one that followed. What was available was selective and intermittent. The reactions of the Soviet Union in the 1920s to the crises of capitalism in Western Europe and the USA, combined with growing Soviet isolationism at home throughout that decade, meant that very few Soviet paintings, drawings or sculptures left the country for foreign collections and museums – an absence that remains almost complete, to this day. Visits to the Soviet Union by critics, writers and intellectuals with a marked interest in the visual arts were few and far between. Exhibitions of Soviet art abroad during the 1920s were significant, taken singly, but few in number. Most have been forgotten, and appear only marginally in accounts of the artistic life of the countries concerned. Who has ever seen more than the occasional scholarly reference to the exhibitions by Robert Falk and David Shterenberg at the 1924 Venice Biennale, to the 1929 'Exhibition of the Association of the Artists of the Revolution' in Cologne, or to the 1924 'Exhibition of Soviet Art' in New York?

An exception is the 'Erste Russische Kunstausstellung' (First Russian Exhibition) at the Van Diemen Gallery in Berlin in 1922, which has proved significant for subsequent Western interpretations. Composed of a stylistically wide variety of work, it was nevertheless the 'avant-garde' section that attracted greatest attention from Western artists and critics; and this was seen largely in terms of the West's own modernist preconceptions of the time, that is, *without* any of the social and revolutionary context from which, and in several cases against which, the work had in fact developed.

Such was the perception of a young artist and critic from the United States, Louis Lozowick. Lozowick was studying at the Friedrich-Wilhelm University in Berlin at the time, and his 1925 book *Modern Russian Art*, though researched partly in Moscow, was based largely upon his experiences of the Van Diemen Gallery show. Lozowick makes such statements as, 'modern Russian art reached its greatest intensity and its greatest fertility during the Revolution'; he also says that

> when the Soviets assumed power they . . . at once found allies in the radical artists, the Futurists as they were called. The alliance was very quickly established before the conservative, recognised Academicians had time to decide what orientation to take. The Futurists on their part were quick to discover an inherent affinity between themselves and the revolutionists; had they not also revolted against old accepted standards and been considered social outcasts?[2]

2. L. Lozowick, *Modern Russian Art*, Société Anonyme, New York, 1925, pp 11, 5.

Here begins the myth that the 'revolutionary' art and the revolutionary politics of the Bolshevik period are in all essentials the same thing. The myth was perpetuated by Alfred H. Barr, who proposed in his influential exhibition and book *Cubism and Abstract Art* of 1936, that abstraction was 'the particular problem' by which artists of the early twentieth century were obsessed.[3] In his notorious diagram charting the 'development' of twentieth-century art, Russian and Soviet art *as a whole* is represented by Suprematism and Constructivism, which

3. A. H. Barr, *Cubism and Abstract Art*, Museum of Modern Art, New York, 1936, p 11.

appear as stepping-stones on the direct road from Parisian Cubism to something Barr calls 'Geometrical Abstract Art' (Figure 1). On the relation of politics to art, Barr neatly assimilates the familiar idea that the Futurists, Suprematists and Constructivists had been 'artistically revolutionary' under the Tsars with the very fact of the social Revolution of 1917. After this date, Barr says, these artists

> came into their own. For three years they dominated the artistic life of the larger cities, taught in the art academies, designed posters, floats in parades, statues to Marxian heroes and gigantic Cubistic facades to screen the Winter Palace during mass celebrations.

Kazimir Malevich's painting 'White on White' of 1918 (Figure 13), asserts Barr, 'might have counted as a *tabula-rasa* upon which to build a new art for a new order, but' – here the argument collapses – 'it was as unintelligible to the proletariat as his earlier Suprematist pictures had been to the bourgeoisie'.[4] Barr says that although left-wing art and literature was supported by 'highly cultivated' Bolsheviks such as Trotsky and Lunacharsky, Lenin branded it an 'infantile disorder'. Toleration turned to impatience. 'Today' (that is, in 1936), abstraction in art 'is still considered a "left deviation" in the USSR and is discouraged.'[5]

Barr's confident oversimplifications here, such as that Trotsky 'supported' left-wing art, that 'White on White' alone might have provided a basis for a new art, that Lunacharsky remained benign, that Lenin, by contrast, was a 'philistine with power',[6] are no less important than the fact that *Cubism and Abstract Art* treats only five or six individuals at all extensively in the post-1917 period: Malevich, Alexandr Rodchenko, Lazar Lisitsky, Vladimir Tatlin, Naum Gabo and Antoine Pevsner. In point of historical fact, however, Soviet artists of this period are to be counted in their dozens, even hundreds, and the ideology of the 'individual artist' was under severe attack from inside the Soviet Union itself.

The myth of a handful of 'great modernists' as constituting the whole of early Soviet art has proved remarkably efficacious. Malevich remains the most widely documented Russian and Soviet artist of his generation. Tatlin and Rodchenko are still paraded as creative demi-gods of 'revolutionary art', as if this was somehow their revolution alone, or as if no questions could be asked about the meaning that this art might have had for those in whose name the Revolution was waged. Nor is anything heard of the other Soviet artists, those who practised figurative or 'realist' styles, or who clung to pre-Revolutionary practices, or who did not join what Western critics called the 'avant-garde'. And because abstraction did indeed enter a period of re-evaluation in the Soviet Union after about 1922, Soviet art as a whole is still represented as if it virtually came to a full-stop after that date. Soviet art which did not conform to the Western idea of the modernist 'avant-garde' has been written out of history as if it did not exist. (It may as well be explained here that I reserve the use of quotation marks for the words 'realist' and 'realism' throughout

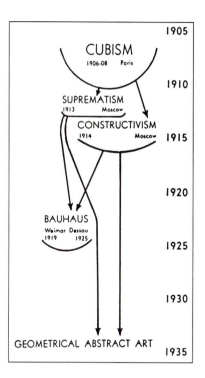

Figure 1
Diagram from A. Barr, *Cubism and Abstract Art*, 1936

4. Ibid., p 16.

5. Ibid., p 17.

6. Ibid., p 18.

this book, except for quoted cases. This is because the terms are at once contentious and much disputed – no less so now than after 1917 – and cannot be taken at face value in the often highly rhetorical prose of the day. The term 'avant-garde' was not much in use, and similarly cannot be taken as descriptive.)

Camilla Gray, too, whose book *The Great Experiment: Russian Art 1863–1922* has done so much since its publication in 1962 to popularise the subject, unfortunately repeats many of Barr's misconceptions (Barr had been one of her mentors). Gray repeats the well-worn nostrum that the Futurists identified themselves with the Revolution (as a group they did not). She reasserts the prominent place occupied by Malevich, Tatlin et al., to the virtual exclusion of most other groups and affiliations. She ends her book with mention of 'an exhibition of abstract art' at the Van Diemen Gallery in Berlin in 1922. In fact the Van Diemen Gallery exhibition was a stylistically eclectic show, in which abstract art was in a numerical minority. And the year 1922 marks the end of Camilla Gray's book. Hence nothing is heard of the founding of such groups as the Society of Easel Painters (Obshchestvo khudozhnikov-stankovistov or OST), Four Arts, or the Association of Artists of Revolutionary Russia (Assotsiatsiya khudozhnikov revolyutsionnoi Rossii or AKhRR), the largest and most problematic art organisation of the period and the one that may be said to have dominated the majority of other art groups before the passage of the April Decree in 1932. By ending her account in 1922, the impression has further persisted that art itself stopped in Soviet Russia in that year. Yet nothing could be further from the truth.

Gray ends her book with the following words:

> In Russia itself, so all over Western Europe, artists were fired by the experiment of Communism which was so convincingly being worked out there; from all over Western Europe artists looked to Russia for the realisation of their 'new' vision, for in Communism they saw the answer to the sad isolation of the artist from society which the capitalist economy had introduced. In Russia, under this new-born regime, they felt a great experiment was being made in which, for the first time since the middle ages, the artist and his art was embodied in the make-up of the common life, art was given a working job, and the artist considered a responsible member of society.[7]

7. C. Gray, *The Great Experiment: Russian Art, 1863–1922*, Thames and Hudson, London, 1962, p 255.

Unfortunately it is not true that Russian artists were universally fired by the experiment of communism, nor that Western artists looked to Russia in anything like the terms described. Communism was by no means being 'convincingly worked out', if that means that its path was easy or that there was general agreement on what forms of organisation it should take. The idea that the artist was suddenly awarded a badge of 'responsibility' after 1917 is sheer nonsense, where this implies that only hooliganism prevailed before, or that there was a clear standard of what 'responsible' artistic behaviour in such circumstances could mean.

It was not like that at all. What I have tried to do in these pages is to construct a picture of artistic life and debate in the Soviet Union which, I hope in some contrast, conveys something of the language in which its virtually intractable problems were discussed and which acted as the vehicle for some of the fiercest aesthetic and political controversy of modern times. Nothing is more startling than precisely the disunity into which this period fell; the myriad forms and devices, the rhetorical flourishes and obscurities, the earnestness of the discussion, the grandeur, the comedy and the tragedy of its results. Perhaps seldom before was so much felt to be at stake in art, with so few sure signposts as to its realisation. It was not modernism that was being pursued; but capitalism that was being tested and contested, both in practice and in theory. Whether Soviet artists could respond to these challenges, and how, is the real story of these books.

*   *   *

Volume One covers the period from the Revolution to the death of Lenin in 1924. In one sense this was indeed a period of dazzling experiment in the visual and other arts. The legacy of Constructivism, abstraction, the machine aesthetic, the fertile *zaum* experiment in poetry, and much more, sent ripples of significance into the West that have still not been forgotten. Great achievements in graphic art, painting, poetry, public decoration and theatre came in the first flush of optimism that a new kind of society was in the making – along with altogether new kinds of men and women. Part, at least, of this 'avant-garde' was persuaded of the link between cultural renewal and the social and political revolution that was then unfolding before them. And yet this is only half, or less, of the story of early Soviet culture. To what extent were these experiments carried out in utopian disregard of the actual facts of the Revolution – which included misery, privation, administrative confusion, Bolshevik coercion and an atmosphere of unfreedom for a sizeable majority? What relationship could the newer forms and rhythms be expected to have with Russian (and other) traditions in art and literature? And what precisely *was* the art of the bourgeoisie in that first post-Revolutionary scene? Could policy be formulated at the level of the state? Could it be made to stick? What could 'the proletariat' – that newest and most vital category – be expected to devise on its own behalf?

The enormous conceptual and organisational problems which lay lurking in these questions were all active and important in the period of Lenin. But there is nothing magical or inviolable about 1924, the date of his death. It has a certain symbolic importance, perhaps, in view of the significant realignments in the upper echelons of the Party which followed his demise. Yet in another sense the death of Lenin is no more than a point in a more or less unbroken chain of reversals and continuities. To draw out only two arguments from the present volume: the apogee of 'avant-garde' art around 1918–21, far from announcing the death-knell of easel painting, figure sculpture, narrative plays and poems, in fact precipitated their revival in a wide variety of both contemporary and traditional forms. Thus, by the time of Lenin's death in 1924, several new groupings in the various arts –

many of them dependent on pre-Revolutionary theories and media – were already viable and flourishing. We shall want to explore whether to ascribe this revival to an international tendency to return to traditional standards in the 1920s – as occurred in France, Britain, Italy and the United States – or to the particular vicissitudes of Soviet power; or perhaps to a mixture of both. Then, secondly, I want to emphasise how Bolshevism as a system of government, particularly in its coercive and warring character, not to mention its tendency to secrecy and factionalism, was well established before Lenin quit the scene. The strained relationship which sprung up between the Party-State and the various artistic groups – at once encouraging and censorious, permissive and stern, tolerant yet demanding – was born long before 1924, and lasted until long after. Bolshevism as a system never did have an unproblematic relation to the arts. And of course that system itself was created from within Lenin's own embattled administration.

While Volume Two covers the period from 1924 to 1932 and hence is concerned with the arts under the post-Lenin administration, it is the continuities that must be stressed as much as the ruptures and changes of direction. But changes of emphasis, of weight, of style, there definitely were. The pre-1924 question that came to dominate discussions of the arts after 1924 was the degree of authority that the Party could and perhaps should exert over cultural discussions. Artists were deeply aware of this, just as they had been in the time of Lenin. But in the period to 1928, the debate was complicated by two facts which lay in contradistinction to each other: one was the restoration of a quasi-market economy, an atmosphere of relative artistic and cultural tolerance, and a margin of material prosperity, which produced, despite Bolshevism rather than because of it, something of a plural market for art; the other was a factional war at the heart of the Communist Party for control of the policy machine, and hence ultimately of the economic and cultural direction of the country.

Therefore, from one point of view, the middle and later 1920s was a period in which Soviet artists enjoyed a relative absence of the turbulence that had characterised the Revolution and the Civil War. The 'avant-garde' was now being reassessed; art could be seen linking hands once more with accessibility, with pleasure, with historical memory, even in some quarters with 'art for art's sake'. Yet this perspective was not to last. Bolshevism was not ultimately hospitable to relaxation and to market standards. To staunch communists, cultural pluralism seemed (at the very least) to imply political pluralism; and having submitted the country to a decisive 'break' with the capitalist world, there were plenty who would object vociferously to the sudden and apparently expedient change of direction. Furthermore, the international economy was on the point of collapse. The struggle inside the Party by the end of 1927 was coming to a decisive head. The so-called 'Left Opposition' was on the point of defeat; grain deficits, according to one analysis, were destabilising the economy. What is termed the 'cultural revolution' of 1928–32 was the result. For the arts, this period saw a highly volatile combination of popular agitation, coercion, and the eventual super-imposition of a limited number of cultural norms.

Thus by 1932 the first phase of revolutionary Bolshevism can be said to have ended, or come to grief. Or was it two phases? Or three? Or five? What were the losses and gains of the twentieth century's first revolutionary administration? And what were its prospects?

In one sense the abiding questions for both the Party and the artists of the Soviet Union throughout this period could be formulated simply: what should the extent of the Party's supervision of the arts be? What could artists do to persuade the Party that its own particular aesthetic convictions were the 'true' convictions of Bolshevism? And what could the Bolshevik Party do to reconcile the apparently irreconcilable demands of political firmness of purpose and the 'freedom' to create? To what extent should 'supervision' mean 'control'? How could you have Bolshevism *without* control? And how could you have had the great days of 1917 without Bolshevism?

Others will judge the extent to which these questions have been fully explored in the pages which follow. In many cases the evidence remains incomplete, or sketchy. In many cases it is distorted intolerably by the biases of cultural policy following 1932, the so-called 'Stalin period', in which Soviet history was rewritten 'from above' in ways that are now becoming familiar to observers both in the Soviet Union and here. But the first fifteen years of Bolshevik rule are undoubtedly relevant as never before. In the rapidly changing world of the 'Gorbachev revolution', the Soviet arts are again experiencing the tensions of being attracted by the allure of the market model of production, at the same time as remaining conscious of their Soviet and Russian past. How the story will end we do not know. My greatest wish is that artists of today and tomorrow – in the Soviet Union and elsewhere – will find something in these pages to assimilate.

*   *   *

I have many debts to discharge. The published accounts of Russian and Soviet literature in the 1920s are nowhere so bleak as are those for the visual arts, and I have drawn extensively from Herman Ermolaev's and Robert Maguire's researches into the novelists and poets of the period, just as I have done from Sheila Fitzpatrick's pioneering work on the Soviet cultural and educational administration, Alec Nove's researches in Soviet economics, and Christina Lodder's account of an important strand of Soviet art in the post-Revolutionary period, that of Constructivism. I have acknowledged my debts to these scholars in the many footnotes to the book, and in the text itself. To other colleagues and friends I owe many types of gratitude: to Genady Dobrov, Evgeny Barabanov, Alexey Sinodov, Andrey Kovalev and John Crowfoot, for discussions they had with me in the Soviet Union; to Mikhail Sokolov, Sergey Klokov and Helena Bespalova, who helped me to see works of art in Moscow; to Robin Milner-Gulland, Colin Bearne, Peter Townsend, Nick

Stephens, Andrew Graham-Dixon, Tom Gilhespy, Charles Darwent, Roxane Permar, Roy Miles, Felix Holzapfel and Paul Pavlikowski for many types of encouragement and moral support during a hectic period of work; to Toby Clark and Neil Edmunds for letting me see unpublished writings of their own; to Christina Lodder and John E. Bowlt for answering letters of inquiry promptly and helpfully; to Brian Wallis of *Art in America*; to Henry Meyric-Hughes, Liz Moloney and Gill Hedley of the British Council for helping with travel arrangements to the Soviet Union; and to the library staff of the British Library and Tate Gallery, London, of the School of Slavonic and East European Studies, London University, of the Museum of Modern Art, New York, of the Getty Centre for the Humanities, Santa Monica, and of the Central Reference Library in Winchester, Hampshire for their unfailingly competent aid in times of scholarly need. Numerous other friends supplied me with books and answered photographic enquiries, and to all these I am grateful. I must particularly thank the following people for unflagging help in obtaining photographs: Lidiya Iovleva, Vitold Petrushenko and Katyana Gubanova of the State Tretyakov Gallery, Moscow; Evgenia Petrova and Julia Dovgard of the State Russian Museum, Leningrad; Ingeborg Sperl of the Austrian Museum of Applied Arts, Vienna; Chris Morgan and Andrew Lord of the Society for Cultural Relations with the USSR, London; the Novosti Press Agency, London; Lynne Green of the City Art Gallery, Southampton; Janet Moore of the Museum of Modern Art, Oxford; David King, Sue Kay and Julia Bearcroft. Permission to publish photographs was generously granted by numerous organisations and individuals, and this is recorded in the picture captions.

The manuscript was read in various of its stages by Elizabeth Hunkin, Colin Bearne, Roxane Permar and Toby Clark, all of whom offered suggestions for improvement which I was happy to accept. A particular debt of gratitude is due to Marianne With, Elisabeth Hunkin, Alys Blakeway, Geoffrey Reynolds, Jeremy Howard and Karen Barratt, who helped me with translations from Russian and German sources and without whom this book would have remained a clear impossibility. I am very grateful to my typists, Frances Childs and Carrie Breach, who shouldered the difficult task of deciphering the text; to my daughters Frances and Camilla Taylor who helped arrange the bibliography; and to my wife Lucy who supported the project with remarkable goodwill. I must finally record my gratitude to Mark Jones, who first suggested I write this book, and to his wife Natalya Jones, who have been generous hosts on two of my visits to the Soviet Union. To them and to my editors at Pluto I offer my deepest gratitude.

Note on Transliteration

Of the available transliteration systems I have chosen the first of those recommended in J. Thomas Shaw's *The Transliteration of Modern Russian for English-Language Publications*, University of Wisconsin Press, Madison, 1967, pp 3–11, as giving a largely accessible pattern which nevertheless looks familiar to the English reader. The exceptions are certain well-known names which already have an anglicised form in widespread use; thus Moussorgsky, Scriabin, Tchaikovsky, Zinoviev; also *Leon* Trotsky, *Joseph* Stalin, Comintern, etc. I have italicised only the names of books, journals, plays and musical works. Groups are left plain; thus *LEF*, but also LEF. In the main I have used the English form for a group name, but in certain cases the Russian seemed to me comprehensible once introduced: thus we have Four Arts, but Pereval. 'October' is used for the writers' group of 1922, 'Oktyabr' for the artists of 1928; and so forth. The now standard acronyms have been used for political and cultural groups, eg. OST, VAPP, NOZh, VSNKh. For expansions the glossary may be consulted.

1

Before October

The Bolshevik Party and the Arts

The Russian Social-Democratic Workers' Party, which met for the first time in March 1898, cannot be said to have been overly concerned with the arts. The manifesto to which this meeting gave rise, written by Peter Struve (who shortly afterwards deserted the Party), did however refer to the right of the Russian working class to 'a share in the administration of the state, freedom of the spoken and written word, (and) freedom of organisation and assembly'[1] – perhaps the earliest suggestion that literature, and by implication the other arts, were to be free and unconstrained in the new social order which would be founded by the rapidly rising proletarian class. In outline, Struve's manifesto followed the 1848 *Communist Manifesto* of Karl Marx and Friedrich Engels in postulating the overthrow of capitalism first by a bourgeois-democratic revolution and then by a proletarian-socialist revolution, as historically inevitable steps on the path to a classless society; and, like the *Communist Manifesto*, carried the suggestion that the interests of the proletariat as a class, including its cultural interests, would at a certain stage diverge from those of the bourgeois class.[2]

But when and by what means they would do so were by no means clear in 1898. When the young revolutionary Vladimir Ulyanov (called 'Lenin' to disguise his identity from the Tsarist police) (Figure 2) took steps to reunite the dispersed and poorly organised Social-Democratic Workers' Party around the magazine *Iskra* (Spark) in the first five years of the twentieth century, it was on a platform of proletarian uprising against exploitation, in concert with the workers of other countries. Lenin's faction within the *Iskra* group was staunchly opposed to the concept of peasant rebellion, spontaneous or otherwise, such as had been promulgated by the Narodniks of the 1870s, and was hostile to economic reform without political agitation to accompany it. This faction was implacably set against the various 'legal' Marxist groups whose interest was likewise in peaceful and gradual reform, and hoped to see the closest possible links between the coming bourgeois revolution and the proletarian revolution which, in Marx's scheme, would soon follow. Lenin believed that Russian Social-Democracy was vitally concerned with

1. *VKP (B) v Rezolyutsiyakh* (1941), i, pp 3–5; E. H. Carr, *The Bolshevik Revolution 1917–23*, Vol 1 (1950), Pelican, Harmondsworth, 1986 edition, p 15.

2. K. Marx and F. Engels, *The Communist Manifesto*, 1848; Penguin Books, Harmondsworth, 1967, pp 79–94.

Figure 2
V. I. Lenin, photograph from police files (photo: *David King*)

1

both the overcoming of feudalism and absolutism by the bourgeois
class (a contest in which the proletariat would have a stake) *and* with
the fight against capitalism, in which the proletariat would quickly
turn against the bourgeoisie themselves.

This conception of rapidly succeeding revolutionary stages was of
great importance to Lenin and the other Bolshevik leaders because it
suggested a period when bourgeois culture and proletarian culture
would have to coexist in a state first of cooperation, then of increasing
antagonism, followed by final separation. Yet there was to be little
unanimity about when, or how, this cycle of events would occur.
Some activists within the Party would argue for the existence of
purely proletarian culture, issuing as it were naturally from the soul
of the working class. Others would argue that such a thing did not,
and could not, yet exist. Others would argue for a period of essentially
bourgeois cultural dominance, until the day came when the time for
the final conversion to socialism was ripe. But since it was acknowledged in almost all revolutionary circles that Russia, compared with
Western Europe, was still a very backward country, one in which the
ground for even a bourgeois revolution had scarcely yet been laid,
much was conceded to depend upon the precise course that social
and political events would finally take.

Another important plank in Lenin's revolutionary theory (and by
1905 he was acknowledged to be the leading theorist of Social-
Democracy, easily capable of challenging the far older Plekhanov on
this ground) concerned the nature of a revolutionary party and its
most effective mode of organisation. Lenin argued consistently that
the political consciousness of the proletariat would not evolve from
within, spontaneously, but needed organising and encouraging 'from
without'.[3] This in turn required a 'theory' of revolutionary action,
which in its turn required the existence of a leading group of intellectuals from whom this theory would flow. It followed from this that
the Social-Democratic Workers' Party, in Lenin's hands, would have
to contain a small, élite group of professional revolutionary thinkers
who would not only formulate theory but who would be charged
with putting it into effect. Further, it seemed to follow from the
relatively undeveloped political consciousness of the proletariat that
such thinkers would for the most part, and initially, be drawn from
the ranks of the bourgeoisie. Such an élite Party group would form
the 'vanguard' of the class whose interests it formulated and represented. Numerically and in class terms this vanguard would necessarily be somewhat distinct from the proletariat, but would 'lead' the
proletariat to the point where, in economic and political theory as well
as in culture, it would prove able to lead itself.

Thus in Lenin's conception the Party would not be identical to the
working mass, but in a certain important sense would stand apart
from it.[4] Just how far apart would become another question of great
importance for the cultural life of the country in the revolutionary
period that was imminent. On the one hand there stood the historic
example of the intelligentsia in Russia in the 1870s whose 'going to
the people' had proved them capable of flexibility and real commitment, at least; on the other hand it would be alleged that an inde-

3. V. Lenin, *Polnoe sobranie sochineniya*,
iv, p 422; Carr, 1950, p 27.

4. V. Lenin, *Sochineniya*, iv, p 465; Carr,
p 30.

pendent revolutionary intelligentsia, drawn from the ranks of the nobility and the disaffected bourgeoisie, would find it impossible to identify completely and genuinely with the consciousness and aspirations of the proletarian (and even more the peasant) class.

It was in organisational terms too that Lenin's early views were to become of decisive significance later. The very nature and extent of Tsarist autocracy made it impossible for a socialist or revolutionary party to lead an open and legal existence. What Lenin himself characterised as the 'police state' under the Tsars was given to arresting and imprisoning revolutionary groups of all shades and degrees of commitment. In Lenin's view this gave rise to the need for a small, tightly organised group of professional revolutionary agitators whose operations would, in Lenin's words, be subject to 'the strictest secrecy', 'the strictest choice of members' and 'complete comradely confidence'.[5] Broad organisations such as trade unions and factory groups (and by implication cultural groups, though these were not yet central to the discussion) would contain very small Party 'fractions' which would receive instructions from the Central Committee of the Party and would consider themselves bound by the strictest loyalty to carry these instructions out.

It was this emphasis on loyalty and discipline which first separated the Bolsheviks (or majority group) from the Mensheviks (or minority group) at the Second Congress of the Russian Social-Democratic Workers' Party in Brussels and London in the Summer of 1903. It was here for the first time that Marx's slogan 'the dictatorship of the proletariat' was mentioned openly in the Party programme, alongside demands for freedom of conscience, speech, press and assembly, and a wide range of social and economic demands. It called once more for the overthrow of the Tsarist autocracy and the convening of a 'constituent assembly', elected by the whole people. Yet on the decisive question of attitude and Party organisation, the Bolsheviks urged intense personal commitment and direct revolutionary participation, while the Mensheviks took the 'softer' line of gradual reform and less centralised leadership and authority. Lenin, for example, came in for the harshest criticism from Georgy Plekhanov, who accused him of 'bonapartism', of 'confusing the dictatorship of the proletariat with dictatorship over the proletariat';[6] while Lenin viewed Plekhanov as willing to make concessions to bourgeois and reformist groups and to let Party unity go to the winds. The young Trotsky at this stage sided with the Mensheviks against Lenin – indeed repeated Plekhanov's accusation.[7] The German revolutionary Rosa Luxemburg accused him of 'ultra-centralism, which could lead easily to conservatism'.[8] Accusations of Jacobinism abounded. Yet Lenin remained convinced that Party unity and Party discipline were essential. In practice the day-to-day life of an active revolutionary was an immensely difficult one. Constant harassment by the police, the need to resort frequently to 'Aesopian' language to conceal one's true intent, makeshift domestic arrangements, imprisonment, and lengthy periods of exile were stock-in-trade. Much of the atmosphere of intrigue which later became characteristic both of Party discussions and cultural debate can be traced directly to this formative experience.

5. V Lenin, *Sochineniya*, iv, p 466; Carr, 1950, p 32; also Lenin, *What is to be Done?*, 1902, passim.

6. G. Plekhanov, *Sochineniya*, xiii, pp 90–1; Carr, 1950, p 44.

7. L. Trotsky, *Our Political Tasks*, 1904.

8. R. Luxemburg, *Neue Zeit*, xxii, Vienna, 1903–4, ii, pp 484–92, 529–35; Carr, 1950, p 46.

The tendency of the Bolshevik Party organisation to exclude – for better or worse – those whom it believed to be antagonistic to its interests is perfectly exemplified in Lenin's article of late 1905 on 'Party Organisation and Party Literature', the first substantial Party statement on artistic and cultural matters and one which came to acquire almost symbolic status in later discussions of literary policy among Party theorists. Published towards the end of the frustrated 1905 revolution in a period in which the hitherto 'illegal' press was suddenly granted rights of publication and dissemination, 'Party Organisation and Party Literature' was in fact concerned both with the publication of Party pamphlets, newspapers and broadsheets and with the authorship of novels, poems and plays; indeed it conflates them. But it is the argument over exclusion which concerns us immediately. Lenin's reasoning is to the effect that literature in general 'must become Party Literature'.[9] In contradistinction to 'literary careerism' and 'individualism' (what Lenin calls 'aristocratic anarchism and the drive for profit'), he urges that the proletariat must put into practice the principle of Party literature 'as fully and completely as possible'.

9.   V. Lenin, 'Party Organisation and Party Literature', *Novaya zhizn*, no 12, November 13, 1905; *Collected Works*, Vol 10, Lawrence and Wishart, London, 1960–70, p 45.

Lenin asks, what is this principle of Party literature?

> It is not simply that, for the socialist proletariat, literature cannot be a means of enriching individuals or groups; it cannot, in fact, be an individual undertaking, independent of the common cause of the proletariat. Down with non-partisan writers! Down with literary supermen! Literature must become *part* of the common cause of the proletariat, 'a cog and a screw' of one single great Social-Democratic mechanism set in motion by the entire politically conscious vanguard of the entire working-class. Literature must become a component of organised, planned and integrated Social-Democratic Party work.[10]

10.   Lenin, 'Party Organisation', p 45.

However he also asserts that

> Literature is least of all subject to mechanical adjustment and levelling . . . [there is] no question, either, but that in this field scope must undoubtedly be allowed for personal initiative, individual inclination, thought and fantasy, form and content . . . [which] shows that the literary side of the proletarian Party cause cannot be mechanically identified with its other sides.[11]

11.   Ibid., p 46.

But in spite of this concession he urges that

> The organised socialist proletariat must keep an eye on all this work, supervise it in its entirety, from beginning to end, without any exception, infuse into it the life-stream of the living proletarian cause, thereby cutting the ground from under the old, semi-Oblomov, semi-shopkeeper Russian principle: the writer does the writing, the reader does the reading.[12]

12.   Ibid., p 46.

13.   Ibid., p 47.

Lenin cautions loudly here against 'any kind of standardised system, or a solution by means of a few decrees'.[13] Yet freedom from 'careerism' and from 'bourgeois anarchist individualism' would come only from the subordination of literature to Party control. And then comes the argument for exclusion:

Everyone is free to write and say whatever he likes, without any restric-
tion. But every voluntary association (including a Party) is also free to
expel members who use the name of the Party to advocate anti-Party
views . . . I am bound to accord you, in the name of free speech, the full
right to shout, lie and write to your heart's content. But you are bound to
grant me, in the name of freedom of association, the right to enter into, or
withdraw from, association with people advocating this or that view. The
Party is a voluntary association which [Lenin candidly confesses] would
inevitably break up, finish ideologically and then physically, if it did not
cleanse itself of people advocating anti-Party views.[14]

14. Lenin, 'Party Organisation', p 47.

It will be immediately apparent that Lenin's 1905 formula was a
complex one, capable of being read as a programme for strict Party
control, yet equally capable of being seen as a plea for 'a broad,
multi-form and varied literature inseparably linked with the Social-
Democratic working class movement'.[15] Conceptually too it had its
inner complexities: 'freedom to associate' is identified with 'freedom
to exclude'; while the agent of exclusion is clearly the 'I' of Lenin's
own voice. What is completely unambiguous is the strength of
Lenin's disquiet with the hypocrisy of the 'freedom' sought by the
bourgeois writer, which is nothing more than 'an anarchist phrase',
a false spirit of libertarianism which in reality is yoked to the demands
of the bourgeois publisher for profits. This is the source of Lenin's
plea for a literature which will serve, 'not some satiated heroine, not
the "upper ten thousand" suffering from fatty degeneration, but the
millions and tens of millions of working people – the flower of the
country, its strength and its future'.[16]

15. Ibid., p 49.

16. Ibid., pp 48–9.

The urgency of Lenin's declamations against 'bourgeois freedom'
in this passage is a useful measure of the distance that the Bolsheviks
would soon establish from the Menshevik side of the Social-Democratic Party. The immediate contest was the 1905 revolution itself –
the massive demonstration led by Father Gapon in January, which
was massacred in St Petersburg, followed by paralysing strikes and
peasant uprisings in the spring and autumn – and the question which
now presented itself in starkly practical terms, whether this had
indeed been the bourgeois revolution which both Bolsheviks and
Mensheviks alike had been predicting. For the Mensheviks it was still
essential to complete a bourgeois revolution and establish a more or
less stable version of capitalism (and with it a wholly capitalist and
bourgeois culture) *before* the socialist revolution could be seriously
entertained. A new constitution had been introduced in October 1905,
sanctioning the existence of a Duma (consultative assembly) form of
government in St Petersburg alongside a workers' 'soviet' or autonomous, elective and self-regulating committee. At the time of the 1905
revolution Lenin too believed some form of bourgeois revolution was
essential to prepare the way for the eventual transition to socialism:
'there is not and cannot be any other path to real freedom for the
proletariat and the peasantry', he wrote, 'than the road of bourgeois
freedom and bourgeois progress'.[17] Yet by the end of the year, despite
his conviction that a major upheaval had indeed taken place, it was
clear to him also that the proletarian revolution, although possibly
imminent, was probably still some way off. The reforms of 1905

17. Lenin, *Sochineniya*, viii, p 104; Carr
1950, pp 65–6.

proved to be short-lived. The St Petersburg Soviet was crushed at the end of the year. The thesis that the bourgeois class in Russia hardly possessed the power to consolidate its revolutionary upheaval was rapidly becoming true. The Bolsheviks, accordingly, would now exaggerate their differences from the Mensheviks; would press for more concerted underground revolutionary activity to prepare for the next time the cataclysm came.

Indeed, despite occasional glimmerings of unity, it must have been clear that Lenin would brook no half-measures with the Mensheviks. Even by the beginning of 1905 he had abandoned the *Iskra* group to found a new journal *Vpered* (Forward), which would declare his determination to make an absolute theoretical and practical break with the reformist wing of the Party. But Lenin's theoretical battle was not only with the Mensheviks. Throughout the days and weeks of the 1905 revolution and then at the third Bolshevik Party Congress in London, in the summer of that year, Lenin had had the full support of two men whose ideas were to prove crucial to post-revolutionary developments in the arts: Alexandr Bogdanov (pseudonym of Alexandr Malinovsky) and Anatoly Lunacharsky. However, between Lenin and these two supporters there soon was to occur a clash of ideas of a kind even more fundamental than his tactical difficulties with the Mensheviks. Both men came to develop views which strongly contrasted with Lenin's own and which led to their eventual expulsion from the Bolshevik camp in 1909 – in Bogdanov's case a departure that was to prove final. Here was another case of Bolshevism's tendency to 'purify' itself from within.

Bogdanov was already known as a philosopher of some originality. The author of two later science fiction novels,[18] his distinctive philosophical contribution was already emerging as a marrying together of concepts derived from medical science (he had graduated as a doctor in 1899) with a utopian conception of 'the collective' as prior to, and over against, 'the individual'. According to Bogdanov's *Empiriomonism: Articles in Philosophy*, published in three volumes between 1904 and 1906, historical reality was not primarily the reality of class antagonism as propagated by Marx, but one in which ideas and ideologies (including the Marxist and positivist concepts of 'matter' and 'materialism') performed an organising role, having no ultimate validity but functioning merely as convenient hypotheses. Bogdanov further argued that capitalist society was dualistic (the contrast between 'self' and 'other') but that in a socialist society the 'I' would dissipate in the generality of the collective – this collective itself being all-powerful and all-knowing. Thus the individual will – so crucial to Lenin's concept of an actively participating revolutionary fighter – could have no ultimate place in Bogdanov's almost mystical scheme.[19]

Lenin had already agreed with Bogdanov to sink their philosophical differences for the sake of revolutionary social-democracy.[20] But in political terms both Bogdanov and Lunacharsky came to take up positions which precipitated a more fundamental split with the Party leader. After 1905 they took an 'ultra-left' stance which compelled them to oppose the Duma elections and press for a recall of the

18. A.A. Bogdanov was the author of *Red Star* (1908) and *The Engineer Menni* (1912).

19. This summary of Bogdanov's early views is indebted to R. C. Williams, 'Collective Immortality: The Syndicalist Origins of Proletarian Culture, 1905–1910', *Slavic Review*, no 3, September 1980, pp 389–402.

20. Lenin, *Sochineniya*, Vol 47, p 142.

Bolshevik delegation, branding Lenin's own support for the Duma as 'Menshevik'. Both men were now (and had been) close to syndicalism, and favoured immediate workers' control through the medium of the general strike – a viewpoint that was at variance with Lenin's idea of centralised Party control and one which accorded far more closely with the West European labour movements in which trade unionism was already strong.

Bogdanov and Lunacharsky's 'deviations' from orthodox Leninist Bolshevism were consolidated in the group established at the writer Maxim Gorky's house on the island of Capri in 1908 and 1909, a group which came to represent a real threat to Lenin as he saw the beginnings of alternative philosophies springing up, philosophies he roundly condemned as 'God-building' and 're-callism'. These were the charges contained in Lenin's *Materialism and Empirio-Criticism*, specifically published against Bogdanov in 1908, while at the same time he managed to preserve friendly relations with Gorky. Gorky reports a conversation between Lenin and Bogdanov on the question of the utopian novel, in which the Party leader exclaimed to Bogdanov: 'If you would write a novel for the workers on the subject of how the sharks of capitalism robbed the earth and wasted the oil, iron, timber and coal – that would be a useful book, Signor Machist!'[21]

The importance of these collectivist and syndicalist leanings, and Lenin's opposition to them, is that they provide the immediate philosophical context for a concept that was to loom large in the arts both during and after 1917, that of 'proletarian culture'. Bogdanov had long argued that the proletariat had 'its own type of thinking';[22] while Lunacharsky had argued – in obvious contrast to the Leninist framework in which the masses would need instructing 'from above' – that 'proletarian culture' followed directly from social-democracy as the spontaneous expression of the masses.[23] Gorky's own writings, according to Lunacharsky, were an example of 'proletarian culture' in the making. In this incarnation 'proletarian culture' equalled the spirit of collectivism transferred to art; it was to be vividly distinguished from individualism; and it was to be based, importantly, in the experience of labour within the life and mode of action of the collective.[24]

It was here that one of the central and indispensable cultural doctrines of post-Revolutionary Soviet socialism had its origins. Joined immediately by P. K. Bessalko, M. I. Kalinin, A. K. Gastev and M. P. Gerasimov, the Proletkult movement (as it became known) attempted from this point onwards actually to assume the mantle of 'true Bolshevism' in direct opposition to Lenin's developing cultural authoritarianism and the marked tendency of his favoured method of revolutionary organisation to imply the removal of Party leaders from the experience of the masses. Accordingly, Bogdanov was expelled from the editorial board of the journal *Proletarii* – now effectively the Central Committee of the Bolshevik Party – in 1909. Lunacharsky left the Party also, to be recalled in 1917. At this point therefore Lenin was attempting to preserve his version of Bolshevism against assailants both on the 'left' – the proletarian culture camp –

21. M. Gorky, 'Days with Lenin', from the excerpt in T. Riha (ed) *Readings in Russian Civilization*, 1964, p 513. Lenin refers here to the ideas of the Austrian physicist and philosopher E. Mach, which were also developed by R. Avenarius. 'Machism' was the thesis that only observable complexes of sensations exist and that science should restrict itself to 'description' rather than attempt 'explanation'. On Mach's principle of the 'economy of thought' Lenin commented that 'it can lead to nothing but subjective idealism. It is more "economical" to "think" that only I and my sensations exist.' (*Pol. Sob. Soch.*, Vol 18, pp 175–6)

22. A. Bogdanov, *Pryklyucheniya odnoi filosofskoi shkoly*, St Petersburg 1908, p 66; Williams, 'Collective Immortality', p 399.

23. A.V. Lunacharsky, 'Zadachi sotsial-demokraticheskogo khudozhvestnennogo tvorchestva', *Vestnik zhizn*, 1907, no 1; Williams, 'Collective Immortality', p 399.

24. There is as yet no adequate publication on the early development of proletarian culture in its national variations. Some of this is briefly adumbrated in Eden and Cedar Paul, *Proletkult*, London, 1921, but without detail.

and on the 'right' – the Mensheviks and gradualists whose main interest was in democratic reform.

The cultural territory in 1909 was also divided into many ideological and artistic groups and allegiances, the most important of which can be related to different social and political positions within the country as a whole. On the 'left' was not yet a genuine proletarian culture movement – such a thing was then only a remote hypothesis – but an inkling existed in literature of what such a thing would be like, namely Gorky and his 'realist' followers whose principal literary themes were the circumstances of the working poor in both city and country.

On the extreme 'right' in the visual arts was the Imperial Academy with its elaborate and rigid system of education, its subservience to the royal household and its court, and its more or less complete absence of interest in the social and revolutionary movements of the day. The Peredvizhniki (Association for Travelling Art Exhibitions) painters of the 1860s and 1870s were now in positions of leadership at the heart of the Academy and were no longer, in the main, concerned with the circumstances of the peasant or proletarian poor. Valentin Serov was an exception. He had witnessed the unprovoked massacre of demonstrators on 'Bloody Sunday', 22 January 1905 (9 January old style), and immediately had attempted to persuade Ilya Repin to join him in resigning from the Academy on the grounds that Grand Duke Vladimir, Commandant of the Imperial troops, was also President of the St Petersburg Academy. Repin refused, later characterising Serov's political views as 'extreme'.[25] As Elizabeth Valkenier points out in her study of the Peredvizhniki, the loyalist affiliations of the artists of this group in the early years of the century contrasted sharply with the pleas of other professional organisations in the sciences and the arts, including playwrights, composers and musicians, for an end to autocratic supervision of the arts by the Tsarist court. Moreover, when middle-of-the-road artists took advantage of the relaxed censorship following the October 1905 constitution and demanded a reform of the Academy, the older Peredvizhniki painters had kept silent.

Somewhere in between the 'left' and the 'right' was the Mir iskusstva (World of Art) group around Alexandr Benois. Demands for a different relationship between art and the state had been supported by Mir iskusstva. Also based in St Petersburg, it had already, in its own way, become concerned with the 'renewal' of man and society and was populated by elegant and on the whole wealthy sons and daughters of the intelligentsia who had been interested in establishing effective communications with other cultural centres in Western Europe. Strongly opposed to the 'realist' naturalism of the Academy and the Peredvizhniki, this formation developed around 1906 or 1907 into a Russian form of Symbolism. The Symbolist magazine *Zolotoe runo* (Golden Fleece), founded in 1906, published occasional criticisms of the bureaucratic control of art by the state, based on the argument that the state itself was merely an arm of a Royal household that was increasingly out of touch with public taste and with the mood of the majority of the population.[26] But it cannot be

25. Repin, *Dalekoe blizkoe*, Moscow, 1937, p 452; E. Valkenier, *Russian Realist Art: The State and Society: The Peredvizhniki and their Tradition*, Ardis, Ann Arbor, Michigan, 1977, p 138.

26. Valkenier, *Russian Realist Art*, p 140.

said that the Symbolist movement was capable of providing a viable alternative programme for the arts. Concerned above all to embrace literature and music, the younger generation of Symbolists, led by the example of slightly older artists such as Viktor Borisov-Musatov and Mikhail Vrubel, immersed themselves in melancholy, in vague colours, in 'other-worldly' tones and stylised drawing, and cultivated an aesthetic which, though staunchly anti-Academic, was in effect apolitical and perhaps even reactionary in so far as it traded in mystical and esoteric ideas. In the Golubaya rosa (Blue Rose) association, which had one exhibition in March and April 1907, the emphasis was heavily upon the transcendence of 'mundane' reality and a sort of indefinable trafficking with 'the absolute'.[27] Any Menshevik who wanted to identify the true face of the 'newest' bourgeois culture in 1906 would have been able to gauge its revolutionary aspirations from articles such as 'Painting and Revolution', published in *Zolotoe runo* in that year: 'New artists will be true prophets and priests', the article stated, 'the heralds of the Universal Soul's inspirations. With a language of phantoms, dreams, colours and sounds they will begin to prophesy when positive scientific knowledge will lapse helplessly into silence.' Speaking of the importance of *tone* in visual art, it encourages 'young artists [who], . . . in their inspired enlightenment, *alien to any kind of literariness or preconceived philosophical ideas*, have advanced as far as unconscious musicality'.[28] Such statements were typical of the backsliding and escapism of much of the post-1905 Symbolist intelligentsia.

This was also the moment of 'primitivism' in Russian art. At the third exhibition of the Golden Fleece society in December 1909, Mikhail Larionov and Natalya Goncharova exhibited works which looked back to the Russian past – to the *lubok* (woodcut) in particular – as well as to the Western European aesthetic of flattened pictorial space and simplified painting technique (Figure 3). Kazimir Malevich joined the 'primitivist' tendency at around this time, specialising in paintings of peasant subjects, generally engaged in work and painted with an incandescent, mystical simplicity. These were the years of the groups and exhibitions much celebrated in Western modernism – the Jack of Diamonds, The Union of Youth, 'The Donkey's Tail', 'The

27. For this and similar statements see J. E. Bowlt, 'The Blue Rose: Russian Symbolism in Art', *Burlington Magazine*, August 1976, pp 566–75.

28. D. Imgardt, 'Zhivopis i revolyutsia' (Painting and Revolution), *Zolotoe runo*, Moscow 1906, no 5, pp 56–8; Bowlt, 'Blue Rose', p 570.

Figure 3
M. Larionov, *Ladies on the Boulevard*, c.1910 (photo: *Novosti*)

29.   For example Gray, *Great Experiment*, Chs 3–5; J. E. Bowlt, 'The Union of Youth', in G. Gibian and H. Tjalsma (eds) *Russian Modernism: Culture and the Avant Garde, 1900–1930*, Cornell University Press, Ithaca and London, 1976, pp 165–87; J. Howard, 'Nikolai Kulbin and the Union of Youth: A History of the St Petersburg Avant-garde, 1908–14' unpublished PhD Thesis, St Andrews, 1989.

30.   V. Markov, *Russian Futurism*, University of California Press, 1968, p 34.

31.   The first and shortest version of Malevich's autobiography is the essay known as *From 1/42, Notes*, published in *Writings* (ed. T. Anderson), Vol II, 1960, pp 147–54; the longer version from which this account is drawn is available is N.I. Khardzhiyev, *Istorii russkogo avantgarda*, Stockholm, 1976; also in *October*, 34, Fall 1985, pp 25–44.

Target', and others, which have been described in several accounts.[29] An early link with writers and poets was provided by Vladimir and David Burlyuk, both of whom were 'primitivist' painters and energetic organisers whose full gifts have not yet been adequately appreciated. In their circle too were poets like Vasily Kamensky and Benedikt Livshits, for whom early 'primitivist' painting resembled a 'renovated vision of the world'.[30]

It is easy to be carried away by excessive enthusiasm for these works which do, however, occupy only one part of the complete artistic spectrum in the period between the 1905 revolution and the outbreak of the First World War. It may also be significant that these works (together with the groups from which they derived) were in political terms outmoded, and perhaps necessarily so, even by the time they were made. Kamensky's early 'novel' *The Mud Hut* (1910) is impressionistic and somewhat fragmented in style, and is concerned with the lyrical qualities of nature and the spontaneity and wisdom of the child. The poets Velimir Khlebnikov and Alexey Kruchonykh were members of this circle, very much concerned to recuperate infantilist, parodic and folk-lore speech patterns for literature. Malevich's much-vaunted attention to the spiritual qualities of the Russian peasant arguably replicated late nineteenth-century Narodism or 'going-to-the-people' which had long since been superseded in contemporary political analysis. Perhaps Malevich was typical of the political consciousness of the 'primitivist'. He had no interest in and little sympathy for the revolutionary events of 1905. At one point he was caught up in pitched battles between members of a Moscow student commune and the Black Hundreds, a notorious armed force with a reputation for repression and terror – an event he describes in his autobiography in some detail. First, the students arm themselves with axes and guns. Finding himself cajoled by revolutionary participants (he describes them as 'my decadent colleagues'), Malevich narrowly escapes being shot and conceals himself in a friend's room while the battle rages on. But he makes no mention of the causes of the disturbance or the wider atmosphere of unrest, and appears relieved to be able to return to Kursk, where the mood was far quieter.[31]

The precise identification of this inventive and formally experimental modernist 'avant-garde' with a particular political standpoint – either of the 'right' or the 'left' – is notoriously difficult to effect. From one perspective, its appropriation of folk culture, of childhood and 'primitive' mentality, of peasant culture, may be said to form the beginnings of an oppositional (yet still bourgeois) art which at least would fashion a challenge to the styles and habits of the Tsarist Academy. That, more or less, has come to be the position of the intellectual and artistic 'left' in the Western democracies from that day until now. From another perspective, the mysticism and the peasant sympathies of this early 'avant-garde', its failure to identify with the situation of the proletariat, may make it appear uncommitted and merely 'experimental' within the spectrum of possible interventions in the arts. Furthermore the financing and patronage of the various 'modernist' groups came largely if not wholly from wealthy bourgeois merchants who had travelled widely in the West and who had made fortunes out of capitalist trade: Ivan Morozov and Sergey Shchukine in the case of the younger painters, the millionaire Nikolay Ryabushinsky in the case of the Symbolists and their journal *Zolotoe runo*, and the businessman and collector Levky Zheverzheev in the case of the Union of Youth.

Where the Mensheviks stood on this question naturally would have depended upon how long or how short a time they believed the bourgeois revolution would endure. In a sense it was the very indeterminacy of this question that made the Menshevik standpoint an impossible one – both in the cultural field and in the wider political arena. This dilemma was to grow worse, not better. At the beginning of 1912 the chances of reconciliation between Mensheviks and Bolsheviks came to an abrupt end when Lenin announced a complete identification of his Bolshevik group and the Social-Democratic Workers' Party. At the same time a new period of industrial unrest began, accompanied by a split between Lenin and Trotsky, the latter of whom had provided sterling leadership of the St Petersburg Soviet in 1905 but was now castigated as a 'Menshevik' for his attempts to unify the Party around a consensus platform.

The contrast of artistic and political events in Russia early in 1912 is as graphic an opposition as one could wish. To take but one example of industrial unrest: this was the moment of the massacre of striking workers in the Lena Goldfields by government troops, an event which attracted the sympathies of Bolsheviks and 'left' Mensheviks alike. Yet this same moment also saw the first real eruption of modernism on Russian soil. Both within the Union of Youth organisation in St Petersburg and in the Jack of Diamonds and Donkey's Tail groups in Moscow, fertile experiments were being conducted with imagery, rhythm systems and word-formation in a new alliance with 'Cubism' and, indeed, with a wide range of international formal precedents and ideas. The second Jack of Diamonds exhibition in February 1912 included works by the Brücke group from Berlin, by Kandinsky from Munich, and by Delaunay, Matisse, Léger and Picasso from Paris. This was a period of rapid and often competitive interchange between the European capitals, and between and within the groups inside the Russian 'avant-garde'.

These 'avant-garde' groups have been extensively described in the Western literature already.[32] Here we shall isolate two important manifestations of how 'Futurists', as they were regularly called, taunted a certain spectrum of bourgeois opinion, and of how they measured themselves in relation to the past. The poet Kruchonykh had been experimenting with novel linguistic forms in poetry for some years; by 1912 his concept of *zaum* or trans-rational poetry had been evolved, in which word-fragments and individual letters, some not even belonging to Russian, would be arranged randomly on the page. The manifesto *A Slap in the Face of Public Taste*, published in January 1913 over the signatures of David Burlyuk, Vladimir Mayakovsky, Kruchonykh and Khlebnikov (the last of whom did not take part in the writing) announces that 'only we are the face of our

32. For example in V. Markov, *Russian Futurism: A History*, University of California Press, 1968; S. Compton, *The World Backwards: Russian Futurist Books, 1912–1916*, London, 1978; V. Zavalishin, *Early Soviet Writers*, New York, 1958, Chapters 1–7; S. Barron and M. Tuchman (eds), *The Avant-Garde in Russia, 1910–1930; New Perspectives*, Los Angeles, 1980, Chapters 1–8; Gray, *The Great Experiment*, Chapters 4–8; etc.

33.   *A Slap in the Face of Public Taste* is reproduced in Markov, *Russian Futurism*, pp 45–6.

34.   Ibid., p 46.

time'; but was concerned less with the social turmoil of 1913 than with the overthrow – symbolically and rhetorically – of previous art. The manifesto announced that 'the Academy and Pushkin are more incomprehensible than hieroglyphics' – in itself hardly a revolutionary sentiment at the time. 'Throw Pushkin, Dostoevsky, Tolstoy, et al. overboard from the ship of modernity', the statement continued.[33] Poets would henceforward have 'rights to enlarge vocabulary in its scope with arbitrary and derivative words . . . to feel an insurmountable hatred for the language existing before . . . '. The manifesto exhorted poets to 'wash your hands of the filthy slime of the books written by all those Leonid Andreevs, all those Maxim Gorkys, Kuprins, Bloks, Sologubs, Remizovs, Averchenkos, Chernyis, Kuzmins, Bunins . . . we look at their nothingness from the heights of skyscrapers'.[34] In fact Gorky, Kuprin, Andreev and Bunin had all belonged to the Znaniye (Knowledge) school of 'realist' writers of several years before, some of whom had been, and were, close to the Bogdanov-Lunacharsky ideal. Blok and Sologub were Symbolists. The list published in *A Slap in the Face of Public Taste* encompassed most popular authors of the day, and thus implied a knowing rejection of the 'proletarian culture' ideal generated by 'left' Bolsheviks.

The second manifestation from 1913 – the year that Vladimir Markov rightly calls the *annus mirabilis* of Russian Futurism – was the 'opera' entitled *Victory over the Sun*, performed in St Petersburg on 3 and 5 December with libretto by Kruchonykh and music by Mikhail Matyushin, to which Malevich contributed stage designs, costumes and lighting (Figure 4). Normally recorded as a key event in the history of the Russian 'avant-garde' – which it may well have been – the production was designed as an under-rehearsed rag-bag of 'episodes' which followed another Futurist production, Mayakovsky's more carefully considered *Vladimir Mayakovsky: A Tragedy*, on the 2 and 4 December. Both productions were sponsored by the Union of Youth. Naturally, both were a sell-out, despite the expensive seats. One of the 'actors' in *Victory Over the Sun*, a certain K. Tomashevsky, wrote later that the opera was designed to attract 'fashionable and philistine bourgeois' rather than the public at large, and that a fair proportion of the audience was made up of policemen and representatives of the gutter press.

The drama on stage took the form of a symbolic capture of the sun by *Budetlyane* or 'Futurelandmen', who then journey to the '10th land', where they find it 'easier to breathe'. In the *dénouement*, however, those of less than perfect disposition go mad or commit suicide in the face of the extreme disorientation which accompanies life in the new land. The sun ('cheap and pretentious') appears to represent rationality and the 'old order'. The implication of the opera is that those with moral courage may survive, but only just. They may succeed in establishing a base-camp in the foothills of the future, but will be uncertain as to how to proceed from there. *Victory Over the Sun* was conveyed in largely *zaum* verse, for example

Figure 4
K. Malevich, costume for *Victory Over the Sun*, 1913

Threateningly loud fastprophesying go-ers will shake.

Appearancechangers of action will go fully armed,
directed by pointermagi of games, in wonderland costumes
showing morning, evening deed-ive . . .[35]

while the lighting and costumes broke up the bodies 'because for
Malevich they were only geometric bodies yielding not only to de-
composition into elements, but also complete disintegration in the
pictorial space'.[36] Real actors were debarred from taking part, and
many of the requisite props never arrived at all. Tomashevsky describes the evening as 'pure nonsense and abracadabra', while the
audience is said to have roared with laughter at the cacophonous
music and thrown fruit at the stage whenever they felt like protest-
ing – interventions which were encouraged by the performers.[37]

What such events tell us about the political affiliations of early
Russian Futurism is only partially clear. In some sense 'revolutionary' in terms of the devices and formalities of art, many Futurist
paintings and plays were drenched in esoteric and mystical symbols
which could have met with little sympathy from any of the political
groupings near to the Bolshevik leadership. That the majority of
Futurist art-works contained no reference to contemporary events
and staged what quickly became a ritual rebellion against the artistic
forms of the past is also implied by such an analysis. There are
references to 'rationality' as a pervasive bourgeois norm in *Victory
Over the Sun*, and the title itself seems to derive from an actual eclipse
of the sun that took place in 1913, but the sorts of transformations that
are envisaged by the leading exponents of the 'avant-garde' remain
largely metaphorical and symbolic. Vasily Kandinsky, in his *Concerning the Spiritual in Art* of 1912, summarised the whole of human life
as a spiritual triangle, the majority of the inhabitants of which are
ignorant and confused. Kandinsky is openly disparaging about 'the
republicans or democrats' who feel 'fear, distaste and hatred' for the
term 'anarchy', about which they know nothing 'except the terrifying
name'. Economically, says Kandinsky, 'these people are socialists:
they sharpen the sword of justice to deal the fatal blow to the capitalist
hydra and cut off the head of evil'. But they

have never managed to solve a problem for themselves and have always
been pulled along in the cart of humanity by their self-sacrificing fellow
men standing far above them; they know nothing of the effort of pull-
ing . . . though they imagine it to be very easy, believing in infallible
remedies and prescriptions of universal application.[38]

At the top of this triangle, says Kandinsky, there stands 'only a single
man: his joyful vision is like an inner, immeasurable sorrow. Those
who are closest to him do not understand him and in their indignation
call him deranged . . .'[39]. He is, in short, an artist, and it is he who pulls
the cartload of humanity onwards and upwards.

Malevich engaged in a number of highly 'transformative' paint-
ings replete with fishes and ladder symbols before presenting his
Suprematist 'Black Square' at Ivan Puni's 'Last Exhibition of Futurist
Painting .0.10' of December 1915. At that time he announced 'I have

35. From the English translation of *Victory Over the Sun* by Ewa Bartos and Victoria Kirby, *The Drama Review*, Fall 1971, pp 107–25.

36. The account is by B. Livshits, who was in the audience; see S. Compton, 'Malevich's Suprematism: The Higher Intuition', *Burlington Magazine*, August 1976, p 580.

37. K. Tomashevsky, 'From *Vladimir Mayakovsky*', *The Drama Review*, Fall 1971, pp 93–100.

38. W. Kandinsky, *Concerning the Spiritual in Art*, Munich 1912; in K. Lindsay and P. Vergo (eds), *Kandinsky's Complete Writings*, Vol 1, Faber and Faber, London 1982, pp 139–40.

39. Ibid., pp 133–4.

40. K. Malevich, *Essays on Art* (ed.
T. Anderson), Vol I, 1908, p 19.

transformed myself in the zero of form [sic] and dragged myself out
of the rubbish-filled pool of Academic art . . . Hurry, for tomorrow
you will not recognise us.'[40] He speaks in a prose-poem of the same
year of striving to achieve one-ness with 'the three-faced God':

> I am the beginning of everything for in my consciousness
> worlds are created
> I search for God, I search within myself for myself

41. K. Malevich, 'I am the Beginning',
Essays on Art, Vol 4.

Malevich says it is necessary to 'embrace the sky . . . [to] remove from
ourselves the weight of the body, to make ourselves lighter, and for
this reason we draw ourselves a supra-image and the forms of its life,
in order to reincarnate ourselves in it'.[41] Such offerings do not belong
within the same frame of reference as the ambition of the Bolshevik
Party to seize power at the moment of maximum civil unrest. Symptomatic of a crisis within the bourgeoisie, Futurism would have been
seen by Bolsheviks as offering nothing to the revolutionary proletariat except a set of signs and languages that might one day become
available for critical appropriation by a dictatorship of workers and
peasants.

But even if such prospects were entertained, it would have to be
said that their realisation was surely a long way off. Lenin in 1912 saw
his task as being to distance the Party from Menshevism, though
Plekhanov and other Mensheviks were not in practice debarred from
contributing to the new Party newspaper *Pravda* when it began
publication in May, and, in practice, the actual policies of the Bolsheviks and Mensheviks may not have been far apart. (Both supported the trade unions in their struggle for improved rights and
conditions, both supported the Socialist International, and both were
committed to the overthrow of Tsarism.[42]) This is why Plekhanov's
1912 lecture 'Art and Social Life', delivered to a small group in Paris
in November, is an important pointer to revolutionary cultural policy
at the time. Plekhanov is implacably opposed to 'art for art's sake',[43]
and to the 'exclusive concern for form', the latter of which he says is
significant of 'social and political indifferentism'.[44]

42. L. Schapiro, *The Communist Party of
the Soviet Union*, Methuen, London 1963,
pp 128–42.

43. G. V. Plekhanov, *Art and Social Life*,
1912 (London, Lawrence & Wishart
edn, n.d.), p 5.

44. Ibid., p 23.

45. Ibid., p 34.

Indeed the chief proposition of Plekhanov's pamphlet is that
'when artists become blind to the major social trends of their time, the
inherent value of the ideas they express . . . is seriously impaired'.[45]
He is in no doubt at all that the ethereal 'verbal music' of the mystical
Symbolist poet Zinaida Hippius is symptomatic of widespread social
decay and should be called 'decadent'. But (and here he signals his
Menshevism) he does not believe that capitalist relations of production, from which such evils stem, have yet had their day; though he
believes that their final decay is brought nearer by the 'infatuation' of
Russian intellectuals with philosophical and aesthetic doctrines from
Western Europe which are themselves symptoms of the more advanced class degeneration already rife in that quarter. In this he
quickly pounces upon *Du Cubisme* by Albert Gleizes and Jean Metzinger,[46] particularly their statements (which were of course not
typical of all 'Cubist' thought) that 'there is nothing real outside of
us', and that 'we seek the essential . . . in our personality'; not to

46. A. Gleizes and J. Metzinger, *Du
Cubisme*, Paris, 1912.

mention their famous remark that the artist 'must speak to the crowd, but not in the language of the crowd', which to Mensheviks and Bolsheviks alike would have been pure ideological heresy.

Yearning for a 'serious attitude to real social life' and for a rich and significant 'idea content' for art – painting in particular is referred to here – Plekhanov berates those who (like the Impressionists) dabble only in appearances and the reality of the ego. Artists must be on guard against what Plekhanov calls 'the feverish hunt for something "new", to which the majority of present-day artists are addicted'.[47] Artists must become aware of the 'new teachings of social life', must cultivate the 'idea content' of art, in particular must 'absorb the great emancipatory ideas of our time'.[48] Citing Marx and Engels' scheme in the *Communist Manifesto* that in the final decline of class culture one portion of the bourgeoisie, those 'who have raised themselves to the level of comprehending theoretically the historical movement as a whole' will cut itself adrift and go over to the proletariat, Plekhanov complains that 'among the bourgeois ideologists who go over to the proletariat we find very few artists'.[49] The reason? That only people who 'think' can thus cut themselves free. Yet, believes Plekhanov, 'modern artists, in contradiction to the great masters of the Renaissance, do extremely little thinking'.[50] In short, for the bourgeoisie, going forward can now only mean sinking downwards. And this fate is shared by its ideologists, the 'most advanced' of whom 'are precisely those who have sunk lower than all their predecessors'.[51]

Aside from his insistence on 'the great emancipatory ideas of our time' as a basis for art, Plekhanov does not yet defend this or that artist as a revolutionary beacon; nor does he develop the theme of how such ideas might become embodied in art. Lunacharsky, who was present at Plekhanov's lecture, argued with his assertion that bourgeois art was in a state of decay, apparently implying that bourgeois art was still ascending rapidly in 1912 or at least that the matter was incapable of proof. In return Plekhanov accused Lunacharsky of promulgating 'proletarian culture' – which he may well have been doing – and of 'associating with his close colleague in thought, Mr Bogdanov',[52] whose advice Plekhanov also declined to take.

This clash of views in late 1912 only partially illuminates the aesthetic perceptions of these very considerable protagonists. Plekhanov was non-plussed by the French and Russian 'avant-garde'. Lunacharsky's attitude to the 'avant-garde' is reasonably clear, though not without contradiction. His 'proletarian culture' platform made him sympathetic to socialist playwrights like Maeterlinck and Verhaeren; we know that he attended workers' choral concerts and Isadora Duncan's dancing, and that he admired the worker-poet Jehan Richtus.[53] He also admired the wandering proletarian violinist Eduard Syrmus, who had met Lenin and Gorky. These were examples of the 'proletarian culture' that he thought would soon erupt. In art, he was cautious. He liked Puvis de Chavannes, but found the Cubists and Futurists intolerable. Chagall was prone to 'pretentious posing and a kind of sick taste' – Chagall was under the sway of Apollinaire and Cubism at the time. The large Italian Futurist

47. G. V. Plekhanov, *Art and Social Life*, p 66.

48. Ibid., p 68.

49. Ibid., p 67.

50. Ibid., p 67. Plekhanov makes an interesting citation at this point, to J. Holl, *La Jeune Peinture Contemporaine*, Paris, 1912, who (pp 14–15) complains of 'the general lack of culture that characterises most young artists . . . they are in general very ignorant . . . Being incapable of understanding, or indifferent to the conflicts of ideas and dramatic situations of the present day, they work drudgingly secluded from all intellectual and social movements, confining themselves to problems of technique and absorbed more and more with the material appearance of painting than with its general significance and intellectual influence.'

51. Ibid., p 68.

52. Ibid., p 72.

53. R.C. Williams, *Artists in Revolution: Portraits of the Russian Avant-Garde 1905–1925*, Scolar Press, London, 1977, p 53.

54.   These affidavits are taken from Williams, *Artists in Revolution*, p 53, in citation of Lunacharsky, *Ob izobrazitelnom isskustve*, Moscow, Vol 1, pp 160, 183, 185.

exhibition in Paris of April 1912 was 'pure subjective chaos'; Boccioni, in particular, was 'nine-tenths artistic hooliganism'.[54] Yet Lunacharsky acquainted himself with the Russian emigré colony of La Ruche (Chagall, Soutine, Kremegne, Zadkine, Altman, Kisling, Koukine and Shterenberg, among others) during his time in Paris. By Shterenberg's work he was impressed (Figure 5), which suggests at least a partially open attitude to 'modernist' art.

Figure 5
D. Shterenberg, *Paris Rooftops*, *c*.1910–11 (photo: *SCR* London)

When the outbreak of war brought a sudden interruption to the activities of the Paris, Moscow and St Petersburg avant-garde, there began a period of some two and a half years – late 1914 to the beginning of 1917 – during which the leaders and principal supporters of the Bolshevik Party were caught up in matters of international scope in the political arena and inevitably expressed themselves little or not at all on questions of culture. Lenin's call for national defeat followed by civil war proved a difficult path to follow for even the staunchest Bolshevik followers. Plekhanov, in contrast, called for a policy of national defence and for gradual and piecemeal reform, and his momentary association with the Bolsheviks came to an end. Most Party leaders were abroad, or in exile, or both, and were consequently removed from substantial contact with Russian ideas in the arts. They were also removed from each other for the majority of the conflict. Trotsky was initially in Vienna, Lenin and Lunacharsky were in Switzerland, and Stalin was languishing with Sverdlov in Siberia.

This relatively extended war-time period of some thirty or so months surely played a more important role in the formation of subsequent Bolshevik Party attitudes to the arts than we normally think. Already very controversial amongst even its closest followers, 'avant-garde' art was by definition incapable of being comprehended thoroughly or consistently by isolated underground revolutionaries who were constantly on the move from one country to another. The very culture of the 'avant-garde' presupposed not only the closest engagement with art, but a relatively fixed routine of meetings, discussions, magazine reviews and gossip; and nothing could have been further from the fragile and nomadic existence of the Bolshevik underground during the war-time years. Lenin, who was by age and temperament a man of conservative artistic tastes, expressed the problem clearly to Clara Zetkin:

> Why worship the new, merely because it is new? That is nonsense, sheer nonsense . . . I have the courage to recognise myself to be a barbarian; I cannot extol the products of Expressionism, Futurism, Cubism and other 'isms' as the supreme revelations of artistic genius.[55]

55. Clara Zetkin, 'My Recollection of Lenin', in *Lenin on Literature and Art*, 1967, p 274.

In a Party in which the views of the highest leadership were to assume extreme importance, such opinions counted for a very great deal. 'I do not understand them and they give me no pleasure'[56] was Lenin's verdict on the movements he had heard about and seen. Echoes of such sentiments would be audible for many years to come.

56. Ibid., p 274.

The Leadership in 1917

On the eve of the Revolution it cannot be said that the Bolshevik Party had anything like as developed a policy for art and culture as it did for social and political revolution. Perhaps no one could have comprehended the import of the extraordinary changes that had occurred in the arts during the course of the war, let alone those immediately before 1914. Nor did Party doctrine supply any certain guidance. The founding fathers of Marxism had said little enough about the arts, and what had been said was said long ago, in very different circumstances. And besides, the war provided enough political and military crises to make any future artistic policy for the Party hardly a matter of the highest priority.

Nor were the leaders of the Bolshevik Party really prepared for government when the time came. Until now an illegal, underground organisation, its modes of organisation and communication had been characterised by secrecy, intrigue, concealment and the most intense vigilance against those who would harm its interests or threaten its sometimes very fragile unity. Furthermore (and necessarily), no one knew in advance when or where the Revolution would take place, or what form it would take. No one was able to say who would lead it, or how, or who the first ministers of any Revolutionary government would be. It is as well to remember these uncertainties, for they bear strongly on the course that events were to take.

It is also worth pausing briefly to remind ourselves who the leaders of the Bolshevik Party were in 1917, what their artistic and cultural predispositions were, and what kind of cultural revolution they were likely to make if and when the opportunity came. In a Party organised around a strong central leadership, too, the proclivities of a few well placed individuals were apt to prove proportionally very influential indeed.

Lenin, the Party leader, was the son of well-educated parents; his father had been a university graduate in mathematics and had become a school inspector. His mother taught him the piano and singing, and the family travelled abroad frequently. His early reading was wide and varied. He occasionally went to concerts and the theatre, though there is no mention in the numerous biographies of his having visited art exhibitions in his youth (nor any account of his having visited art museums in his adult years, the accounts of which are more detailed). His intellectual interests as a university student were dominated by politics and economics, and one quickly senses that real immersion in cultural matters was not Lenin's *forte*, nor his particular wish. Drawing a contrast later between Lenin and Plekhanov, Lunacharsky described the latter as one 'with a noble desire to defend culture and its further progress from Tsarist and bourgeois barbarism . . . Lenin, on the contrary, was above all a political fighter'.[1] A biographer who knew Lenin says that 'when the conversation turned to literature and art, Plekhanov found the young man [Lenin] unimaginative and uninspired'.[2] During a period of exile in Siberia, Lenin was described by his companion G. Krzhyzhanovsky as 'not a great admirer of good literature [who] patiently bore with my jeering remarks about his undeveloped literary tastes.'[3] Lenin was later reported (by Nikolay Valentinov) as having read Goethe's *Faust*, but no other works by him; as having never read Shakespeare, Byron, Molière or Schiller. 'He divides literature into two parts: what he needs, and what he doesn't need', Valentinov relates. Dostoevsky was 'rubbish'; *The Possessed* was 'reactionary filth', according to Lenin: 'I looked through the book and threw it away.' But he liked *War and Peace*, and greatly admired Nekrasov, often quoting

> The green sounds drone
> The green sounds, the spring sounds
> The cherry orchards, looking as if
> Milk had been poured over them . . .[4]

As an exile Lenin devoted his time constantly to political literature, and became instantly recognised as a brilliant theoretical and organi-

1.   Lunacharsky, cited in D. Shub, *Lenin*, 1948 (Penguin Books, Harmondsworth, 1966), p 42.

2.   D. Shub, *Lenin*, p 42.

3.   Ibid., p 54.

4.   N. Valentinov (N. N. Volsky), *Encounters with Lenin*, Oxford University Press, London, 1968, p 50.

sational mind; but never a man of wide or discriminating cultural experience. During the war Lenin spent several months in Berne, and then in 1916 moved to Zurich, one of the homes of European Dada with a vivid tradition of cabaret and satire. But all the evidence points to a strong dislike for experimental work in the arts, however icono-clastic. Occupied for the most part in Zurich in writing *Imperialism as the Highest Stage of Capitalism*, there is no mention in his biographies of any contact with, or sympathy for, the European 'avant-garde' then partially exiled in that city. Solzhenitsyn in his novelistic *Lenin in Zurich* surmises that:

> Through all his years as an emigré Lenin had hated cafés, those smoke-filled dens of logorrhoea, where nine-tenths of the compulsive revolution-ary windbags were in permanent session. During the war Zurich had drawn in another dubious crowd from the belligerent neighbours. It was because of them that the rents had gone up – this mob of adventurers, shady businessmen, profiteers, draft-dodging students and blethering intellectuals, with their philosophical manifestos and artistic demonstra-tions, in revolt against they knew not what. And there they all were – in the cafés.[5]

5. A. Solzhenitsyn, *Lenin in Zurich*, Bodley Head, London, 1976, p 95.

Lenin was culturally isolated in Western Europe. He could attract few followers, and was considered by many to be a crank. The remainder of the Bolshevik organisation was widely dispersed, and communi-cation with the other members was erratic at best.

Trotsky's background and cultural experience had been in some ways comparable, though his interest in the arts and especially in literature was far greater than Lenin's. Born in 1879 the son of industrious Jewish farmers in the Ukraine, Lev Bronstein (as he then was) had lived for part of his childhood with a cultured Odessa family who taught him, among other things, Russian lit-erature: Pushkin, Lermontov, Nekrasov and Tolstoy; also Goethe and Dickens. It was through this family with its frequent visits from local newspaper editors and literary men that Trotsky first formed the view that 'authors, journalists and artists always stood for a world more attractive than any other, open only to the elect'.[6] As one biographer comments, 'This world [he] beheld with a thrill known only to the born man of letters when he first comes into contact with the men and the affairs of his predestined pro-fession.'[7] It was in Odessa too that Trotsky first explored the theatre and Italian opera, briefly falling in love with an opera singer Guiseppina Uget, whom Trotsky says 'seemed to me to have descended straight from heaven to the stage boards of Odessa'.[8] Little attracted to politics in his teens, Trotsky intended to pursue mathematics at university and only encountered socialist ideas in his later school years, spent in Nikolaev. At first more interested in the Narodnik movement than Marxism, he turned abruptly to social-democracy only as an undergraduate, as he became aware of the powerful mixture represented by revolutionary political ideology combined with Russian and Western European cultural ideas. He then graduated to the clandestine political movement led

6. L. Trotsky, *My Life*, p 86; I. Deut-scher, *The Prophet Armed: Trotsky 1879–1921*, Oxford University Press, London and Oxford, 1954, p 16.

7. Deutscher, *The Prophet Armed*, p 16.

8. Trotsky, *My Life*, p 85; Deutscher, *Prophet Armed*, p 17.

by Lenin, and like all active Bolsheviks suffered the experience of harsh imprisonment without trial (Figure 6).

As an exile in Siberia Trotsky read Russian and West European literature voraciously and published critical appraisals of writers such as Nietszche and Ibsen in the Irkutsk newspaper *Eastern Review*, in which he supported their contempt for the fragility and corruptibility of bourgeois morals, while yet distancing himself from the concept of 'the superman' which is found in unequal degrees in both.

Figure 6
Trotsky (second left) en route to exile in Obdorsk, January 1907(photo: *David King*).

He expressed admiration for Dobrolyubov and Belinsky. In the course of an essay on Hauptmann he expresses dissatisfaction with the ideal of 'art for art's sake', which he says 'like a paper kite can soar to heights from which all earthly matters are drowned in grey indifference'. Even after it has reached the clouds, Trotsky flourishes, 'this poor "free" art still remains tied to a strong rope, the earthly end of which is tightly gripped by the philistine'.[9] Elsewhere in these early writings he takes issue with the Symbolist movement which was then becoming fashionable. He believed that although all art, however 'realistic', remains symbolic, the Symbolist school was attempting to turn the means into an end, and in the process was degrading the symbol from an expression of human experience into a means of escape from it. The purpose of art, says Trotsky, 'is not to copy reality in empirical detail but to throw light on the complex content of life by singling out its general typical features . . . '[10], a formula that suggests a close reading of Engels.

But Trotsky was a natural literary critic, and it was his high regard for literature that brought him later to the conviction that the Revolution was one of words as well as deeds. Brilliant in debate and equally brilliant with the pen, he was perhaps apt to forget that a verbal victory was not always sufficient to carry the day in practical terms. But the close connection between literature and revolution was

9. L. Trotsky, *Sochineniya*, Vol XX, pp 170–81; Deutscher, *Prophet Armed*, p 51.

10. L. Trotsky, *Sochineniya*, Vol XX, pp 167–70; Deutscher, *Prophet Armed*, p 51.

second nature to many revolutionaries in hiding, in prison, or in exile. Of course their circumstances of confinement removed them from any real contact with visual art, and as with Lenin there is no record of Trotsky having taken a real interest in painting or sculpture, either in his early years or in the decade after 1917. Thus literature was and would remain the central cultural resource of the Bolshevik leaders, and it was from standards forged in this field that much subsequent artistic policy would flow.

Nikolay Bukharin was younger than the other future leaders who have been mentioned so far (Figure 7). His cultural and class background is also highly relevant to later Soviet policy in the arts. A sixteen-year-old student in 1905, Bukharin's background and temperament deserve comparison with those of Lenin and Trotsky. Bukharin's father, like Lenin's, had been a university graduate in mathematics, and helped foster in his son a life-long interest in animals which would lead much later to the formation of a considerable menagerie in the rooms and basement of the Kremlin.[11] But Bukharin was broadly educated, fond of literature, and considered a career as an artist before political and economic interests took over. (After 1917 he was to become known in Bolshevik circles for his political cartoons). Art, for Bukharin, was a 'passion' that took only second place to his revolutionary work. He knew some foreign languages, and even by 1905 was well versed in non-Marxist social theory from Western Europe, as well, inevitably, as in social-democratic doctrine at home.

The older Lunacharsky, too, though never to become a Party leader, was of a very different breed to the robust working-class revolutionaries who were agitating for the Party inside Russia. Brought up largely by a cultured and well-educated mother (his step-father died when he was nine) Lunacharsky had become attracted to Marxism as a school student, and had left home at the age of twenty to study with Axelrod and Avenarius at the University of Zurich, to which Plekhanov was a visitor. A further period in Paris acquainted him with the galleries and museums of the French capital. Arrested for revolutionary activity once back in Russia, he spent time in a Kiev jail before a period of exile in Kaluga, where he met Bogdanov, whose sister he married. He also met the philosopher Nikolay Berdyaev, who like others of his generation (Tolstoy, Sergey Bulgakov, Merezhkovsky) was turning to religion as a source of ethics. It was Bogdanov however whose ideas he liked, and it was Bogdanov's allegiance to Lenin that propelled Lunacharsky to Paris, where he met Lenin, and to Geneva, where he helped edit *Vpered*, moving for a short time to Florence where, apart from helping to edit the new Party journal *Proletarii*, he studied Italian art and literature. By the time the 'proletarian culture' concept emerged within Gorky's group on Capri some years later, Lunacharsky was very well versed in European art and literature as well as an experienced member of the Bolshevik underground. His famous self-description as 'an intellectual among Bolsheviks, and a Bolshevik among intellectuals',[12] fitted him fairly exactly from this time. As already noted, Bogdanovism was not popular with Lenin's group, and even less popular in the

Figure 7
Nikolay Bukharin, June 1909
(photo: *David King*)

11. This and other formative influences are detailed in S. Cohen, *Bukharin and the Russian Revolution: A Political Biography, 1888–1938*, London, 1971 and Wildwood House, New York, 1974, pp 66 ff.

12. See S. Fitzpatrick, *The Commissariat of the Enlightenment: Soviet Organisation of the Arts under Lunacharsky*, Cambridge University Press, Cambridge, 1970, pp 1–2.

faintly religious form that Lunacharsky gave it. Excluded from the Bolshevik Party in 1909, Lunacharsky migrated from the Capri school via Bologna to Paris (Lenin was still there), where he arrived late in 1911, at a crucial moment in French avant-garde art, and this, as already stated, he came to know extensively, if not to admire. When war broke out he retired to neutral Switzerland and lived an apparently comfortable existence supported by his mother's inheritance.

In the war-time years Lenin scarcely knew Joseph Stalin, who was in exile for revolutionary activities in the inhospitable Arctic village of Kureika in Siberia, with Sverdlov and other Bolsheviks. The two men had collaborated on defining Bolshevik policy on the national question, and Stalin had a reputation for forthright organisational work, but that is all. His background and experience were very different from Lenin's. One of the few working-class members of the then Bolshevik Party leadership, Stalin had been born a Georgian with an ancestry from the north Caucasian mountains. The grandson of serfs and the son of an alcoholic shoe-mender, himself born in serfdom, Stalin had been beaten mercilessly at home and had developed into an alert yet evasive schoolchild.[13] His mother sent him to an ecclesiastical school, and thence to the Theological Seminary in Tiflis, a grim environment regulated by strict discipline and, so it is said, mutual suspicion and intrigue among the pupils.[14] His reading in Russian and foreign literature (Hugo, Chekhov, Gogol and Thackeray) was absorbed alongside socialist literature, Darwinism and history; yet his biographers emphasise how different was his identification with working-class oppression compared with that of the other Bolshevik leaders. Born among the oppressed rather than looking down upon them from the distance which education bestowed upon the middle and upper classes, Stalin grew up with a first-hand, fighting hatred of the possessing and ruling classes. Lacking the moral sensitivity and intellectual refinement of Lenin, Trotsky, Bukharin, Lunacharsky or Kamenev, his socialism from the beginning was 'cold, sober and rough'[15](Figure 8). Deutscher draws a sharp contrast between the intellectuals among the Party leaders, 'all of whom were highly gifted orators or writers, thinkers with great élan, imagination and originality', and Stalin, whose acumen and commonsense were not matched either by originality or imagination. His acquaintances and friends were to be of a different caste to theirs. And he already suffered from a deep sense of inferiority which such comparisons could only exacerbate.

With these qualities Stalin had entered the socialist underground and had excelled both in evading the police and in organising workers' groups sympathetic to revolutionary struggle. (His later detractors tend to play down his early revolutionary accomplishments, while his allies seek to glorify them beyond the facts.) Adopting the name 'Koba', meaning 'Indomitable', he was an active organiser in the Black Sea oil port of Batumi, including the refinery owned by the Rothschilds and financed by British and French capital; he suffered imprisonment and exile before resuming work in the Baku oil region on the Caspian and gaining the recognition of the Party leader for his 'hardness' of attitude and for his organisational success and energy.

13. I. Deutscher, *Stalin, A Political Biography*, Oxford University Press, 1949 (London, 1966), p 23.

14. Ibid., p 33.

15. Ibid., p 44.

Figure 8
J. Stalin in 1905 (photo: *SCR* London)

success and energy. In the period of reaction which followed 1905 and throughout the war period Stalin was mostly in prison, in exile, in deportation, or in hiding. 'Two years of revolutionary work among the oil workers of Baku hardened one as a practical fighter and as a practical leader', he was to write later; 'In the storm of the deepest conflicts between workers and oil industrialists . . . I first learnt what it meant to lead big masses of workers.'[16] His exile from mid-1913 onwards in sub-Arctic Siberia was one devoted to physical survival, primitive hunting and fishing and, no doubt, long days and weeks of boredom. Opportunities for culture in any shape or form were nil. He wrote to his future mother-in-law Olga Alliluyeva that he wanted picture postcards because the 'stark ugliness' of the tundra offered nothing to the eye (Figure 9). 'I have been overcome by a silly longing to see some landscape', he wrote, 'be it only on paper.'[17] Meanwhile, modernist experimentation was aflame in the cities; 'landscape' was

16. Ibid., p 108.

17. Stalin, 25 November 1915;
M. Hyde, *Stalin, the History of a Dictator*,
Rupert Hart-Davis, London, 1971, p
122; I. Deutscher, *Stalin*, p 137.

Figure 9
The village of Kureika, Siberia
(photo: *SCR* London)

already a thing of the past. Stalin thus came to the Bolshevik Party with none of the cultural experience of the principal leaders. While Trotsky immersed himself in Ruskin, Maupassant and Ibsen, Stalin remained uncomprehending about Western literature. Whereas Bukharin kept animals as pets and dreamt about being an artist, Stalin hunted animals for food, and wrote for postcards. In comparison with Lunacharsky he was gruff, boorish and devoid of art. Yet he and other working class revolutionaries – Sverdlov, Shlyapnikov, Kalinin – were to rise to positions of prominence in the Bolshevik Party. And it behoves us to remember this; for it was to be their revolution too.

Such, indeed, were the men who in some form of co-operation were to make not only the Revolution in Russia but also a cultural and artistic policy for the new state. In 1917 itself the insurrection of February began as a spontaneous eruption of dissatisfaction at the privations of war and the manifest inequalities still remaining within Russian society. It was accompanied by a resurrected Petrograd Soviet of Workers' Deputies compounded of several different parties (Social-Revolutionaries, Mensheviks and Bolsheviks) that made for an unstable and even precarious relationship with the 'official' or Provisional Government that had become the immediate successor to the now fallen Romanov monarchy. (Social-Revolutionaries or SRs were concerned chiefly with mollifying the bourgeois aspirations of the peasants.) From abroad, the Bolshevik leaders had called for a conversion of the imperialist war into civil strife, and now urged the establishment of a revolutionary government of the working class, free and universal suffrage, and a thorough denunciation of the Provisional Government which they believed to be little more than 'a government of landowners and capitalists', to quote *Pravda* for March 1917.[18] Soviets were created or sprang up in several other cities; but generally the tactical question among Bolsheviks was somewhat confused – Kamenev, for example, advocating a cautious policy of 'watchful control' over the Provisional Government. On hearing the news of the February insurrection, Stalin, Trotsky and Lenin took immediate steps to return to Petrograd. Lenin's appearance in April 1917 with his message of outright opposition to the Provisional Government reaffirmed in his wavering and poorly coordinated colleagues the conviction that the bourgeois revolution embodied in the Provisional Government – if that is what it finally was – must prepare for its end. He did not declare its termination there and then, for he was not quite in a position to do so. Yet he called upon Bolsheviks quickly to gain control of the Soviets and to prepare themselves for power. The Menshevik conception of 'dual power' was impossible. 'There cannot be two powers in the state', he said.[19]

The theses which Lenin read to the Social Democratic conference at the Tauride Palace in April were felt to be incredible, even by the Bolshevik Party. Bogdanov, Lenin's one-time ally, now in purdah and yet leader of the recently formed Proletkult (Proletarian Culture) organisation, greeted Lenin's call for the proletariat to take the reins of power with cries of 'delirium, the delirium of a mad-man'.[20] Yet Lenin won over the Petrograd Party and the all-Russian meeting of the Party (also in April), persuading it to oppose fiercely continued support of the war and calling for 'the transfer of all state power in all belligerent countries into the hands of the revolutionary proletariat'.[21]

From now until October events played successively into Bolshevik hands. The involvement of the Petrograd Soviet in a reformed Provisional Government in May had the effect of splitting the SRs and Mensheviks into those who supported and those who opposed the war policy, and revealed the Bolsheviks as the only revolutionary party with a clear-cut policy amounting to peace at any price. Strengthened by the return of Trotsky from America in May, Lenin's Party was still in a minority in the Soviets, and thus took only a small number of seats at the All-Russian Central Executive Committee of the Soviets or VTsIK, which was now created to coordinate the action of individual soviets but which at this stage still voted, against the Bolsheviks, for the continuance of the Provisional Government. An attempt to arrest Kamenev, Lenin and Zinoviev in July resulted in the flight of the latter two to Finland. Trotsky, Lunacharsky and Alexandra Kollontai were arrested, and tension between the Provisional

18. Carr, 1950, p 84.

19. Lenin, Vol XX, p 114; Carr, 1950, p 93.

20. Carr, 1950, p 90.

21. Ibid., p 94.

Government and the Bolsheviks visibly heightened. With the soviets now compromised by cooperation with the Government and with Lenin himself in hiding, the position looked fraught. A failed right-wing coup led by Kornilov in August helped precipitate Bolsheviks into majority positions in the Petrograd and Moscow Soviets, even though SRs and Mensheviks still dominated VTsIK. Peasant disorder accumulated. Demobilised or disaffected soldiers showed a positive sympathy for the Bolsheviks, and it became clear to Party leaders, even those absent from the action, that conditions for an end to the bourgeois interregnum were rapidly maturing. By September Lenin believed the time was ripe for the seizure of power by force. Trotsky was released from prison and took over the leadership of the Petrograd Soviet. Lenin himself returned from hiding in disguise to counsel the Party to prepare for armed insurrection, and to appoint a 'political bureau' to carry it out when the time came – though in the event the military preparations were supervised by Trotsky and the Bolshevik-dominated Petrograd Soviet. On the morning of the planned meeting of the second All-Russian Congress of the Soviets – 7 November (25 October old style) – Bolshevik forces occupied key positions in Petrograd, with Party members assigned to organise the railways, food supplies, postal and telegraphic communications, thus forming an embryo administration functioning alongside and on behalf of the Soviet. The Provisional Government was taken captive or fled. At the meeting of the All-Russian Congress of the Soviets in the evening, all power was proclaimed to be now transferred 'throughout Russia' to Soviets of Workers', Soldiers' and Peasants' Deputies. The next day – 8 November (26 October old style) – the Council of People's Commissars (Sovnarkom) was appointed by VTsIK and the world's first Workers' and Peasants' Government was, at least tentatively, in place.

2

Revolution and Civil War
1917–1921

The Arts and Soviet Power

From the point of view of intellectuals in the bourgeois democracies some two or three generations later, it has seemed as if there were then scores of artists in Soviet Russia who were doing extraordinary and brilliant work in the days following the fall of the Provisional Government. But this is open to misunderstanding if seen solely in terms of Western European concepts of 'creativity' and individual 'achievement'.

For that is not what counted in the stricken days of 1917 and 1918. The artistic work of the months after the seizure of power must be seen against a background of very considerable uncertainty for the Soviet government. The range of influence of the government initially extended no further than the main cities, certainly not into the countryside except in isolated pockets. Even in the cities the seizure of power by the Bolsheviks was greeted with fierce opposition from landowners, employers, merchants and managers of industry and production – many of whom came out on strike. The withdrawal of Soviet Russia from the European war on apparently disadvantageous terms met with derision and resentment from allies in the capitalist countries; consequently few observers in the West believed that Soviet power could last for more than a few days or weeks. Lenin himself did not believe that the new government could hold out indefinitely unless supported by wide-scale socialist uprisings in the rest of Europe. Furthermore, after only a few weeks had passed, Cossack armies pledged to the overthrow of the Soviet regime were gathering in the Don, the Kuban and the Urals. The economy of the country was at a standstill: economic management had been seriously interrupted by the war, and industrial production in the final months of 1917 slumped virtually to nil. Socialism was very far from being established; the chances of its survival looked very slender indeed.

There was a particular difficulty for members of the artistic and cultural intelligentsia, who were confronted with real dilemmas of allegiance and affiliation following the victory of October. For the fact is that October signified an intersection of three forces; a motivated individual, a political party, and a representative chamber elected 'from below' (the All-Russian Central Executive Committee of the

Soviets, or VTsIK). Each one possessed a different kind of authority: Lenin as a revered and charismatic leader; the Party as his instrument and forum for ideas; and the soviets, as democratically elected bodies comprised of representatives of working people and peasants. Theoretically these should have been distinguishable, as organs of Party and state. But were they? And who was really in power? The fact that October was a victory for all three undoubtedly made attempts to conceptualise the Revolution confused and difficult.

This was only one problem. What was the status of the other parties – perhaps those with different viewpoints on the arts? How much credence was to be accorded to the still considerable body of Menshevik opinion that the socialist revolution had come too quickly on the heels of an incomplete bourgeois revolution only months before? It has to be reckoned with that the intelligentsia generally had not been prepared for revolution, and regarded the Bolsheviks with extreme suspicion. In the first months of the new dispensation little was known about the extent or the pace of the changes which were to come. The economy itself was tottering. Who therefore would administer publishing, the practice of the arts, education and the museums? How much was to remain of the old culture of painting, sculpture and decoration, of the literary forms of the poem or the novel, of the symphony and the sonata, of the theatre and the circus? What would become of the works of Rachmaninov, Ostrovsky, Tolstoy, Repin? For a group of people more used to speculative and creative work than to practical politics or organisation, the uncertainties must have seemed overwhelming. What did Lenin think about the arts? What did the Party say? What was to be the contribution of the soviets, and through them of the workers and peasants? Particularly for Bolshevik supporters, what precedents, if any, were there for a culture based upon the dictatorship of the proletariat? What would be the fate of artists and intellectuals who did not, or could not, wholly subscribe to the principles of the new government?

One of the persistent and perhaps tragic themes of early Soviet social and cultural life is the extent to which the functions of the Soviet Government – that is, the All-Russian Congress of the Soviets, with its Central Executive Committee (VTsIK) and its Council of People's Commissars (Sovnarkom) – very soon overlapped with, or became subordinate to, the apparatus of the Bolshevik Party. It is no exaggeration to say that little of what will occupy us in the artistic life of the period from 1917 to 1932 can be understood without an insight into the importance of this question.

Here, after all, was a form of government that had no parallel in modern history, at least not since France in 1789 (the Bolsheviks were fully aware of the comparison). Nowadays we are apt to think of Soviet power by analogy with the bourgeois constitutions of the West, with VTsIK as a kind of parliament, with Sovnarkom as an inner cabinet, and with the 'Party' as a kind of prime-ministerial think-tank. But such analogies can be misleading.

At the beginning of December 1917 the Bolsheviks (despite their support for such a body) were still in a minority in the Constituent Assembly. This had been established under the Provisional Government as an elected meeting place for different parties and it had, notionally, a higher authority than the Soviets. Nor were Bolsheviks yet predominant in VTsIK or Sovnarkom, over which Lenin nevertheless presided. Yet Lenin was highly concerned that if the SRs and surviving Mensheviks and Kadets were allowed to pursue their opposition to Bolshevism, his Party could fail to survive. 'Resistance has to be suppressed', Lenin wrote, 'and we shall suppress it by the same methods by which the propertied classes suppressed the proletariat',[1] that is, by expropriation and repression. He was personally convinced that the Constituent Assembly was a bourgeois forum, and that it had to be superseded by revolutionary Social-Democracy and an unfettered republic of soviets. Henceforward, too, other socialist parties who did not accept the basic premises of the proletarian revolution would be defined as counter-revolutionary, and vilified as such. The Constituent Assembly would have to go; thus by tactical means and by a little force the termination of the Assembly was engineered in January 1918.[2] This was only the beginning of a process – in reality a continuation of the policy of before 1917 – whereby the Bolsheviks would brook no opposition from parties outside its ranks so long as it controlled the Soviets. Arrests and imprisonments (particularly of right SRs, Kadets, Mensheviks and anarchists) swiftly followed. The principle of 'all power to the Soviets' (of workers', soldiers' and peasants' deputies) was now regularly and repeatedly proclaimed.

But what of the role of the state, which Lenin had predicted would 'wither away' in the course of the transition to a classless society? This famous doctrine derived from Marx, who viewed the state as the instrument of exploitation by the propertied classes and hence as the expression of class conflict, which would necessarily die away with the passage to Communism. Lenin, too, had written in *State and Revolution* as recently as August 1917 (not published until 1918) that the proletarian state would be 'so constituted that it will at once begin to die away and cannot help dying away'. It would not die away at once, he pointed out, but gradually, beginning immediately after the assumption of proletarian power, 'since in society without class contradictions [that is when the dictatorship of the proletariat itself becomes unnecessary] the state is unnecessary and impossible'.[3] The function of the bureaucracy, likewise – defined in Engels' words as an administrative machinery 'proceeding out of society but standing above it' – would gradually devolve to the mass: 'Under socialism *all* will administer in turn and will quickly become accustomed to nobody administering.'[4]

In practice, the extent to which the state was capable of being disbanded in the first months and years after October 1917 was radically constrained by events; first, the insecurity of the Bolshevik Party's hold on power; second, the centralised organisation's need to recover economically from the war; and third, the onset of protracted civil strife which began in 1918. Lenin held to the ideal of the disappearance of a centralised organising function all his life: he became particularly concerned about the growth of bureaucracy within both state and Party in his final years. But in the immediate aftermath of

1. Lenin, *Sochineniya*, Vol xiii, pp 109–10; Carr, 1950, p 123.

2. See the account of the closing of the Constituent Assembly by its leader, Viktor Chernov, who left Russia in 1920, in 'Russia's One-Day Parliament', *The New Leader*, New York, 31 January 1948; reprinted in T. Riha (ed) *Readings in Russian Civilisation*, Chicago and London, 1964, pp 505–8; also the account by L. Trotsky, *On Lenin: Notes Towards a Biography* (1924) George Harrap and Co, London 1971, Chapter 5.

3. Lenin, *State and Revolution*, Soch xxi, 388; Carr, 1950, p 247.

4. Lenin, *State and Revolution*, Soch xxi, 452; Carr, 1950, p 249.

the October Revolution it was an ideal which had to be reconciled with the exercise of ruthless power over the opponents of Bolshevism in the interests of establishing the conditions under which the state could even begin to decline in importance.

This apparent contradiction between self-determination on the one hand and disciplined subservience to a Bolshevik 'line' on the other is one of the animating preconditions for most cultural life in Soviet Russia between 1917 and 1921, and beyond. Lenin was certainly aware of how the need for financial management and the requirements of minimal economic, educational and legislative organisation would tend to concentrate state power at the centre rather than at the periphery or the base. But the role played by the Party in consolidating its own power increased markedly as well. Defending the practice of peremptory imprisonment and execution of Bolshevik opponents, Trotsky told VTsIK in December 1917:

> You protest against the mild terror which we are directing against our class enemies. But you should know that not later than a month from now the terror will assume very violent forms, after the example of the French Revolution. The guillotine will be ready for our enemies and not merely the jail.[5]

Days after this statement, the Military-Revolutionary Committee of the Petrograd Soviet was transformed into the All-Russian Extraordinary Commission (or Cheka) under Felix Dzerzhinsky, 'for the purpose of combating counter-revolution and sabotage'(Figure 10).[6] Here was another agonising dilemma for Bolshevism. A minimum of force was clearly desirable. And yet there were enough

5.   Bunyan & Fisher, *The Bolshevik Revolution, 1917–18*, University Press, Stanford, California, 1934, p 362; Carr, 1950, p 166.

6.   Decree of Sovnarkom, 7 December (Old Style) 1917; Carr, 1950, p 167.

Figure 10
Cheka brigade on Rostov-on-Don, 1 May 1920: 'In the struggle against economic wreckers we know of no limitation on the workers' time.' (photo: *David King*)

antagonists aligned against the Soviet state to make such a measure at least understandable: Cossack armies in the South, an incipient counter-revolution in the Ukraine, hostility from the British and the French abroad, as well as on Soviet soil, and German forces in the West. Everyday life was in a state of hiatus. Education, already primitive, was at a standstill. Cold and hunger were widespread. Looting and food hoarding were practised on a wide scale. As Lenin put it graphically, ' . . . until we apply the terror – shooting on the spot – to speculators, we shall achieve nothing.'[7] In a similar frame of mind, Lenin would urge all around him against falling prey to 'softness', to pacifism, to easy-going trustfulness in consolidating the proletariat's dictatorship. 'Where is our dictatorship?' he stormed. 'Well, show it to me. We have a mess, not a dictatorship . . . Do you really think we shall come out victorious without any revolutionary terror?'[8]

7. L. Trotsky, *On Lenin: Notes Towards a Biography*, p 118.

8. Ibid., p 118.

How would artists and writers respond to such an administration? Already the arts were divided into an enormous number of different interests, aspirations and styles. Yet now, in the late part of 1917, an entire range of functions, from theatre managers to critics, 'avant-garde' and traditional artists, designers, writers and musicians, had somehow to be brought within the sphere of Bolshevik influence. Yet most institutions of the 'old world' were still in place. The Imperial Academy, its teaching methods and professors, had not yet been reformed. Young proletarians and refugees from the bourgeois class would need educating in establishments of a totally new kind. Painting and sculpture would presumably have to continue on some terms; but how, and why, and where, were thus far unknown quantities. Also, the new regime would need to establish itself not just in the minds but in the hearts of the working class. It was soon appreciated that this would require a panoply of speeches, parades, spectacles, commemorative and propagandistic events – in short a number of new cultural forms having a whole urban population as its audience. This much was clear. But beyond this the Bolshevik leadership had as yet no policy on what part the arts should play in national life, how they were to be administered, or what style or content the full panoply of the arts under incipient socialism would have. Obviously such events would need organising, designing, festooning. Here were tasks for artists – not the traditional tasks associated with the easel and the studio, but broadly-based, participative, exhortative tasks which would need to be carried out alongside, and to some extent in competition with, the remnants of the older Tsarist and bourgeois cultures that were by no means dead or even lifeless. How the relationship between the old and the new was to be structured was an urgent and perhaps intractable difficulty. So was the larger question of censorship and control. How these problems were negotiated, and how they intersected with the theoretical debate about art in the period up to 1921, will occupy us for the remainder of this chapter.

'Left' and 'Right' in Art

Something of the urgency the new government felt for the incorporation and progress of the arts is evident from the establishment on 8 November (26 October old style) 1917 of a People's Commissariat of Enlightenment (Narodnyi komissariat prosveshcheniya, or Narkompros), headed by Lunacharsky, which would take administrative charge of education and the arts. Despite his record of previous dissension from the Bolshevik Party, Lunacharsky was considered a natural for the post, one of the most important in the new government. Temperamentally romantic rather than partisan, he was both highly cultured and a practised and persuasive orator. Lunacharsky had reconverted to Bolshevism in the year of the Revolution and now fully supported the aims of the Soviet government, becoming a personal confidant of Lenin despite the obvious fact that their views on art diverged considerably. Education policy was in every sense a key issue for Lenin. Here there existed truly enormous scope for improvement and reform. The linkage of education with art under a single ministry is also significant. After the February/May Revolution there had been proposals for a Ministry of Fine Arts, and though this was never formed a variety of artists' societies and trade unions had sprung up to represent and protect artists' interests.[1] The merging of art with education in a single commissariat after the October Revolution may reflect Lenin's (thus far unarticulated) belief that the arts, particularly literature, should have a pedagogical, reforming function; that likewise education should have a cultural role.

In the first months of its existence Narkompros met with considerable resistance from artistic groups who were either inhospitable to or suspicious of the Bolsheviks. It was bitterly attacked by Gorky's internationalist newspaper *Novaya zhizn* (New Life) whose correspondents at that time included the painters Kuzma Petrov-Vodkin (Figure 11) and Nathan Altman and the poet Mayakovsky. Narkompros was also deeply resented by the Union of Art Workers (Soyuz deyatllei iskusstv), which had been set up in Petrograd after the February Revolution and which now refused to cooperate with Lunacharsky unless he guaranteed it complete autonomy from the state and freedom to carry out its own plan to reform the powerful Academy of Arts and its associated institutions.[2] The Union of Art Workers was a diverse organisation, whose left wing, sympathetic to Bolshevism, appeared as anxious not to be engulfed by the machinery of state as the right, which consisted of more traditional artists who had previously belonged to the Palace Ministry, and who were now led by the Symbolist poet Fyodor Sologub. But it must have presented a powerful challenge to Lunacharsky's plans. In November 1917 it appealed to the already doomed Constituent Assembly for funds to support art schools and museums, declaring itself to be 'the only organ which has the right to direct the artistic life of the country'[3] – the first of several such appeals by powerful artistic lobbies to *unilaterally* determine the direction of art in the new state.

It is conventionally asserted that 'left-wing' art enjoyed a position

1. See V. Makovsky, 'Ministerstvo iskusstv', *Apollon* (Petrograd), no 2/3, 1917, pp 1–16.

2. C. Lodder, *Russian Constructivism*, Yale University Press, London and New Haven, 1983, p 48, n 10.

3. Fitzpatrick, *Commissariat of the Enlightenment*, Cambridge University Press, 1970, p 114.

Figure 11
K. Petrov-Vodkin, *Self-Portrait*, 1918 (photo: *Novosti*)

of hegemony in the Soviet Union between 1917 and about 1920; that there occurred a dramatic 'flowering' of the 'avant-garde' which suddenly vindicated the presumed connection between radical artistic style and radical political thought. Yet while it is true that 'left-wing' artists and critics enjoyed freedoms and opportunities which they did not have (or did not take) before 1917, it can also be argued that their situation was insecure, certainly problematical, from the first days of Bolshevik power onwards.

Whatever it may mean to say that 'the October Revolution liberated the arts',[4] it is also a fact that none of the Bolshevik Party leaders had any real sympathy for 'left-wing' art and were, therefore, for the first 24 months after October 1917, more or less seriously compromised between their need to see visible signs of support from the younger intellectuals, and their conviction, frequently enough expressed before 1917 as well as in certain cases after, that 'radical' art of the 'avant-garde' was a product of bourgeois society and should sooner or later be replaced.

This conflict was most evident in the person of Lunacharsky himself, for more than a decade a convinced member of the Proletkult theory of 'art for and from the proletariat', but now suddenly catapulted into the impossible role of supervising education and the arts in a war-torn and economically ravaged country. Lunacharsky's attitude to the 'left-wing' artists initially was not so much one of sympathy, but of tolerance and compromise. They were, after all, young and energetic, and the handful that had declared their open support for the Bolshevik government were considered useful allies.

Thus certain artists belonging to what became known as the artistic 'left' were prepared to support, even to work within, Narkompros, at this point the sole official state body for the organisation of the arts. Among visual artists, Tatlin, Rodchenko and Ivan Puni were enthusiastic. As Tatlin said: ' . . . to accept or not to accept . . . there was no such question for me. I organically merged into active creative, social and pedagogical life'.[5] Among writers and dramatists, Blok and Mayakovsky were enthusiastic supporters of the new regime, Blok being a late convert from the ranks of the Symbolists and whose poems 'The Twelve' and 'The Scythians' of 1918 (the former of which is quoted here) were widely regarded as major revolutionary utterances (they were not, however, followed by similar politically conscious works):

> The wind plays up: snow flutters down.
> Twelve men are marching through town.
> Their rifle butts on black slings sway.
> Lights left, right, left, wink all the way.
> Cap tilted, fag drooping, every one
> Looks like a jailbird on the run
> Freedom, freedom,
> Down with the cross![6]

Along with Blok and Mayakovsky, the young theatre director Vsevolod Meyerhold was among the few to accept an invitation from

4. E. Valkenier, *Russian Realist Art*, Ardis, Ann Arbor, Michigan, 1977, p 143.

5. Tatlin, *Kratkii obzor*; cited by Lodder, *Russian Constructivism*, 1983, pp 47–8; from a private archive, Moscow.

6. A. Blok, 'The Twelve', 1918, in the translation by J. Stallworthy and P. France, *Alexander Blok, The Twelve & Other Poems*, London, 1970, p 145.

Lunacharsky to attend a meeting in November 1917 to discuss the reorganisation of the arts – most of the 120 invitees declined.

Meyerhold, unlike Blok, had already been sympathetic to Bolshevism for some time. He had witnessed the brutal suppression of a student demonstration in 1901 and had stated then that

> the theatre is capable of playing an enormous part in the transformation of the whole of existence . . . I am irritated by those comrades of mine who have no desire to rise above the narrow interests of their caste and respond to the interests of society.[7]

In the intervening years he had not always followed the implications of this statement; he had become a devotee of 'marvels and enchantment . . . breathless joy and strange magic'.[8] Yet in 1917 he went over to the Bolsheviks and threw himself into collaboration with Mayakovsky, taking up an important post within the theatrical section of Narkompros and becoming a Party member in 1918.

Mayakovsky is the poet who is now most firmly identified with the Revolution, at least since being lavishly praised by Stalin in the 1930s. Mayakovsky had been interested in political agitation since his teens, had been imprisoned for associating with the Bolsheviks, and was in 1917 considered a leading member of 'Futurism' since being introduced into that milieu by David Burlyuk in 1912. Temperamentally and by conviction he hated the vague sentimentalism of the Symbolists, and had the deepest disregard for the 'lyricism' and affectation of 'bourgeois' poetry. Loud and rebellious in tone and style, Mayakovsky fused Futurist techniques – broken metres, assonance, novel punctuation and staccato abruptness of diction – with topics of unquestionable contemporary relevance, both impassioned and timely. Vivid figures of speech had become his *forte* even before 1917 – now he would compare his heart with 'a bordello on fire', and his words with 'prostitutes leaping from its blazing windows'. He was also a fine painter (Figure 12). Equally concerned with visual art from the early years of the Revolution, Mayakovsky published on 15 March 1918 a 'Decree Concerning the Democratisation of Art (Writings on Hoardings and Painting in Public Places)', signed also by Kamensky and Burlyuk, declaring 'all art for all of the people' and urging artists to

> seize their paintpots and use the brushes of their trade to illuminate and bedeck all the flanks, foreheads and breasts of cities and stations, and the endlessly running flock of railroad trucks. From now on, the citizen will at every moment savour the colourful brilliance of today's joyful beauty and listen everywhere to the music – melodies, thunderous or noisy – of superb composers.[9]

But it is the fact that Mayakovsky's techniques were forged not in the Revolution itself but in the circles of literary and artistic Futurism and specifically in the period of political and social reaction before 1917, that is of significance. As already noted, Futurist intellectual activity had flourished in the period before 1917 almost independently of politics. It had been concentrated in the very heart of bourgeois life,

7. V. Meyerhold, Letter of 18 April 1901; E. Braun, *Meyerhold on Theatre*, Methuen and Co, London 1969, p 159.

8. V. Meyerhold, *Teatr*, 24 October 1913, p 5; Braun, *Meyerhold*, p 159.

9. V. Mayakovsky, *Gazetta futuristov*, 15 March 1918.

Figure 12
V. Mayakovsky, *Self-Portrait*, c.1915
(photo: Coll. *V. V. Katanyan*)

in uproarious café discussions, poetry readings and displays of iconoclastic behaviour, in both Moscow and Petrograd. Mayakovsky himself, unlike other Futurists, openly and enthusiastically welcomed the Revolution when it came. However the 'Futurist' label that he had accepted before 1917 was one that he would find it increasingly hard to live down. When Lenin learned that Lunacharsky had arranged for a printing of 5,000 copies of Mayakovsky's poem '150,000,000' he wrote to his Commissar in a fury: the poem is 'nonsense, stupidity, double-eyed stupidity and affectation', said Lenin. 'I believe that such things should be published one in ten and not more than 1,500 copies, for libraries and cranks. As for Lunacharsky, he should be flogged for his Futurism.'[10]

Futurism in general was an uncertain quantity for Narkompros. In the visual arts, the attitude was one of compromise and accommodation. A Fine Art Department (Otdel izobrazitelnykh iskusstv or IZO) was established within Narkompros in January 1918 with Vladimir Tatlin in charge in Moscow and the painter David Shterenberg as its general head in Petrograd. Despite the fact that Shterenberg was not a Futurist, IZO Narkompros for a time became a haven for experimental or 'avant-garde' artists, together with other groups. Several less 'progressive' artists who refused to cooperate with the new state agreed nevertheless to work in the Department of Museums and Conservation of Antiquities.

Several prominent modernist emigrés returned to the Soviet Union before 1917 and played a variety of somewhat ambiguous roles in the new artistic administration. Marc Chagall, who had enjoyed the stimulus of Apollinaire's circle in Paris before 1914 but who had no interest in politics, returned to Russia in that year (largely by accident – he had travelled to visit his fiancée and had intended to return to Paris) and painted in a semi-mystical vein derived from his Hasidic Jewish religion, producing paintings which suffused daily life with an atmosphere of ecstasy and celebration. Throughout the events of summer and autumn 1917 Chagall had been on holiday with his wife, but returned to his home town of Vitebsk in November, having shied away from the prospect of an appointment alongside Mayakovsky and Meyerhold in the capital.[11] (Chagall was sympathetic to Bolshevism's pledge to promote Jewish artists, who had hitherto suffered appalling victimisation.[12] He had worked with Lisitsky on the promotion of Jewish artistic life in Petrograd before the Revolution.) Kandinsky too, though avowedly uninterested in politics, had returned to Russia in 1914 and despite having done very little painting in the war years was active from 1918 onwards within Narkompros, contributing plans for a network of contemporary art museums and attempting to gain acceptance for his ideas in various art schools and research institutes.[13] Yet it was necessary for Kandinsky repeatedly to stipulate that he would have nothing to do with practical politics. As he himself said, 'I have absolutely no interest in politics. I am totally unpolitical and was never active in politics. I have never read newspapers.'[14]

From this evidence alone we can say that although international modernists came to be considered to belong to an artistic 'left', they

10. Lenin, letter to A. V. Lunacharsky, May 6, 1921; *Collected Works*, Vol 45, pp 138–9; *Lenin on Literature and Art*, p 235.

11. F. Meyer, *Marc Chagall*, New York, n.d., p 254.

12. In fact it was not the Bolsheviks who had inaugurated citizens' rights for Jews. Shortly after the February (March old style) Revolution of 1917, the Provisional Government of Lvov and Kerensky had issued a decree (March 20 old style, that is, April 2) removing all inequalities from Jewish people and declaring them, in effect, equal citizens with the non-Jewish population. This was entitled *On the Revocation of Religious and National Disabilities* (see R. Browder and A. Kerensky (eds) *Provisional Government of 1917: Documents*, Princeton University Press, 1961). A Jewish Congress was quickly formed – it never met, owing to the October Revolution – which declared the new status given to Jews to have 'no parallel in Jewish history for two thousand years'; see S. Baron, *The Russian Jew under the Tsars and Soviets*, p 168, who cites L. Chasanowitsch and L. Motzkin (eds) *Die Judenfrage der Gegenwart: Dokumentensammlung*, Stockholm 1919, pp 35 ff. The Bolshevik revolution of October 1917 confirmed this tolerance of Jews; in fact the Bolshevik party contained many Jews in its top echelons. See Baron, pp 169–70, who gives a list.

13. On the former, see Kandinsky's articles: 'The Museum and the Culture of Painting', 'The Great Utopia' and 'Steps taken by the Department of Fine Arts in the Realm of International Art Politics', published in *Khudozhestvennaya zhizn* (Artistic Life) from 1919 to 1920, and translated in K. Lindsay and P. Vergo (eds) *Kandinsky's Complete Writings*, Faber and Faber, London, 1982, Vol 1, pp 434–54.

14. W. Kandinsky, in *Artists Write to W. Grohmann* (ed K. Gutbrod), Cologne, 1968, p 46.

Figure 13
K. Malevich, *Suprematist Composition: White on White*, c.1918 (photo: *Museum of Modern Art, New York*)

15.   V. Lobanov, *Khudezhestvennye gruppirovki za poslednie 25 let*, Moscow, 1930.

stand in no simple correlation either to the revolutionary centre of the Bolshevik Party or to the political 'left' within Bolshevism. Like the overwhelming majority of the Russian 'intelligentsia', most were covertly either opposed or indifferent to the new regime. Another obstacle to any neat arrangement of categories is that even among the modernist artists who supported (or who were supported by) the new regime, the kinds of theoretical and aesthetic programmes put forward by the various groups varied wildly, offering a series of highly contrasting formal analogies for the Revolution in terms of art. Much more needs to be said about the metaphorical and/or metonymic relationship in which these formal devices stood to the Revolution, and something will be said in succeeding chapters. In practice, Narkompros was eager to encourage most artistically 'left' manifestations, at least for a time. Between 1918 and 1921 Lunacharsky and his Commissariat gave licence for a series of 'State Exhibitions' of new art,[15] each of which was nevertheless dominated by this or that group with vested interests of its own. In-fighting was rife. Rhetoric was keen, and sometimes absurd. The central question hovering above and in the background of most of those activities – many of them taken up enthusiastically, but for different reasons, by members of the Western European 'avant-garde' – was how to produce and carry into effect an artistic programme which would in some sense 'correspond' to the new life which was being formed about them in the most hazardous of conditions.

Just what kind of tentative, experimental culture this amounted to is best appreciated by a few examples. Malevich, to take the case of an ostensibly 'spiritual' modernist, had gained some notoriety before the Revolution with his Suprematist system, and now claimed some degree of affinity with the Bolshevik regime (he had become chairman of the art section of the Moscow Council of Soldiers' Deputies after the February revolution of 1917). Following the October Revolution Malevich was active in teaching and in exhibitions, and was widely employed in public decorations, graphic design and environmental adornment generally. Although the '0.10' exhibition of 1915 had been received with some puzzlement even within the 'avantgarde', Suprematism by 1918 had become so widely visible that, as one report had it, 'Suprematism has blossomed throughout Moscow. Signs, exhibitions, cafés, everything is Suprematist. One may say with assurance that Suprematism has arrived.'[16] Malevich by now had become more confident and more ambitious than before about the applicability of his new system of coloured rectangles, circles and squares. By 1918 he claimed to equate Suprematism with the foundations of an entire new spiritual and artistic culture.

His painting 'White on White' of that year (Figure 13) is symptomatic of the strengths and limitations of the new transcendental system. 'The Whites' were counter-revolutionary forces who were engaged in civil war with the Red Army until late in 1920; nevertheless Malevich equates White with a transcendent, visionary future. He writes at this time that mankind will achieve 'whiteness' when the Revolution is finally complete.[17] White, he says, will be the colour of the future. By 1918, all colours (including black) had come to represent to Malevich the world of objects and the world of the senses. Green was anathema to him, just as it was for Kandinsky and Mondrian, suggesting the old idea of nature and the natural world. Blue represented sky, which by then Malevich had also 'gone beyond'. White on the other hand was the colour of ice, of the frozen north where the free bear of Russia could roam;[18] the colour of the chasm into which the aviators of the future could fly. 'Infinity', declaims Malevich, 'is before us'.[19]

Chagall, after October 1917, had returned to the relative quiet of Vitebsk to pursue his painting. Yet by August 1918 he had obtained permission from Lunacharsky to establish a school of art; and on 12 September he was appointed Commissar of Art for Vitebsk, with responsibility for art schools, museums, lectures and theatre, not only in Vitebsk but in the surrounding region.[20] The appointment was less than a happy one. At first, he set about his task with enthusiasm, organising the decoration of the entire town for the first anniversary of the Revolution in 1918 (Figure 14). In successive issues of *Vitebsk Gazette*[21] he summoned artists to submit designs for banners and decorations, and organised a jury to select the best. Shops were painted. Hundreds of banners were prepared. Red bunting decorated the streets. The decorations were on the whole well received, though the scheme was attacked in the local *Izvestiya* in an article which asked how many pairs of underwear could be made from the fifteen thousand metres of cotton used for the bunting.[22] As Chagall noted later

16. N. Punin, 'V Moskve. O novikh khudozhestvennikh gruppirovkakh', *Iskusstvo kommuny*, no 10, 9 November 1919; cited in Gray, *'Great Experiment*, p 209.

17. A. C. Birnholz, 'On the Meaning of Kazemir Malevich's White on White', *Art International*, XX1/1, 1972, p 14.

18. Malevich, *Essays on Art*, Vol I, p 40.

19. Malevich, Vol I, pp 121–2.

20. This was another decision which his wife Bella urged him – this time unsuccessfully – not to take. 'Unfortunately she is always right', Chagall laments on p 134 of *My Life*, when he realised how much less time he would have to devote to painting.

21. *Vitebskii listok*, from September 12 to October 28, 1918; see Meyer, *Marc Chagall*, pp 264–5 and notes 2–9, p 605.

22. *Izvestiya of the Soviet of the Representatives of the Peasants, the Workers, the Red Army and the Farm Workers of the Vitebsk region*, October 19, 1918; Meyer, *Marc Chagall*, p 266.

Figure 14
M. Chagall, panel display for a public building, 1918

in his autobiography, certain people, including Party officials, were unsympathetic to his schemes. 'Why is the cow green and why is the horse flying in the sky? Why? What has that to do with Marx and Lenin?' were among the questions asked.[23]

It is typical of the twentieth-century modernist 'avant-garde' that in conceptual terms there was a straying away from practical political debate into the margins of religion, 'philosophy' and so on. That had a definable purpose in relation to non-revolutionary bourgeois culture; but under a regime known as the 'dictatorship of the proletariat' it is important to consider the extent to which these relationships became necessarily unfixed. Unfortunately there was (and is) no special formula for these relationships. A glance at the collection compiled by George Costakis and exhibited widely in Europe and the United States in recent years [24] shows one thing relatively clearly; just how stylistically various this abstract and experimental 'avant-garde' was, and how problematic was its relationship with the ostensible concerns of the Bolshevik administration as well as with the cultural level of the exhausted and materially disenfranchised proletariat (Figures 15, 20). The terms on which such a variegated 'avant-garde' could continue to exist were bound to be very controversial indeed.

Only a particular sub-group within the Futurists, the so-called Komfut (Communist Futurist) group, consciously attempted to forge exact conceptual connections between Communism as an economic, political and social goal and Futurism as an artistic ideology. Centred round the IZO-supported magazine *Iskusstvo kommuny* (Art of the Commune) which had a brief life between December 1918 and April 1919, Komfut was formally founded in January 1919. Komfut was particularly strongly opposed to Italian Futurism and particularly wished to denounce the already visibly fascist tendencies of that movement. Including such eminent names as Boris Kushner, Osip Brik, Natan Altman, Vladimir Mayakovsky and David Shterenberg, Komfut required membership of the Bolshevik Party and enjoined study of 'cultural communist ideology' at the group's own school.[25] An initial Komfut statement in *Iskusstvo kommuny* heralded that

> a Communist regime demands a Communist consciousness. All forms of life, morality, philosophy, and art must be re-created according to communist principles. Without this, the subsequent development of the Communist Revolution is impossible.[26]

The statement goes on to accuse Narkompros of still cleaving to the cultural habits of the gentry and the bourgeoisie, of failing to create a real communist ideology. 'It is essential to summon the masses to creative activity', the statement ends.[27] Kushner himself was implacably opposed to the remnants of bourgeois culture being smuggled into the new Soviet life, or of being retained there under another guise. 'They used to think that art was beauty . . . divination, revelation, incarnation, transubstantiation', he wrote; (whereas) 'to the socialist consciousness, a work of art is no more than an object, a thing.'[28] Or, as the Formalist critic Nikolay Punin suggested in his lectures to art students in the summer of 1919, artistic creation was as

Figure 15
V. Lebedev, *Woman Ironing*, 1920

23. Chagall, *My Life*, p 139; Meyer, *Marc Chagall*, p 266.

24. *Russian Avant-Garde Art: The George Costakis Collection* (ed. A. Rudenstine), Thames and Hudson, London 1971.

25. It may be symptomatic that neither Komfut nor Boris Kushner are referred to in the 527 pages of the *George Costakis Collection* volume cited earlier, except for a single brief reference to Kushner in the chronology at the end of the book. This is characteristic of Western scholars and collectors who have tried to wrest Communist ideology – and all the problems attendant on that connection – away from the work of abstract and experimental artists.

26. 'Programmnaya deklaratsiya', *Iskusstvo kommuny*, no 8, 26 January 1919, p 3; Bowlt, *Russian Art of the Avant Garde, Theory and Criticism 1902–1934*, The Viking Press, New York 1976, p 165.

27. 'Programmnaya deklaratsiya', Bowlt, *Russian Art of the Avant-Garde*, p 166.

discoverable in mathematical terms as the workings of a steam engine, in particular

$$S (Pi + Pii + Piii + \ldots \ldots P\pi) Y = T$$

where P are artistic principles, Y is intuition and T is artistic creation.[29] Obviously this is primitive mathematics, and perhaps not usable as science. Yet such formulations had the effect of suggesting metaphorically that art could be assimilated to science; that 'modern art criticism in general and any modern judgement on art must once and for all finish with those arbitrary, individual and often capricious impressions that spectators get from the work of art.'[30] Highly articulate and successful as polemicists, the Komfut group developed a fervent critical manner that became the scourge of government organisations and more moderate Futurists alike. It was in the circle close to Komfut and *Iskusstvo kommuny* that the ideas central to 'Constructivism' were first elaborated, ideas that were later taken up in an international context. Yet their eventual failure to acquire and secure long-lasting patronage in their own country, let alone popular support, is one of the decisive structural facts of early Soviet culture. It was in the efforts of the Komfut group that many of the dilemmas of international modernism vis-a-vis 'left' politics were most graphically contained.

It should be noted that the very rhetoric commanded by the different art groups of the Civil War period had its own qualities. Desperate and yet romantic, embattled and yet utopian, even when its model was science, it is notable how often this rhetoric sought to do down or malign the programme of some other group in addition to advertising its own. Relations between every sector of the visual arts community seemed strained and battle-strewn in the Civil War of 1918 to the end of 1920. Futurists, almost by second nature, were given to high-flown attacks on other parties. The Futurists within IZO Narkompros singled out for particular attention the members of Mir Iskusstva (World of Art), the most middle-of-the-road group in Russia in both artistic and political terms; reserving greater vehemence only for the traditional 'realist' artists, even though several of them, such as Kustodiev and Malyutin, had joined the Bolshevik cause in their own manner (Figure 16). Shterenberg of the Petrograd IZO was himself capable of being uncompromising. In an article of Autumn 1918, he said:

> We must speak directly; he who is not with us is against us . . . let only those who break and destroy forms in order to create new ones be with us, because they and we have a single thought – Revolution. Long live the proletariat! Long live the revolution in art![31]

Yet Mayakovsky's attacks on classics like Pushkin and the necessity for destroying all artistic precedents from the past, published in *Iskusstvo kommuny*, caused Lunacharsky considerable embarrassment. He reiterated once more his defence of many artistic approaches; but took the opportunity of gently rebuking the Futurists for their implied assumption that they were necessarily superior to everyone else.

28. B. Kushner, 'Bozhestvennoe proizvedenie' ('The Divine Work of Art'), *Iskusstvo kommuny*, no 9, February 2, 1919, p 1; Bowlt, *Russian Art of the Avant-Garde*, pp 167, 170; reprinted in I. Matsa (ed) *Sovetskoe iskusstvo za 15 let, materialy i dokumentatsiya*, Moscow–Leningrad 1933, pp 169–71.

29. N. Punin, *Pervyi tsikl lektsii*, Petrograd, 1920; extracted in J. E. Bowlt, *Russian Art of the Avant-Garde*, pp 170–6; see also Bowlt, 'Russian Formalism and the Visual Arts', *20th Century Studies*, no 718, December 1972, pp 131–46.

30. Punin, *Pervyi tsikl lektsii*; Bowlt, *Russian Art of the Avant-Garde*, p 174.

31. *Shterenberg*, cited in Fitzpatrick, *Commissariat*, p 124.

Figure 16
B. Kustodiev, *Old Man and his Money*, 1918, Brodsky Museum, Leningrad (Photo: *Novosti*)

32. Fitzpatrick, *Commissariat*, p 126, no reference supplied.

It would be a misfortune indeed [Lunacharsky said] if the artistic innovators finally imagined themselves to be a state artistic school, to be official exponents of an art which, although revolutionary, was dictated from above.[32]

What was Lunacharsky's attitude then to the 'right' artists, those who clung to traditional styles, or who tried to infuse them with contemporary content? Certainly Narkompros attracted a moderate amount of support from some artists of more traditional persuasions, and in Moscow, shortly after the Revolution, managed to persuade the artists' union Izograf, which was mostly comprised of 'realists' and easel painters, to cooperate on working out a plan for artistic life in the city including the protection of the art collections and historical monuments and devising a plan for the Moscow Academy of Arts. So varied was the task with which Narkompros was entrusted that it was possible to elicit support from many different segments of artistic opinion, even those that might have been mutually incompatible with each other.

So far as the Mir iskusstva group was concerned, only a few members, such as Igor Grabar and Alexandr Benois, took up the invitation to cooperate with the Commissariat. Of the Association for Travelling Art Exhibitions or Peredvizhniki, many had quickly emigrated at the time of the Revolution, and the majority of those who remained in the country refused to support the Bolsheviks and sank into hostile silence. Repin may be characteristic. He had found the turmoil of 1905 distasteful and wanted nothing more than to consolidate his newly-won status as a property owner and darling of the rich. He and the other Peredvizhniki who sulked in indignation after October 1917 only hastened the summary closure of the Academy of Art in April 1918 and the dismissal of its professors, many of whom were Peredvizhniki members or supporters.

When the Free State Art Studios (SVOMAS) were founded in 1918 only a small number of the older Peredvizhniki (such as Arkady Rylov) transferred to them from the Academy. This was despite the fact that 'realism' still retained a considerable measure of popularity among students, and many younger artists, who had been trained in 'realist' techniques, came forward either as teachers or students (Figure 17). Those of an academic persuasion, however, had to endure

Figure 17
A. Rylov, *In the Blue Expanse*, 1918, Tretyakov Gallery, Moscow (photo: *Tretyakov Gallery*)

the invective of the Futurists, Suprematists and others who were stridently proclaiming the necessity to 'burn Raphael' and uncompromisingly overturn the art of the past. Nevertheless, large numbers of exhibitions were held, both under the aegis of Narkompros and otherwise, in which considerable numbers of easel paintings and 'realist' works were shown.[33] The psychological boycott of Narkompros activity by the Peredvizhniki was one that was probably

33. See V. Lobanov, *Khudozhestvennye gruppirovki*, 1930.

genuinely regretted within the Commissariat. As Shterenberg himself put it (and he was an easel painter, although not a 'realist'), 'I will not make reference to . . . the so-called political sabotage [by the non-Futurist groups] for fear of hurting either this or that trend'.[34] But the implied accusation of sabotage was, to some, a hurtful one. Vladimir Makovsky's son, himself a Peredvizhniki painter, wrote to his friend the poet Baksheev saying how 'we sit in our holes, hungry and cold, and dream of how to make a penny'. Remaining members of the Peredvizhniki continued to meet and discuss their situation, and, says Makovsky, decided to participate in some Narkompros exhibitions, in part 'not to be accused of sabotage', but also in part to respond to popular demand for their work, demand which they considered, and probably with good reason, was still high.[35]

It is significant that even some supporters of the 'avant-garde' recognised that for the mass of the people, paintings still needed to be pictures. As Nikolay Punin admitted in an article of April 1919, there seemed to exist an affinity between Peredvizhniki 'realism' and the mass of the Soviet people. In his lectures of that summer he confessed:

> It is possible that many of you would like to read something more in modern artists' pictures than they can and should give. That is understandable because there still dwells in you, and probably will dwell for a long time yet, the desire to see in the artist a man of letters, a philosopher, a moralist . . . [36]

Punin tries to distinguish between the philistine *lumpenproletariat* and the genuine proletariat who will immediately identify with the 'avant-garde'. 'For the mob', says Punin loftily, 'painting as a pure art form, painting as an element, is unintelligible unless it is diluted with literary and other aspects of artistic creation.'[37] Yet his statements may be taken as an admission that the new formal art and its criticism had, after almost two years of fervent activity, no broad appeal.

It must be apparent that 'left' and 'right' in artistic parlance were only partly descriptive terms. Their use was largely rhetorical, too. They characterised only the extremes of the spectrum – abstract, experimental and perhaps 'formal' on the one hand, and traditional, conservative and perhaps 'popular' on the other. Between these extremes were many shades of opinion and many ways of gauging the relative distance between one opinion and another. That there were such differences, shades, distances, is a central fact of Soviet art in the years immediately after 1917. There was no single 'left' position, nor a single 'right' or even 'centre' standpoint. And even though what was termed 'left' was in some sense ascendant in certain quarters, this is not to be taken to imply that other opinions, tastes, proclivities and dispositions, many of them deeply traditional, were not still active – several in latent as well as overt form.

Lenin's own confessedly conservative opinion should be borne in mind once more. According to Lunacharsky's recollections, he valued 'the art of the past, especially Russian realism, including the Peredvizhniki'.[38] But how widely was this opinion known? And – the

34. D. Shterenberg, 'Otchet deyatelnosti otdela Izobrazitelnykh Iskusstv Narkomprosa', *Izobrazitelnoe iskusstvo*, no 1, 1919, p 70; Valkenier, *Russian Realist Art*, p. 146.

35. Makovsky to Baksheev, Letter of 4 Feb 1919; Valkenier, *Russian Realist Art*, p 146.

36. N. Punin, *Lectures*, 1919; published as *Pervyi tsikl lektsii*, Petrograd 1920; in Bowlt, *Russian Art of the Avant-Garde*, p 176. Punin, *Iskusstvo kommuny*, April 13, 1919, p 1; Valkenier, *Russian Realist Art*, p 146.

37. N. Punin, *Lectures*; Bowlt, *Russian Art of the Avant-Garde*, p 173.

38. A. Lunacharsky, 'Lenin i iskusstvo', 1924, in A. Lunacharsky, *Ob izobrazitelnom iskusstve* (ed I. A. Sots), Moscow 1967, Vol 2, p 11; or in English in the excerpt 'Lenin and the Arts' in *Lenin on Literature and Art*, Moscow, 1967, p 285.

crucial question – how was Bolshevism to be measured against the plurality of artistic form that had now arisen? For what had just been born and was still being strenuously fought for was the creation of a single political and economic ideology, a single code of civic and private behaviour, a single standpoint vis-a-vis the capitalist world of the present and the bourgeois world of the past. It was the appearance of a yawning gap between the singularity of this world-view and the diversity of its cultural expressions that lay at the root of many of the cultural dilemmas of this and the immediately later period. Most aesthetic manifestos were appeals to represent a *singular* world-view precisely with a *singular* artistic code. Yet it was the very *plurality* of these singular appeals that pitched the art of the period into more or less ceaseless controversy and turmoil both for participants and observers alike.

Proletarian Art, Literature and Music

A complete picture of Soviet art in the years immediately after the Revolution is impossible without an insight into the work of the Proletkult (Proletarskaya kultura) organisation, founded after the February Revolution on the basis of ideas laid down some ten years earlier in the circle of Bogdanov, Lunacharsky and Gorky. A Proletkult conference took place in Petrograd days before the October Revolution in 1917 and a similar event was held in April 1918 in Moscow. Covering literature, art, music, education, club-work and theatre, Proletkult grew rapidly during its first year, based on the principles of proletarian consciousness, independence from government, and collectivism. As a resolution at the First All-Russian Conference of the Proletkult held in Moscow from 15 to 20 September 1918, explained:

> Art organises social experience by means of living images, not only in the sphere of cognition, but also in the sphere of feeling and desire. As a consequence it is a most powerful weapon for the organisation of collective forces, and in a class society, of class forces.
> The proletariat must have its own class art to organise its own forces in social labour, struggle and construction. The spirit of this art is that of labour collectivism: it perceives and reflects the world from the point of view of the labour collective.[1]

The Proletkult organisation was probably the most important specifically Soviet agency for the practice of the arts after 1917, and at its height involved literally hundreds of thousands of people in education, workshops, artistic practice and training. Organised chiefly by Alexandr Bogdanov, Platon Kerzhentsev (real name P. M. Lebedev) and P. Lebedev-Polyansky (real name P. I. Lebedev), its relations with other art groups were strained from the beginning. Proletkult came into sharp conflict with the Futurists, with Narkompros, and most importantly with Lenin.

It is worth examining a little more closely what kind of organisation Proletkult was. From 1918 Proletkult had some 1,000 studio

1. Quoted by N. Brodsky, V. Lvov-Rogachevski and N. Sidorov, *Literaturnye Manifesty*, Moscow, 1929, pp 130–1. See E. Brown, *The Proletarian Episode in Russian Literature 1928–1932*, Columbia University Press, New York, 1953, p 7.

workshops throughout the relatively small territory then under the control of the Bolsheviks, with some 400,000 members. The Proletkult published some twenty journals, including *Proletarskaya kultura, The Future, The Furnace, The Siren* and others. As one correspondent wrote, 'Proletkult has its cells in every factory.'[2] Clearly its organisational base and its membership were considerable. Despite its disagreements with Narkompros over the question of the participation of the intelligentsia and the role to be played by previous art, Proletkult still received encouragement from Narkompros for both its basic policy of encouraging studio work and attempting to uncover genuine talent among the urban workforce, in painting, sculpture, literature and the other arts.

2.   Quoted in Fitzpatrick, *Commissariat*, p 98.

So far as the Bolshevik Party was concerned the major anxiety over Proletkult was its platform of independence from government as an autonomous organisation removed from economics and politics; this raised a controversy which we shall examine shortly. On the question of the content of proletarian culture it is less easy to be exact, because by its very nature it took many forms and did not fall immediately into the rhetorical categories of 'left' and 'right'. Some Proletkult work was inspired by traditional examples. Some of it was led by Futurists within its ranks. All of it, necessarily, was amateur, and was staunchly opposed to the concept of a professional artistic élite.

Among artists, suffice it to say that there was no unanimous approach that was considered suitable for adoption in the Proletkult studios. Several Futurists, for example Olga Rozanova, were sympathetic to Proletkult and worked within it; yet 'realistic' and 'popular' styles were influential there too. In literature and poetry the position was equally complex. Perhaps the dominant general aspiration was that the writing and reception of literature should be stripped of its mystical and spiritual associations and made amenable to materialist, Marxist analysis. Terms like 'genius' and 'inspiration' were no longer to apply, or, rather, they were to be analysed into so many simple, comprehensible ideas.

Poetry was to be treated accordingly. From before the Revolution the so-called Formalist school grouped around Viktor Shklovsky and Roman Jacobson had advocated the analysis of language into its elemental structural units, and Futurist poets like Khlebnikov and Kruchonykh had split words into smaller segments and taken them out of the sentential context for poetic ends. Now, a mechanical view of poetry was developed which stood apart from the contemporary Futurist poetics of Mayakovsky, Gastev, and their followers. The 'imagist' group led by Vadim Shershenevich and Anatoly Marienhof proposed a radical separation of the poem into self-contained 'image-units' which did not connect with others: the poem could be read backwards, or in part, just as a painting by Yakulov or Erdmann (whom they admired) could be hung upside down without loss. Imaginists were particularly active in the field of anti-religious poetry, and the Bryusov Institute was formed to put these ideas into practice. Here, writers of all kinds, including poets, were trained according to materialist methods, and aimed eventually to spread the ability to write effectively, even artistically, 'to the entire Soviet people'.[3]

The demystificatory and democratising ideals of the Bryusov Institute poets – though not their methods – were also common objectives of those who attempted to infuse their writing with actual revolutionary sentiments and who were sympathetic to the Proletkult ideal. Of these, Mayakovsky is the best known, and it is interesting to note how he was attracted by the monumentalising spirit exemplified by schemes such as Lenin's for sculpture in public places, the Plan for Monumental Propaganda. Monumentality was not to be achieved by lengthy or epic verses so much as by broadly sketched images of the whole proletariat in its forward march. Mayakovsky's poem '150,000,000', which Lenin so disliked, is declamatory, enthusiastic and even aggressive:

> Down with the madness of possession in all its forms! . . .
> Be athletically valiant, with tense muscles,
> Full of the religion of action!
> Your soul!
> Steam, compressed air, electricity . . .

or, a few lines later:

> Onward!
> Drive your elbows into ribs like iron spikes,
> Crash your fists into the jaws of the elegant charity
> gentlemen tightly buttoned into frockcoats!
> Your knuckle-dusters into their noses!
> Tabula rasa!

The poem is dedicated to the creative force of the masses:

> One hundred and fifty million:
> That is the name of the composer of this poem.
> The rattling of shot and shell:
> That is its rhythm . . . [4]

Demyan Bedny is the other poet who was widely identified as the glorifier of the struggle and achievement of the proletariat (Figure 67). Trotsky later averred that whereas works by the likes of Kruchonykh are 'merely exercises in technique, like the playing of scales and passages',[5] more than anyone else, Bedny

> has the right to be called the poet of revolutionary Russia. . . . there is nothing of the dilettante in his anger and his hatred. He hates with the well-placed hatred of the most revolutionary Party in the world . . . Demyan Bedny did not and will not create a school; he himself was created by a school, called the Russian Communist Party, for the needs of the great epoch which will not come again.[6]

Bedny's poem 'The Highway' ends with the words

> March, March!
> The bourgeois state is a rubbish heap

3. R. Fülöp-Miller, *Mind and Face of Bolshevism: An Examination of Cultural Life in Soviet Russia*, G. Putman & Sons, London & New York, 1927, pp 153–4. Georgy Yakulov was an avant-garde painter who taught at the Svomas and took part in the 3rd OBMOKhU exhibition, and many other activities. Erdmann I have so far been unable to trace.

4. V. Mayakovsky, '150,000,000' in E. J. Brown, *Russian Literature since the Revolution*, revised edition, Harvard University Press, Cambridge, Mass, and London, 1982, p 33.

5. L. Trotsky, *Literature and Revolution* (1923), Ann Arbor, Michigan, 1966, pp 248–9.

6. Ibid., pp 212–14.

The proletariat has taken over the Government
Interfere not! [7]

7.   Quoted in Fülöp-Miller, *Mind and Face of Bolshevism*, p 157.

In order to aid the mass consumption of these and similar proletarian poems, vast crowds were addressed through loudspeakers in an atmosphere of almost ecstatic revolutionary enthusiasm. In the years following the October Revolution poetry above all can be said to have struck a chord with the Soviet masses, whether proletarians or otherwise. Poets rapidly became national institutions in ways which workers in the other arts did not.

The work of the Proletkult literary studios was based on the ideal of giving instruction in literature from the point of view of the urban working class. This was to include a study of the literature of the past. In the words of the First All-Russian Proletkult Conference,

> In order to acquaint Proletkult members with the literary heritage of past epochs, courses should be given in ancient and modern literature, both Russian and foreign . . . and in the history of culture . . . All of these courses should be given from the point of view of the working class.
> The writer and the reader should become acquainted with the technique of literary creation, and for this purpose theoretical courses and practical exercises should be given in metrics, rhythm and the general theory of versification, in the theory of dramaturgy, artistic prose and criticism. [8]

8.   See Brown, *Proletarian Episode*, p 8.

No doubt these formulations were extremely ambitious at the time. Much work produced in the Proletkult workshops would be necessarily crude and awkward – in one sense that was its purpose – but the work of the leading poets of the movement shows a real willingness to celebrate and perpetuate the Revolution in poetical terms. In his popular *Dynamo Verses* which went through six editions in 1918 and 1919, the somewhat wordy Ilya Sadofyev spoke thus of the collective life:

> By dint of our collective effort
> By labouring with might and main
> We've raised a temple to Apollo
> We have built cities on the plain [9]

9.   Quoted in *Novy chtets-deklamator*, Moscow, 1923, Vol 1, p 364; V. Zavalishin, *Early Soviet Writers*, New York, 1958, p 146.

Mayakovsky's companion Alexey Gastev now contributed to the Proletkult movement with enthusiastic hosannas to industry and the machine. In a very different vein, a number of Symbolist poets joined the movement and infused proletarian poetry with the metaphor of space conquest and the exploration of the stars. This tendency, known as 'Cosmism' or 'Planetarity' was heavily discouraged by Trotsky and included such transcendental sentiments as

> One must be dull-witted in the extreme
> not to see windows on infinity [10]

10.   V. Kirillov, 'Razgovor so zvyozdami', *Stikhotvoreniya, 1913–23*, Moscow, 1924, p 123; Zavalishin, *Early Soviet Writers*, p 149.

from a poem by Vladimir Kirillov. Kirillov on other occasions worshipped labour as if it were a religion. The widely read Mikhail Gerasimov drew a direct parallel – here relying on Lunacharsky's earlier ideas – between socialist collectivity and the teachings of

Christ. The factory and the church in Gerasimov's verses are frequently combined:

> I, stripling, in a temple grew
> Where candles were of molten steel
> And visions of a starry cross
> Before me rose and made me reel.[11]

11. M. Gerasimov, *Severnaya vesna* (Northern Spring), Moscow, 1924, p 14; Zavalishin, *Early Soviet Writers*, p 154.

Hence in much proletarian poetry the break with the past was seldom decisive, and strange hybrid forms that attempted to construct a bridge between one epoch and the next were plentiful.

In music, partially similar tensions were visible from 1917 onwards. On the one hand, there continued to be regular performances of concert classics by Bach, Mozart and Liszt, as well as Russian composers of all periods, irrespective of their class allegiance. There was, once more, the unsolved problem of how to link the past to the future and how to devise new forms that were nevertheless intelligible to the widest mass. Yet here too one senses the influence of the relatively conservative tastes of Lunacharsky and Lenin. For Lunacharsky, Beethoven was a supreme figure – a view he shared with Lenin – while Tchaikovsky was considered 'a bit flabby', too 'countryish', too 'salonish', too 'perfumed',[12] though evidently still appropriate for a Russian audience. Such bulwarks of pre-Revolutionary Russian musical life as the Bolshoi Opera continued to perform works from the repertoire, including performances of Verdi's *Aïda* and Saint-Saens' *Samson and Delilah*, very shortly after the momentous events of October. Concerts continued to be played, though in sometimes unimaginably adverse conditions. Electricity was often not available, and heating in concert halls, necessary for soloists and audiences alike, was frequently non-existent. Payment for performers often took the form of bread or bags of flour, and concert halls in the outlying districts of the large cities were even more sparsely provided for than the central halls and theatres. The composer Grechaninov recalls: 'my health was undermined to such an extent that I could hardly drag my feet. My hands suffered from frost bite and I could not touch the piano.'[13] Nevertheless, music was assigned a vital part to play in the life of the country during the years of the Civil War. Lunacharsky sent groups from the Bolshoi theatre to sing for military units, not only at mobilisation points in Moscow and the cities but also at the front. The repertoire on these occasions comprised mostly Russian and patriotic songs, but increasingly embraced the Western European vocal repertoire as well – Wagner, Grieg, Sibelius and Schubert.[14]

12. S. D. Krebs, *Soviet Composers and the Development of Soviet Music*, George Allen and Unwin, London, 1970, p 37.

13. A. Grechaninov, *My Life*, New York 1952, p 125. I owe this reference to N. Edmunds, 'The Politics of Music: The Development of Soviet Music, 1917–1939', unpublished MA dissertation, University of Sussex, 1988, p 9.

14. S. Migai, 'Concerts for the People', *Sovetskaya muzyka*, no 11, 1957, pp 29–33, in W. Rosenberg (ed), *Bolshevik Visions, First Phase of the Cultural Revolution in Soviet Russia*, Ardis, Ann Arbor, Michigan 1984, pp 456–8.

Some of this activity overlapped with the work of the Proletkult. Amidst the hurly-burly and confusion of the Civil War it was apparently still possible to devote time to the question of what new musical forms should or could be evolved in the new state. Marxists and communists sympathetic to proletarian culture, such as the influential Bukharin, were naturally opposed to replaying the works of the bourgeois epoch, particularly since they emphasised the cult of the individual composer, performer and conductor. The question became how to define a Bolshevik type of music that was appealing to and expressive of the proletariat, while at the same time being in a certain sense monumental in its scope and range.

Lenin himself recognised the difficulty of this dilemma. On hearing Beethoven played in recital, Gorky reports him as saying:

> I know of nothing more beautiful than the *Appassionata*. I could hear it every day. It is marvellous, unearthly music. Every time I hear these notes, I think with pride and perhaps childish *naïveté* that it is wonderful what man can accomplish. But I cannot listen to music often, it affects my nerves. I want to say amiable stupidities and pat the head of anyone who can create such beauty in such a filthy hell. But today is not the time to pat heads; today our hands must descend to split skulls open, split them open ruthlessly – although opposition to all violence is our ultimate ideal. It is a hellishly hard task. [15]

15. Quoted in Fülöp-Miller, *Mind and Face of Bolshevism*, p 176.

Proletkultists such as Bukharin, however, viewed music as a social activity whose instruments and techniques were essentially dependent on conditions of production and on the economic conditions affecting the performance and reception of works. Bolshevik music, therefore, should reflect these realities. Music was:

> an embodiment of the prevailing psychology and ideology, the expression of feelings, thoughts, moods, and that faith, those impressions, that are in the air . . . Style is influenced to a considerable extent by the . . . quality of the instruments and the form of organisation of musical associations. But all these factors depend upon the laws of social evolution.[16]

16. Ibid., p 178.

Clearly, Bukharin's demand was for a contemporary materialistic, as well as revolutionary, musical form.

One answer proposed in the Proletkult in the early years after the Revolution was a music which contained, not the rhythms of the classical sonata, but those of the modern machine city: the clattering of engines, the din of the factory, the hooting and screeching of busy traffic. These, of course, were to be regarded as the universal and impersonal cadences of the new Soviet (and twentieth-century) environment, ones which encouraged the masses to regard 'culture' and everyday life as indistinguishable. It followed that special orchestras had to be created containing instruments which gave the sounds of sirens, whirring machines, cranes and railway stock. There are echoes here of the *tuonarumori* (noise machines) invented by the Italian Futurists and brought to Moscow on their visit in 1914 – though the Bolshevik noise machines were intended to summon up harmony between man and his environment, not to make a mockery of it or poke fun at the older conventions of the orchestra. A group called the 'Engineerists' performed some of the first works in this austere new idiom at a concert of motors, turbines, and hooters at the Moscow Trade Union Palace.[17] The conducting was carried out by a choirmaster positioned on a balcony with some complex signalling devices.

17. Ibid., p 183.

One variation on the noise machine orchestra which was tried soon after 1917 was the symphony for factory whistles which, as Mayakovsky and Gastev both pointed out, could take a whole district for its audience and which, because of its reliance on everyday sounds, could remind the proletariat of the sensory rhythms of its real home, the factory. According to reports, however, the difficulties of this new form were that compositions tended to be overcomplicated, and conductors sometimes found it hard to keep the music to time. Certainly the individual whistles were not tuned with any precision, and it became extremely difficult to achieve any sense of overall orchestral sound, albeit of the new sort. Here at any rate was a further attempt to achieve a monumental artistic effect in line with revolutionary and proletarian life.

But these developments took some time to emerge. Initially in the Proletkult the emphasis was upon learning to play instruments such as the violin and the piano, in spite of the fact that they were invented historically for solo performance and were expensive to purchase and maintain. It was soon realised that Proletkult's distinctive contribution would be to encourage singing, and particularly folk-singing: this at least was cheap, and the resources for it were plentiful. Choral singing was also deemed appropriate, especially if accompanied by instruction in how to understand music, how to listen and eventually how to create. The Moscow Proletkult argued that choral singing was 'a means for the harmonious union of all', and admitted only workers and children to their studios. The history of music was also taught, and they managed to form a string orchestra and devise a plan for a competition to compose suitable revolutionary songs. (It was pointed out that the 'Internationale' required a many-part choir, while most Proletkult choirs possessed two parts at most.)[18] The two-part *Varshavyanka* or 'Warsaw Song', composed by Krzhyzhanovsky in 1897 and revived for the Proletkult in 1923 (Figure 18) illustrates the genre.

In the theatre, the viewpoint of the Proletkult theorists was, in the words of Valerian Pletnev, that culture could be built in the first instance by the proletariat, unaided by the backward peasants and certainly without the assistance of 'brilliant bourgeois actors' or, for that matter, of traditions from the bourgeois past.[19] Kerzhentsev, for his part, argued that proletarian culture should be allowed to prevail over other forms – this he deduced from the leading role of the proletariat in the new state, and from the fact that all works of art produced in feudal and bourgeois times must be tainted. 'Theatrical politics must be imposed forcibly',[20] he urged; though in practice he appeared willing to allow bourgeois specialists a role in helping amateur groups to organise their work.

In practice, too, many of the theatres within the control of the Proletkult made use of classic pre-Revolutionary plays, since there was a distinct dearth of new scripts and since the old plays were still considered popular by those to whom Proletkult was trying to appeal. Proletkult support for the mass open-air spectaculars was intense.[21] In the theatre they urged the principle of amateurism and hence for ignoring, wherever possible, the 'expertise' of professional actors and managers. Many thousands of amateur theatres sprang up throughout the country under the sponsorship of Proletkult, and these put on improvised performances with makeshift resources, but with extraordinary enthusiasm for the victory of the Revolution and

18. This is the report of Comrade B. B. Krasin at the First All-Russian Conference of the Proletkult, September 17, 1918; in W. Rosenberg (ed), *Bolshevik Visions*, pp 453–4.

19. V. Pletnev, *Gorn*, 1919, no 1, p 6; C. Rudnitsky, *Russian and Soviet Theatre: Tradition And The Avant-Garde*, Thames & Hudson, London, 1988, pp 45–6.

20. P. Kerzhentsev, *Izvestiya*, 27 October 1918; C. Rudnitsky, *Russian and Soviet Theatre*, p 46.

21. See the following section, pp 63–75 below.

№ 2. Варшавянка.

Обраб. П. К.

Вих_ри вражде́б_ны_е ве_ют над на_ми,

Тем_ны_е си_лы нас злоб_но гне_тут.

В бой ро_ко_вой мы всту_пи_ли с вра_га_ми, Нас е_ще судь_бы без_

for the principle of mass participation in culture. The Red Army and Navy theatre clubs, also very numerous, gave performances in the immediate vicinity of the front line, in virtually any building that came to hand, shell-damaged or not, or by the light of camp-fires in the open air. Here too the mood was one of popular heroism, enthusiasm and colour. To make up for the lack of suitable plays, new ones were rapidly penned by commissars, commanders and ordinary soldiers, and performed in accompaniment to rallies, speeches and agitational events.

In content and mood, these enormously popular 'agit-plays' were capable of both sober factual description as well as high flights of revolutionary romanticism. The hard drudgery of a worker's or a peasant's life in pre-Revolutionary times could be contrasted with the cruelty of landowners and gendarmes. The ruthlessness of the White armies in the Civil War period could be contrasted with the selflessness of the Red Army cadres. Equally, the enthusiastic and forward-looking plays and verses of Mayakovsky bubbled over with allegorical imagery, powerful symbolism and fantastic possibilities for life in the new epoch.

Despite the immense practical and conceptual difficulties, the beginnings of Proletkult activity were ambitious, though perhaps uneven in their results. At the First All-Russian Conference of the Proletkult in September 1918, speeches were made summarising the work completed so far and planning for the years ahead. In the musical field it was felt that some progress had been made, but that much more needed to be done to create a specifically proletarian music. A number of complaints were articulated against the musical culture of the past. Specialists in music seemed competent only in technique, but not in understanding, complained the prominent critic and performer Nadezhda Bryusova: 'Music must not be built by the intellect alone, but by internal sensations. Music should give a capacity to live and a capacity to build life.'[22] Another speaker proposed that 'we . . . resolve to carry on the struggle against the anti-artistic music of restaurants, cabarets, gypsy music and so on.' This is

> only bourgeois music which has poisoned real music. Gramophone records have spread it everywhere . . . but it is a difficult struggle, since now everything is hurrying to dress itself in revolutionary garb. Writers of revolutionary songs too often write revolutionary words to the most banal tunes.[23]

Here the unanimous call was for better revolutionary songs and more of them.

Another speaker complained that at the local or factory level it was impossible to form choirs or orchestras; there were simply not enough people able to perform. A delegate from the Petrograd Proletkult again expressed the overriding demand: not just for resources, but for new music. 'Tchaikovsky is melancholic', this speaker suggested,

> penetrated through and through with the specific psychology of the intelligentsia, expressing the grief of an unsuccessful life . . . We do not need it. In order to lift us to new heights, music must scrutinise all

22. N. Bryusova, Report to the First All-Russian Proletkult Conference, 17 September 1918; in Rosenberg (ed), *Bolshevik Visions*, p 453.

23. B. B. Krasin's 'Report to the Proletkult Conference', in Rosenberg (ed), *Bolshevik Visions*, p 453.

Figure 18 (opposite)
Proletkult setting of the *Varshavyanka* or 'Warsaw song' for tenor and bass parts, Moscow 1923 (photo: *David King*)

proletarian life [and] . . . call us to light, to struggle, to the stars . . . We hope that . . . soon, a symphony of labour will ring out, in which the voices of machines, sirens and motors will join in one chorus with the voice of victorious workers.[24]

In the theatre a central problem was perceived to be lack of genuinely proletarian actors: 'there are still no actors for the proletarian theatres', complained Kerzhentsev; ' . . . however talented and sensitive a bourgeois actor is, there will always be psychological boundaries separating him from the proletariat'.[25] Another major difficulty was the repertoire. 'This business of the repertoire is very nasty', said Kerzhentsev,

> In truth, nowhere in European literature is there a repertoire for proletarian theatre. The number of authors and works which express the needs and strivings of the proletariat is extraordinarily negligible. Socialist plays can be counted not in twos but in ones.

(Kerzhentsev mentioned the selection by the Moscow Proletkult after much deliberation of Verhaeren's play *The Dawn*, but reflected that 'in its basic concept it is far from our needs. The entire play is structured around the role of the hero, while the masses, the people, just make up the background to the play.')[26]

Other matters debated included the extent to which the Proletkult could 'completely reject bourgeois culture and begin to build from scratch',[27] what the psychology of the proletarian actor should be, how the expertise at the Maly, Arts, Kamerny and Komissarzhevsky theatres could be spread to a wider audience; how great singers like Shalyapin could be heard by the broad masses, how theatre in any form could reach the villages and remoter districts of the union.

In visual arts and literature, just as in music and the theatre, the claim was at least capable of being made in 1918 that proletarian culture, the culture fashioned by the proletariat for its own self-development and self-awareness, was 'no longer merely a dream, but a reality',[28] to quote the words of Lebedev-Polyansky, himself both a member of Narkompros and President of Proletkult until 1920. Yet much of the rhetoric still concerned the future. Proletarian culture would be the 'opposite' of bourgeois culture, Lebedev-Polyansky said; would defeat the anarchistic and individualistic elements so typical of bourgeois and capitalist culture. Lebedev-Polyansky made the interesting claim that the knowable content of contemporary life was incapable of being apprehended by individuals working alone: 'the content of contemporary experience is so great that it is inaccessible to individual knowledge, does not even fit into existing forms of cognition.'[29] What was needed were 'new forms . . . which can freely embrace and combine the entire content of experience in its constant development',[30] a task that only the proletariat with its 'culture of collective labour' could accomplish.

The appeal made in Lebedev-Polyansky's address was frankly and openly romantic. Anarchistic bourgeois culture must be overcome first by knowing it, and then by subjecting it to merciless criticism from a class standpoint, he said. In general, art could be defined in

24. V. T. Kirillov at the Proletkult Conference; in Rosenberg (ed), *Bolshevik Visions*, p 455.

25. P. M. Kerzhentsev, *Report at the First All-Russian Conference of the Proletkult*, 17 September 1918; in Rosenberg (ed), *Bolshevik Visions*, p 428.

26. P. M. Kerzhentsev, *Report*; in Rosenberg (ed), *Bolshevik Visions*, p 430.

27. This was E. Bogdateva from the Petrograd Proletkult; in Rosenberg (ed), *Bolshevik Visions*, p 431.

28. P. Lebedev-Polyansky, 'Revolution and the Cultural Tasks of the Proletariat', in *Protokoly pervoi vserossiiskoi konferentsii proletarskikh kulturno-prosvetitelnykh organizatsii, 15–20 September 1918, Moscow, 1918*; in Rosenberg (ed), *Bolshevik Visions*, p 63.

29. Lebedev-Polyansky, 'Revolution', pp 63–4.

30. Ibid., p 64.

bourgeois life 'merely as a diversion', whereas for the proletariat it would become 'the means to organic life'.[31] He gave an example of this organising and inspirational power. A worker feels himself incapable of participating in a forthcoming demonstration. Personal apprehensions, as well as other factors, keep him away.

> But the strains of the Marseillaise penetrate his wretched hut and seize him . . . He joins the demonstrators and is no longer able to cut himself off from this collective. No arguments – home, wife, children, prison – can stop him. Perhaps afterwards he is sorry, but at this moment he forgets everything.[32]

Thus would art help organise life:

> . . . the proletariat will better understand its ideal when it experiences its beauty and grandeur under the influence of an art form: literary, musical, in painting or in architecture.[33]

Lebedev-Polyansky must have been aware of the unpolished and even naive quality of much work produced under the aegis of the Proletkult; yet he claimed in 1918 that at present it was 'entirely unimportant that our undertakings do not always end with success'. What was important was that

> the working class feels an organic need to imprint its life experience and its emotions in formal systems and images, and to oppose them to the bourgeoisie, with its dying culture.[34]

On the vital matter of the relationship between Proletkult and 'professional' artists, particularly the socialist intelligentsia (some of whom were installed in Narkompros), the attitude of the conference was instructive. Lebedev-Polyansky himself was cautious, even sceptical. Perceiving a distinct threat from the professionals to Proletkult's 'culture from below' principle, not to mention its 'collective' platform, he urged that non-proletarians could at best be of 'temporary assistance', but no more.

> Whom do we have in mind here? Primarily the socialist intelligentsia. It has come over to us and has a record of cultural service. But we will take from it only its special skills, putting its cultural influence under strict control.[35]

Further, he argued that if the workers themselves were not yet free of bourgeois habits, even when at their most revolutionary, then the socialist intelligentsia must be in an even worse position. The proletariat must develop 'a critical nose' in its relations with other social groups. This was one more argument for the slogan of cultural independence.

The nature and extent of Proletkult's work in the visual or 'fine' arts can be judged from the report by A. A. Andreev, himself a prominent member of the Petrograd organisation. It is clear from everything Andreev said at the 1918 Conference that very little had yet been achieved in this field. He pointed out that there were hardly

31. Lebedev-Polyansky, 'Revolution', p 65.

32. Ibid., p 65.

33. Ibid., p 65.

34. Ibid., p 64.

35. Ibid., p 65.

36. A. Andreev, 'On the Question of the Fine Arts'; *Protokoly*, etc, in Rosenberg (ed), *Bolshevik Visions*, p 393.

37. Andreev, 'On the Question', p 394.

38. Ibid., p 394.

39. Ibid., p 394.

40. Comrade A. I. Ivanov, cited by Andreev, 'On the Question', p 394.

41. Andreev, 'On the Question', p 396.

42. Ibid., pp 398–9.

any studios, few materials, little coordination – and yet a brief and very tentative beginning was visible in the works shown at the exhibition which was held in conjunction with the conference. These were works 'by self-taught proletarians', Andreev explained.[36] Now what was needed was unification, and materials. Art materials which had been found in the premises of the old bourgeois art societies should be turned over to the local Proletkults without delay. Instructors were needed, but not from the intelligentsia. Along with materials, an entire programme of 'university-factories' was required where one could learn about art, but also produce; 'otherwise we will not be raising the level of culture in the area of the fine arts.'[37] On the basic level of informing the working masses about the role which art can play in life, Andreev said that 'we must issue a series of propagandistic artistic posters in millions of copies', since books on the subject go unread, whereas the picture-poster is 'pasted on chests and on walls; children are raised on them.'[38] If we can organise all this on an all-Russian scale, Andreev suggests, 'then we will have solved our problem.'[39]

But in September 1918 the problem was far from solved. In the debate which followed Andreev's address it became instantly clear that little could be agreed upon and that very little of any substance had been done. One questioner pointed out that although the concept of collective creativity was sound, no one seemed available to carry it out; that 'drawing a picture is more difficult with two people than with one.'[40] Another asked whether politics should necessarily be part of art. Another questioned whether the projected new art schools should study from art, or from nature. Another asked whether art should not merely picture the revolution, but *be* a revolution in itself. Andreev conceded that 'we do not know now what proletarian collective creativity [in the visual arts] will mould into. When we fall and make mistakes, we will learn.'[41]

After discussion, the meeting passed resolutions expressing the preliminary state of development of the Proletkult art sector. It aimed to unify proletarian artists in 'learning-labour and instructional-propaganda communes'; to organise these communes into workshops; to promulgate the doctrine of 'social communism' by the means and forms of representational art; to create university-factories, as discussed; to take energetic measures to

> decorate cities, buildings and monuments, participate in festivals, in industrial production, in the press, on the greatest possible scale . . . to execute pictures of the Revolution, agitational broadsides, illustrations, posters, portraits of public figures, monuments, etc., for which materials will have to be provided.[42]

The meeting also resolved to keep such masterpieces in common as the property of the entire proletariat and its state organisations, and to see in the products of representational art created on the basis of proletarian revolutionary ideology 'a source of the joy, beauty and wisdom of the life of the proletariat as well as a mighty propaganda weapon of class consciousness in the international proletarian revolution'.[43] However, significantly, a resolution to the effect that 'All pre-Revolutionary bourgeois enlightening and educational societies who own movable and immovable possessions and capital be liquidated, and all possessions and means be shifted to the Proletkult . . .' was defeated. The argument proposed was that such action would be premature; that until proletarian art was better established it would be preferable for Proletkult and those other groups to function in parallel.

Such was the disposition of the Proletkult organisation late in 1918: uncertain of its methods, short of materials, yet fervently of the belief that proletarian consciousness could generate a new art, and determined not to join forces either with the state organisations (Narkompros or the art schools) or with the professional artists of either 'right' or 'left', the latter of whom were now increasingly well regarded by the state.

Whether such fierce independence from other groups was a tenable position for the Proletkult could not be clearly foreseen in 1918. Certainly some members close to the 'left' Futurists were prepared to argue for a merging of their interests with the Proletkult. In an article in *Iskusstvo kommuny* for December 1918 Natan Altman seemed eager to heal the wounds inflicted on the professionals by the Proletkultists. He referred to the 'abuse' recently received from the Proletkult, to the taunts of being 'bureaucrats' and 'house artists' to which Futurists had been subjected.[44] But he proposed a deeper link between Futurism and the Proletkult than arose from the mere fact that Futurism was a 'revolutionary' art which overthrew the rules of the past. Nor did he think proletarian art should be construed as pictures of heroic workers with red banners: 'this is proletarian art to the same extent as a member of the Black Hundreds who has got into the Party and can show his membership card is a communist.'[45] The real link, Altman believed, was the *collectivist* foundations of proletarian art, which paralleled the Futurist picture since the Futurist picture itself 'lives a collective life'.[46] By this, Altman appears to have been pointing to the 'integrated', internally connected character of Futurist art, the fact (more properly the argument) that each part of the Futurist picture works only in conjunction with all the other parts (Figure 19).

But it must surely be doubtful whether such an argument could have cut much ice with the Proletkults in 1918. They remained, until the personal intervention of Lenin near the end of 1920, repositories of relatively humble aesthetic formulations and of earnest desires to overcome the organisational problems of forging a genuinely working-class art, and were not a real testing ground for aesthetic theory. The much wished-for independence of Proletkult artists and organisers from the main organs of government was at bottom a class viewpoint, and one that implied an attitude of hostility to the bourgeois intellectuals who were so active inside Narkompros. It was the question of independence above all that was to provide the pivot around which the life or death of the proletarian culture movement was later to revolve.

43. Andreev, 'On the Question', p 399.

44. N. Altman, '"Futurism" and Proletarian Art', *Iskusstvo kommuny*, no 2, 15 December 1918; in Matsa, *Sovetskoe iskusstvo*, 1933, pp 167–88; also Rosenberg (ed), *Bolshevik Visions*, pp 400–1.

45. Altman, 'Futurism'; Rosenberg (ed), *Bolshevik Visions*, p 400.

46. Ibid., p 401.

Figure 19
A. Vesnin, *Composition*, 1922, Shchusev Museum of Architecture, Moscow

Lenin's Plan for Monumental Propaganda

An important project over which the Party leader exercised even greater personal supervision had been initiated in the winter of 1917–18. Sometime during those dark days Lenin had told Lunacharsky that he planned to remove and destroy the many statues of Tsars and Tsarist officials in the public squares of the Soviet Union and replace them with monuments to the Socialist Revolution. The painter and historian Igor Grabar later recalled how Lunacharsky conveyed news of the plan to a group of artists and sculptors at that time: 'I've just come from Vladimir Ilich', Lunacharsky excitedly related'

> Once again he has had one of those fortunate and profoundly exciting ideas with which he has so often shocked and delighted us. He intends to decorate Moscow's squares with statues and monuments to revolutionaries and the great fighters for socialism. This provides both agitation for socialism and a wide field for the display of our sculptural talents.[1]

1. Grabar on Lunacharsky; Lodder, *Russian Constructivism*, p 275, fn 52.

Lunacharsky's excitement here can be explained in the light of the generally dismal prognosis for both Soviet socialism and Soviet sculpture in the winter of 1917–18. Socialism, to be sure, was under heavy attack in the early months of 1918, and the prospect of a specifically public display of revolutionary symbols must have had a grandiose and inspiring ring. And Soviet sculpture was certainly in need of a fillip. What Lunacharsky describes as 'our sculptural talents' were not conspicuous by their numbers early in 1918. Russian sculpture in general had been virtually dormant for thirty years – a few figures such as Anna Golubkina (b. 1864), Alexandr Matveev (b. 1874) and Sergey Konenkov notwithstanding – and the 'avant-gardists' like Rodchenko and Tatlin had largely forsaken the idea of public sculpture in favour of studio experiments and pictorial 'reliefs'.[2] In practice, Lenin's plan – popularly known as the Plan for Monumental Propaganda – had a specific rationale which is only partly suggested in Lunacharsky's report: to pull down the public remnants of Tsarist culture and celebrate the 'victory' of socialism in a way that would engage the skills of the intelligentsia and public opinion alike, and to erase once more the distinction between public art and private belief which had been so carefully cultivated in the period of bourgeois rule. One of the earliest accounts of Soviet artistic planning says that Lenin's idea was also to create a kind of revolutionary *Siegesallee* or Victory Avenue in Moscow to celebrate the ascendency of Bolshevik power.[3] However, this may describe only the intention and not the result of the plan as it was actually carried out. In practice, matters were more confused.

2. On the dormancy, see the early pages of J. E. Bowlt, 'Russian Sculpture and Lenin's Plan of Monumental Propaganda', in H. Millon and L. Nochlin (eds), *Art and Architecture in the Service of Politics*, MIT Press, Cambridge, Massachusetts, 1982, pp 182–93.

Trotsky gave a military interpretation. 'We are erecting monuments to our great men, the leaders of socialism', Trotsky said in November 1918.

3. R. Fülöp-Miller, *Mind and Face of Bolshevism*, 1927, p 90.

> We are sure that these works of art will be dear to the heart of every worker and the active mass of the people. Along with this, we must say to every one of them in Moscow, Petrograd and in the more out-of-the-way places:

'see, the Soviet power has put up a monument to Lasalle. Lasalle is dear to you but if the bourgeois breaks through the front and comes here, he will sweep away that monument, together with the Soviet power and all the achievements that we have won. That means that all workers, all to whom Soviet power is dear, must defend it in arms'.[4]

In November 1918 the prospect of defeat by White and counter-revolutionary forces was at its height. Both the timing and the language of Trotsky's statement call attention to the fact that the main period of the Plan for Monumental Propaganda was precisely the time between the signing of the Brest-Litovsk Treaty in March 1918 and the full-scale mobilisation of the Civil War. This was the period of 'war communism' in which emergency measures were needed to prop up the ailing economy and regiment civil life by constant vigilance and hard work.

Also implied in Trotsky's statement is a widening in scope of the plan to include Petrograd and other cities as well as Moscow. Certainly as published the plan appears to have been aimed not solely at the construction of a Victory Avenue, nor merely the mounting of a series of monuments to the leaders of socialism. On 12 April 1918, shortly after the Allied intervention on the side of the White armies and following the move of the capital to Moscow (Lenin thought Petrograd too vulnerable to attack from the North and West), the Council of People's Commissars accepted a decree entitled 'The Removal of Monuments Erected in Honour of the Tsars and their Servants and the Production of Projects for Monuments to the Russian Socialist Revolution', known also by a shorter title, 'On the Monuments of the Republic'. It was published in *Izvestiya* and *Pravda* on 14 April. This decree, to 'commemorate the great Revolution', resolved that 'the monuments erected in honour of Tsars and their minions and which have no historical or artistic value are to be removed from the squares and streets and stored up or used for utilitarian purposes' (in other words destroyed). A special commission made up of the People's Commissar for Property of the Republic, together with Lunacharsky and Shterenberg from IZO Narkompros was

> instructed to determine through agreement with the Art Collegium of Moscow and Petrograd which monuments shall be pulled down . . . [and] is instructed to mobilise artists and organise a broad competition in designing monuments to commemorate the great days of the Russian Socialist Revolution.

It was specified that

> by May the First some of the most monstrous idols be removed and that models of new monuments be put in their place for the public to judge . . . [as well as] to prepare at short notice May Day decorations for the city and to change the old inscriptions, emblems, names of streets, coats of arms, etc., to new ones reflecting the ideas and sentiments of the revolutionary working population of Russia.[5]

It appears that little was done initially to implement this plan. Lenin wrote to Lunacharsky on 13 May complaining 'I am surprised and

4. L. Trotsky, speech at the Sixth Congress of the Soviets, Moscow, 9 November 1918; from *How the Revolution Armed*, New Park Publications, London, 1979, p 463; cited in C. Lodder 'Lenin's Plan of Monumental Propaganda', *Sbornik nos 6–7, Study Group on the Russian Revolution*, Leeds, 1981, pp 69–70.

5. In I. Grabar, et al (eds), *Istoriya russkogo iskusstva*, Vol II, Akademia Nauk SSR, Moscow 1957, and in *Decrees of Soviet Power*, Russian ed, Vol II, 1959, pp 95–6; in *Lenin on Literature and Art*, Moscow 1967, p 245. See also the excerpts given in J. E. Bowlt's 'Russian Sculpture and Lenin's Plan of Monumental Propaganda', 1982; and J. E. Bowlt's 'Introduction' to V. Tatlin and S. Dymshits-Tolstaya, 'Memorandum From the Visual Arts Sections of the People's Commissariat For Enlightenment to the Soviet of People's Commissars: Project for the Organisation of Competitions for Monuments to Distinguished Persons', 1918, in *Design Issues*, Vol 1, no 2, Fall 1984, pp 70–4.

6. *Lenin i Lunacharsky. Perepiska, doklady, dokumenty*, Izdatelstvo Nauka, Moscow, 1971, p 61; Lodder, 'Lenin's Plan of Monumental Propaganda', 1981, p 69.

7. Lenin, Collected Works, Vol 44, p 105; in *Lenin on Literature & Art*, Progress Publishers, Moscow 1967, p 222.

8. *Izvestiya VTsIK*, no 155, 14 April 1918; Lodder, 1981, p 70.

9. *Izvestiya VTsIK*, no 163, 2 August 1918; in *Lenin on Literature & Art*, p 247.

10. Bowlt, 'Russian Sculpture and Lenin's Plan', says that 'a more haphazard list of historical luminaries could scarcely be imagined' (p 186). Bowlt also (p 189) speaks of 'the monumental failure of the monumental plan' – a conclusion that I believe is far too harsh.

indignant at your inactivity.'[6] On 15 June an even more direct letter was sent, asking him to 'submit information without delay as to what exactly has been done' to implement the 12 April decree. 'Two months' procrastination in carrying out the decree – important both as propaganda and as providing work to the unemployed – is unpardonable.'[7]

The original decree published in April 1918 stated that the monuments should be 'to outstanding persons in the field of revolutionary and social activity, philosophy, literature, science and art'.[8] A later version specified a wider and more specific brief. As published in *Izvestiya* on 2 August 1918 following extensive consultations with the sculptor Konenkov, the list of persons to whom monuments were to be erected contained names of 31 revolutionaries and public figures ranging from Spartacus to Volodarsky, the latter of whom was people's commissar of the Press, Propaganda and Agitation after 1917 and was murdered shortly before the Decree on monuments was announced. Twenty writers and poets, three composers and two actors were on the lists with seven names reserved for artists.[9] The list of revolutionaries and public figures included many foreign revolutionaries such as Robert Owen, Marat, Danton, Garibaldi, Saint-Simon and Fourier, as well as Marx and Engels; and Russian figures like Bakunin, Zhelyabov, Sofia Perovskaya, but also Plekhanov, who had had an uneven relationship with the Bolshevik Party. The writers and poets were all Russian, including Tolstoy and Pushkin but also Dostoevsky and Lermontov, who were not considered specifically revolutionary and of whom Lenin personally did not approve (see his remarks on Dostoevsky quoted earlier). Even non-Marxist writers like Mikhailovsky were included, alongside others of revolutionary persuasion such as Pisarev, Dobrolyubov and Chernyshevsky. The 'philosophers and scientists' were Skovoroda, Lomonosov and Mendeleev. The composers were Moussorgsky, Scriabin and Chopin – a strange and seemingly arbitrary list, even though all were popular figures from the late nineteenth century. The list of artists was also curious. Apart from the fourteenth- and fifteenth-century icon painter Andrey Rublyov, the list comprised the eighteenth-century sculptors Shubin and Kozlovsky and the architect Kazakov, and the nineteenth-century artists O. Kiprensky (1782–1836) and A. Ivanov (1806–1858), and the Symbolist painter Mikhail Vrubel, who had died in 1910. Pioneering Russian 'realists' of the Peredvizhniki formation of the 1860s and 1870s, men like Vasnetsov, Repin and Surikov, were conspicuous by their absence. Other names, including Cézanne, Lord Byron, Voltaire and Rimsky-Korsakov were shortly added to this already highly heterodox list. In full, it constituted a diverse assembly of 67 persons with no obvious bias either to extremely popular artists in the public imagination, or to any particular tradition within pre-Revolutionary art. Conceivably it was precisely the *absence* of specific figures in either 'realist' or modernist art – perhaps omitted so as not to offend any of the contending groups of mid-1918 – which constituted the real selection. If so, the motives enshrined in the final selection are more subtle than is normally given credit.[10] Certainly the choice of figures is more firmly focused on 'culture' than on 'socialism'. But whose culture? Did Lenin and the commissariat suffer from too much advice, or was not enough time allowed for the debate? At present we do not know.

Certain conditions were laid down for the submission of designs. They were to be made initially in cheap materials such as plaster, wood, or cement, and the public would be allowed to give their judgement on the merit of the works before some were converted into more permanent materials such as bronze, granite or marble. There was to be no official jury; and the height of monuments, including the pedestal where one was needed, was to be 5 arshins or 11 feet 8 inches. In stylistic terms the sculptor was to have complete freedom, and payment would be in the region of 8,000 rubles.

It seems clear that 'left' artists were not intended to be the primary beneficiaries of this plan. The Moscow branch of Narkompros, headed by the enthusiastic Tatlin, nevertheless assigned the awarding of commissions to the Moscow Union of Sculptors, then headed by Konenkov and Korolev. Tatlin's interpretation of the commission brief emphasised repeatedly that 'the greatest and youngest talents' should be employed, those who were 'young and fresh'. Yet Tatlin felt constrained to say that a sculptor 'must work up a design or project in the form of a bust, a figure or a bas-relief',[11] a condition which would have excluded non-figurative work. At least he himself did not submit a proposal.

11. V. Tatlin and S. Dymshits-Tolstaya, 'Memorandum', pp 73, 74.

Furthermore, the pace at which the scheme was pursued showed few signs of the enthusiasm and zeal so characteristic of the younger artists. The implementation of the Plan, even after August 1918, was extremely slow, prompting Lenin to write again to Lunacharsky in September in the harshest terms:

12. Lenin, telegram to A. V. Lunacharsky, 18 September 1918; *Collected Works*, Vol 35, p 360; in *Lenin on Literature and Art*, Moscow, 1967, p 223.

> I have heard today of Vinogradov's report on the busts and monuments, and am utterly outraged; nothing has been done for months; to this day there is not a single bust . . . There is no bust of Marx on display, nothing has been done in the way of propaganda by putting up inscriptions in the streets. I reprimand you for this criminal lackadaisical attitude, and demand that the names of all responsible persons should be sent to me for prosecution. Shame on the saboteurs and thoughtless loafers![12]

Several unveiling ceremonies took place soon afterwards. A monument to Radishchev by L. Shervud was unveiled in Petrograd on 22 September; this was followed by monuments to Lassalle by Sinaisky (7 October) (Figure 20), to Dobrolyubov (27 October), to Marx (4 November), to Chernyshevsky and Heine (17 November) and to Taras Shevchenko (29 November). Before the end of the year Moscow was graced with monuments to Marx, Engels, Robespierre, Plekhanov and Heine. The removal of old Tsarist monuments must have been completed by the summer of 1918. Other new monuments followed in 1919. As late as June 1920 other monuments were being prepared, for example to Rosa Luxemburg and Karl Liebknecht in Petrograd's Uritsky Square. By 1921 a total of 25 monuments were unveiled in Moscow, 15 in Petrograd, while some 47 remained in model form.

Lenin is said to have been shocked when he first saw the results of

Figure 20
V. Sinaisky, *Ferdinand Lasalle*, 1921

Figure 21
A. Zlatovratsky, *M. Saltikov-Shchedrin*

his decree. Although monumental in scale, a small number were done in quasi-Futurist styles that made them all but unrecognisable. Others were more classical, while several were romantic in conception (for example, Zlatovratsky's monument to the satirist Saltykov-Shchedrin – Figure 21), depicting their subjects with awesome, visionary expressions. Since the idea of the Plan was to make only the most popular monuments permanent, and since in any case materials were in short supply and the standards of casting in bronze or carving were not high among Soviet sculptors at this time, several of the monuments erected were made in poor or inappropriate materials, even for a temporary project, and were consequently 'washed away by downpours of rain'.[13] The Bakunin statue designed by Boris Korolev became a particular *cause célèbre* in the debate on sculptural style. Conceived in a Cubo-Futurist manner, and erected in 1919 on Ploshchad Turgeneva in Moscow, it immediately met with resistance from the public (Figure 22). Fülöp-Miller relates that

> the responsible authorities, conscious of the unpopularity of such experiments, for long did not dare to unveil the statue at all, and kept it permanently behind a wooden partition. But some poor people in the cold winter days carried away the boards for firewood, and one fine morning, to the general consternation, the unveiled monument became visible, and the sight of it caused a real revolt of the populace. The general indignation was so great that, rather than face it, the political authorities preferred to have the monument immediately demolished.[14]

Such reports do much to suggest that public statuary, which after all had to show a recognisable portrait image, proved difficult to treat successfully in the Cubo-Futurist style. (The transfer of Cubism into three dimensions also proved problematic in Western Europe, where there was greater tolerance of experimental art.) They were also unpopular with the public; similar criticisms were levelled at the Heine statue by Georgy Motovilov in Moscow, the Perovskaya statue by Grizelli, and the Saltykov-Shchedrin statue by Zlatovratsky. Another sculptor, Merkurov, devised a project for a statue of Karl Marx, 'standing on four elephants';[15] while another monument in Moscow represented Marx and Engels in a 'kind of swimming-pool', as Lunacharsky recollected, nicknamed by Muscovites 'the bearded bathers' [16] (Figure 23).

Figure 22
B. Korolev, *Monument to Bakunin*

These misgivings must have done much to fuel Lenin's personal conviction that traditional 'realist' work by sculptors like M. Bloch (designer of the Volodarsky statue and the 'Red Metalworker' figure in Petrograd) or N. Andreev (who sculpted Lenin himself) was more reliable; that 'left' artistic experimenters should learn from the best work of the past. Equally – and this perhaps was the dilemma for Soviet public statuary – some 'realistic' proposals were clumsy in the extreme, or at best a hybrid of incompatible elements. One sketch for a monument called 'The Collosus of Iron' shows a gloomy-looking industrial worker some fifty feet high leaning with both elbows on two large iron pylons, standing on top of a doric temple with a rusticated basement (Figure 24). It is likely that several such works of 'symbolic naturalism' were executed, but have not survived. Other

Figure 23
V. I. Lenin speaking at the unveiling of a temporary monument to Karl Marx and Friedrich Engels in Revolution Square, 7 November 1919 (photo: *Novosti*)

13. R. Fülöp-Miller, *Mind and Face of Bolshevism*, p 91.

14. Ibid., p 95.

15. Fitzpatrick, *Commissariat*, p 126.

16. Ibid., p 126; Lunacharsky, *Lenin & Art* (reminiscences).

17. N. Punin, 'O pamyatnikakh', *Iskusstvo Kommuny*, no 14, 9 March 1919, p 2; Bowlt, 'Russian Sculpture', p 187.

monuments were too small. 'Left' critics were certainly not amused. As Nikolai Punin noted disparagingly of Shervud's Radishchev monument: 'every day I walked past the Radishchev monument, but only on the eighth day did I notice that it had fallen over.' [17]

Drawing firm conclusions on the success or otherwise of the Plan is fraught with difficulties. The obviously unsatisfactory nature of many of the monuments must have been all too visible. For those close to the administration it must have been clear that the planning was sometimes haphazard. Yet in more general terms the Plan for Monumental Propaganda must be seen against the background of the Party's real need to replace the Tsarist monuments with cultural and/or socialist ones, and to achieve a 'monumental' propaganda impact on the new city proletariat. Lacking a consistent theory for

Figure 24
Plan for a monument: 'the Colossus of Iron', *c*.1919

public sculpture in the new revolutionary situation, the plan attempted to combine the Party's need with an opening up of the stylistic question for public debate. The removal of the old monuments was easily achieved.

To a certain extent the 'monumental' propaganda effect was probably achieved as well. The unveiling of a statue or monument normally took place on a Sunday, and provided the occasion for speeches by Party leaders, their very appearance in public likewise constituting an important symbolic gesture which was recognised as such by the assembled crowds. The public demonstration that Bolshevism was concerned with culture as well as with narrowly practical politics functioned in at least two ways: to 'soften' the image of implacable revolutionary discipline, and to inspire frequent accusations of wastefulness, given that all resources were at that time incredibly scarce. By all accounts the idea of monumentalism – of decorating the public city in a thorough-going propagandistic way – was extended to the adornment of houses with bas-reliefs, posters, frescoes, panels, lettering and the like, generally on a vast scale often 'from thirty to forty feet high', during the course of 1918 and 1919.[18] (This is the origin of the 'monumental art' studios that are still active in Soviet art schools today.) The frescoes, panels and posters related to the latest events of the Revolution and Civil War, and were frequently in satirical form. Caricature was considered an important tool, supported at the time by the theory worked out by certain Bolshevik scholars of 'the revolutionary laugh'. This theory said:

18. R. Fülöp-Miller, *Mind and Face of Bolshevism*, p 91.

> The attention which is stored up in the human brain after concentration on an object may, on further investigation of the thing considered and on recognition of its valuelessness, be dissolved in laughter. Laughter is thus a sign of the valuelessness of a thing, an attribute of superiority. Laughter is, therefore, a weapon which can destroy an opponent, and which if systematically used by a gifted mind, may become terrible.[19]

19. Ibid., pp 91–2.

It is significant that the weapon of caricature was not part of the armoury of those who worked on the Plan for Monumental Propaganda. Caricature, so far as one can tell, was confined to the printed page and to the Revolutionary hoarding. In stylistic terms the Plan for Monumental Propaganda was carried out in an atmosphere of a real lack of confidence, unsure of its language and insufficiently confident of its means in a significant number of cases.

Yet it is not to be doubted that the Plan succeeded in opening up the stylistic question in an immediate and far-reaching way. It did not resolve the question of whether experimental or traditional art was more appropriate to the new socialist state; rather, it (perhaps inadvertently) posed the question and for a time made it a living issue with government officials and the public alike. Even though the results of some of the sculptors' work were not entirely happy, and even though many of the monuments were destroyed either by the elements or the indirect effects of public ire, the Plan demonstrated something of the importance that the Party and the government attached to the encouragement of public art, to reviving the fortunes of Russian and Soviet sculpture, and to conceiving of its display and

Figure 26 (opposite)
Decoration on the agit-train,
'The October Revolution', 1919

execution on a truly ambitious scale. Given the truly immense economic and military difficulties the new administration were grappling with at the height of the Civil War, one may come to see the overall result of the Plan as a significant if even somewhat flawed achievement.

Festivals, Street Theatre and Tatlin's Tower Project

Within the atmosphere of the Civil war art of every kind achieved a public dimension as part of its very *raison d'etre*. A prime example of two-dimensional art devoted to raising public awareness was the famous Russian Telegraph Agency (ROSTA) window posters designed with wonderful elegance and the minimum of means by Mayakovsky and Vladimir Lebedev (Figure 25), among others. Another type of artistic activity that raised questions of style, resources and medium were the street festivals and mass spectaculars, together with the agitational ships, steamers and trains that were planned and executed during the period of the Civil War (Figure 26). These activities, the former especially, demonstrate the existence of a different kind of creative upsurge after 1917. The mass spectacles involved literally hundreds of thousands of people in events of public participation and performance, and constituted a form of public and popular art that had perhaps not been seen on such a scale in Russia since the Middle Ages.

Figure 25
V. Lebedev, ROSTA window: 'Setting to work, keep your rifle at hand', 1921

The slogan attached to these activities was 'the theatricalisation of life': a practice, or set of practices, of great importance within the new state and one which was administered by the State Theatrical Department, with the help of specially appointed National Celebration Commissars and sub-commissions attached to them.[1] The concept of 'theatricalisation' had traditionally been important in Russian life. Now, in the wake of the October Revolution, it offered the idea that by involving the public on a vast scale the individual might lose his sense of isolation and experience a real identification with the events and aspirations of the new society. To judge from surviving documentary photographs, considerable human and material resources were poured into these spectaculars at a time of often devasting economic hardship (Figure 27).

The main festivals whose anniversaries were celebrated regularly

1. Fülöp-Miller, *Mind and Face of Bol-shevism*, p 133.

Figure 27
Theatricalised storming of the Winter Palace, Petrograd, November 1920

between 1917 and 1921, both in Moscow and Petrograd and in other cities, were the 1 May or Workers' Day celebrations which had begun in 1917 after the February revolution; the anniversary of the October Revolution itself, from 1918 onwards; and the anniversary of the founding of the Red Army on 23 February, from 1919 onwards.

Other topical and very important problems such as the rationing of food, the electrification of the country, the introduction of motor ploughs on the farms, and the much hoped-for alliance between workers and peasants, were theatricalised in like fashion. The future socialist utopia, the mechanised age and the machine, the world-wide victory of Bolshevism – these themes too were subject to spectacular festival portrayal. Here was an opportunity for all types of artist to contribute to the design of processions, monuments, panels, the decoration of bridges and public buildings, and, from a formal viewpoint, to conceive their work on a massive scale in relation to the imposing classical and Imperial buildings of the major cities.

All shades of artistic opinion within IZO Narkompros were offered responsibility for some festival decoration. The appeal of this work was particularly strong among the 'left' and abstract groups, a tendency summarised in Mayakovsky's statement of late 1918 that 'the streets are our brushes, the squares our palettes.'[2] Perhaps the most celebrated design for a civic monument was by Natan Altman, for the base of the Alexander Column in Petrograd, which was executed in 1918. Painted orange, pink, yellow and predominantly red, the futuristic shapes thrusting dynamically against each other were designed to symbolise the progressive and revolutionary qualities of the new society. Coloured to resemble a fire at the base of the column, they were clearly capable of being read both as beacon and as a destructive incendiary device (Figure 28). Altman was also capable of more literal

2. V. Mayakovsky, 'Prikaz po armii is-kusstva', *Iskusstvo kommuny*, no 1, 1918, p 1.

3. A. Blok, 'The Twelve', in *Alexander Blok: The Twelve & Other Poems*, p 141.

Figure 28
N. Altman, decorations for the base of the Alexander column, Palace Square, Petrograd, 1918

designs, however, as his huge panel designs for the façades of the Winter Palace demonstrate. Conceived to be some fifty or more feet in height, they showed workers and peasants holding banners proclaiming 'Land for the Workers' and 'Factories for the Workers' (Figure 29). Apparently no expense was spared in providing material for these decorations: some 20,000 arshin (15,000 square yards) of canvas alone were used for Altman's scheme. Such profligacy was bound to attract comment. In Blok's 'The Twelve', already referred to, an old lady regards a massive poster across the street which announces 'All Power to the Constituent Assembly'. She is weeping, 'worried to death . . . that banner, for God's sake, so many yards of cloth! How many children's leggings it would make, and they are without shirts, without boots.'[3]

From 1920, Palace Square in Petrograd which Altman's panels overlooked was the scene of several public theatrical spectacles on a truly epic scale. One of these was the 'Liberation of Labour' on May Day of that year, held in front of the Exchange building, with designs

Figure 29
N. Altman, panel decoration for the Winter Palace: 'he who was nothing will become everything'

by Yury Annenkov and Mstislav Dobuzhinsky. The written scenario gives an impression of the scale of the event.

> The scene is a wall, in the middle of which is an enormous golden gate. Behind the wall strains of joyful music sound, bright beams of light in all the colours of the rainbow dart higher and further; the wall hides a world full of joyous life. Before the closed door stand cannon to prevent entrance into the radiant realm of freedom, equality and fraternity. On the steps in front of the door are slaves engaged in heavy work, driven on by overseers with long knouts. On all sides moans and groans may be heard, the clang of rattling chairs, and whistling, the curses and shrieks of the slaves and the savage marching laughter of the overseers. For a little while this terrible noise of human misery is silenced, and the bewitching strains of the distant music become clearer. The slaves stop work, excited by the notes which come through the gate, some slaves expressing their longing for the unattainable country of happiness by joyful shouts . . .

After a lavish meal taken by the 'rulers' of this unhappy kingdom, the strains of the kingdom of the future are heard again.

> The feasting guests jump up from their seats, a foreboding of the coming catastrophe fills them with terror. The slaves raise their arms rapturously, as if in prayer, towards the golden gate, which is to open the way to the land of freedom.

The rulers' table is attacked by swarms of Roman slaves led by Spartacus, by a horde of peasants led by Stenka Razin, and the 'Marseillaise' accompanies a new column wearing Phrygian caps.

> With a clap of thunder the high wall falls back . . . there is the great tree of freedom wreathed in red ribbons; now the Red Army lays down its arms, and exchanges them for sickles, scythes, hammers, pitchforks and other tools. All the nations join in a joyous dance in an apotheosis of fraternity. The 'International' sounds forth in mighty strains, and the whole stage is covered in a rain of fireworks.[4]

Another mighty spectacular was the re-enactment in November 1920 of the storming of the Winter Palace. This had a cast of 10,000 and an audience of ten times that number.[5] Annenkov's sketch once again gives an idea of the scale of the drama (Figure 30). The white Winter

4. A full description of the projected performance is given in Fülöp-Miller, *Mind and Face of Bolshevism*, pp 142–4.

5. S. Bojko, 'Agit-Prop Art, The Streets were their theatre'; in S. Barron and M. Tuchman (eds), *The Avant-Garde in Russia, 1910–30, New Perspectives*, MIT Press, Massachusetts, London and Los Angeles, 1980, p 77.

Figure 30
Y. Annenkov, sketch for a re-enactment of the storming of the Winter Palace, November 1920

Palace is portrayed as a single set. On the left is a Red Stage, occupied by Bolsheviks. On the right is a White Stage, held by Kerensky, the bourgeoisie, Capital, and Kerensky's Battalion of Women. In the actual performance the sky was lit by searchlights from naval vessels in the river behind the Palace. After a cannon-shot at 10 pm, a trumpet call and an orchestral rendition of 'Robespierre' by Litolsky, the massed audience saw Kerensky receiving ovations from generals, courtiers and capitalists, then a cry of 'Lenin' from the Red Stage, followed by revolutionary songs, and eventually an armed 'struggle' on a connecting bridge between the two stages. The remnants of Kerensky's force flee into the Winter Palace, but are pursued by armoured cars and canons which enter the square following a salvo from the nearby *Aurora*, anchored on the river. The lighted windows of the Palace are extinguished amidst rocket displays and 'singing from many thousand throats' as the victory of Communism was achieved.

The May Day festivals can be illustrated by the one in Petrograd in 1918 based on illuminations, fountains and fireworks on the Neva river, with the participation of flotillas and bands. Concerts were organised of factory sirens and ships' bells and hooters – such as had been called for by the Proletkult – with a conductor standing high above the proceedings to 'orchestrate' the various sounds. Apart from May Day celebrations, Civil War victories of great significance were dramatised in public, such as the 'Revolutionary Tribunal Judgement Over Wrangel in Stanitsa Krymskaya' which was staged in the Kuban in 1920. Or, to take a different example, a cast of 4,000 enacted 'Towards a Worldwide Commune', also designed by Altman and directed by four people (N. Petrov, N. Radlov, V. Soloviev and A. Pyotrovsky), also in front of the Exchange Building in Petrograd in 1920.

From early eye-witness accounts it appears that festivals and pageants responded to an almost innate sense of participatory theatre in the Soviet public. Demonstrations staged for any and every occasion met with apparently extraordinary popular enthusiasm. Fülöp-Miller gives a vivid description:

> On such occasions, from all quarters and corners stream workers, soldiers, Soviet officials, whole organisations, unions and schools, and soon even the most spacious squares are full of people. Motor cars and all passing carriages are stopped and turned in a second into moving speakers' platforms, from which soldiers, workers, agitators, or students make flaming speeches to the people. Here, too, they immediately proceed to scenic representations, and performances are improvised everywhere with the aid of living pictures . . . lectures are held, revolutionary songs are sung, the orchestra plays operatic music, the ballet from the Bolshoi Theatre is requisitioned. The great poets of the day recite their latest efforts to the populace; from the balconies of Government offices, from the platforms, and from the roofs of motor cars the People's Commissars address the masses. A swarm of flags and banners makes gay the houses and the swaying crowd; radio concerts, torchlight processions, and cinematograph performances are held. The speeches are broadcast for immense distances by means of loud speakers, while on the roofs of the tramway-cars rowdy Punch-and-Judy shows are given for the children.[6]

6. Fülöp-Miller, *Mind and Face of Bolshevism*, p 137. He cites (p 138) one parade during an industrial festival which contained a huge tablet carried aloft by the Association of Chemists. On the tablet was written in large letters a receipt: 'For the sick proletariat of Western Europe: one part General Strike, one part United Front, and one part Soviet Republic as ordered by Dr Vladimir Ilych Lenin. Dose: Quantum Satis.'

The contributions of 'left' artists to the festivals and spectaculars were by all accounts ambitious, though not always successful in practical terms. Artists like Lyubov Popova, Alexandr Vesnin, Rodchenko and Tatlin are known to have been involved, but little of their work remains, even in photographs. A contemporary comment suggests that proto-Constructivist ideas did not transfer easily onto a public scale:

> Those very counter-reliefs and constructed combinations of planes and materials which seem so acutely revolutionary at exhibitions, appear inadequate, too individual and even painterly when they are taken out onto the streets and squares. They seems like paintings hung out of doors.[7]

7. V. Dmitriev, 'Pervyi itog', *Iskusstvo kommuny*, no 15, 1919, pp 2–3; Lodder, *Russian Constructivism*, p 51.

The reasons for the precariousness of 'avant-garde' design must remain a matter of speculation. One reason may lie in the 'openness' of the new method, in which sparseness and clear articulation might well have lapsed into flimsiness. Or perhaps the transfer of small studio designs onto the huge scale required by public exhibition proved too great a demand. At the very least, the experience of working on a monumental scale outdoors must have impelled those who would later become Constructivists to consider carefully the practicality of the newly evolving aesthetic.

Particular mention should be made at this point of Tatlin's plan for a Monument to the Third International (the Communist successor to the First and Second Internationals, set up in 1919) which stands somewhere between the Plan for Monumental Propaganda, the concept of spectacular public theatre, and utopian studio designs on paper. In fact the Monument was never built, and probably never could have been built given its huge proportions and technical complexity. But the cultural context of the Tower project remains something of a mystery.

During the first part of 1918 Tatlin was the head of the Moscow branch of IZO Narkompros, and as such was in charge of the administration of the Plan for Monumental Propaganda in the city. In a report to Sovnarkom of June 1918 Tatlin warned of the dangers of executing new monuments too speedily lest this should impede the artistic quality of the work: 'The state in its present form cannot and should not be the initiator of bad taste.'[8] He expressed his dislike of the idea of the state imposing its taste through juries, and made a plea that 'young and fresh artistic talents' should be employed.[9] In a letter written probably in August he suggested that as well as monuments to public figures, there should be 'monuments to the Russian Revolution, monuments to a relationship between the state and art which has not existed until now'.[10] It is not yet clear whether this is a reference to the famous Tower that he was to build over 15 months later. It is possible that the idea for a monumental tower (as opposed to a figure or bas-relief in a public square) had formed itself in Tatlin's mind even before the Revolution,[11] though to what design is thus far uncertain. At any rate Tatlin removed himself from his role in administering the Plan when he resigned from IZO Narkompros in August 1918. His commission by Narkompros in January 1919 to execute a

8. V. Tatlin and S. Dymshits-Tolstaya 'Memorandum' (written 18 June 1918, published in *Izvestiya VIsIK*, no 155, 24 July 1918); p 73.

9. V. Tatlin and S. Dymshits-Tolstaya, 'Memorandum', p 74.

10. Letter from Tatlin to Lunacharsky, August 1918, in *Lenin i Lunacharsky*, p 80; Lodder, p 55 and p 276, n 75.

11. This was suggested to me by Robin Milner-Gulland of Sussex University.

project for a monument to the Revolution may therefore be loosely connected to the main impulses of the Plan, but whether it should be strictly considered part of the Plan is more doubtful. Given that the ground-rules of the Plan required projects to be submitted actual size and to be completed within three months of receiving an advance from Narkompros, presumably not.

Tatlin's project was of a quite different type to the monuments and busts being erected in city squares. The design of the monument occupied most of 1919, and a wooden model was built between March and November 1920. In an article of March 1919 by Nikolay Punin (himself a sarcastic observer of the Monumental Propaganda statues) revealed the basic concept of Tatlin's monument. The form of the monument 'would correspond to all invented artistic forms at the present time . . . cubes, cylinders, spheres, cones, segments, spherical surfaces, pieces of these, etc.'; in other words it would not be figurative, or even based on the figure.[12] It would be dynamic, functional, and agitational:

> As a principle it is necessary to stress that, first, all the elements of the monument should be modern technical apparatuses promoting agitation and propaganda, and secondly, that the monument should be a place of the most intense movement; least of all should one stand still or sit down in it, you must be mechanically taken up, down, carried away against your will, in front of you must flash the powerful laconic phrase of the orator-agitator, and further on the latest news, decrees, decisions, the latest inventions, an explosion of simple and clear thoughts; creativity, only creativity.[13]

The structure would include lecture halls, gymnasia and agitational rooms, but not libraries and museums, on account of the constant internal movement of the structure. The exclusion of cultural material from the past was symptomatic of the conception of the Tower. Other facilities would include a squad of motorcycles and cars for the distribution of agitational literature, a telephone exchange, a projector for throwing messages onto the clouds, a painting shop, and so on. The entire design would be based on the spiral and the diagonal, and the internal chambers would be glass structures, rotated on their axes. By December 1919 the design of the Tower was in its final form (Figure 31). Envisaged as being four hundred metres high and straddling the river Neva in Petrograd, Tatlin appeared confident that it could be built, notwithstanding the absence of prototypes or any clear indication of how the constructional and labour resources could be obtained. Not until later, probably mid-1920, was the project dedicated to the Third International, which had been inaugurated in 1919.[14]

A small model of the Tower was exhibited in both Petrograd and Moscow in December 1920, amidst meetings and discussions on its qualities and on its appropriateness both as a symbol and as a utilitarian construction for the new state. Mayakovsky welcomed the project as 'the first monument without a beard'; however others, such as Lisitsky and Gabo, were critical. So was Lunacharsky, whose support for 'left' artists within his organisation often seems to have

12. N. Punin, 'O pamyatnikakh', *Iskusstvo kommuny*, no. 14, 9 March 1919.

13. N. Punin, 'O pamyatnikakh'.

14. Lodder, *Russian Constructivism*, 1983, p 56. A full description of the functions of the Tower is contained in N. Punin, 'Tour de Tatline', *Veshch*, nos 1–2, 1922: 'The monument consists of three great rooms of glass, erected with the help of a complicated system of vertical pillars and spirals. These rooms are placed on top of each other and have different, harmonically corresponding forms. They are to be able to move at different speeds by means of a special mechanism. The lower storey, which is in the form of a cube, rotates on its axis at the speed of one revolution per year. This is intended for legislative assemblies. The next storey, which is in the form of a pyramid, rotates on its axis at the rate of one revolution per month. Here the executive bodies are to meet . . . Finally, the uppermost cylinder which rotates at the speed of one revolution per day, is reserved for information services: an information tower, a newspaper, the issuing of proclamations, pamphlets and manifestoes, in short all the means for informing the international proletariat; it will also have a telegraphic office and an apparatus that can project slogans on to a large screen. These can be fitted around the axes of the hemisphere. It should be emphasised that Tatlin's proposal provides for walls with a vacuum (thermos) which will help keep the temperature in the various rooms constant.' See also Lodder, 'Lenin's Plan', 1981, p 71.

Figure 31
V. Tatlin, proposal for a
monument to the 3rd International

Figure 32
17th century landscape
drawing in the Stroganov style
(illustration: *I.M. Zinoviev,
Iskusstva Palecha, Leningrad 1975*)

deserted him when faced with the practical difficulties involved. Trotsky was also to be dismissive of the project in his slightly later *Literature and Revolution*, claiming that the Tower was impractical and romantic.

Tatlin's design has been exhibited and discussed more widely than perhaps any other single work of the Soviet 'avant-garde'. Yet stylistically and conceptually both its antecedents and more immediate context remain still open for discussion. In 1921 Tatlin himself emphasised the origins of the design in his own earlier experiments in the culture of materials, specifically the counter-reliefs he made before 1915:

> This investigation of material, volume and construction made it possible for us, in 1918, to move towards creating an artistic form of a selection of the materials iron and glass as the materials of a modern classicism, equivalent in their severity to marble in the past.[15]

In terms of previous buildings Tatlin's tower has been related to the Tower of Babel, the Chateau of Blois, a staircase by Gropius and Meyer, the Eiffel Tower, the minaret of the Great Mosque at Samara, and the Dome of the Rock (Qubbat as Sakhra) in Jerusalem.[16] In terms of painted or sculpted representations there are examples such as the diagonal and spiral forms of Boccioni's 'Extension of a Bottle in Space' (1912), Rodin's 'Tower of Labour', and others. To these may be added the fifteenth- to seventeenth-century landscape paintings of rocks and mountains by artists of the Russian Palech school (Figure 32). No less than their Western European medieval counterparts, such images suggest that form itself could have inspirational, transcendent qualities. Certainly known by Tatlin and other members of the 'avant-garde', they provide a range of two-dimensional precedents along-side the better known revolutionary towers and spirals upon which he may also have drawn.

But in 1919 and 1920 there was another context for 'tower' designs as embodiments of upward revolutionary aspiration. One of the side-effects of the early work in the Plan for Monumental Propaganda had been that Boris Korolev was detailed to head a Commission for the Resolution of Questions Bearing on the Synthesis of Sculpture and Architecture, or Sinskulptarch, created in May 1919 and attached to IZO Narkompros. Opposed to the classicism of the dominant Zholtovsky faction within the architecture section of Narkompros, Korolev's Commission elaborated a number of plans for a fusion of sculpture and the built environment, concentrating initially on plans for a Temple of the New Cult ('a building for communication among nations')[17] which was also intended for use in the performance of mass spectacles. At the end of 1919 the Commission changed its name to Zhivskulptarch or Commission for the Synthesis of Painting, Sculpture and Architecture, including within its aegis the architects and designers N.A. Ladovsky, A. Rodchenko, Mapu, V. Krinsky, S.V. Dombrovsky and A. I. Gegello. It was this Commission that produced a large number of 'dynamic tower' compositions, thrusting upwards without symmetry or rectangularity, which were deemed precisely to express the world-reforming revolutionary aspirations of the new Soviet state. There exist dozens of designs by Ladovsky, Gegello, Chernikov, Korolev, W.I. Fidman, A.V. Shevchenko, Dombrovsky and Istelnov which all more or less rehearse (or anticipate) Tatlin's Tower design, with the signal difference that the majority communicate on the plane of fantasy only and make no pretence at embodying functional form (Figures 33 and 34). The designs by Ladovsky, Korolev, Chernikov and Shevchenko of 1919, for example, are openly described as fantasies. No less extraordinary than Tatlin's project, they evoke a scale, a style, and a massing of forms that one can just envisage realised in some remote future utopia. Korolev's drawings are highly organic, and lack the somewhat clumsy engineering appearance of Tatlin's scheme. Some, such as Gegello's, are functional. At once both monument and building, natural form and man-made edifice, these designs look forward into the future and back into the remote past. They show that Tatlin was not alone in being concerned with the idea of a revolutionary spiral tower in 1919. At the very least, they deserve to stand alongside his heavier and more cumbersome quasi-functional design in the context of futuristic architecture during the Civil War.

Probably in the final analysis it will be necessary to look again at the unchallenged reputation which Tatlin's project has acquired as a

15. V. Tatlin, T. Shapiro, I. Meerzon and P. Vinogradov, 'Nasha predstoynay-ashchaya rabota', *VIII sezd sovetov. Ezhed-nevny byulleteni sezda VTsIK*, no 13, 1 January 1921, p 11; Lodder, *Russian Constructivism*, p 64 and p 277 n 113.

16. See J. Elderfield, 'The Line of Free Men. Tatlin's "Towers" and the "Age of Invention"', *Studio International*, no 11, 1969, pp 162–7; and R. Milner-Gulland, 'Tower and Dome: Two Revolutionary Buildings', *Slavic Review*, Spring 1988, pp 39–50.

17. S. O. Khan-Magomedov, *Pioneers of Soviet Architecture*, Thames & Hudson, London, 1987, pp 67–8.

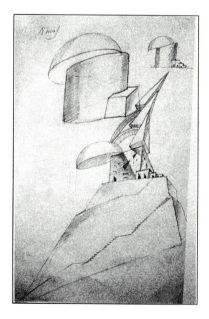

Figure 33
N. Ladovsky, *Architectural fantasy for a public building*, 1919, Tretyakov Gallery, Moscow

Figure 34
A. Gegello, *Competition design for the Petrograd Crematorium*, 1919, Shchusev Museum of Architecture, Moscow

unique revolutionary monument. Despite its role in stimulating discussion and acting as a model for a utopian yet functional socialist architecture, it is arguable whether Tatlin's project achieved as much in practical agitation and propaganda terms as the mass spectacles, the various monuments erected under Lenin's plan, or even the widespread poster designs and cartoons that so forcefully animated the public. Further, it may have to be said that the model was displayed at a particularly unfortunate time, late in 1920, when the state authorities were widely known to be becoming impatient with utopian conceptions in public sculpture and manifestations of artistic Futurism generally. In any event Tatlin's tower became a revolutionary symbol predominantly in the modernist-orientated West; to a lesser extent within that section of the Soviet 'avant-garde' to whom it was offered for discussion. As a widespread symbol of revolutionary Soviet culture neither it nor any other single work could have attracted, and then retained, the significance with which the Tower is often endowed.

A final example of the gigantism and utopianism of the 'avant-garde's' contribution to the mass spectacular was the 'theatrical military parade' designed by Lyubov Popova and Alexandr Vesnin to celebrate the Third Congress of the Third International (Comintern) on the Khodinskaya Field in Moscow in May 1921 (Figure 35). Popova and Vesnin's design shows a 'fortress of capitalism' on the left, with a 'City of the Future' on the right, connected by a network of revolutionary messages suspended from airships. Fülöp-Miller describes the project in the following terms:

> Two hundred riders from the cavalry school, 2300 foot soldiers, 16 guns, five aeroplanes with searchlights, ten automobile searchlights, several armoured trains, tanks, motorcycles, ambulance sections, detachments of the general recruiting school, of the associations for physical culture, and of the central direction of military training establishments were to take

part, as well as various military bands and choirs. In the first five scenes the various sections of the revolutionaries were to have combined to encircle the capitalist fortress, and, with the help of artillery camps, to surround it with a curtain of smoke. Concealed by this dense screen, the tanks were to have advanced to the attack and stormed the bastions, while the flame-throwers were giving out an enormous fireball of changing outline. The silhouette of the illuminated smoke would finally have represented a factory with the watchword of the fight inscribed on the walls: 'What work has created shall belong to the workers.' After a great parade of troops, the gymnastic associations on motor vans were to have shown the people of the future engaged in throwing the discus and gathering the hay into sheaves. Then a general dance, with the motto 'Hammer and Sickle', was to introduce motions representing industrial and agricultural work, the hammer bearers from time to time crossing their instruments in a friendly way with the sickles of the other group. Rhythmic movements performed by the pupils of the public training schools were to have symbolised the phrase 'Joy and Strength – the victory of the creators'; now nearing, now retreating from the tribunal, they were finally, in conjunction with the troops, to have been effectively grouped in the 'City of the Future'. The final item of the performance was to have been provided by a display of flying by aeroplanes, with searchlights, fireworks, and a great choral singing, accompanied by the orchestras.[18]

18. Fülöp-Miller, *Mind and Face of Bolshevism*, pp 148–9.

The fact that the project was abandoned 'because of the difficult economic situation of the country' comes as no particular surprise. The designers must have been encouraged by the knowledge that spectacles of similar magnitude had already been staged, arguably (as in the November 1920 spectacular in Petrograd) at times of even greater economic hardship. Yet by the spring and summer of 1921 a different economic climate prevailed. Also, the fact that neither the Tatlin project nor the Third International project in Moscow were realised may indicate that the Party authorities were becoming by that time less favourably disposed to 'Constructivist' design and 'left' artistic activity in general. Those parades and spectaculars that did successfully take place in 1920 and early 1921 depended upon a

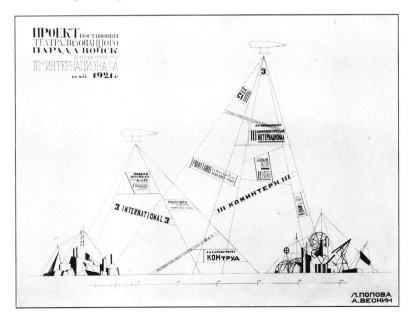

Figure 35
L. Popova and A. Vesnin, project for a theatricalised military parade for the Congress of the 3rd International, entitled 'The End of Capital', May 1921, Tretyakov Gallery, Moscow (photo: *Tretyakov Gallery*)

mixture of readily accessible symbolism, much of it portrayed naturalistically, with only a modicum of 'Cubist' influence visible. However fertile 'avant-garde' design could become in the safety of the studio, its difficulties in the public sphere remained real ones; and they were not to be easily overcome.

In sheer quantitative terms alone however there is no doubt that 'theatricalisation' in Soviet life was widespread and intense after 1917. Fülöp-Miller emphasises how internal this was to the behavioural standards of the day. Describing an ordinary Russian speaking on the street, he observes that

> Suddenly, he sends a gesture into space, like an arrow from a bow, and at the same time giving the cue to another in the circle, who immediately becomes an actor in the drama . . . soon, many emphatic gestures and words creep in as an increasing number of bystanders begin to take part in the scene. Suddenly the performance takes on living form: chairs and tables are shifted with a few touches, and soon stand in a particular relation to each other and to the events being enacted. Men and things are now subject to new and different laws. Those taking no part look on in astonishment and soon become an audience, just as the story, which was at first merely related, becomes reality and attains complete actuality in the people acting and the improvised scenery . . . if an improvised play of this kind takes place on the street among a group of chance-met passers by, then everything which passes, pedestrians, vans and motor-cars, are drawn in to the action and must take part in the play . . . [19]

19. Fülöp-Miller, *Mind and Face of Bolshevism*, pp 135-6.

Regarding the organised spectacles and events, *Vestnik teatra* (Theatre Bulletin) wrote in 1919 that 'the quantitative side is staggering. The future historian will record how, throughout one of the bloodiest and most brutal revolutions, all of Russia was acting.'[20] It should be noted too that the mass spectaculars of 1918–21 contained a careful blend of 'factual' re-enactment, imaginary embellishment, and pure symbolism. 'Towards a Worldwide Commune' of 1920 traced events from the Paris Commune to the Civil War, but embroidered the actual course of events with choral singing, crowds of girls in red dresses holding golden trumpets, rockets, searchlights, and other devices. Even with such a drama as 'The Storming of the Winter Palace' it must have been obvious that events were not precisely as depicted. Yet it was beside the point whether the Provisional Government was actually defeated in that way. The purpose of the event was participatory, symbolic and didactic, and served to teach vast numbers of people recent history – 80 per cent of the population could still neither read nor write – in a period of almost unparalleled political, economic and cultural instability.

20. *Vestnik teatra*, 17 November 1919; cited in Rudnitsky, *Russian and Soviet Theatre*, p 44.

Nor, apparently, was physical hardship or civil chaos any impediment to the organisation of such festivals. On 1 May 1919, as Petrograd was suffering the most extreme privations and as Yudenich's armies were on the outskirts of the city, a mass spectacular 'Pageant of the IIIrd International' was performed in the city, apparently well-attended and undisturbed. Naturally, too, the participatory nature of such events was highly attractive to the leaders of the Proletkult organisation. Platon Kerzhentsev, one of the principal theorists of the Proletkult, published a book in 1918 entitled

Tvorcheskii teatr (Creative Theatre) in which he argued that Revolutionary theatre should have various characteristics which were already possessed by the mass spectacular. Spectators must be turned into actors, he argued, while drama must answer to the 'creative, artistic instinct of the masses'. Professional actors and permanent companies should be relegated to the past. Creative amateurism would become the norm. Art would cleanse and enthuse, and bring into being the harmoniously developed individual well-attuned to the mass.[21]

But here too was an opportunity for an opening rift between Proletkult and the Narkompros organisation. Lunacharsky was in favour of the principle of mass participatory theatre, but not, it would seem, to the exclusion of all else. As a playwright himself he was all too aware that what was gained in quantity was perhaps sacrificed in quality: with a fully amateur cast the subtlety of an individual performance or the gradual unfolding of a plot could too easily be lost. Lenin, too, was concerned lest enthusiasm for mass participation would drown out the possibilities for 'art'. 'There's no harm in the spectacles', he said to Clara Zetkin. 'I don't object. But it must not be forgotten that the spectacle is not truly great art, but only a pretty entertainment. Our workers and peasants really do deserve something greater than that.'[22]

21. See P. Kerzhentsev, *Tvorcheskii teatr*, Petrograd, 1918, passim.

22. *Lenin o literature i isskustve*, Moscow, 1969, p 665; Rudnitsky, *Russian and Soviet Theatre*, p 45.

Narkompros, Proletkult and Lenin

The policy within Narkompros of attempting to give a measure of support for many different styles and philosophies of art caused it to come into open and bitter conflict with those groups and individuals who believed – however benign the policies of 'tolerance' and 'arm's-length support' may seem now – that this was not an appropriate path for an organ of the Communist State to pursue.

One such conflict was with the Komfut group around Boris Kushner and Osip Brik. The Komfut Declaration of January 1919 had stated that

in their activities the cultural-educational organs of the Soviet government show a complete misunderstanding of the revolutionary task entrusted to them. The social-democratic ideology so hastily knocked together is incapable of resisting the century-old experience of bourgeois ideologies, who, in their own interests, are exploiting the proletarian-cultural organs.[1]

Under the guise of immutable truths, the Declaration stated,

1. 'Programmnaya deklaratsiya', *Iskusstvo kommuny*, no 8, 26 January 1919; in Bowlt, *Russian Art of the Avant-Garde*, p 165.

the masses are being presented with the pseudo-teachings of the gentry . . . it is essential to wage merciless war against all the fake ideologies of the bourgeois past. It is essential to subordinate the Soviet cultural-educational organs to the guidance of a new cultural communist ideology . . . that is only now being formulated.[2]

2. 'Programmnaya deklaratsiya', p 166.

In practice however the Komfut group was too small to have any major impact on the policies or practices of Narkompros. It remained one group among others in a wide spectrum of choices and possibilities, all of which were tolerated to some degree.

Another such conflict developed between the Party leader, Narkompros and the Proletkult organisation. Finding itself in its earliest days without much sympathy either in the Union of Art Workers or in the Petrograd intelligentsia generally, Narkompros, perhaps expediently, had turned to the Petrograd Proletkult. The Proletkult organisation had had its first national conference in that city a week before the October Revolution to discuss how to put into practice the 'proletarian culture' philosophy of Bogdanov, Gorky, and Lunacharsky. It must be remembered that Proletkult had been established as a mass working-class organisation, devoted to the generation of specifically 'collectivist' cultural work, with full independence from government. Lunacharsky, along with Kalinin, Lenin's wife Krupskaya and Larissa Reisner were initially among the members of the Proletkult Central Committee; and Kalinin and Krupskaya, together with Lebedev-Polyansky, had also joined Narkompros immediately it was set up, so links between the two bodies were already close. (Krupskaya at that point had left Proletkult and continued her work inside Narkompros alone.) In fact Narkompros gave the Petrograd Proletkult full departmental status within the new Commissariat, and yet guaranteed Proletkult freedom of action and full independence from the Party. As Narkompros proclaimed on 29 October,

> the people themselves, consciously or unconsciously, must evolve their own culture . . . the independent action of . . . workers', soldiers' and peasants' cultural-educational organisations must achieve full autonomy, both in relation to the central government and to the municipal centres.[3]

3. Fitzpatrick, *Commissariat*, p 89.

And yet it was this tolerant support for Proletkult that proved to be Lunacharsky's undoing. It turned out that Proletkult did not want such support. For Lunacharsky personally, it came to be impossible *both* to supervise patronage from above *and* to cleave to the original Proletkult platform of genuine independence. Something had to give.

It soon became apparent that the policy of Proletkult was not consistent with the liberal and tolerant policies pursued by Narkompros. Proletkult had been opposed to bourgeois culture in its pre-Revolutionary form, and both before and after the October Revolution declared that they would abolish and destroy it, replacing it with forms of cultural activity which were thoroughly and firmly based in the proletariat. Now, both the Petrograd and Moscow Proletkult quickly realised that Lunacharsky and Narkompros (aided efficiently by Krupskaya) were prone to involving the bourgeois specialists in theoretical and artistic work and to that extent denied 'full power in cultural questions' to the proletariat themselves. In so far as 'leftist' artists within Narkompros attempted to influence the work and direction of Proletkult, for example, the Proletkult could claim to feel contaminated. The percolation of Futurist ideals into Proletkult, also, was described by one Proletkult zealot as having brought with it 'the

putrid poison of the decaying bourgeois organism'.[4] Proletkult therefore was the second organisation which sought to establish exclusive
rights over the direction of art in the new state: its ideology was to be
thoroughly and exclusively that of the working class. Because of this
principle, its relations with Narkompros (and through Krupskaya
with Lenin) became strained from the beginning. Some three years
later, in 1920, Lenin was to declare in no uncertain terms that the
artistic policy of Proletkult was erroneous, and that it should be
brought directly under state control.

The evolution of this controversy is worth examining. The crucial
question at issue between Narkompros and the Proletkult centred
upon the independence of the latter. Despite full departmental status
within Narkompros having been given to Proletkult, in combination
with guarantees of independence and freedom of action from the
Party, the tension between the two camps soon became considerable.
In March 1918, Krupskaya, commenting from within Narkompros on
the reluctance of the Petrograd Proletkult to take part in an education
conference, reported that 'there has been a definite decision in Petrograd (that Proletkult) must not exist as an autonomous organisation.'[5]
A month later, in April 1918, Lunacharsky himself pointed out that
in any case Proletkult had enrolled many intellectuals and had hence
compromised its class position. He proposed that Proletkults be
made immediately accountable to Narkompros and to the government, and to the Central Committee of the Communist Party. The
Central Committee, he said, was in fact 'the sole bearer of proletarian
culture' and 'stands on the position of class war', that is, war against
bourgeois and non-Party elements.[6] Yet the State Education Commission, in spite of Lunacharsky's proposal, maintaining its brief to
educate and bring culture to the whole population, seemed satisfied
to let Proletkult continue to exist as an autonomous body, a viewpoint
accepted by *Pravda*'s editor Bukharin on the occasion of the first
number of the Proletkult journal *Proletarskaya kultura* in July 1918.
Bukharin, in fact, as one of the leading Bolshevik theorists in the years
after 1917, was an enthusiastic supporter of Proletkult in all its forms,
the more so as it assumed a radical posture towards the art of the past
and an uncompromising class identity in its relations with the bourgeoisie and the old intelligentsia. 'The old theatre must be smashed'
a later *Pravda* article stated[7] – an attitude incompatible with the
conciliatory posture towards past culture taken by Narkompros and
by Lunacharsky himself.

At the First All-Russian Conference of the Proletkult on 25
September 1918 the thesis of autonomy of strict proletarian culture
had been endorsed from within the organisation by the most
popular speakers present, including Bogdanov. He had argued
that

> art organises social experiences by means of living images with regard
> both to cognition and to feelings and aspirations. Consequently, art is the
> most powerful weapon for organising collective forces in a class society –
> class forces.

4. Zalovsky article, *Izvestiya*, 29 Decem
ber 1917, reported in Fitzpatrick, Commissariat, p 123.

5. Fitzpatrick, *Commissariat*, p 92.

6. Lunacharsky, 8 April 1918; Fitzpatrick, *Commissariat*, p 93.

7. N. Bukharin, 'Mstitel', *Pravda*, no
282, 16 December 1919, p 1

The proletariat, Bogdanov urged,

> needs a new class art. The spirit of this art is collectivism of labour: it assimilates and reflects the world from the viewpoint of the labour collective, it expresses the relevance of its feelings, of its fighting spirit, and also its creative will.[8]

On the question of past, bourgeois art, Bogdanov may have tried to reconcile himself at this point with Lunacharsky. A statement by Lunacharsky published in *Proletarskaya kultura* No 2 in July 1918 had argued not only that the intelligentsia must play a part in developing proletarian culture, but that proletarian culture must draw on the art of the past in order to create its own. 'The treasures of the old art should not be accepted passively' Bogdanov himself now asserted; the proletarian must 'accept the treasures of the old art in the light of his own criticism . . . there they will prove to be a valuable legacy for the proletarian . . . a weapon in the organisation of a new world.'[9]

Lenin's position is relevant here as well. The prohibition on the export of works of art 'possessing a specific and historical value', which 'could lead to a loss of the people's cultural treasures' had already been decreed by the Central Committee and signed by Lenin in the week before the Proletkult conference opened in September. The Party leader had also been elected honorary president of the Proletkult organisation and, though unable to be present at the conference in person, sent a message which was read out to the assembled delegates. In inviting Lenin to address the conference Bogdanov perhaps believed that a compromise on autonomy was still possible. Lenin's message to the conference urged that Proletkult make its priority the participation of the proletariat in government, hence renouncing or at least softening their original line on autonomous operation. However the substance of Lenin's argument appears to have been ignored in the immediate discussion on practical and organisational questions;[10] in any event, as the discussion revealed, it was not clear in every case whether the call for 'collective and working class' culture actually implied a complete divorce from the past, or not.

But it must have been clear to all concerned that the state took a specific view of the relationship between the 'new' Soviet culture and that of the pre-Revolutionary past. Several decrees now made it necessary that the bourgeois art collections of before 1917 should be retained and used, rather than exported, sold or otherwise disposed of. Lenin himself took an important step in this direction just three months after the Proletkult conference when he signed a Decree of the Central Committee 'On The Nationalisation of Art Collections'. This resolution brought the private collections of Ivan Morozov, Ilya Ostroukov and Mikhail Morozov – those same collections from which the pre-Revolutionary 'avant-garde' had learned so much – within the perimeter of the new state and under the control of Narkompros in particular. At this stage, in December 1918, Lenin and the Party apparatus appeared to place a good deal of

8. Address by Bogdanov to the All-Russian Conference of the Proletkult, 25 September 1918; printed as 'Proletariat i iskusstvo', *Proletarskaya kultura*, no 5, 1918, p 32; Bowlt, *Russian Art of the Avant-Garde*, p 177.

9. Bogdanov, 'Proletariat', p 177.

10. See above pp 51–5

confidence in Narkompros, while continuing to regard Proletkult as an organisation to be carefully watched.

Yet it should be noted that the artistic policies of Proletkult at the end of 1918 and during 1919 were not, in practice, completely tuned to the exclusion of past art, no doubt because of the difficulty of evolving a proletarian style *de novo*, but also because of the continuing popularity of older works. Even Kerzhentsev, who was capable of implacable hostility to past art, now said that

> the working class should by no means reject the rich cultural heritage of the past, the material and spiritual achievements made by classes which are alien and hostile to the proletariat. The proletarian must look over it critically, choose what is of value, elucidate it with his own point of view, use it with a view of producing its own culture.[11]

However, in proposing that the Proletkult should be 'class-restricted, workers' organisations, completely autonomous in their activities',[12] Kerzhentsev implied disagreement with the 'Party principle' which all Bolshevik leaders except Bukharin and Lunacharsky had consistently stressed.

But on the question of style the matter was essentially flexible. In the field of literature Bogdanov himself made an exception to his ban on previous artistic forms when it came to very popular Russian writers from the nineteenth century such as Pushkin, Lermontov and Tolstoy, whom he recommended against the rival claims of Mayakovsky, Blok, Andreev and others that poets should follow more contemporary rhythms. On the other hand, many would-be proletarian poets were hypnotised by Mayakovsky's recitations, and were even impressed with Symbolists like Bely. In visual art a similar attraction was exerted by Tatlin and Rodchenko and their followers. Clearly, a stylistically homogeneous 'line' would have been impossible within an organisation as large as Proletkult, even if it had been desirable.

Notwithstanding this diversity, Proletkult inevitably became something of a haven for Futurist artists, whether these were Constructivists, Suprematists or so-called Formalists in the field of literature and poetry. Lunacharsky observed that the Futurists showed a greater willingness than the easel painters and 'realists' to work alongside workers in an instructional setting.[13]

But the degree of influence exercised by Futurists over the Proletkult became something of a battlefield from 1919 onwards. The now very influential Zinoviev, for example, addressing a conference of proletarian writers in Petrograd in the autumn of 1919, voiced an irritated protest at the 'excesses' of Futurist art:

> At one time we allowed the most nonsensical Futurism to get a reputation as the official school of communist art. We let doubtful elements attach themselves to our Proletkult. It is time we put an end to this. We must give the promising worker-writer the chance to study in earnest. Dear Comrades, my wishes to you are that we should bring more proletarian simplicity into our art.[14]

In a similar form Petrograd Proletkult leader Pavel Bessalko had

11. P. M. Kerzhentsev, 'Out of School Education and the Proletkults' early 1919, from *Oktyabrskii perevorot i diktatura proletaryata*, Moscow, 1919; in Rosenberg (ed), *Bolshevik Visions*, p 343.

12. P. M. Kerzhentsev, 'Out of School Education', p 344.

13. Lunacharsky, 'Ideology on the Eve of October', *Vospominaniya i vpechatleniya*, 1922; Fitzpatrick, *Commissariat*, p 100.

14. Zinoviev; Fitzpatrick, *Commissariat*, p 100–1.

15.   Bessalko; Fitzpatrick, *Commissariat*, p 100.

already spoken out strongly against those who, in his view, 'were to the left of common-sense'.[15]

Bogdanov himself, who by training was a scientist and wanted a far more organised policy for proletarian culture, began to lay less emphasis on the classics and more on 'practical' approaches to art from the middle of 1919 onwards. He wanted to extend Proletkult activity beyond studios and literary workshops, into education. He founded a Proletarian University in Moscow in 1919, run on the basis of short courses and practical experiment. ('Its work has partly the character of a laboratory experiment' were words that recall the slogans of what would become Productivist art.) This was then replaced by the Sverdlov Communist University in Moscow and the Zinoviev Communist University in Leningrad in the same year, both of which had a strongly class-conscious policies for recruitment and training.

Recruitment in such establishments was mixed to begin with, admitting members of the old intelligentsia as well as the working class; but entry was soon restricted to worker and peasant students (Figure 36). The intelligentsia were henceforward 'class enemies':

Figure 36
Enrolment of students at the
Sverdlov University, Moscow

instruction was in mental and manual skills, and included factory work and military drill. Courses were short, partly because lecturers were scarce. Lectures were replaced by discussion seminars, in which topics included the history of revolutionary movements, elementary science, Russian language and culture, and oratory, that is, the ability to stand up and speak to groups of workers and peasants in the service of agitation and propaganda. Government grants were low, and living standards among students were as meagre as their enthusiasm was high:

the students have set up a special recruitment exchange for daily jobs, which secures to needy students five or six days' manual work a month. During the Agricultural Exhibition in Moscow (1923) many students, men and women, acted as guides, porters and mechanics; at present many of them support themselves by selling cigarettes in the streets.[16]

16. Fülöp-Miller, *Mind and Face of Bolshevism*, pp 240–1.

But these new working-class universities provided important precedents. For, in spite of the controversial nature of extending proletarian art activity into general education (this was opposed for example by Lunacharsky), graduates trained in these establishments later would become the core of the new Soviet intelligentsia by dint of their greater knowledge of Marxism–Leninism and their claims to irreproachable class origins and educational experience.

In the sphere of art itself however Bogdanov stuck to his proletarian principles, against most of the odds. In *Proletarskaya kultura* in 1920 he published his essay 'Paths of Proletarian Creation' in which the fundamental comparison between art and physical labour was fully and finally asserted. Here it is Bogdanov the neurologist who speaks. Labour is collective experience, he argues once more, of which 'creation' is obviously a component part. Creativity in art combines materials in a new way, and is superior to what is called 'spiritual' labour since 'almost all "fortuitous" and unnoticeable discoveries have been made through a selection of material combinations',[17] and not through the mere selection of images that is associated with 'spiritual' labour. Bogdanov was still firmly against 'old culture', most of which he believed was based on the individual 'I' and on unconscious methods such as 'inspiration'. The new proletarian art, he argued, will combine monism (the fusion of art and life) and collectivism:

17. A. Bogdanov, 'The Paths of Proletarian Creation', *Proletarskaya kultura*, no 15/16, 1920; in Bowlt, *Russian Art of the Avant-Garde*, p 179.

> the old artist sees the revelation of his individuality in his work; the new artist will understand and feel that within his work and through his work he is creating a totality – collectivism . . . The old artist need or need not value artistic clarity; for the new artist, this means nothing less than collective accessibility, and this contains the vital meaning of the artist's endeavour.[18]

18. Bogdanov, 'Paths of Proletarian Creation'; in Bowlt, *Russian Art of the Avant-Garde*, p 181.

Bogdanov's anti-modern position on artistic individualism is accompanied by a definite attitude to materials. Here, he takes a stance close to that of the Constructivists. The technical methods of the old art, he says,

> have developed in isolation from the methods of other spheres of life; the techniques of proletarian art must seek consciously to utilize the materials of all those methods. For example photography, stereography, cinematography, special colours, phonography, etc., must find their own places as media within the spectrum of artistic techniques. From the principle of methodological monism it follows that there can be no methods of practical work or science that cannot find a direct or indirect application in art, and vice-versa.[19]

19. Ibid., p 181.

At the very end of 'Paths of Proletarian Creation' Bogdanov inserted the merest of favourable references to 'the old art'. 'In the art of the past', he ventured, 'there are many concealed collective elements', though he does not specify what they are. 'By discovering them', he continues, 'the proletarian critics provide an opportunity for creatively assimilating the best writers of the old culture in a new light, thereby adding immensely to their value.'[20] But this smallest of concessions to Lenin's own policies was not enough to stem the tide of Party feeling against the Proletkult, or the views of those within Narkompros who saw assimilation of the few remaining independent organisations as the only acceptable path.

Lunacharsky, for his part, continued his policies of appeasement and (wherever possible) tolerance for the Proletkult view of art, however much he may have wished to confine its efforts to 'studio work' and not let it spill over into general education. On these terms alone he supposed its autonomy might just be preserved. Yet Krupskaya remained firmly against a separate existence for Proletkult, since she felt it could not sustain its 'laboratory' character, and in any case would lay itself open to pollution from petty-bourgeois elements as soon as it really began to take its work to the masses. In any case she could see little difference 'either in method of work or class composition between Proletkult and Narkompros'.[21]

Lenin's criticisms of the ideological pretensions of the Proletkult had already been implicit at the September 1918 Proletkult Conference, and had surfaced again at the First All-Union Congress on Adult Education in May 1919. Here, Lenin touched on a theme that was dear to his heart: the gap, an ever-widening one, between the pretensions of an educated urban 'avant-garde' and the illiteracy of the Russian peasant, in whose name, after all, the Revolution had largely been waged. Referring to the decree of 10 December 1918 'On the Mobilisation of the Literate and the Organisation of Propaganda of the Soviet System',[22] he said:

> we shall have to draw the conclusion that we have done very little [to educate the illiterate], and that our duty in this field is to realise that the organisation of proletarian elements is essential. It is not the ridiculous phrases which remain on paper that matter, but the introduction of measures which the people need urgently and which would compel every literate person to regard it as his duty to instruct several illiterate persons.[23]

He admitted that industrial chaos was partially to blame: 'we have no fuel, of course; our factories are idle, we have little paper and we cannot produce books.' All this, Lenin said, was true. But it was also true that they could not organise the distribution of the books that were available – and of these there were plenty. 'At present', he said,

> we must combat the survivals of disorganisation, chaos, and ridiculous departmental wrangling. This must be our main task. We must take up the simple and urgent matter of mobilising the literate to combat illiteracy . . . If [our revolution] fails to carry out this task, if it fails to set about creating a really systematic and uniform organisation in place of our Russian chaos and inefficiency, then this Revolution will remain a bourgeois revolution . . .

Speaking then of the other obstacles that lay in the way of 'organisation and instruction, spreading knowledge, combating that heritage

20.   Bogdanov, 'Paths of Proletarian Creation'; in Bowlt, *Russian Art of the Avant-Garde*, p 182.

21.   Krupskaya, 'A Few Words about Proletkult', *Pol sob soch*, Vol 7, p 60; Fitzpatrick, *Commissariat*, pp 105, 342.

22.   *Izvestiya*, no 272, 12 December 1918.

23.   Lenin, First All-Union Congress on Adult Education, *Pravda*, 7 May 1919; reprinted in *Lenin on Culture and Cultural Revolution*, 1966, pp 80–1.

of ignorance, primitiveness, barbarism and savagery that we took over' [from the days of capitalism], he referred to the

> plethora of bourgeois intellectuals, escapees from the bourgeois intelli-
> gentsia, who often looked at the newly created workers' and peasants'
> organisations as the most convenient field for their own personal fantasies
> in the sphere of philosophy and culture . . . and smuggled in something
> supernatural and foolish in the guise of pure proletarian culture.

Although pardonable and perhaps natural in the early days, Lenin said, 'I hope that, in the long run, we shall try to get rid of all this and shall succeed.'[24] In addition to its relations with past art, it was obviously necessary for the Proletkult to review the real success of its efforts to induce, by whatever means, the participation of a semi-literate population in cultural work.

On the question of what measures actively to take against Prolet-kult the Adult Education Congress had been divided. On the one hand it voted for assimilating Proletkult into Narkompros; and on the other hand it had supported Bogdanov's ideas for a Proletarian University. On the last day of the Congress Lenin had made an unscheduled speech 'On the Deception of the People by Slogans of Freedom and Equality' which, though directed against anti-Communist elements in the liberal intelligentsia, contained yet another reference to Proletkult as an artistic and cultural phenomenon. The dictatorship of the proletariat was inevitable, Lenin said; and this meant not only force but 'a higher level of labour organisation than before . . . and that is why I regard all intellectual fantasies of "proletarian culture" with such ruthless hostility'. The tone of Lenin's attack was characteristically practical and organisational: 'To those [proletarian] fantasies I oppose the ABC of organisation. The task of proletarian discipline is to distribute bread and coal . . . If we solve this very simple, elementary problem, we shall win . . . the basic fact of proletarian culture is proletarian organisation.'[25] This emerging discourse of 'discipline' and 'organisation' had already gripped the Party organisation. Very soon it was to become a major structural factor of all Soviet life and culture, and one that was to pervade discussions in the artistic and literary fields for at least the next 15 years.

In spite of the Congress's final decision to absorb Proletkult into Narkompros, Lunacharsky strategically intervened at a subsequent meeting of the Narkompros organisation to ensure that Proletkult 'conducts its work independently, with its own separate budget', another diplomatic gesture on Lunacharsky's part that was surely designed to head off an immediate crisis. Lunacharsky freely admitted that the Proletkults had perhaps not understood their tasks, especially where education was concerned. 'But what of it?' he asked obligingly; 'All the Soviet organs get entangled with each other, and it is impossible to avoid interdepartmental friction.'[26]

However, Lunacharsky's conciliatory attitude was not to survive indefinitely unscathed. In October 1920, after some 17 months of further quasi-autonomous operation for Proletkult, there assembled in Moscow another congress, the First All-Union Congress of the

24. Lenin, First All-Union Congress on Adult Education, p 82, 79.

25. Lenin, *Sochineniya*, Vol 38, pp 368–9; Fitzpatrick, *Commissariat*, p 107.

26. Lunacharsky, *Proletarskaya kultura*, 1919, nos 9/10, June/July, p 63; Fitzpatrick, *Commissariat*, p 108.

Proletkult, at which Lenin was to make a further statement, this time one affecting both Proletkult *and* Narkompros. By this time it could be said that Narkompros and Lunacharsky had weathered the storm of the Civil War astonishingly well, considering the chronic shortage of materials and the lack of means to distribute books and educational matter, as well as the attacks periodically made upon the Commissariat by both the 'left' and the 'right' of the Party. But Narkompros had still come under fire for its inefficiency, and was already under discussion for full-scale reorganisation. In this sense the continued support of the Party leader was essential.

In the months since the Adult Education Congress Lenin had kept abreast of developments within the Proletkult with the help of Krupskaya, but (like her) was still unhappy with its autonomous status and the fact that it continued to enjoy regular financial support from Narkompros. Perhaps the very idea of such an arrangement was evidence of organisational and ideological inefficiency within the Commissariat. Lenin, at any rate, had never been well disposed towards Bogdanov's opinions, and now picked upon Proletkult as a way of demonstrating his dislike of his 'proletarian culture' philosophy, while at the same time voicing his disapproval at Narkompros' performance. Thus he instructed Lunacharsky to go to the Congress and announce that Proletkult must henceforward come under the aegis of Narkompros and renounce its autonomy. This was on 7 October 1920. But when Lenin read the report of Lunacharsky's speech in *Izvestiya* the next day, he was surprised by what he read. He penned an immediate and angry reply: 'Comrade Lunacharsky said things that were *diametrically opposed* to what he and I had agreed upon yesterday.' Immediately, he added a resolution subjugating Proletkult to the machinery of Narkompros, had it passed by the Central Committee and sent it back to Narkompros the following day.

In this resolution Lenin emphasised first of all that Marxism,

> far from rejecting the most valuable achievements of the bourgeois epoch, has, on the contrary, assimilated and refashioned everything of value in more than two thousand years of the development of human thought and culture. Only further work on this basis, inspired by the practical experience of the proletarian dictatorship as the final stage in the struggle against every form of exploitation, can be recognised as the development of a genuine proletarian culture.

This said, he proposed that the Congress

27.   Lenin, 'On Proletarian Culture', in *Lenin on Culture and Cultural Revolution*, Progress Publishers, Moscow, 1966, pp 147–8.

> reject in the most resolute manner, as theoretically unsound and practically harmful, all attempts to invent one's own particular brand of culture, to remain isolated in self-contained organisations, to draw a line dividing the work of the People's Commissariat for Education and the Proletkult, or to set up a Proletkult 'autonomy' within the People's Commissariat for Education, and so forth. On the contrary, the Congress enjoins all Proletkult organisations to fully consider themselves as duty bound to act as auxiliary bodies of the network of establishments under the People's Commissariat of Education, and to accomplish their tasks under the general guidance of the Soviet authorities . . . and of the Russian Communist Party, as part of the tasks of the proletarian dictatorship.[27]

Following the Congress the Party set up a commission to prepare an ideological statement on that organisation, though excluding Bukharin. The result was a letter (apparently drafted by Zinoviev) which sought to explain to the Proletkult that it would remain artistically autonomous but that for its own good it would receive scrutiny from Narkompros and the Party – in Lenin's earlier words, 'for the struggle against clearly bourgeois deviations'.[28] The Zinoviev letter appeared as a communication of the Central committee in *Pravda* for 1 December 1920 and made clear the Party's concern to protect Proletkult from 'Futurists, decadents, supporters of idealist philosophers hostile to Marxism and . . . mere idlers . . .'.[29]

The essence of Lenin's intervention was to ensure that no cultural body of any significance would henceforward be allowed to operate wholly outside of the sphere of influence of government. And, since government and Party had become well nigh indistinguishable, this in effect inaugurated the principle of at least partial overall supervision of the cultural field by the apparatus of the Party. It also signified on a more general level the deep desire of the Bolshevik administration to unify the still very disparate aspects of Soviet life within a single ideological framework.

Of course, what form that supervision would take, what the framework would be like, would depend inevitably on the utterances of Marxist doctrine as reinterpreted in the circumstances that then obtained. Of doctrine itself there was no shortage within the Party, either now or throughout the years until 1932. The question was *whose* doctrine would prevail. In 1920 it was the doctrine of the Party leader. Whether we now regard Lenin's policy on culture in 1920 as a timely check on the exuberance of 'revolutionary' youthful experiment, or whether we see it as a voice of reaction in a time of necessary change, there is no doubt that his moderating influence was as important here as it was on political or economic questions. On all questions of artistic and literary experiment his first impulse to 'let them have their way' was immediately checked with 'and yet, people should be reasonable'. Here was dialectics in action; and no doubt it coloured the perceptions of the Party, both now and during the period of his succession.

Educational Organisations: OBMOKhU, INKhUK, and the VKhUTEMAS

Lenin had amply demonstrated his awareness of the importance of education in the new state when he set up Narkompros under Lunacharsky so soon on the heels of the October Revolution in 1917. However, arrangements in higher education took a little longer to evolve than the policies urgently needed for schoolchildren, and in the case of education in art and design the first steps were not formally taken until late in 1918.

In Moscow on 11 and 13 December 1918 what had formerly been the Stroganov School of Applied Art and the Moscow School of

28. Lenin, *Sochineniya*, xlii, p 12; Fitzpatrick, *Commissariat*, p 186.

29. 'On the Proletkults', statement drafted by Zinoviev as a letter from the Central Committee, *Pravda*, 1 December 1920; Fitzpatrick, p 186.

1. 'Afisha pervykh gosudarstvennykh svobodnykh khudozhestvennykh masterskikh', private MS cited in Lodder, *Russian Constructivism*, p 109 and pp 284–5 n 6.

Painting, Sculpture and Architecture, together with some surviving private studios, were regrouped to constitute the First and Second State Free Art Studios or SVOMAS (Svobodnye gosudarstvennye khudozhestvennye masterskie). The aim of the Free Studios was to provide free artistic education to all students irrespective of previous educational qualifications and irrespective of artistic inclination. This, combined with the doctrine of individualism, was the crucial principle that would now render the rigid regime of the old Imperial Academy obsolete. A contemporary statement proclaimed that training would be available in painting, architecture and sculpture, but not in other branches of design, and that, 'recognising within their walls the free existence of all defined artistic trends, the studios give every student the opportunity of developing his individuality in whatever direction he wishes'.[1] The catholicity of the alternatives offered by the Free Studios is a measure of how widely they were intended to appeal. All shades of artistic opinion from Impressionism, Cubism, Futurism, Neo-Cézannism and 'realism' were to be available for instruction. A list of possible teachers in each of these fields was drawn up by a special commission, and students were asked to vote for which option they preferred, adding candidates of their own choice if they wished.

The result of this process was that although two representatives of each style were selected to teach, the most popular by far were the 'realist' and the Neo-Impressionist tutors. The voting list was as follows:

'Realism'/Naturalism	Arkhipov (88) and Malyutin
Neo-Impressionism	Mashkov (78) and Konchalovsky (34)
Impressionism	Korovin (66) and Kuznetsov (35)
Post-Impressionism	Rozhdestvensky (21) and Falk
Futurism	Tatlin (8) and Kandinsky
Suprematism	Malevich (4) and Morgunov

This result suggested that student preferences were conservative and oriented towards painting; also that a school run wholly on student choice would have allowed few opportunities for the modernist groups to emerge as teachers and hence develop their ideas with the younger generation. The implication may also be that student choices were still very much what they might have been had the Revolution never taken place. In practice, the functioning of the Free Studios appears to have been another skilful administrative compromise on Narkompros' part between the far greater level of student interest in the 'realists' and Impressionists on the one hand and the half-concealed desire of the Commissariat to let the Futurists have their say.

The method and character of the teaching was entirely new. Under the Imperial Academy courses in art had been extremely long, up to six years for an initial course, with much time spent in the studio, drawing from antique busts and casts. Painting in oils had been restricted to specific themes only, and examinations for both entrance to and graduation from the Academy had been excessively and pedantically demanding. Now, in the Free Studios, a whole panoply of styles could be attempted, apparently within the confines of one studio. The moderate Mashkov, for example, who was in overall charge of the studios as well as a leader of the Neo-Impressionist group, gave his students the opportunity to paint in a pointillist, naturalistic, or Neo-Cézannist manner.[2] Malevich is said to have taught his students the style of Cézanne and Van Gogh as well as Cubism, Futurism, and Suprematism; though given his well-attested single-mindedness and his previous theoretical statements about the redundancy of Cubism and Futurism, it is likely that the aim of his method was ultimately to suggest the all-encompassing nature of his own Suprematist system.

2. Lodder, *Russian Constructivism*, p 110–11.

The atmosphere of free-ranging discussion which was encouraged within the SVOMAS system gave rise directly or indirectly to a number of results. One of these was a realisation in some quarters that merely learning to follow the system of this or that master did not necessarily lead towards artistic practices that were adequate to the revolutionary situation of the country, the exigencies of the Civil War or the need to defeat the White armies and overcome the prevailing climate of economic and material disarray. *Mere* modernism, particularly, might well not be capable of corresponding to such conditions.

Another result was a tendency to a polarisation of attitudes, in which artists began to adhere to a single line of activity and develop views which were hostile to any others. At any rate, it became clear to many younger artists that not both of two stylistically opposed methods could represent the true or necessary art of the new Soviet Republic at that particular historical moment. There *was* such a thing as a historically adequate and appropriate style, and that would have to be fought for and found.

Thus an organisation known as the Society of Young Artists (Obshchestvo molodykh khudozhnikov or OBMOKhU) was set up in Moscow early in 1919 by a group of artists all of whom had been students at the State Free Studios. Several of OBMOKhU's members – initially they included Nikolay Denisovsky, S. Kostin, Mikhail Eremichev, Konstantin Medunetsky, Nikolay Prusakov, S. Svetlov and the brothers Georgy and Vladimir Stenberg – had already taken part in the street decorations in Moscow in May and October 1918. The group now became oriented to the carrying-out of what they called 'production tasks from the point of view of the new consumer in art',[3] which meant agitational work in general and poster production in particular, though it also included the design of sets for theatrical productions for Moscow and the provinces. Posters were produced for the Committee for the Eradication of Illiteracy, and other commissioned work was done at the behest of Lenin's wife Krupskaya in her role at Glavpolitprosvet (Central Political Education Committee of Narkompros), as well as for the travelling rural theatre of Zinaida Raikh.

3. Ibid., p 67.

The first spring exhibition of the OBMOKhU Group in 1919 consisted entirely of posters and designs for agitational work, and nothing was signed except with the word 'OBMOKhU', to demonstrate the importance of the group's collectivist philosophy and their staunch opposition to individualism. A second exhibition was held in 1920, again preponderantly of posters, and the third and final exhibition of the group, held in May 1921, displayed work by Rodchenko and Karl Ioganson (who had joined the group since its inception) as well as by OBMOKhU's original members. This was the exhibition dominated by very refined constructions based on elementary geometrical shapes which sought to revise traditional assumptions about the nature of sculpture and its base (Figure 42).

The generation of such original practices within the post-Revolutionary debate on the nature of the socialist environment was partly the result of a new freedom from oppressive educational regimes, but also the consequence of a considerable number of debates on art all within the general ambit of IZO Narkompros, where specific alternative theories and approaches were actively discussed. The idea of 'production' art, for example the application of utilitarian, OBMOKhU-type design principles to actual design tasks, was first discussed in the official magazine of IZO Narkompros *Iskusstvo kommuny* or *Art of the Commune*, published between December 1918 and April 1919. *Iskusstvo kommuny* had been a forum for an entire range of 'avant-garde' opinion, expressed in openly agitational language, on behalf of one or another 'revolutionary' artistic or aesthetic position, including those of the Komfut group organised by Boris Kushner which was examined earlier. The programme favoured within Proletkult of sweeping away the art of the past as bourgeois and counter-revolutionary also found an important mouthpiece and discussion forum in *Iskusstvo kommuny*. Such theories, which placed extreme emphasis on the eradication of the boundaries between 'art' and 'work', and 'art' and 'life', played a prominent part in the bringing together of 'art' and 'production' into 'production art', an outlook which constituted a completely fresh approach to the function, structure and material nature of constructive materials.

The work of the OBMOKhU group, though dependent on this magazine debate, was by no means the only offshoot of this debate or of the work of the State Free Studios. Another important centre of theoretical discussion was the Institute of Artistic Culture (Institut khudozhestvennoi kultury or INKhUK), established in Moscow in March 1920, again under the aegis of IZO Narkompros. INKhUK was concerned initially with the investigation of questions belonging within 'the science of art in all its aspects',[4] based on the recognition of the importance of artistic elements including material (surface, texture, density); colour (saturation, strength, transparency); space (volume, depth); time (movement); form (interaction of the other elements, and composition); technique (painting, mosaic, reliefs, sculpture), and the possibility of synthesising them into a complete and systematic discourse.

Osip Brik had advocated the setting up of such an establishment in the pages of *Iskusstvo kommuny* in 1918, arguing for an organisation 'where artists could be trained for work in the creation of new objects for proletarian use, and where they would work on creating the prototypes of these objects'.[5] In practice INKhUK had a more theoretical orientation, and seems to have been the brainchild of Kandinsky, along with Vladimir Franketti, Rodchenko, Varvara Stepanova, Vik-

4. Lodder, *Russian Constructivism*, p 79, p 279 n 39.

5. Brik, 'Drenazh iskusstvu', *Iskusstvo Kommuny*, 1918, p 1; Lodder, *Russian Constructivism*, p 279 n 36.

tor Shestakov and others, following discussions among them in late 1919 and the early months of 1920.[6] Theoretically it closely followed several concerns which had been crucial to Kandinsky in his writings at the time of the Blaue Reiter Group in Munich, such as his *Concerning the Spiritual in Art* which in turn in its conception dates back to the early years of the century and Kandinsky's earliest Symbolist work. The impact of colour, shape, form and even sound upon the emotions and attitudes of observers were now, within INKhUK's programme, subjected to a far more scientific appraisal. Once understood purely intuitively, Kandinsky now proposed the creation of a completely systematic method for codifying the affective and cognitive functions of the various aesthetic elements.

Initially INKhUK was agreeably eclectic and energetic, entrusting the investigation of painterly elements to Kandinsky, the sculptural to Boris Korolev, the poetic to Rozanov, and the music to others. The correlation of musical and plastic forms, for example, such as had already been investigated in the Blaue Reiter formation and in the paintings of Curlionis and Kupka, was now the subject of extensive examination. Kandinsky's famous questionnaire, circulated to INKhUK members on the question of the relationship of form to colour, clearly prefigured his later Bauhaus work and his *Point and Line to Plane*, published in Germany in 1926. However, after only a few months, in the autumn of 1920, an argument arose within INKhUK to the effect that Kandinsky's approach, however apparently scientific, was overly psychologistic and subjective. Rodchenko, Stepanova, Alexey Babichev and Nadezhda Bryusova were especially active in promoting the Productivist-inclined view that the object itself in its material construction was the only relevant focus of study. Such became the pressure upon him that Kandinsky felt obliged to leave INKhUK in January 1921, briefly to become the vice-president of the Russian Academy of Artistic Sciences, where he pursued the same goals of establishing the 'inner laws' of art in order to arrive at a synthesis of creative elements, before he finally left the Soviet Union for Germany in 1922.

From November 1920 the 'object' group around Babichev and Rodchenko (named the General Working Group of Objective Analysis) and which included Popova, Karl Ioganson, Stepanova, Korolev, Nikolay Tarabukin, Rodchenko, Altman, Ivan Klyun, Nadezhda Udaltsova and Alexandr Drevin, pursued a study of the elements of the art object and an active, laboratory approach to analysis. According to Tarabukin, the General Working Group was devoted to an analytical investigation of

> those real forms which, created by the artist, are found in the already finished work. Consequently the form of the work and its elements are the material for analysis and not the psychology of creation, nor the psychology of aesthetic perception, nor the historical, cultural, sociological or other problems of art.[7]

The approach taken was logical, based on observation, and independent of subjective elements or the taste of individuals or 'schools';

6. Lodder, *Russian Constructivism*, p 279 n 36.

7. N. Tarabukin, 'Polozhenie o gruppe obektivnogo analiza', quoted in Lodder, *Russian Constructivism*, p 82.

8. Tarabukin, 'Polozhenie o gruppe', in Lodder, *Russian Constructivism* p 82.

it attempted to be systematic, to constitute what was called 'the science of art'.[8] It was planned that the work of analysis should proceed by means of separation and investigation of the distinguishable elements of art: colour, volume, space, construction, texture, material and form, line, plane and volume. Also included was *faktura*, a concept which at this point meant the method of working the surface and included techniques of joining materials.

The difficulties of defining the elements and the means of objective analysis were naturally felt to be considerable. Heated debates took place in the General Working Group throughout January, February and March 1921, and it began to emerge that some members placed far greater emphasis on the actual use of materials in production, not necessarily confined to the two-dimensional plane. Building on ideas that had been already foreshadowed in *Iskusstvo kommuny* early in 1919, a new group which reflected these principles was formed on 18 March 1921 called the First Working Group of Constructivists, organised within INKhUK by Rodchenko, Stepanova and Alexey Gan. Those still interested in easel painting or in any other way hostile to the productivist approach were edged out of INKhUK, and its leadership was assumed by Brik, with the active encouragement of Arvatov and Kushner, who were all adherents of a materialist Marxist approach to production without a trace of subjective thinking. Thus it was that in INKhUK as well as in OBMOKhU an extremely uncompromising position was reached by the early part of 1921 that advocated a highly utilitarian conception of artistic materials and an absolutely necessary marriage between a study of these elements and the laws of technical manufacture in the service of a new Marxist and materialist environment.

Before we turn to an examination of the attitude taken to these activities by the political leadership of the state it is important to survey the early workings of the organisation known as the Higher State Artistic and Technical Workshops (Vysshie gosudarstvennye khudozhestvenno-tekhnicheskie masterskie or VKhUTEMAS), which was established in Moscow in 1920 as an attempt to promote practical design and education in design, alongside the more theoretical work of INKhUK. The of VKhUTEMAS arose directly out of the reorganisation of the State Free Studios after September 1920, which by that date had not progressed beyond the liberal principle of tolerance for all groups and had even become, to a certain degree, internally divided. The establishment of VKhUTEMAS was approved as a desirable initiative by Narkompros in the autumn of that year and was formally instituted by a State Decree signed by Lenin on 29 November 1920.

The initial declaration of the aims of the VKhUTEMAS was unambiguous:

9. *Izvestiya VTsIK*, 25 December 1920; Lodder, *Russian Constructivism*, p 112.

The Moscow VKhUTEMAS is a specialised educational institution for advanced artistic and technical training, created to prepare highly qualified master artists for industry as well as instructors and directors of professional and technical education.[9]

The task of encouraging instruction in design was deemed of great importance by certain sectors of the government at this point, particularly since the most acute hostilities of the Civil War were now over and the task of economic reconstruction, glimpsed clearly by Lenin as an urgent priority, had now to begin. (For example food supplies must still have been short, since it is known that students and teachers at the VKhUTEMAS became eligible for food rations and deferral of military duty until their studies were completed.)[10] But the regeneration of industry was considered vital, and production art, which gave the appearance of having abandoned the aesthetic sphere altogether, was considered to be a potentially valuable and practical initiative. In practice it was the very *separation* of production art from the more traditional practices and concerns of painting and sculpture that made it possible for the state to lend its support, around 1920 and the beginning of 1921, to both types of work. Production art was briefly championed, and easel painting and sculpture were able to enjoy a period of renewed confidence and activity; while pure Constructivism, with its opposition to easel painting and its 'abstract' and experimental aesthetic, was left increasingly without official support. This parting of the ways was a significant moment in the relationship between 'left' art and the state.

What was the teaching curriculum of the VKhUTEMAS? Initially the VKhUTEMAS admitted students irrespective of their educational and artistic background, as had the State Free Art Studios. Providing a Basic Course for one year, it then permitted students to specialise for three years in one or another of the faculties of Painting, Sculpture, Textiles, Ceramics, Architecture, Woodwork and Metalwork. Yet the programme of creating a 'production art' school for the express purpose of stimulating quality on the industrial front was by no means a simple one; nor was it easily, if ever, very fully achieved. As the division of the VKhUTEMAS into faculties suggests, not all of the studios were devoted either to production art as such, or to Constructivism, or indeed to other forms of 'Futurist' or experimental art. Although the Basic Course was on the whole oriented to Constructivism, the Painting and Sculpture Faculties were wedded to a concept of 'fine art' and contained a mixture of staff, some sympathetic to new approaches but many not, together with some who held intermediate positions, or a liberal, eclectic, approach. In the first period of the VKhUTEMAS the staff of the Painting Faculty included Klyun, Rodchenko, Popova and Alexandr Vesnin among those of Productivist and/or Constructivist persuasion, but also many others (such as Baranov-Rossiné) who were not so inclined or who favoured a definitely figurative approach. Furthermore the Productivist and Constructivist artists were soon replaced by members of the 'realist' groups, such as Sergey Gerasimov, Ilya Mashkov, Pavel Kuznetsov, Robert Falk, Abram Arkhipov, Alexandr Shevchenko, Pyotr Konchalovsky (Figure 37), Konstantin Istomin, Alexandr Drevin, Alexandr Osmerkin and David Shterenberg,[11] many of whom would shortly begin to argue for a regeneration of more traditional approaches based on the easel picture, which they would claim to be in tune with the new Soviet reality. Other parts of the VKhUTEMAS Painting

10. On obtaining a specified age, students were considered to be in military reserve, and, if they did not attend the VKhUTEMAS, could be considered deserters and prosecuted accordingly.

11. Lodder, *Russian Constructivism*, p 115.

Figure 37
P. Konchalovsky,
Still life with Samovar, 1916
(coll. *Y.B. and A.F. Chudnovsky*)

Faculty were devoted to the practice of monumental art, frescoes, wall-paintings and mosaics, and to the design and execution of decorations for the mass festivals and spectacular anniversary celebrations, as well as theatre sets.

Sculpture at the VKhUTEMAS operated from its very beginning without reference to the new approaches, to production art, or to abstraction. Completely committed to various forms of monumental 'realism', the most experimental approach was that of Korolev, who still practised a version of Cubo-Futurism; but others, like Sergey Konenkov, Iosif Chaikov and Ivan Efimov taught a traditional type of monumental sculpture in its relation to specific architectural projects or urban schemes. Only in Graphics, Textiles and possibly Ceramics did 'modernist' design concepts intrude into the VKhUTEMAS with any regularity. Architecture was in theoretical terms the most advanced section of the VKhUTEMAS, and devoted itself to devising ever more daring and utopian solutions to the task of achieving 'the fusion of art with life and full artistic expression of the social and spiritual stirrings of contemporary society' [12]; although it, too, contained a number of specialists in traditional approaches who had formerly been in the Architecture Faculty of the Moscow School of Painting, Sculpture and Architecture before the State Free Studios had been formed. Even in the early years the work of the Architecture Faculty was somewhat marred by extreme differences of opinion between the different artists and instructors concerned.

The work of the VKhUTEMAS as a whole was undoubtedly damaged by the atmosphere of in-fighting between the different groups and the drastic differences in aesthetic approach that characterised the institution. Here once more we encounter the central dilemma of art and literature under Bolshevism. Very many aesthetic pro-

12. 'Programma arkhitekturnogo fakulteta'; Lodder, *Russian Constructivism*, p 118 and p 287 n 106.

grammes claimed correspondence to the Bolshevik world-view; and yet there was nothing in Bolshevik doctrine – nor for that matter in Marx and Engels – that encouraged the simultaneous existence of many 'socialist' styles. 'Pluralism' in those days stood for as little in the field of art as it did in politics; it was no less precarious. It was not possible, nor could it have easily become possible at this early date, for all artistic tendencies to receive support from the Party and state authorities in equal measure. With only the smallest group of Party leaders taking time to interest themselves in art, and at most only one of them, Bukharin, in any way sympathetic to 'radical' experiment in culture, it seems inevitable that patronage should have been un-equally dispensed and that some tendencies would find it more difficult to flower than others.

There is an interesting report by Sergey Senkin on an unexpected visit made by Lenin to the VKhUTEMAS, which helps give some idea of the Party leader's attitude to one section of the VKhUTEMAS' work. Senkin (b. 1894) had been a student with Malevich in the Second State Free Art Studio in Moscow and had joined VKhUTEMAS in 1920, setting up a studio with Gustav Klutsis by November of that year, apparently carrying out investigations into form after the manner of UNOVIS.[13] As Senkin relates, it was late at night, on 25 February 1921:

13. There is a short biography of Senkin in Lodder, *Russian Constructivism*, p 259.

our cell meeting had just finished . . . and I was quite surprised to see a car standing by our building at such a late hour . . . By the light of the match (he had just then struck a match) I glimpsed the very evocative face of Lenin . . . Vladimir Ilich looked us up and down attentively and with cheerful craftiness, and asked 'Well then, tell me, how are you?' We answered in chorus 'All right! Now that everything's in full swing.' 'Well, to judge by your appearance at any rate', Lenin replied, 'I can't say that things are going so very well . . . And how's your work going?' 'Work's going well . . . ' we replied. We all vied with each other to try and praise what we in the students' collective had achieved in the VKhUTEMAS; 'Just today, Vladimir Ilich, we decreed in our meeting that the professors are to work out all the programmes with the students' participation, otherwise they only talk about it and do nothing; but now something will be done.' We stopped, waiting to see what effect we had made. Vladimir Ilich glanced slyly at us: 'Only today, you say?' Again, general confusion . . .

Lenin then asked what they did in the college: 'Surely you argue with the Futurists?' Senkin's group replied in chorus: 'Certainly not, Vladimir Ilich, we ourselves are all Futurists.' But Lenin declined the opportunity to debate Futurism with them on the grounds that he hadn't read enough. They burst out:

we will get the literature for you, Vladimir Ilich; we're sure that you too will be a Futurist. It's impossible for you to be on the side of that rotten, old trash, the more so because the Futurists are a united group, while the rest have gone over to Denikin.

They show him the first issue of their wall newspaper. Senkin continues his account:

Vladimir Ilich purposely takes a long time to read Mayakovsky's slogan 'We are hawkers of a new truth, which gives an iron tone to beauty, so that the public gardens may not be defiled by living nature – we shall hurl reinforced concrete buildings to the skies'. 'Hurl, yes, well, that's not really Russian, is it?' Lenin answers. Then someone produced my drawing, done for the collection in memory of Kropotkin. Vladimir Ilich, with a venomous glance at both the drawing and its author, asked 'And just what does this represent?'[14]

14.   The verb Mayakovsky uses here is *sharakhaem* which appears to be an invented word from the Russian *shar* or ball. 'Ballisticate' might be an English equivalent.

Senkin at this point attempts to cover his nakedness by explaining that it did not represent anything; that the older generation were deceiving themselves into thinking they could represent; and that he and his comrades were still learning how to connect art with politics.

Vladimir Ilich allowed me time to draw breath, and then asked a tiny little question: 'Well, but just how do you connect art with politics?' He turned the drawing round and round, as if looking for this connection in it . . . '

The students then enthuse about Mayakovsky's *Mystery-Bouffe* and Kamensky's *Engine Mass*; Lenin replies by asking what they think of Lunacharsky's work, for example his play *Magi*. The students confess they do not know it. Senkin continues:

We asked Vladimir Ilich's opinion. He laughed and replied, 'Well, tastes differ'; and unexpectedly asked us 'And do you go to the opera?' They reply: 'For us here, Vladimir Ilich, there is absolutely nothing interesting in it.' 'How so?', he answered, 'but Comrade Lunacharsky is always going on about presenting opera.'

At this point Lenin taunts them by remarking 'After all, you yourselves show nothing new. How can this be?' At this, Senkin and his group protest:

'we are still learning . . . [and] in our different ways we even understand these new ideas; but on the other hand we are with one mind against *Eugene Onegin*. *Eugene Onegin* has been pushed down our throats.' 'Well', says Vladimir Ilich, 'I shall have to be for it then, for after all I'm an old man . . .'[15]

15.   S. Senkin, 'Lenin v kommuny Vkhutemasa', *V. I. Lenin on Literature and Art*, pp 624–30; V. Perelman (ed), *Borba za realizm*, Moscow 1962, p 90–4.

What is perhaps revealing about this account is not merely that it confirms Lenin's suspicious attitude towards Futurism; nor that it shows him to be close to Lunacharsky in matters of art and aesthetics, even to the point of defending Lunacharsky's artistic work; but that it suggests that Lenin associated Futurism with utopianism, with intemperance and with zeal, with youth, and with the dangers of pretentiousness in art. It is also striking how willingly he plays the avuncular figure who cannot sympathise with the artistic role-models of the young, and who is prepared to admit that he does not expect them to share his tastes in poetry, opera or art. A few days after his visit to the VKhUTEMAS, Lenin is reported to have said:

I simply cannot understand their enthusiasm for Mayakovsky. All his work is cheap mumbo-jumbo to which the label 'Revolution' has been attached. I am quite convinced that the Revolution doesn't need comic buffoons who flirt with it, such as Mayakovsky . . . If, however, they think that even those buffoons are necessary, let them have their way. And yet, people should be reasonable and not have the impudence to put buffoons, even if they swear by the Revolution, above the 'bourgeois' Pushkin, and they should not keep asserting that Mayakovsky is three times superior to Béranger.[16]

16. Lenin's, remark to P. A. Krusikov, reported in Valentinov, *Encounters*, p 52.

The episode raises the question whether Lenin's views on art around 1920–21 did not stem partly from his sense of distance from the values and aspirations of a 'younger generation' of students and artists – those who saw the Revolution in very different terms than he.

Conceivably too Lenin's visit may have been prompted by rumours that some students were unhappy with the experimental teaching of the college. Following Lenin's published letter condemning the Proletkult organisation in December 1920[17] and perhaps encouraged by it, a group of students at the VKhUTEMAS, led by chairman of the students' organising committee S. Bogdanov (no relation to Alexander Bogdanov), together with the Academy teacher Evgeny Katsman, had written a letter to the Central Committee of the Bolshevik Party stating that

17. See pp 84–5.

> from the first days of the Revolution, matters in artistic education in the republic, which is led by the art department at Narkompros (IZO) under director D. Shterenberg and in which the Futurists have a majority . . . have taken a completely wrong path, and in direct contradiction to the people's interests . . .

adding that 150 students of the VKhUTEMAS had been not only unattracted by the Futurist methods of teaching, but had actually refused to follow them.[18]

At the same time, however, the disparaging attitude taken by the leadership towards 'pure art' was not carried over wholesale into 'production art' or design. This was still regarded as an urgent priority, notwithstanding the theoretical problems of deciding how design should in practice be improved. The Scientific and Technical department of Sovnarkom set up an Art and Production Committee towards the end of the Civil War period to raise standards of industrial manufacture and hence to increase trade. Lenin himself personally supported the Central Institute of Labour (TsIT), set up in 1921 under the poet Alexey Gastev, in an effort to make the industrial process more technically efficient.[19]

18. H. Gassner and E. Gillen, *Zwischen Revolutionskunst und Sozialistischen Realismus: Dokumente und Kommentare: Kunstdebatten in der Sowjetunion von 1917 bis 1931*, Dumont Verlag, Cologne, 1979, p 264.

19. For Gastev and TsIT, see the following chapter, pp 120–6.

After the spring of 1921 the country's economy was organised on a different basis however, and the artistic and cultural ethos of the dominant groups changed radically, away from 'pure art' back towards easel painting and, to some extent, towards the design effort. VKhUTEMAS both reflected and participated in this change. But its status as a breeding ground for an 'experimental' approach to form in the years between 1918 and 1921 cannot be doubted. In point of modernity it was probably the most advanced in the world. But it was that very 'modernity' towards which Bolshevik leaders retained a very ambivalent attitude indeed.

Artistic Policy in the Theatre

A brief look at circumstances in the theatre immediately after the Revolution is also instructive, since here, too, there were tensions between a desire for a single artistic style under state control and a tolerant mixture of many competing methods. A difference is that in the theatre, several voices believed that a Bolshevik administration should end its tolerance for all groups, and began to call for centralised direction for the arts generally soon after 1918, long before the political climate suggested the possibility of such a change. Furthermore the call for centralised direction in the theatre came principally from the 'left', where antagonism against traditional practices was perhaps even stronger than in the visual arts.

In the main, the form and style of amateur theatre in the Proletkult had not been inclined to new techniques, either in acting, directing or production. An amateur theatre group simply had no time for formal experimentation above and beyond what may have been forced upon them by expediency or by the shortage of materials.

The position of the older theatres – the Maly, the Alexandrinsky and the Moscow Art – had initially been one of confusion. These traditional theatres had been dubbed 'academic' by the Bolsheviks in 1919, to which others, such as the Bolshoi Drama Theatre and the Kamerny in Moscow and the Marinsky in Petrograd, were added. They all specialised in the traditional repertoire of plays by Shakespeare, Schiller, Gogol, Ostrovsky and (latterly) Gorky, and had placed emphasis on professional acting, stage-craft and direction. Initially the academic theatres had experienced considerable uncertainty about how the new public would respond to the classics; indeed how the Bolshevik administration would react. In fact they were quickly reassured. Not only did they attract protective patronage from the state, but the new audiences appeared to like the classic plays, particularly if they were produced to show a consonance between the class struggles of earlier times – as was possible with Shakespeare, Ostrovsky, Gogol, Chekhov and others – and those of the present day. It turned out that Goethe, Molière, Sophocles and Schiller were all capable of being staged in a traditional form yet in full harmony with the revolutionary atmosphere of the war communism period. Gogol's *The Government Inspector* was deemed particularly suitable, along with older classics like *The Merchant of Venice* or Molière's *Don Juan*, and it was this play that had helped bring round the most conservative theatre – the former Alexandrinsky – to the newer post-Revolutionary methods. Even the Maly theatre, with its tradition of fine acting and classic productions, began to intersperse its repertory with the works of Gorky and even Lunacharsky himself, whose historical melodrama *Oliver Cromwell* conveyed the events of the English bourgeois revolution in topical form.

The Moscow Art Theatre, under Stanislavsky, had also been forced gradually to change its programme and its methods. 'The Revolution found us, the older generation of the Art Theatre, in a state of some confusion', Stanislavsky wrote. 'At a time when we did not understand all that had happened, the government did not force us to change our colour to red at any price, to become what we were not.'[1]

However the issue quickly arose as to whether the pace of change was sufficiently fast. Having previously been champions of psychological subtlety and dramatic 'humanism', the Moscow Art Theatre now attempted a range of romantic works in addition to its usual fare of Gorky and Chekhov; this included Bryon's verse tragedy *Cain*, *Prometheus* by Aeschylus, and even *The Rose and the Cross* by the Symbolist Alexandr Blok. This initiative did not come until April 1920, the date of the production of *Cain*, and was then reckoned somewhat unsuccessful. *The Government Inspector* was given a successfully updated production, with sets designed by the painter Konstantin Yuon, in 1921; but even supporters of the Moscow Art Theatre were heard to complain, by the spring and summer of 1921, that it showed 'few signs of its participation in Revolutionary contemporaneity . . . [it] had become a sort of museum, a monument to past culture, carefully preserved and protected.'[2]

Lunacharsky showed ostensible sympathy for all groups, just as he had done in the visual arts. He formed good personal relations with the older generation of theatrical managers like Stanislavsky, as well as remaining sympathetic to the experimental 'left'. In practice, theatre workers of both 'right' and 'left' seemed keen on nationalisation, or at least on municipalisation, in order to ensure a special relationship with the state (the argument of the 'right') or increased penetrability (the argument of the 'left'). Narkompros was more cautious. Only in August 1919 did Lunacharsky initiate the handing-over of theatrical property to the state; but this had not meant full-scale proletarianisation, since he granted managerial autonomy only to those theatre managers who were able to manage their own affairs successfully and 'whose cultural value is recognised as incontrovertible'[3] – an attitude which was shared by Lenin. By the end of 1920, attempts to bring the work of the theatres closer to socialist ideals, by whatever means, had been limited.

The attitude of Lunacharsky and Lenin to the theatre is instructive. Both men believed that proletarian theatre was best created, not through the rejection of the past and the ushering in of experimental forms, but in the mastery and development of traditional themes and techniques. Lunacharsky claimed that the proletariat 'actually preferred the classics'; frequently citing the statement sent to him by the Kronstadt sailors that they preferred Gogol and Ostrovsky to 'revolutionary' Futurist spectacles.[4]

In this, however, Lunacharsky was opposed by both Bukharin (then editor of *Pravda* and a zealous supporter of Proletkult in the theatre) and Kerzhentsev. Bukharin, for instance, wrote a bitter attack on Lunacharsky in *Pravda* on the grounds that a play written by a wounded Red Army commander entitled *Krasnaya Pravda* (Red Truth) could not get a decent theatrical building, while traditional theatre such as *The Cherry Orchard* was greeted with yawns and boredom by the masses. Bukharin charged that this official conservatism was a remnant of the old 'slavish respect for aristocratic culture' and of the continued dominance of 'bourgeois ideologies'.[5]

1. K. Stanislavsky, *Sobranie sochinenii*, Moscow 1954–61, Vol 5, pp 249–50; Rudnitsky, *Russian and Soviet Theatre*, p 48.

2. Y. Sobolev, *Teatr*, 1922, no 2, p 39; Rudnitsky, *Russian and Soviet Theatre*, p 52.

3. Lunacharsky, *Izvestiya*, 3 August 1919; Fitzpatrick, *Commissariat*, p 144.

4. Lunacharsky, 'In the name of the Proletariat', *Vestnik teatr*, no 51, 5–8 February 1920; Fitzpatrick, *Commissariat*, pp 146–7.

5. Bukharin, *Pravda*, 16 October 1919.

Lunacharsky, for his part, replied that in fact militant Proletkult productions were not that popular with the broad masses, and that a small studio theatre was more appropriate.

One of the many ironies of Soviet cultural policy in the early years after 1917 is that the government itself was responsible for a turn to the 'left' in several areas, despite what may have been its better judgement. One example of this was Lunacharsky's appointment in the autumn of 1920 of Vsevelod Meyerhold to the post of head of the theatre department of Narkompros (TEO Narkompros). Meyerhold had been an innovator in the theatre in 1918–19 and an early enthusiast of the Revolution, hence his appointment was welcomed enthusiastically by the 'left', and by the Proletkult. However he had not been a strident polemicist, and for this reason he may have been acceptable to Lunacharsky also. In fact Meyerhold on his appointment proved far more iconoclastic than Lunacharsky suspected, and far less sympathetic to the traditional theatre than he must have hoped.

Of the pre-1920 productions organised by Meyerhold, a play by Mayakovsky had been of particular significance. His *Mystery-Bouffe* had been selected to celebrate the first anniversary of the October Revolution, but had been boycotted by the vast majority of actors in Petrograd, themselves still uncertain about the new theatre, and the casting had been completed after a public appeal for volunteer students to fill the roles. Mayakovsky himself had taken three parts for the opening performance on 7 November 1918, and had also designed costumes (Figure 38). The play itself is a parody of the biblical story of the Ark, with the flood representing world revolution and the international proletariat overthrowing the exploiters and being led to the promised land of socialism, in which, significantly, everything is mechanised and all menial work is done by tools and machines. Malevich had designed costumes and settings in the Suprematist style, but these were not to Mayakovsky's liking and he had replaced them with designs of his own. *Mystery-Bouffe* closed after three nights, and was not repeated until 1921. Meyerhold himself became ill and left Moscow, and after his recovery worked with the Red Army Theatre in Novorossisk during the most strenuous period of the Civil War.

On his return to Moscow after a period of imprisonment by the Whites and a narrow escape from execution, Meyerhold was summoned to return to Moscow in 1920 by Lunacharsky to work in Narkompros. Meyerhold immediately began to advocate 'revolution' in the theatre, including full nationalisation of all theatres, liquidation of specially protected state theatres, and the introduction of revolutionary plays and revolutionary techniques. This was to mean, in practice, the abandonment of representational 'realism' and the use of Cubist, Futurist and Suprematist techniques – a wholly unexpected bid for alliance with the artistic 'left' which was greeted by some Proletkultists and most unattached 'leftists' with obvious enthusiasm. Competition between Meyerhold and Lunacharsky suddenly became intense, particularly since Lunacharsky himself was a playwright who could (in his weaker moments) turn to mysticism, mythology, and religion as suitable topics for drama. His defence of melodrama as a popular form, one that 'recommends itself to healthy, monumental, simple, clear and strong taste'[6] was also unattractive to 'left' critics like Kerzhentsev, who found it incomprehensible that the Soviet Commissar for Education could turn out such tired formulations. Lunacharsky's explanation that he wrote the plays at night, as relaxation – 'to forget myself and go away into the Kingdom of pure images and pure ideas'[7] – seemed scarce justification.

At the same time, following his appointment to TEO Narkompros, some of Meyerhold's Futurist theatrical productions were attacked by traditional-minded commentators like Krupskaya for being too difficult and too far removed from the comprehension of the proletarian masses. Such a treatment was meted out to Verhaeren's *The Dawn* in November 1920 at the Sohn Theatre, performed by Meyerhold's own company, the RSFSR Theatre No. 1. Although admission was free and the meaning of Verhaeren's play sufficiently simple and direct – it concerns the transformation of a capitalist war into an international proletarian uprising – Krupskaya found Meyerhold's

6. Lunacharsky, 'What Kind of Melodrama Do We Need?', *Sobranie sochineniya*, vol 2, p 789, Fitzpatrick, *Commissariat*, p 153.

7. *Magi*, Moscow, 1919, p 1; Fitzpatrick, *Commissariat*, p 152.

Figure 38
V. Mayakovsky, costume design for the first performance of *Mystery-Bouffe*, 1918

8. For a description see E. Braun, *Meyerhold on Theatre*, London, 1969, p 164.

adaptation, in which he had up-dated the text to make it fit the circumstances of the Russian Revolution, problematic. She may also have disliked the set design by Vladimir Dmitriev, which was in geometrical Futurist style and thoroughly non-illusionistic, with red, gold and silver cubes and triangles and only the occasional recognisable object such as a graveyard cross or a gate (Figure 39).[8] She associated Meyerhold with Lunacharsky, for having supported him;

Figure 39
Verhaeren, *The Dawn*,
produced by Meyerhold,
November 1920 (photo: *SCR*
London)

so in effect Lunacharsky was being reproached from two directions at once. Kerzhentsev, together with Bukharin, wanted to discipline Lunacharsky for his 'rightism', and thought to whip up enthusiasm for an end to the policy of tolerance for all groups. But Krupskaya's (and by implication Lenin's) attack on Meyerhold's Futurism gave the debate a political significance which it would never lose. The 'left' wanted hegemony over all the arts and an end to the liberal dispensation at Narkompros. The 'right' wanted an end to Futurism and a cleansing of the Narkompros stable. The issue in both cases was the appropriateness of both Futurism and the traditional forms of art for the new socialist society, given that in the dictatorship of the proletariat the people would need to be both the producers and consumers of art. Could revolutionary reality be transmitted through the tolerance of all artistic forms, or was corrective discipline needed to purge the traditional arts of bourgeois mentality in order to encourage the dominance of the new? Or were the new Futurist forms, as Lunacharsky and Krupskaya may both have thought, themselves merely the remnants of the bourgeois pre-Revolutionary era, which neither before nor immediately after 1917 had had any genuinely popular socialist appeal?

Such questions had far-reaching resonances in 1920 and 1921. They affected the other arts no less than the theatre. Opinion was extraordinarily fragmented. The result inevitably was a mixture of styles and approaches, one tendency coming into view as quickly as it was overtaken by another, contrary impulse. The overall state of technique in the theatrical profession was a medley of innovations and cautious reworkings of the past, depending inevitably upon where one stood. Meyerhold himself would forge ahead with a series of innovations in production and acting technique. The older theatres however effected a series of compromises between the classics and the need for 'genuine' revolutionary drama. The change in the economic mood of the country in 1921 would cause yet further changes still.

The Balance of Forces in 1920

As these debates and conflicts will have shown, the situation in the arts by the end of 1920 was in part very clear and at the same time very confused. The principle of creative freedom for diverse approaches was defended by some of the more traditional artists, and by Lunacharsky; while voices like Mayakovsky, Bukharin and Kerzhentsev were avid to clear the decks of the liberal approach and impose various forms of Futurist art by fiat – a policy Lunacharsky rejected as 'red sycophancy'.[1] Yet it must also be recognised that the jostling for position on the level of theory did not always match the practical reality. Administrative muddle was widespread. Much was talked of that was never done. Crippling cold, near-starvation levels of subsistence and material shortage were daily facts of life that had to be reckoned with. In his own defence Lunacharsky cited the fact that the Civil War was at its height, that paper and materials were scarce, and that completely open state support of all artistic groups, however desirable, was impossible to achieve in practice. Economic realities had to impinge.

The need for administrative simplicity during a time of national crisis was undoubtedly one of the factors which lay behind the Central Committee's letter condemning the Proletkults which was published in *Pravda* on 1 December 1920. For outside the area surrounding Moscow, and in the south particularly, the task from the middle of 1918 had been to preserve the socialist Revolution from collapse. Lenin's civil force, the Cheka, had had to resort to mass arrests of anarchists and opponents of the regime, just as 'White terror' had become the term applied to the ferocious attacks on government forces by opponents in the field. Military needs during the Civil War had crippled the balance of the economy, in which production in any case was far lower than before the Revolution, in some cases close to zero. Hunger and disease were widespread among the population (Figure 40), particularly in winter. Schools had few supplies of paper and books. Teachers were reported to Narkompros as being 'without clothes and without shoes . . . terrible cases of poverty among teachers, suicide from want, have been reported . . . '.[2] Prostitution, madness and death among the profession were being alleged.

1. Lunacharsky, *Pravda*, 28 November 1920; Fitzpatrick, *Commissariat*, p 157.

2. Fitzpatrick, *Commissariat*, p 164.

Viktor Shklovsky gives an example of the winter conditions during the Civil War:

> I was giving lectures at the Institute of Art History [in Petrograd]. The Institute apparently had wood, but not enough money to have it sawed. You froze. The curtains and stone walls of that luxurious house froze. The typists in the office were puffy from cold and hunger . . . Before me sat a student from a family of workers – a lithographer. Each day he became more transparent. One day he gave a report on Fielding. His ears were translucent – white, rather than pink. After leaving the class, he fell in the street. He was picked up and taken to hospital – hunger.[3]

3. V. Shklovsky, *A Sentimental Journey: Memoirs 1917–1922*, Cornell University Press, Ithaca, New York, 1970, pp 234–5.

In another example he relates how

> tables, chairs, cornices, butterfly chests had all been burned up. A friend of mine burned his library. That was horrible work. You have to tear all the pages out of the books and wad them up. He nearly died that winter, but the doctor came to see him one day when the whole family was sick. He told them all to move into one tiny room. They warmed it with their breath and survived. In that little room, Boris Eikhenbaum wrote his book *The Young Tolstoy*.[4]

4. V. Shklovsky, *A Sentimental Journey*, p 235.

At this stage, too, the situation in the Party was a troubled and troubling one. Some alleged that the atmosphere had been slowly changing; that the real conditions of the workers and peasants were being ignored and that Party pronouncements frequently bore no relation to the actual state of affairs. Victor Serge, for example, reports a feeling of danger 'from within the very temper and character of victorious Bolshevism'. He recalls that he was 'continually racked by the contrast between the stated theory and the reality, by the growth of intolerance and servility among many officials and their drive towards privilege'.[5] Real facts such as the rampant growth of the black market or the repressive measures often taken by the Cheka were all but ignored by minor officials. 'The wonderful lucidity of these Marxists was beginning to be fuddled with theoretical intoxication bordering on delusion,' states Serge; 'they began to be enclosed within all the tricks and tomfooleries of servility.'[6]

Certainly the Party apparatus, which had already shown a tendency to centralised organisation during the emergency period of the Civil War, was becoming in the latter period of the fighting even more concentrated at the centre than in the first months after the Revolution. The Annual Congresses of the Party were proving to be cumbersome instruments for reacting to unpredictable crises. This at least was the ostensible reason why, at the Eighth Congress of the Party in March 1919, the Central Committee was elaborated to include several extra bodies designed to improve efficiency and increase the Party's capacity for responding to change. In addition to a 'Politburo' for urgent decision-making, an Orgburo was created to oversee the organisational work of the Party, as well as a Central Committee Secretariat, with undefined functions. Several Party leaders sat on more than one committee, to ensure smooth communication (Krestinsky as first Party 'secretary' sat on the Orgburo; Stalin sat on both the Orgburo and the Politburo, and so on). The main task devolved to the Secretariat became Party discipline. Opposition factions *within* the Party rather than outside it now became a cause for concern; and to this end a further body, the so-called 'Control Commission', was added in September 1920 to examine reports of misconduct and to discuss corrective measures with the Central Committee. In the period immediately following, the 'Workers' Opposition' led by Shlyapnikov and Alexandra Kollontai was the main faction against which disciplinary measures were deemed to be necessary. The Workers' Opposition urged a radical de-centralisation of the Party and the handing of more control to the trades unions, a purge of intellectuals from the Party and their replacement by workers, together with free elections to the Party and free discussion within its ranks. It demanded equal wages, free clothing, travel and education. But this utopian platform proved to no avail. Soon after the Tenth Congress of the Party in March 1921 the Workers' Opposition was effectively crushed, following an oration from Trotsky in which he asserted that

> the Party is obliged to maintain its dictatorship, regardless of temporary wavering in the spontaneous moods of the masses, regardless of temporary vacillations even in the working class . . . The dictatorship does not base itself at every given moment on the formal principle of a workers' democracy, although the workers' democracy is, of course, the only method by which the masses can be drawn more and more into political life.[7]

Thus discipline and an ever firmer grasp of control at the centre of the Party came to be considered imperative throughout the stricken days of war communism and the Civil War. Organisation and

5. V. Serge, *Memoirs of a Revolutionary, 1901–1941*, London and Oxford, 1963, pp 112–3.

6. V. Serge, *Memoirs*, p 113. A good first-hand account of the treatment meted out by the Cheka is G. Poppoff, *The Tcheka: The Red Inquisition*, London, 1925.

Figure 40 (opposite)
Starvation conditions during the Civil War (photo: *David King*)

7. Deutscher, *The Prophet Armed*, p 509.

Bolshevik 'firmness' seemed paramount everywhere. With education in some areas at a standstill, and with factory workers hungry almost to the point of death, food detachments were sent into the countryside to collect grain from kulaks (so-called rich peasants) who were suspected of hoarding. In the spring of 1919 when the Civil War was at its height, general conscription was introduced which soon came to include the drafting of labour for essential work. The famous 'communist Saturdays' or *subbotniks* called for by Lenin were introduced in May 1919, in which thousands of workers in Moscow and Petrograd gave free overtime in order to speed up the movement of supplies to the front. The decline of industry was exacerbated by a massive loss of population from the cities between 1917 and 1920, either to the Red Army, or to the countryside in search of food and work. Moscow lost 44.5 per cent of its population between these dates; the figure for Petrograd was 57.5 per cent.[8]

8.   Carr, *The Bolshevik Revolution*, 1950, p 24.

Added to these difficulties, news of the Revolution had scarcely reached the peasants in some distant areas, despite the agit-trains and boats already mentioned. Far-flung peasants were resistant to such experiments as the collective and state farms, the first of which were set up in 1918 and 1919.

It behoves us to remember too that ideological understanding of the Revolution was multi-faceted and diverse – this is what ultimately explains the drive for discipline and loyalty within the Party. We can point out at least two main strands of Revolutionary thinking concerning the events of October 1917. One, the Revolution led by Lenin and the intellectuals of the Party, was premised upon a wide network of connectedness with other impending revolutions in other European states. The emigré leaders of the Bolshevik Party had, through their wide experience of Germany, Austria, France, Britain, Italy and elsewhere, learned to view events not merely on a national scale, and not merely in terms of particular local grievances. Russia was to be the first Revolution out of many and, having ignited the flame, would then bask in its growing heat: the working class of the world would eventually unite in international cooperation.

Another October Revolution was very differently conceived. This was the purely national upheaval based on squalid inequalities and injustices at home; upon labour disputes and declining work conditions; upon the wretchedness of political unfreedom and upon constant surveillance by the security police. This perhaps was where the Revolution of 1905 had begun, in the oilfields of Batumi and Baku, when the determined Caucasian workforce was being marshalled by the likes of Ordzhonikidze, Yenukidze and Stalin at the very time when Lenin and his entourage was still hiding in Geneva and had lost touch, so it was said, with the reality of events in their own country. These hard-working organisers had next to no experience of the theoretical debates taking place in the Party abroad, and probably no aptitude for them either. They were not interested in the revolutionary schools at Longjumeau or Capri, and in fact came to resent them. In the years of reaction, from 1906 to 1912, these local Bolsheviks had undoubtedly become deeply involved in workers' grievances and in the rallying of underground Party cells at a time when the revolutionary spirit (as well as its organisation) was in danger of collapse. By them, October 1917 came to be perceived as a victory won not just by Lenin and the philosophical leadership, but by the Baku oilmen and the tireless organisational efforts of countless Party workers who regarded the Revolution as primarily a Russian, national affair which should bring benefits to the populace irrespective of the higher philosophical and cultural aspirations of the Party leaders. The fact that October 1917 can be seen as a populist revolt inside a socialist revolution as well as a socialist revolution inside a populist revolt is largely responsible for the different sets of cultural expectations which different groups expressed after 1917, both in the cultural field and more generally. It helps to explain the appearance of avid intellectualism on the part of the Suprematists, Futurists and Formalists on the one hand, very much centred in the international atmosphere of Paris, Munich and Berlin; and the avid anti- or pre-intellectualism of the millions of semi-educated workers and peasants in whose name the Revolution was waged, on the other.

These two factors taken in combination – the importance of discipline and Bolshevik 'firmness' in the midst of Civil War, and a lingering ambiguity as to what or for whom the Revolution had really been undertaken – had a devastating impact on events and attitudes within the cultural field. In particular, the decline of cohesion among the proletariat as a class, combined with the already low cultural standard of the peasantry, seems to have persuaded Lenin and most leaders of the Party that artistic Futurism, indeed 'experimentalism' of any kind, could not form a viable cultural prospectus for the country. It was perhaps in the nature of things that the 'administrator' and the 'practitioner' came to see the arts from very different perspectives. In a centrally organised administration, it was a contest that the practictioner could not win.

However by the time the Polish invasion had been quelled in the autumn of 1920, the situation began to change once more. The population was exhausted, and the harsh discipline of the war period could no longer be sustained. Now, a different set of arguments began to present themselves. For those on the 'left' like Bukharin, the war had demonstrated that a socialist economy was possible and that goods could be distributed according to need rather than the market, that industry could function on government orders, and that labour could respond to genuine demand rather than the behest of the bourgeois employer. The battleground of culture, in this view, could be taken with emergency tactics and the involvement of the whole of the leading class (the proletariat) in the creation of absolutely new forms.

On the other hand Lenin was to view such Revolutionary optimism still as a utopian fallacy – in spite of the fact that the war had been won. In fact Lenin did not live long enough to see that the reconstruction of the economy would be immeasurably painstaking and uncertain. But he could see that – for better or worse – the days of youthful Revolutionary enthusiasm were now over; and yet 'leftists' were still pressing that their voices should be the first and most frequent to be heard.

Lenin's cultural conservatism – or caution – has already been noted at several points. Another attack on 'left-wing' or 'avant-garde' art is contained in his pamphlet '"Left-wing" Communism, an Infantile Disorder', written in the early part of 1920 and published in the course of that year. This pamphlet broadens and elaborates Lenin's cultural views within the context of an overtly political discussion.

The inverted commas which Lenin places around 'left-wing' are as important as the charge of 'childishness' of which he accuses certain forms of communist agitational activity. 'Left' doctrinairism is no less a 'disease', he claims, a 'disorder', than 'right' doctrinairism. No less than against 'rightism', Bolshevism was engaged in an unremitting struggle against what Lenin calls 'petty-bourgeois revolutionism', that is, agitational activity not based on the leadership of the Party and aimed at attempting to whip up revolutionary activity among the masses by any and every means, however uncoordinated, including arbitrary political terrorism and assassination. All this smacks of anarchism, Lenin argues.

In a speech to the Komsomol in 1920 Lenin had placed a pre-Revolutionary intellectual in the same category as a 'small owner, a petty employee, a petty official' – that is, 'a man who is concerned only with himself, and does not care a whit for anybody else'.[9] That he also applied this definition to post-Revolutionary intellectuals is reasonably clear. He says in the '"Left-Wing" Communism' pamphlet, that the petty proprietor, the type that Marx had characterised as a small manufacturer or artisan, always suffers oppression under capitalism and is easily driven to revolutionary extremes, but is 'incapable of perseverence, organisation, discipline and steadfastness', that is, 'he does not measure up to the conditions and requirements of a consistently proletarian class struggle',[10] one led by the vanguard of its revolutionary Party.

> A petty-bourgeois driven to frenzy by the horror of capitalism is a social phenomenon which, like anarchism, is characteristic of all capitalist countries. The instability of such revolutionism, its barrenness, and its tendency to turn rapidly into submission, apathy, phantasms, and even a frenzied infatuation with one bourgeois fad or another,

this, alleges Lenin, is its 'infantilism and childishness'.[11]

He argues that a recent eruption of 'left' childishness was the debate on the Brest–Litovsk Treaty, which had succeeded in concluding the war but on very harsh terms to the Soviets. 'Left' communists like Trotsky – joined by Radek and Bukharin – had argued strenuously in favour of prolonging the war, at all costs of not compromising with the imperialist powers. Lenin, however, as the architect of Brest–Litovsk, had urged compromise then and the necessity of flexible compromise now, in all revolutionary actions. But he finds no difficulty or contradiction in quashing 'left-ists' (the German Communist Party as an example) who distinguish rigidly between the dictatorship of the masses and the dictatorship of the leaders, between dictatorship of the class and dictatorship of the Party. He still stands irresolutely on the principle of the Party, interpreted in a

9. Lenin, 'Bourgeois and Communist Morality', Speech to the Third All-Russian Congress of the Komsomol, 2 October 1920; Collected Works, 4th edn, Vol 31, Moscow, 1966, pp 290–6; *Pravda*, 5, 6, 7 October 1920; this quotation is from the translation in Rosenberg (ed), *Bolshevik Visions*, p 35.

10. Lenin, '"Left Wing" Communism, an Infantile Disorder', 1920 (Moscow 1950 edn), p 17–18.

11. Lenin, '"Left-Wing" Communism', p 18.

certain way. The distinction between the Party and the masses testifies, he believes, to

> the most incredibly and hopelessly muddled thinking . . . [since] classes are led by political parties, and political parties, as a general rule, are run by more or less stable groups composed of the most authoritative, influential and experienced members, who are elected to the most responsible positions, and are called leaders. Why replace this with some kind of rigmarole, some new Volapük?[12]

Repudiation of the Party principle and of Party discipline adds up, he says, to 'petty-bourgeois diffuseness and instability, that incapacity for sustained effort, unity and organised action' which would destroy the proletarian revolution.

In characterising inflexible and doctrinaire 'left-ism' as a 'sell-out' to the bourgeoisie, Lenin undoubtedly had cultural 'left-ism' in mind here too, in spite of the fact that it is not explicitly mentioned. The concept of Party leadership of the masses, through its instrument, the working class; the concept of flexible compromise as opposed to 'thinking up some kind of recipe for the workers which would provide them with cut-and-dried solutions for all contingencies';[13] the concept of 'taking the bourgeoisie at its word and utilising the machinery it has set up';[14] all these are cultural concepts too, ones that organised the ground for Lenin's disparagement of 'leftist' art in general and Proletkult independence in particular. Only in one rather marginal place in '"Left-wing" Communism' (in a long footnote to an appendix added to the main text) does Lenin concede that 'left' communists are very good at agitation among the masses, at least in Germany, and in Russia at a local level. In 1907–8, he says, 'on certain occasions and in certain places', 'left' Bolsheviks were even more successful in this than the centre of the Party; Lenin explains this by suggesting that 'at a revolutionary moment, or at a time when revolutionary recollections are still fresh, it may be easier to approach the masses with tactics of sheer negation.'[15] But this does not prove the correctness of such a tactic, he says quickly. Notwithstanding the importance of comprehensible, simple and vivid agitation and propaganda, the central argument remains that of tactical hostility to quasi-anarchistic 'leftism' in all its forms and varieties. From the appearance of the '"Left-Wing" Communism' onwards, if not before, 'left' became a term of stern disapprobation in the Bolshevik Party – quite unlike its usage by socialists in the West – that would be used again and again to vilify and abuse all those who naively gloried in its name.

There is thus no evidence that Lenin softened his line on 'left' culture just because the war had come to an end. Indeed it was precisely because the population would have more time for cultural pursuits that it may have seemed all the more necessary to him now that they become acquainted with the work of the past and sharpen their critical faculties upon it. The letter condemning Proletkult at the end of 1920 was precisely in line with this assault.

In terms of the debate around the political appropriateness of different forms of art, however, the Party's intervention over the

12. Lenin, '"Left-Wing" Communism', pp 26–7. 'Volapük' was an artificial 'universal' language invented primarily for business and commerce by Johann Martin Schleyer in the nineteenth century. See his *Volapük. Die Welt Sprache. Entwurf einer Universal-Sprache fur alle Gebildete der ganzen Erde*, Sigmaringen, 1880, etc.

13. Lenin, '"Left-Wing" Communism', p 23.

14. Ibid., p 83.

15. Ibid., footnote to p 92.

Proletkult, as well as its regular cautions on 'left' art, suggested several other things. It suggested that the 'left' was not to be allowed a monopoly in culture, however energetic and original their efforts may have seemed to some. Nor, of course, was a monopoly to be given to the traditional artists of the 'right'; yet by pronouncing more regularly on the misdeeds of the 'left' it must have appeared that the principles of tolerance had been abandoned – if indeed they had ever been really embraced. Secondly, it offered a precedent for direct *political* intervention in the debate around aesthetics, and established explicitly what had so far lain beneath the surface, namely that the Soviet government was deeply interested in the direction taken by art and culture and regarded them as vitally important components of national life, however great the crises in the economy or the military position may have been. But perhaps most of all it acted as a reminder to artists of every shade that, at a time of bitter devastation on every front, what the 'left' had hopefully described as 'revolutionary art' was far in excess of the ability of the proletariat to comprehend. At a time when schoolchildren still had no paper to practise writing, what franchise could realistically be expected for Kerzhentsev's 'culture of the new'?

3

The Beginning of NEP
1921–1924

The Introduction of NEP

By the beginning of 1921, well over two years of siege conditions had reduced the Soviet people to exhaustion; notwithstanding the well justified claim that it was precisely their stoicism and their endurance that had finally won the day. Conditions both in town and country had been exceptionally harsh. Economically, war communism had involved a mixture of centralised management for heavy industry and the formation of a 'national' rather than a 'market' economy for the Soviet Union's most important product, grain. Prices of grain had been fixed, its use immediate, and payments for it frequently made in kind rather than in currency – a practice which was seen by some as the beginnings of a truly moneyless, communist economy. After the end of the fighting the immediate need was for reconstruction on every front; yet this was believed to require still further discipline and organisation.

Grain, for example, after the end of the fighting, was for a time still requisitioned on the basis of a strict war-time economy. Even Lenin himself, in 1920, showed some sympathy for Trotsky's doctrine of the militarisation of labour, and right up until the opening months of 1921 seemed determined that the market should be suppressed and extreme labour discipline maintained. In this sense alone we may see the closing months of 1920 – the time of the move against Proletkult – as a period of extremism, in which things were said that were fairly soon renounced. Proletkult itself however remained an object of the gravest suspicion.

Lenin became persuaded of the harshness of war communism only in the first months of 1921. Peasant dissatisfaction at the government practice of confiscating grain surpluses (hence suppressing any incentive to produce more) was leading to uprisings in the countryside. A revolt in the naval base at Kronstadt in February 1921, against miserable conditions and what the sailors saw as the unsatisfactory trend of Party policy, acted as a further sign that economic change was urgently needed. The 'mutiny' at Kronstadt – as the Bolshevik leaders called it – was ruthlessly and viciously suppressed by the Red Army, an action supported by both Lenin and Trotsky. Yet just as this act of butchery was being carried out, the long-awaited Tenth Party

Congress of March 1921 was debating a new set of proposals presented by Lenin, known as the New Economic Policy or NEP.

The NEP principles announced a fundamental reversal of the policy of war communism. The essence of the new policy was that the peasants would be encouraged to produce grain by being permitted to sell part of their output under market conditions once their quota had been delivered to the state. Middle peasants and kulaks would be allowed to trade and make profits wherever they could. (Some trade had inevitably flourished in black market conditions before 1921, but the permissions now given were legal.) Conversely, heavy industry would remain under the aegis of the state, but lighter industry and manufacture would be encouraged to supply the demand created by the new capital now in the hands of the peasantry. 'Bourgeois specialists' – those with managerial and entrepreneurial skills from pre-1917 – would be encouraged more than ever to help in the regeneration of the economy. The rouble was stabilised, and production in both industry and agriculture started to pick up.

Party policy was now to be concerned overwhelmingly with the place of the peasantry in relation to the proletariat, and since it was this same policy that was to become crucial for developments in the arts, it is important to realise how it operated. The simple fact was that the rural workforce had not yet reached the economic, material or political stage attained by the proletariat, and this was a gap of which Lenin became ever more aware as he sought measures to marry together the interests of the two segments of the population. Thus NEP policy was an attempt to reflect these different stages: the proletariat still waging a fight against bourgeois market conditions and capitalism, and the peasantry now for the first time emerging from a semi-feudal state into a period of bourgeois and petty-bourgeois aspiration. An element of private trade across the economy would at least raise the conditions of the peasant and bring a little prosperity to the towns – such was the theory. This new 'link with the peasant' was the key policy of the NEP period. As Lenin put it when he saw the beginnings of dissent in the countryside, 'only an agreement with the peasantry can save the socialist revolution in Russia until the revolution has occurred in other countries.'[1]

With the reintroduction of trading under NEP, important changes also took place in the orientation of the Party to questions of education, technical training, and the policy of the cultural sphere. In the field of art, it was perhaps inevitable that the Revolutionary enthusiasm of 1917 and 1918 was beginning to subside. Moreover pre-Revolutionary forms of art such as easel painting had quite clearly survived – not unscathed, perhaps, but still ideologically intact, in spite of the furious attacks launched against them by Futurists and 'left-wing' artists. Policy would now have to reflect precisely the survival of older forms amidst the new. Perhaps the upheaval engendered by the Revolution had even made it more likely, rather than less, that traditional artistic techniques would survive. At any rate, on the assumption that the Revolution and the Civil War had been causes both of iconoclastic experimentation and of a retreat to the safety of traditional forms, it began to seem desirable to several

1. Lenin at the 10th Party Congress, 1921; cited in E. H. Carr, *The Russian Revolution from Lenin to Stalin, 1917–1929,* Macmillan, London and Basingstoke 1979, p50.

people within the Party that more than one approach to 'Revolution-ary art' should be encouraged. Thirdly, Lenin's intervention against the Proletkult at the end of 1920 signalled not merely that the Party took an interest in the arts, but that it was now prepared to make its position known on what course the arts should follow.

But over the practice of the economy and the arts there began to hover a vital question: was the introduction of the New Economic Policy to be understood as a retreat from Revolutionary forms, or merely as an expedient and temporary cessation of extreme measures? Many communists came to regard the NEP economy as a blatant denial of the Revolutionary principles for which they had fought. The view taken by Lenin however was that since war com-munism had itself been an exceptional policy, designed to meet the needs of an exceptional situation, the abandonment of war commun-ism and the very gradual release of the market could not strictly be called a backsliding into capitalism, wholesale or otherwise. Yet he had the proletariat and a whole new generation of younger commun-ists to convince. This tension between the desire to continue imple-menting the Revolutionary policy of October and the more conciliatory *realpolitik* of the Party leader was eventually to grow into a sizeable ideological rift, and one of extreme importance to the arts. At the time of its introduction, at any rate, Lenin described NEP as 'a retreat – for a new attack';[2] but a retreat nonetheless. The question was whether the retreat was to be of short duration, or prolonged; and, if short, when the next advance would be.

2. Carr, *The Russian Revolution from Lenin to Stalin*, p 37.

One of the vitally important concomitants of the 'retreat' engen-dered by NEP, and again one that held enormous significance for the future, was Lenin's insistence upon the maintenance of a completely new type of discipline in the conduct of the government. As he put it, 'discipline is a hundred times more necessary during a retreat.'[3] He meant, above all, the discipline of the Party.

3. Ibid., p 34.

The background to this signal development is that the Tenth Party Congress of March 1921 had been pervaded by a sense of the insta-bility of the Bolshevik regime: falling food supplies, strikes, disturb-ances and – most of all – increased levels of disagreement within the Party, which seemed to render any progress impossible. The crushing of the Kronstadt riot had perhaps been a sign of the government's sense of its own vulnerability. But now, at the Tenth Congress, Lenin referred to the increasing 'factionalism' within the Party, by which he meant the Workers' Opposition on the one hand and Trotsky's group, who advocated the subordination of the trades unions, on the other – both of whom had hitherto been allowed to indulge in free debate and criticise the decisions of the Party once they had been taken.

Now, these groups seemed to threaten the very coherence of the Party. Lenin spoke at the Congress of 'the luxury of discussions' that had become customary:

For a Party which is surrounded by the strongest and most powerful enemies embracing the whole capitalist world, for a Party which carries on its shoulders an unheard-of burden, this luxury was truly astounding.

I do not know how you will assess it now. Has this luxury in your view been fully consistent with our material and moral resources?[4]

Of course the question was entirely rhetorical. Straight away he urged in the strongest terms that 'we need no opposition, comrades, now is not the time; either on this side or on that . . .'[5] Henceforward, decisions arrived at must be strictly obeyed. A resolution 'On the Unity of the Party' insisted that no independent 'platforms' would be allowed, over and above individual or group contributions to debate:

> The Congress prescribes the immediate dissolution of all groups without exception forming themselves on this or that platform, and instructs all organisations to insist strictly on the inadmissibility of any kind of factional activities. Non-fulfillment of this decision of the Congress must entail unconditional and immediate exclusion from the Party.[6]

Even members of the Central Committee could be demoted to candidate membership or expelled. It is significant too that in order to enforce this new administrative fiat the central organs of the Party were provided with new powers to discipline and exclude. The Control Commission under A.A. Solts, particularly, took on new powers. Meanwhile the Secretariat of the Party was deprived of Krestinsky, Preobrazhensky and Serebryakov – all of whom had supported Trotsky against the leadership over the trade union question; they were replaced by V. Molotov, E. Yaroslavsky and L. Mikhailov, all of whom also attained to the Central Committee in place of disgraced incumbents. Two of these were to become (may already have been) staunch supporters of Stalin, and one of them, Yaroslavsky, was to play an important role in the organisation of policy for the arts.

The new atmosphere of Party discipline after 1921 also meant that the balance between the central Party apparatus and the membership underwent a decisive change. The Tenth Congress initiated the first full-scale 'purge' of the rank-and-file membership. This was designed rigidly to exclude 'non-communist elements', following a review of each member's standards of behaviour and firmness of conviction. Disloyal Bolsheviks were peremptorily excluded: a total of 24 per cent were removed by the time of the Eleventh Congress in 1922, a high proportion of whom were intellectuals.[7] Mensheviks and remaining SRs were arrested, tried or sent abroad.

But loyalty and discipline were not the only behavioural standards required of conscientious Party members in the early days of NEP. Inevitably, communist 'culture' was also to embrace the conduct of private life, dress and personal adornment. A.A. Solts, Chairman of the Control Commission which purged the Party, gave a speech at Sverdlov University in 1922 in which he attempted to define the 'correct' attitudes. The burden of his address was to consign the concept of 'private life' decisively to the past. As the leading Party, Solts argued, the Bolsheviks were fighters through and through, committed to the struggle against the bourgeoisie; and anyone who ceased to be such a fighter would cease to be a member of the Party. He pointed out that for the bourgeoisie, dress and manners were

4. Lenin, *Sochineniya*, Vol 26, p 200; in E. H. Carr, *The Bolshevik Revolution, 1917–1923* (3 vols), Penguin, Harmondsworth, 1950; London, 1966, p 205.

5. Lenin, *Sochineniya*, Vol 26, p 227; Carr, *Bolshevik Revolution*, p 206.

6. *VKP(b) Rezolyutsiyakh* (1941), i, pp 366–8; Carr, *Bolshevik Revolution*, p 207.

7. Carr, *Bolshevik Revolution*, p 213. The figures given by Carr for Party membership before the purge are 8,400 (1905); 23,600 (Feb 1917); 115,000 (Feb 1918); 313,000 (early 1919); 431,000 (Jan 1920), 585,000 (Jan 1921);650,000 (October 1921);which then declined to 500,000 (March 1922); from A. S. Bubnov, *VKP(b)*, 1931.

considered 'beautiful' when they testified to success in bourgeois life. But what he called 'our aesthetics, our beauty' (that is, Bolshevik aesthetics and Bolshevik beauty) was grounded on 'respect for labour, on a striving to place workers ahead of everything'. Therefore, he said,

> if the external appearance of a Party member testifies to a full rift with working life, then that must be ugly, and it must encounter such an attitude as to make the Party member not wish to dress in such a way ... Such a comrade thinks that there exists some sort of personal life in which he is completely free to follow his own tastes ... [8]

Generally, it was the 'elegance' of the bourgeoisie that Solts held up to ridicule; adding 'I consider it ugly for a person to wear rings, bracelets, gold teeth – in my view that must arouse aesthetic indignation.'[9]

Does this imply that Party members should dress like slobs? Of course not, Solts pointed out. One may dress beautifully, but the beauty must be of a different sort. Bolsheviks are

> not against joys and pleasures, but we are against the distribution of them such that half the day is spent in the role of a devout Party member while the other half is spent living one's 'personal life'. One cannot separate private life from Party life ...

A visit to the theatre cannot be considered 'private life' while other types of work are thought of as 'public', he said.[10] Sexual relations were to come under similar strictures. The Bolsheviks, he emphasised, were not ascetics and if anything adhered to the views of 'free-thinkers'. Yet

> a disorderly sex life undoubtedly weakens each Party member as a fighter ... we must observe some proportion ... great variety in this area will take too much energy, feeling and intellect from a person ... Looking for diversity [in sex] shows that ... his head is occupied more with this side of life than with the interests of the struggle.[11]

There are signs too in Bukharin's early writings that behaviour that passed as 'anti-bourgeois' before the Revolution was quite inadmissible now that the proletariat was in power. (It hardly needs to be stressed that if applied to the arts this argument would have had drastic results.) In a speech to the Komsomol in October 1922, Bukharin singled out smoking as an example. In his own school days he himself

> smoked as a form of demonstration ... and by this small deed we destroyed the discipline of the old system. This was a protest which ... carried over to the organisation of all society ... This frivolity led to various revolutionary movements.[12]

But now in 1922, conditions were utterly different. To think otherwise, argued Bukharin, would be 'an uncritical transfer of the methods of destruction of the bourgeois system to our own organism'.[13] Bukharin urged that the same was true of alcohol and sex. As

8. A. A. Solts, 'Communist Ethics', 1922 in E. Yaroslavsky (ed), *Kalim dolzhen byt 'kommunist'*, Leningrad, 1925; in W. Rosenberg (ed), *Bolshevik Visions First Phase of the Cultural Revolution in Soviet Russia*, Ardis, Ann Arbor, Michigan, 1984, p 49.

9. Solts, 'Communist Ethics', p 49.

10. Ibid., p 50.

11. Ibid., p 52.

12. Bukharin, 'Speech to the Fifth Komsomol Congress', 11–19 October 1922, published in *Pyatyi vserossiiskii sezd RKSM 11–19 Oktyabrya 1922 goda Stenograficheskii otchet*, Moscow–Leningrad 1927, pp 113–23; Rosenberg (ed), *Bolshevik Visions*, p 88.

13. Bukharin, 'Speech to the Fifth Komsomol Congress', p 58.

an alternative to excesses in either, he advocated football and chess as games which induced intellectual, social and competitive training. 'Any game is to some extent a rehearsal for current actions . . . a preparation of the hand and mind . . . you must introduce the principle of competitiveness in all games.'[14] Amidst the uncertainties of NEP, he proposed, these principles were required more than ever before, in order to overcome the class enemy: the kulak and the bourgeoisie. He spoke of making 'cadres of excellent fighters in the field of cultural struggle'[15] – military language that would be revived with a vengeance after 1928. No clearer condemnation of the mores of artistic bohemia could possibly be imagined.

This watershed was also accompanied by structural changes in the administration of the arts. Following the attack on Proletkult and the insinuations of 'Futurism' within IZO Narkompros in October 1920, Proletkult and IZO Narkompros, together with the publishing houses Gosizdat and Tsentropechat, and the State Circus administration, were all brought within the ambit of a reformed Narkompros body – that for extra-mural education – known as the Chief Political Education Committee (Glavnyi politiko-prosvetitelnyi komitet or Glavpolitprosvet) under a *protégé* of Trotsky, E. A. Litkens. This was at the end of 1920. In appearance this subordination may have seemed drastic; but in practice Lenin and the Central Committee were happy for Proletkult to retain some independence within its new home, largely at the behest of Bukharin, who had argued in the Proletkult Congress that Proletkult should not necessarily be required to 'assimilate bourgeois culture' on Lenin's terms. At the same time, relations between Narkompros and the Party became strained. To what extent was the Party (through Sovnarkom) to dominate the affairs of Narkompros, and (through Narkompros) to supervise Proletkult?

Though urgent, it appears that these questions were left unresolved. The December 1920 letter in *Pravda* had been a shot across the bows of the bourgeois 'leftists' within Proletkult as well as those still in Narkompros, and a warning that the Central Committee recognised how 'endangered' had Proletkult's efforts become by the influence of certain bourgeois groups. But the statement on Proletkult was to some extent conciliatory: it assured the Proletkult that it had the Central Committee's full support for proletarian activity in the arts, and that 'full autonomy' within the ambit of Narkompros was guaranteed. The real butt of the Central Committee's letter were the 'Futurists, decadents . . . the renegades from the ranks of bourgeois publicists and philosophers' who had crept into the arts. The Central Committee recognised

> that up to the present time Narkompros itself, in the artistic sphere, displays these same intellectual trends . . . The Central Committee is managing to get rid of these bourgeois tendencies within Narkompros as well . . . [16]

Thus by the beginning of the NEP period in March 1921 the political education department Glavpolitprosvet had formally absorbed the art department (IZO) of Narkompros, having in theory taken to itself

14.   Bukharin, 'Speech to the Fifth Komsomol Congress', p 60.

15.   Ibid., p 61.

16.   'On the Proletkults', Fitzpatrick, *Commissariat*, p 187.

'the right to veto from the political point of view all work in the arts'. Yet in the first instance it could attract few managers of real experience and standing. Along with other large Commissariats, Narkompros' workforce was to be reduced by half during 1921 in a move to divert money to heavy industry. Most former IZO Narkompros employees such as Altman, Shterenberg and V. Bryusov moved elsewhere. The painter Pyotr Kiselis was appointed as head of Glavpolitprosvet's own IZO department, and Alexandr Serafimovich moved to Glavpolitprosvet's LITO or Literature Department; but on the whole this was a far less notable arts and literature administration than Narkompros had had before. And yet ironically, many of the replacements now being made within Narkompros were more favourably inclined to Futurism and Bogdanov than either Lunacharsky (of Narkompros) or Lebedev-Polyansky (of Proletkult) had ever been. Thus Valerian Pletnev, who replaced Lebedev-Polyansky as President of Proletkult after December 1920, was already in close agreement with Bogdanov and Bukharin, and as a playwright came increasingly under the spell of the Futurists in the first half of 1921, being appointed to lead the arts sector of Glavpolitprosvet in February in succession to Kiselis. Indeed Proletkult under Pletnev now came under the sway of Futurism *despite* the Central Committee's criticisms and *despite* Lenin's own misgivings. (Bogdanov had himself withdrawn from Proletkult in December 1920 under pressure from the Party leader.) But by this time Narkompros as a body had ceased to exert any real control over the visual arts. The refashioned Narkompros was administratively more complex than before, and cultural liberals like Lunacharsky were replaced by undistinguished administrators or iconoclasts, despite the best intentions of Krupskaya, now president of Glavpolitprosvet, and Lenin himself. Thus Lunacharsky, though still active in education and in the theatre, was no longer so prominently occupied with the administration of the visual arts.

It is of course ironic that several of the attempts to move arts organisations to the centre or to the right – at any rate away from extreme 'left' positions – resulted in management appointments which in practice had the reverse effect: first Meyerhold in the old TEO Narkompros and now Pletnev in the Proletkult and in Glavpolitprosvet. Lenin, for his part, must have been dismayed at how ineffective some of his (and the Central Committee's) decisions in practice really were. In several cases there was a failure to follow up an ambitious statement with practical and effective action. Lenin is reported as saying 'such is the sad state of our decrees; they are signed and then we ourselves forget about them and fail to carry them out.'[17]

But the confusion within Narkompros was perhaps significant of a more general trend after 1920 and the beginning of 1921: a marked decline in the influence of the Bolshevik 'old guard' and an increase in the part played by younger Party trainees, working within the context of larger and more complex administrative structures yet without the broad educational advantages and competences of the older Bolsheviks. This change from experience to youth, from liberal attitudes and a belief in discussion to dogmatism and a reluctance to

17. Lenin, *Collected Works*, Vol 32, p 22. Compare the counter-revolutionary journalist and mystic P. O. Ouspensky in his *Letters From Russia*, 1919: 'If we begin to examine what is left of Russia today, we observe primarily that everything in it acts according to one general rule, which I may call the Law of Opposite Aims and Results. In other words, everything leads to results that are contrary to what people intend to bring about and towards which they strive . . .' (London, 1973 edition, p 3).

discuss was a gradual yet perceptible one around 1921. The Bolshevik Party had not necessarily intended these revisions in the form they actually took; yet it had been responsible for them, and it would have to endure the consequences.

Constructivism and the Labour Process

Within the hiatus of changing policy at the end of 1920 and the beginning of 1921, what was the role played by 'left' or 'modernist' artists within the state bodies for higher education and research?

As we saw in the last chapter, the state-supported programme of INKhUK had split into two main parts at the very end of 1920: on the one side Kandinsky's psychological programme, which fell out of favour and resulted in his departure in January 1921, and on the other side the programme of the General Working Group of Objective Analysis (Obshchaya rabochaya gruppa obektivnogo analiza), which became dominant after Kandinsky's departure and which was organised by Alexey Babichev, soon to be replaced by the First Working Group of Constructivists, organised by Rodchenko, Stepanova and Alexey Gan.

Early statements by members of the First Working Group suggest some unanimity of commitment to the ideals of three-dimensional construction characterised by 'the best use of the materials [and] the absence of any superfluous elements'. Construction, this statement goes on, is 'the combination of lines, and the planes and forms they define; it is a system of forces'.[1] The purpose of these statements was partly for those so inclined to dissociate themselves from others within the General Working Group of Objective Analysis who favoured, not construction in three dimensions, but composition. Composition, according to artists like Klyun, Popova, Drevin and Udaltsova, was essentially the distribution of elements on a flat surface without any pretence of practical construction (Figure 41). Popova, for example, defined composition as 'the regular and tasteful arrangement of material',[2] at this stage showing considerable distrust of the principle's practical applicability. Drevin said composition was the 'distribution of parts'.[3] However Stepanova, of the First Working Group of Constructivists, said of composition that it is based 'precisely on the excessive ... the greater the quantity of excess material and excess elements a composition has, the subtler it is in respect of taste and the more visually it disassociates itself from construction' – she is perhaps describing some of Popova's paintings of that date – and affirmed that 'only construction demands the absence of both excess materials and excess elements ... we are following the lines of reducing the excessive ... and are drawn clearly to construction.'[4]

With easel artists like Drevin and Udaltsova wedded to two-dimensional art, and with the architects Krinsky and Ladovsky following their own professional path, the much more closely-knit Constructivist group within INKhUK firmly followed the path of 'construction in real space'; quickly gaining control of the organisation of INKhUK and effectively forcing many others to leave. Brik

1. 'Protokol zasedaniya INKhUKa' 11 March 1921; C. Lodder, *Russian Constructivism*, Yale University Press, New Haven and London, 1983, p 84, to whom this section is indebted.

2. 'Protokol', 21 January 1921; Lodder, *Russian Constructivism*, p 88.

3. 'Protokol', 4 March 1921; Lodder, *Russian Constructivism*, p 85.

4. 28 January 1921; Lodder, *Russian Constructivism*, p 88, no reference supplied but presumably 'Protokol'.

Figure 41
L. Popova, *Spatial Force Construction*, c.1920–21.

became president, Tarabukin became secretary, and Rodchenko became the clearest and most outspoken theoretical voice. The theorists Arvatov and Kushner soon joined INKhUK to reinforce its by now very solid Productivist platform. Klyun, Drevin and Udaltsova soon left the institute.

Easel painting was momentarily under a heavy cloud, at least here; although Popova, who still practised it, remained formally within the Constructivist circle. For approximately two years, up until 1923, those associated with the Constructivists at INKhUK were extremely active in exhibitions, debates, articles and books. Almost at once they declared their aims to be 'revolutionary inventive activity . . . to realise in practical terms the communistic expression of material structures'.[5] Their programme stood firmly and implacably against 'aesthetics' and against 'individualism', indeed against 'art' as a whole as then and previously understood. With or without the consent of the Party they laid emphasis on establishing

5. 'Programma uchebnoi podgruppy rabochei gruppy konstruktivistov *Ermitazh*, no 13, 1922, cited in Lodder, *Russian Constructivism*, p 282 n 103.

> the materialistic understanding of the world, the philosophy and theory of scientific communism, realising the practice of Soviet construction, and of determining the place which the intellectual producer of Constructivist constructions must occupy in communist life . . .[6]

6. 'Programma uchebnoi podgruppy', Lodder, *Russian Constructivism*, p 282 n 105.

The exhibitions of the Constructivists over the period 1921–3 were important in establishing the methods and results of the new programme. These included the third and most celebrated exhibition of the OBMOKhU group in Moscow in May 1921, in which Rodchenko and Ioganson took part; the September 1921 exhibition known as '5x5=25', with five works each by Alexandr Vesnin, Popova, Rodchenko, Stepanova and Alexandra Exter; and the January 1922 exhibition entitled 'The Constructivists' at the Café Poetov in Moscow, involving the Stenberg brothers and Medunetsky. In the catalogue to '5x5=25' Rodchenko explained how he had first showed three-dimensional constructions at 'Abstract Art and Suprematism' in 1919; then line as a constructive factor; and now monochrome canvases in the primary colours. Stepanova decried 'composition' as a merely contemplative tool; and Popova and Exter too stressed the 'experimental' nature of their works – which in effect were analyses of the effects of colour and their constructive possibilities.[7] But two-dimensional planar work went hand in hand with actual constructions. Working under the banner of 'intellectual production', Constructivists produced objects both in natural materials such as wood, and in manufactured materials such as steel and iron, worked in an engineering fashion and structured around the principles of balance, tension and compression. Many of these designs were conceived as models of actual structures, both architectural and otherwise. The works shown at the May 1921 OBMOKhU exhibition, for example, were designed to be efficient in engineering terms. Described as 'laboratory work' and 'utilitarian art', and ostensibly opposed to all varieties of studio aesthetics, particularly easel painting and carved or modelled sculpture, the central principle adopted by OBMOKhU in this exhibition was that of extremely refined, economical and even elegant construction, designed to demonstrate the

7. Catalogue to '5x5=25'; in Gassner and Gillen, *Zwischen Revolutionskunst und Sozialistischem Realismus: Dokumente und Kommentare: Kunstdebatten in der Sowjetunion von 1917 bis 1934*, DuMont Verlag Cologne, 1979, pp 116–17.

8. See the catalogue *Russian Constructivism Revisited*, The Hatton Gallery, Newcastle-upon-Tyne, 1974.

constructive possibilities inherent in ordinary geometrical shapes of the utmost simplicity (Figure 42). Even the bases on which the structures were placed for exhibition – although superficially resembling the plinths of traditional sculpture – were conceived of as part of the unity of the work.[8] The event constituted an early demonstration of the radical potential of materials when treated in a Constructivist way. With this development, the sphere of 'artistic activity' had been effectively vacated. The distinction between 'art' and 'work' had been made to disappear.

Figure 42
3rd OBMOKhU Exhibition,
May 1921.

9. A full list is given in Lodder, *Russian Constructivism*, pp 93–4.

10. 'Institut khudozhestvennoi kultury v Moskve (INKhUK) pri otdele IZO NKP', p 86; in Matsa, *Sovetskoe iskusstvo*, p 126; Lodder, *Russian Constructivism*, p 281 n 86.

11. 'Institut khudozhestvennoi kultury', Lodder, *Russian Constructivism*, p 281 n 86.

A diverse programme of talks and debates took place throughout 1921 and 1922 which articulated and consolidated the Constructivist point of view, given predominantly by Tarabukin, Brik, Kushner, Boris Arvatov and Rodchenko, but also by the architect Vladimir Krinsky and artists such as Malevich and Altman.[9] By the end of 1921 Brik, among others, was advocating that artists begin 'real practical work in production'.[10] Twenty-five INKhUK members accepted his proposals and rejected 'pure' easel art as fruitless and futile, now committing themselves to working in industry 'under the pressure of the revolutionary conditions of contemporary life'.[11] Now it became the avowed task of INKhUK to address itself specifically to the problems of working in industrial manufacture. Strong links were immediately established with the VKhUTEMAS, and several members took active steps to work in industry on practical problems of design and production, as well as to work for Trade Union and State committees. Arvatov and Tatlin set up a 'production laboratory' in a Petrograd factory, and several INKhUK members, including Arvatov, Brik, Kushner and Tarabukin, became active in attempting to reorganise the Proletkult along 'Productivist' lines.

Relations between 'Productivism' and the attitudes of the state authorities to engineering, work and industry are highly instructive.

The argument of the Constructivists was based on two principles: one concerning the nature of all labour under communism, and the other concerning the exclusive validity of the Constructivist platform within the new Soviet reality. Naturally, both arguments could be run together. In one of the early statements of the First Working Group the task envisaged was

> to arrive at the problem of work; to elucidate the position of work in its historical perspective (slaveholding societies, feudalism, capitalism); to establish the stages of work: before the Revolution – slave work; at present – the liberation of work; and after the final victory of the proletariat – the possibility of exultant work.[12]

12. 'Programma uchebnoi podgruppy', Lodder, *Russian Constructivism*, p 282 n 105.

Equally, the leading Constructivists were in no doubt that Constructivism and Constructivism alone was now, in 1921 and 1922, the only direction that art in Soviet society could usefully take. Brik, for one, was prepared to be quite uncompromising about rejecting any co-operation with other artistic groups, including those supposedly on the 'left'. Easel painting, which in INKhUK circles was by 1922 regarded as lying to the 'right', he claimed was 'fundamentally opposed to the state's point of view, the activities of government bodies in the field of art, and to our activity as a circle of the Party'.[13] In Alexey Gan's book *Konstructivizm*, published in 1922, he too argued that Constructivism was the art of the socialist state. Basing his case on the writings of Marx, Engels and Lenin, Gan was convinced that the eradication of the distinction between 'artist' and 'factory worker' was essential to the eventual development of communism, and that all other forms of art were left-overs from the feudal, pre-industrial or bourgeois eras. Industrial culture he identified as the culture of the new revolutionary period of the proletariat, which had as its purpose the cultivation of practical, communal, machine-based and, eventually, joyous work. Constructivism was to become 'the first culture of organised labour and intellect'. Art was merely

13. O. Brik, 'What are artists to do now?', 13 April 1922; cited by Lodder, *Russian Constructivism*, p 100.

> part of the spiritual culture of the past . . . we should not reflect, depict and interpret reality but should build practically and express the planned objectives of the newly active working class, the proletariat . . . It is now that the proletarian revolution has conquered . . . that the master of colour and line, the combiner of spatial and volumetric solids, and the organiser of mass action – must all become Constructivists in the general business of the building and movement of the many-millioned human mass.[14]

14. A. Gan, *Konstruktivism*, p 53; Lodder, *Russian Constructivism*, pp 98–9.

It is difficult to judge whether theorists like Brik and Gan were really speaking here on behalf of the Bolshevik Party or whether they were attempting to justify their efforts in the eyes of the Party, whom they knew to be sceptical. Elements of both manoeuvres were probably present. Certainly Brik was taken to task over his reference to 'our [that is, INKhUK's] activity as a circle of the Party'. Some of those present at his talk objected to the identification. As Lodder reports it, Vesnin and Ladovsky wanted INKhUK to remain a 'theoretical' institution, however much they may have subscribed to the overall spirit of October. Babichev, who was also present, apparently felt that Brik was importing the tactical language of politics into art, particularly in his insinuation that the 'right' wing of easel painting was somehow opposed to the government's view.[15]

In one very important respect however the views of the INKhUK Constructivists and Productivists on the nature of the work process mirror very closely the priorities of at least a section of the Party leadership and may even have been close to those of Lenin himself. Certainly much is to be learnt about the place of Constructivism in the new state from the repeated use by artists and theorists of concepts like 'organise', 'utility', 'expediency', and 'the absence of superfluous elements'. For such phrases also expressed widely-held attitudes to work and labour organisation at the highest levels of the Party, and are to be found repeatedly in programmes for industrial reorganisation in the period of the New Economic Policy.

Admittedly, to begin with, the talk was of 'efficiency' and 'raising productivity' rather than of 'liberating labour' – let alone of 'exultant work'. Lenin himself, after earlier doubts, had become much impressed with the theories of F.W. Taylor and Frank Gilbreth, who had introduced time-management, the analysis of labour and the adoption of progressive piece-rates into the industrial system in the United States (albeit against considerable opposition from political radicals and trade unionists).[16] At a meeting of the Supreme Council of the National Economy (Vysshyi sovet narodnogo khozyaistva or VSNKh) on 1 April 1918, at which a decree on labour discipline was being discussed, Lenin had declared that

> we must definitely speak of the introduction of the Taylor system, in other words, of using all scientific methods of labour which this system advances. Without this, it will be impossible to raise productivity, and without this we will not usher in socialism.[17]

However it was Alexey Gastev (Figure 43) who took such sentiments to a logical extreme. Gastev, at the time of the Revolution a worker-poet in a similar mould to Mayakovsky, had turned his attention in 1918 to industrial organisation methods in order to develop programmes of highly regulated and supposedly 'efficient' labour. Time-and-motion studies in the Taylorist and Gilbrethian manner quickly became Gastev's *idée fixe*, and in a number of publications after 1918 he expounded his ideals for a scheme which became known as 'the scientific organisation of work' (nauchnaya organizatsiya truda, or NOT), which in turn led to the opening of the Central Institute of Labour in Moscow in 1920, of which he became the director.

Gastev's views were first published in 1919 in *Proletarskaya kultura*, the journal in which proletarian art and literature were hotly discussed. In Gastev's view proletarian culture could not be adequately defined without reference to the new industrial process. 'It is necessary to be a kind of engineer,' Gastev proposed;

> it is necessary to be an experienced social constructor and to take one's scientific methods not from general presuppositions regarding the development of productive forces, but from a most exact molecular analysis of the new production, which has brought into existence the contemporary proletariat . . .[18]

15. Lodder, *Russian Constructivism*, p 160 and p 280 n 135.

16. See, for example, F. W. Taylor, *Shop Management*, New York, 1911, and *Principles of Scientific Management*, New York, 1911.

17. V. D. Banasyukevich, 'V. I. Lenin i nauchnaya organizatsiya truda', *Istoriya SSSR*, 1965, p 108 no 2; quoted by K. E. Bailes, 'Alexey Gastev and the Soviet Controversy over Taylorism, 1918–1922'; *Soviet Studies*, Vol XXIX, no 3, July 1977, p 376.

18. Gastev, 'O tendentsiyakh proletarskoi kultury', *Proletarskaya kultura*, 1919, no 9–10, p 36; K. E. Bailes, 'Alexey Gastev', p 377.

Figure 43
Alexey Gastev

In fact Gastev believed that mechanisation and standardisation were likely to eliminate both heavy labour and creative decision-making, producing (and requiring) a work-force that was itself a vast machine, each human part of which was doing routine and anonymous work. The proposal sounds Orwellian; yet Gastev took a benign view, indeed he devoted much time to defining how labour could become ever more productive and efficient. Collectivism, not individuality, would be the hall-mark of this system:

> the psychology of the proletariat is already now being transformed into a new social psychology where one human complex works under the control of another . . . This psychology reveals a new working-class collectivism which is manifested not only in relations between persons but in relations of whole groups of people to whole groups of mechanisms . . . The manifestations of this *mechanised collectivism* are so foreign to personality, so anonymous, that the movement of these collective complexes is similar to the movement of things, in which there is no longer any individual face but only regular, uniform steps and faces devoid of expression, of soul, of lyricism, of emotion, measured not by a shout or a smile but by the pressure gauge or the speed gauge.[19]

19. Gastev, 'O tendentsiyakh', pp 44–5; Bailes, 'Alexey Gastev', p 378.

Although Bolshevik leaders were never to endorse the idea of 'mechanised collectivism' in anything like Gastev's terms, they were nevertheless enthusiastic to introduce changes in working practices speedily and comprehensively and to eliminate unegalitarian labour schedules under which some would work short hours in comfort and light while others were condemned to strenuous and lengthy days. Already committed to the mechanisation of agriculture and the electrification of the Soviet Union, the Party leadership now addressed itself to the proposition that work itself was to be 'Taylorised' and improved. Lenin himself authorised NOT sections as a means of rooting out sluggish bureaucracy in the state administration, while Gastev was commissioned to head a Time League, with cells in every town and village, which would press for the scientific organisation of work and issue programmes and instructions on how this could be achieved. Every adherent of the Time League kept a 'chronocard' to record latenesses and dilatoriness, with fines for wasted time as a penalty. Slogans were issued in short, sharp messages to demonstrate the benefits of the economical use of language. 'Discover the mechanism of time and then reform!' and 'Calculating time means a longer life!' were examples.[20]

20. R. Fülöp-Miller, *Mind and Face of Bolshevism*, pp 206–7.

Gastev's instructions for 'efficiency' were to be applied to every department of life. Everyone would get up, go to bed and have meals at regular times. Workers would become like cogs in a vast machine. Proletarian psychology would be equivalent to anonymity; as Gastev put it, this would 'permit the classification of an individual proletarian unit as A, B, C, or 325, 0–075, O, and so on'. Technicism would permeate 'even his intimate life, including his aesthetic, intellectual and sexual values'.[21] Language would be cleansed of lengthy and cumbersome expressions (hence the gradual introduction of abbreviations like Narkompros, VTsIK, Komsomol, etc). Work slogans were issued in poster form with telegraphic messages like 'Sharp Eye, Keen

21. Gastev, 'O tendentsiyakh', pp 44–5; Bailes, 'Alexey Gastev', p 378.

Ear, Alertness, Exact Reports!', 'Mighty Stroke, Calculated Pressure, Measured Rest', 'Unremitting Struggle, Mastery of the Body!' and so on.[22] Gastev's Central Institute of Labour devoted itself to the analysis of movement and behaviour by means of chrono-cyclographic photography. The measurement of the balance and pressure of the limbs as well as every aspect of working conditions were in theory subject to measurement and analysis (Figure 44). Everything superfluous was

22. R. Fülöp-Miller, *Mind and Face of Bolshevism*, p 210.

Figure 44
Cine-photograph of the labour process at the Central Institute of Labour

to be removed, in order that energy output could be higher for the same mechanical effort. 'All the limbs must be individually trained,' said Gastev,

> statics and dynamics will be taught, as well as the handling of tools, the movements making up the stroke, the exercise of hand, elbow, shoulder ... After practice, the right and left hands must be made equally skillful. This will be followed by intensive practice with hammer and chisel, and here, too, the pupil must be taught to be ambidextrous. This method produces the greatest efficiency in all kinds of fitting and machine work, and can be devoted to a system of instruction and organisation which will lead to a new civilisation.[23]

23. Gastev quoted by Fülöp-Miller, *Mind and Face of Bolshevism*, p 211–12.

Predictably, Gastev's Constructivist-like methods led to great controversy within the Proletkult. Bogdanov accused Gastev of reducing the worker to an automaton, whereas the aim should be to raise up new standards of creativity and skill. Bogdanov also suspected that Gastev was presupposing an élite of creative engineers who would stand over the proletariat and control it from above.[24]

24. A. Bogdanov, 'O tendentsiyakh proletarskoi kultury (Otvet A. Gastevu)', *Proletarskaya kultura*, 1919, no 11–12: in Bogdanov, *O proletarskoi kulture 1904–1924*, Moscow, 1925, p 326; Bailes, 'Alexey Gastev', p 380.

Lenin, for his part, seems to have supported the continued existence of engineering specialists – and of bourgeois specialists in general – despite the infamy and 'baiting campaigns' to which they were subjected by groups such as the Democratic Centralists and the Workers' Opposition, not to mention Proletkult leaders like Bogdanov. But Lenin's argument here was characteristically pragmatic. At the Eighth Congress of the Party in 1919 he had attempted to put an end to disagreement on the matter within the Party by coming out firmly in favour of a conciliatory and even favourable attitude to all specialists, such as managers and engineers, even to the point of paying them preferential salaries and offering better working conditions:

> We must immediately, without awaiting help from other countries, increase the forces of production. To do this without the bourgeois specialists is impossible. This must be said once and for all . . . When they [bourgeois specialists] see in practice that the proletariat attracts the wide masses more and more to help in their tasks, they will be convinced morally, and not simply politically severed from the bourgeoisie . . . They will be attracted to our *apparat* and make themselves part of it.[25]

In giving advice to Narkompros, Lenin had urged that they 'learn from the Red Army' how to catch their specialists. He had reminded them that the Red Army caught specialists 'in anti-Soviet acts', punished them, and then released them into employment on its own terms.[26] So it was to be in industry. Specialists would have to be employed, even if only to counteract the reputation of the Russian worker for laziness and Oblomov-like indifference to practical tasks. Thus the re-designing of the work process became a high priority for Lenin. He was apparently planning to write a book on scientific management at this time. No doubt he did not go as far as Gastev's plans for 'mechanised collectivism'. But he could still support Gastev's requests for funds for the Central Institute of Labour in 1921, and appeared to think that its efforts were for the most part worthwhile.

Contrariwise, knowledge of and interest in this debate about the status of engineers and the correct attitude to work must be partly responsible for the emphasis placed in early Constructivist writings on the role to be played within industry by the new artist-intellectuals. Here, too, was a potentially far-reaching programme for improving the quality of industrial goods, and here, too, was a programme with many significant implications for the nature and conduct of work. Here, too, were specialists; yet they were specialists in the service of an idea of 'art' as part of an efficient production cycle.

But how to put Constructivist ideas into practice was the essence of the problem. Early in 1922 Rodchenko proposed (against Brik) that INKhUK organise a series of talks by invited engineers so that its members could begin to become acquainted with actual problems of production. There had been several voices, after all, who had complained that designs like those of the OBMOKhU exhibitions were impractical and could not be made use of in a genuinely functional way.

Boris Kushner was heavily occupied with the problem of industrial production in 1922. In talks given at INKhUK he theorised extensively on the nature and function of design, and in his third paper, on 'The Role of the Engineer in Production', he attempted to find a role for artists within the existing engineering profession. To Kushner there appeared to be three types of specialist – the workshop supervisor, the designer/technologist, and the production organiser.[27] All

25. Lenin, *Sochineniya*, xxxviii, pp 166–7; K. Bailes, *Technology and Society under Lenin and Stalin*, Princeton University Press, New Jersey, 1978, p 51.

26. Lenin to Preobrazhensky, 19 April 1921; Fitzpatrick, *Commissariat*, p 222.

27. These were defined as the engineer-technologist, the engineer-constructor, and the engineer-organiser. See the account in Lodder, *Russian Constructivism*, p 101, to whom I am once again indebted.

three roles, however, Kushner felt were led by the demands of industry as a whole, and he believed that the position should be reversed so that the designer/technologist, in particular, could be aided if not actually replaced by the Constructivist-trained artist. This, he argued, would decisively assist the nation's need for better standards of design. Kushner seems to have recognised here that Constructivists, for all their energy and enthusiasm, were not trained in mathematics or engineering, nor for that matter in industrial management, and would therefore have to occupy a limited function in the total industrial process.

Brik, too, recognised a creative role for the artist in industry; and like Kushner he did so out of a desire to humanise the purely mechanical role of the worker put forward in Gastev's programme. 'By artistic production', Brik said, 'we mean simply a consciously creative relationship to the production process . . . not a beautifully decorated object but a consciously made object.' But he agreed with Bogdanov that the worker must achieve a role in both executive as well as organising roles. 'We want the worker to cease being a mechanical executor of some type of plan unfamiliar to him. He must become a conscious and active participant in the creative process of producing an object.'[28]

28. O. Brik, 'V poryadke dnya', *Iskusstvo v proizvodstve*, Moscow, 1921, pp 7–8.

Thus there were at least two views being promulgated on the question of how to define 'work' in the Soviet state, and on what sorts of objects should result from the work process. Gastev and the Institute of Labour addressed themselves principally to the first question, while the Constructivists became vitally interested in both. There was, nevertheless, general agreement that industrialisation was the key to the country's future and that the worker's role in this process, like the artist's, needed to be radically redefined.

In practical terms it has to be admitted that the Constructivists, who urged the closest links between the artist and the industrial process, evolved no very coherent programme for how this should be carried out. Arvatov, Kushner, Brik and Tarabukin continued to proselytise for 'Production Art' for many years, and several 'left' journals such as *Krasnaya nov* (Red Virgin Soil), *Zhizn iskusstvo* (Life of Art), *LEF*, and the Proletkult magazine *Gorn* (Furnace) took a 'Productivist' stance in 1922 and 1923. Yet for the most part Constructivist ideas remained on the level of designs only, and substantial industrial links were few. The majority of the most fruitful designs were in two-dimensional work, in graphics and textiles, even though the development of Constructivist ideas in the VKhUTEMAS produced some highly original ideas for modernist furniture and interior design in the mid-1920s.[29]

29. These are covered most extensively in Lodder, *Russian Constructivism*, Chapter 5.

By the end of 1922 and the beginning of 1923, certainly a new stage had been reached in the debate about the usefulness of Taylorism to Soviet society. Gastev had already come under fire for being petty-bourgeois in his approach, and for restricting his methods to those of the industrial metal-worker, of whose union Gastev had been secretary in 1917–18. One critic wrote:

His [Gastev's] aim is the ideal petty-bourgeois craftsman . . . his aim is to make man a hammer, a file or a knife. But the new proletarian epoch stands in the sign of the great modern machines; the mass man is to be part of a mighty aggregate of turbines, and not transformed into an antiquated cobbler's awl.[30]

Now, at a conference of the Moscow Group of Communists Actively Interested in Scientific Management in January 1923, Gastev was reproached for not paying sufficient attention to the psychological and physiological aspects of labour, and for reducing the worker to 'an unreasoning and stupid instrument without any general qualifications or adequate all-round development'.[31] The protection of workers' interests, too, had been at a minimum in Gastev's plan. In March 1924 the issue came to a head (at least temporarily) at the Second All-Union Conference on Scientific Management. By this time Gastev had called various high-ranking officials to his support, including *Pravda* editor Bukharin and trade union leader Mikhail Tomsky, and had been supported in print by no lesser figures than Zinoviev and Andreev, as well as by Lenin in some of his utterances. Gastev's critics in the Moscow Group of Communists relied upon a spirited statement by former Proletkult leader Kerzhentsev, who had just written a popular book on efficiency methods.[32] Kerzhentsev supported general improvements in working conditions, including wage rises, and had been critical of Gastev's laboratory methods which aimed at increasing productivity irrespective of the human consequences. Kerzhentsev and the Group of Communists now demanded control of the NOT cells and an integration of their work with measures to protect labour rights and conditions. In their view, Gastev's Central Institute of Labour appealed only to the technocratic élite – plant managers, specialists, and the like.

But in spite of the weight of evidence against him, it appears that Gastev managed to persuade the Conference delegates that his methods were moving forward from the early concern with metal cutting and trimming, and that the Institute was not in fact indifferent to questions of industrial psychology.[33] Production engineers were certainly sympathetic to Gastev's line, or so it was claimed, and in any case it was surely generally known that the Party was sympathetic to Gastev's methods.

From this point on, what Gastev called 'Soviet Americanism' became an established fact within Soviet industry – but with a difference. The Party continued to view the industrialisation of the country and the modernisation of agriculture as an important priority. As Lenin insisted, modernisation based upon the technical and industrial skills of capitalism was necessary in order precisely to defeat capitalism. Yet Taylorism had presupposed a classless society in which all work could be organised by science. Whether this was being achieved in America was obviously debatable; yet in the Soviet Union, such a process could not be truly egalitarian while the cultural and scientific level of the country remained so low. From every point of view the actual situation seemed to presuppose a stratum of scientific managers who could direct the work-force and give shape to its efforts. It also had to be doubted whether the Constructivist

30. Fülöp-Miller, *Mind and Face of Bolshevism*, p 212. Gastev had indeed written: 'We must bring the hammer and knife into the foreground. Whoever can handle the hammer skillfully has grasped the secret of the rotary press. Whoever handles the knife skillfully knows the secret of all cutting machines . . . every man must be able to cut and file metals. Every man must be able to fell, plane and cut up wood. This exercises the capacity for organisation.'

31. *Pravda*, 11 January 1923; Bailes, 'Alexey Gastev', p 386.

32. P. Kerzhentsev, *Printsipy organizatsii*, Moscow, 1924.

33. See Bailes, 'Alexey Gastev' pp 389–91.

ideal of efficient, liberated work, applied piecemeal and with widely differing degrees of support, could ever hope to make a substantial impact on a country still dominated by nineteenth-century industrial techniques and Tsarist behavioural patterns.

Thus in the discussion on working methods, a series of compromises was reached in the early 1920s in which Taylorism became something like official policy, while the extremism of Gastev's 'mechanised collectivism' became in practice diluted. Yet the importance of the questions remains immense. For it can at least be argued that the status of Bolshevik 'modernisation' was (perhaps still is) indistinguishable from its wider ideological aims and aspirations; provides even a litmus test of its historical and practical credibility. This raises the question of whether Bolshevism was primarily a set of startling and novel ideas, or whether it was primarily a coercive political strategy capable of generating rapid and fundamental change. The gap between theory and practice was never more complex or difficult to negotiate than in this, the field of labour policy and industrial design. And within this problematic, Constructivism occupied a doubly ambiguous place. For alongside the question of its practicability in the real world of manufacture, questions inevitably lingered over its previous associations with Futurism and the artistic 'left'. Perhaps too it personified the gap between theory and practice that became visible within Bolshevik culture in such a multitude of other ways.

The Politicisation of Music, Theatre and Literature

A tendency to mechanised, efficient forms was also visible in the other arts, and in a general sense went hand in hand with a policy of functional, collective expression that could be associated with Bolshevism itself. In music, the campaign against bourgeois mystification in the guise of the cult of the individual composer (performer, conductor), the campaign against the language of 'genius' and 'inspiration', and the promulgation of a policy of collective, contemporary expression, was already under way before the beginning of NEP. A proletarian, factory-inspired orchestra of sirens and factory whistles had been attempted in 1918. In the NEP period the first performance of a factory symphony on a large scale took place in Baku, on 7 November 1922. This involved the foghorns of the whole Caspian fleet, all the factory sirens of the city, two batteries of artillery, several infantry regiments, a machine-gun section, hydroplanes, and several choirs in which all spectators were invited to participate.[1] Audible far beyond the walls of Baku, the performance is said to have been impressive, and no doubt inspired other large-scale performances elsewhere.

However, concert music using the traditional orchestra by no means disappeared. The Association for Modern Music, formed in Moscow in 1923, included several composers such as Nikolay Myaskovsky and Samuel Feinberg who were aware of modernist music in Western Europe and who developed methods of orchestration that

1. Fülöp-Miller, *Mind and Face of Bolshevism*, p 184.

were designed to express a revolutionary and modernising mood. Unusual chords and key structures and a series of explosive, uncomfortable harmonics and complex rhythms were among the methods regularly employed. The young Sergey Prokofiev quickly became celebrated as an operatic composer not only with Bolshevik sympathies but also with a significant new conception of rhythm and dynamic effect. In ballet, a series of new choreographers, such as Baron Nikolay Forreger, began to experiment with ways of radically modernising the classical canon. In his case this led to a form of 'machine dancing' in which the body was made to function like a machine, mechanically and functionally, strictly geometricised. The spectator was intended to recognise each movement as part of the whole stage dance into which the dancer's body fitted.

In the theatre, Stanislavsky's 'realism' had already radically modified the practices of direction and performance dominant in the nineteenth-century theatre.[2] His extremely austere and demanding methods of training for actors, and the very thorough attempts he made to induce his actors to completely identify in mind and body with their parts, are now legendary. His pupils Evgeny Vakhtangov and Alexandr Tairov extended and modified Stanislavsky's methods, the first by breaking down the conventional barriers between the stage and the auditorium with a series of quasi-Brechtian devices, and the second by turning back to exotic and decorative drama which verged on the baroque and the expressionistic. Neither, however, had any interest in political drama or the events of the revolutionary period. As Tairov put it during a debate in 1920, 'A propagandist theatre after a revolution is like mustard after a meal.'[3]

Yet what Vakhtangov did achieve was a certain reinterpretation of older plays which could sometimes be paraded as allegories of Revolutionary themes. As director of the First Studio of the Moscow Art Theatre, he had spoken firmly in favour of revolutionary theatre, not as propagandist or Futurist spectacle, but as a kind of dramatic portrayal that was rooted in all the people. In order to create the new and obtain victory, Vakhtangov said, the artist needs 'the firm ground of the people ... all of us are the people. We speak here of the people who are the creators of the Revolution.'[4] With this somewhat indefinite programme and an armoury of anti-naturalistic devices Vakhtangov had already produced such works as Strindberg's *Eric XIV* – an anti-monarchist tragedy that expressed the insurgent power of popular disaffection – and in 1921, as director of the newly created Third Studio in Moscow's Arbat (where the Vakhtangov theatre is now located), *The Miracle of Saint Anthony* by Maeterlinck, rewritten by Vakhtangov in a satirical vein. In Maeterlink's version the play is concerned with the misunderstanding which greets St Anthony's saintly deeds. 'Now,' wrote Vakhtangov in 1922, 'the theatrical means which we use in Anthony to brand the bourgeois [he depicts them as insolent dullards, incapable of understanding Anthony's powers] have coincided with the demands of life, the demands of contemporaneity.'[5]

One senses nevertheless that these words would have rung slightly false to the zealots of the Proletkult organisation as well as to

2. A lively text is N. M. Gorchakov, *Stanislavsky Directs* (1950), Limelight Edition, New York, 1985.

3. Tairov, Reported in *Vestnik teatra*, Moscow, 1920, no 78–9, p 16.

4. E. Vakhtangov, *Materialy i stati*, Moscow, 1959, p 168; Rudnitsky, *Russian and Soviet Theatre: Tradition and the Avant-Garde*, Thames and Hudson, London, 1988, p 52.

5. E. Vakhtangov, 'Materialy', 209; Rudnitsky, *Russian and Soviet Theatre*, p 54.

those demanding new forms and themes for the revolutionary theatre: Vakhtangov's colourful production of Gozzi's fairy-tale *Princess Turandot* early in 1922 seemed flouncy and irrelevant, except as an expression of the new mood of relief from the harshness of war communism that was then pervasive.

However it was the appointment in 1920 of another of Stanislavsky's pupils, Meyerhold, to the post of head of the theatre section of Narkompros that had brought with it the most innovative wave of experiments in the early revolutionary theatre. In August 1920, at the Second Congress of the Third International in Moscow, a resolution had been passed requiring Meyerhold to set up 'a theatre of the International Proletkult'. Because of this, Meyerhold explained, 'I have vowed to have as little as possible to do with the professional theatres.'[6] And yet Meyerhold had had immediate difficulties with Lunacharsky and Krupskaya, particularly over his production of Verhaeren's *The Dawn*, and in February 1921 resigned as head of TEO Narkompros.

In the debate surrounding *The Dawn*, however, Meyerhold's conception of revolutionary theatre emerged even more fully. 'Bourgeois stage illusion' was now definitely out. The public had changed, Meyerhold insisted, and would stand for no nonsense. Footlights and other apparatus would have to go. The stage was to be used as a forum for propaganda, for speeches, for denunciation of the bourgeoisie, and for Party and revolutionary rhetoric. Sets were to be reformed. 'Decoration,' said Meyerhold,

> is for the restaurants of Munich and Vienna . . . we have only to talk to the latest followers of Picasso and Tatlin to know at once that we are dealing with kindred spirits. We are building, just as they are building. What do we want with pleasing pictorial effects? What the modern spectator wants is the placard, the juxtaposition of the surfaces and shapes of *tangible materials*: To sum up, both we and they want to escape from the box of the theatre on to the wide-open stage.

We want our setting to be 'an iron pipe or the open sea', he said elsewhere: 'our artists will be delighted to throw away their brushes and take up axes, picks and hammers and hack stage sets out of the materials of raw nature.'[7]

The second play produced by Meyerhold's RSFSR Theatre Number 1 was a new production of Mayakovsky's *Mystery-Bouffe*, rewritten for the occasion. Despite continued charges of obscurity by the critics, this production was a popular success and ran for five months, up to the end of May 1921. However the financial difficulties associated with the uneasy beginnings of NEP resulted in accusations by the Moscow Soviet of overspending, and the theatre was closed in September. Meyerhold and some of the members of RSFSR Theatre Number 1 moved to the newly formed State Higher Theatre Workshop in Moscow, of which Meyerhold was appointed Director.

A new phase of Meyerhold's work now began, for it was at this time that he was developing his system of theatrical 'bio-mechanics', which required a concentration of technique upon the body rather than on the mind, as had been Stanislavsky's practice. Meyerhold

6.   V. Meyerhold, 'On the Contemporary Theatre', *Vestnik teatra*, Moscow, 1920, no 70, pp 11–12; in E. Braun (ed), *Meyerhold on Theatre*, Methuen & Co., London and New York, 1969, p 167.

7.   V. Meyerhold, *Vestnik teatra*, no 72–73, 7 November 1920, pp 9–10.

believed that in Stanislavsky's theatre, the spiritual had been elevated too far and that the actor's physique had degenerated. Now, he wanted physically fit actors who had complete control over all their gestures and actions and who could eliminate superfluous, unintended movements. As he put it, 'only via the sports arena can we approach the theatrical arena.'[8] The link with Taylorism – or with Gastev's concept of efficiency – was intentional. 'We are always dealing in art with the organisation of material', Meyerhold wrote in 1922; 'Constructivism demands that the artist becomes an engineer as well. Art must be based on scientific principles; all the work done by the artist must be conscious.'[9]

It is apparent from this description that Meyerhold embraced what he took to be the ideological and propagandistic programme of the Soviet state, and for the moment his doing so won him its moral and financial support. In Meyerhold's conception theatre would present the ideal proletarian worker, well organised, well trained, purposeful and efficient, whose inner communist soul was effortlessly externalised in his actions and gestures. Indeed, these formulations became the basis of Constructivist theatre at its most effective.

Meyerhold's theatre was, in effect, the state theatre at this time. As a director and producer however it was essential that the propagandistic dramas he put on would enjoin real reaction. To this end he needed non-illusionistic scenery, and good plays. The latter were possibly more difficult to come by than the former.

Many plays, classical and modern, needed to be radically rearranged to suit Meyerhold's new methods and aims. The best-known Constructivist reinterpretation was that provided for Fernand Crommelynck's play *The Magnanimous Cuckold*, performed at Meyerhold's theatre on 15 April 1922 on a stage machine designed by Lyubov Popova (Figures 45 and 46). Meyerhold had seen the '5x5=25' exhibition in Moscow late in 1921, and had realised that efficient,

8. V. Meyerhold, *Teatralnaya Moskva*, Moscow, 1922, no 45, pp 9–10; Braun, p 200.

9. V. Meyerhold, 'Akter budushchego', *Ermitazh*, no 6, 1922, pp 10–11; Lodder, *Russian Constructivism*, p 170.

Figure 46
Igor Ilinsky in a scene from
The Magnanimous Cuckold, 1922
(photo: *SCR*, London)

Figure 45
L. Popova, drawing of the set for
The Magnanimous Cuckold, 1922,
Tretyakov Gallery, Moscow
(photo: *Tretyakov Gallery*)

utilitarian designs could easily be adapted to a stage setting. Also, as he recalled later, uncertainties about which (if any) theatre would be available made him seek a set which could be erected anywhere, if necessary out of doors. With this production

> we hoped to lay the basis for a new form of theatrical presentation with no need for illusionistic settings or complicated props, making do with the simplest objects which came to hand and transforming a spectacle performed by specialists into an improvised performance which could be put on by workers in their leisure time.[10]

Popova's stage-machine was a combination of those purely utilitarian functions with a variety of simple imagery, which suggested a city, a house, the windmill in which the play was supposed to be set, and the internal wheels of the mill. Moving platforms, revolving doors and opening windows were linked mechanically to the action of the play. In the conception of the set, Popova wrote,

> utilitarian suitability must serve as the criterion, and certainly not the solution of any formal or aesthetic problems . . . the movement and speeds [of the windows and doors] were to underline and intensify the kinetic value of each movement of the action.[11]

Nevertheless, it soon became apparent that there was a tendency for utilitarian simplicity and mechanical efficiency to constitute their own aesthetic, and in the minds of some quickly became identified with the imperatives of the new state in the fields of industry and the economy. In such a way, 'Constructivism' became both a style and a metaphor, a set of forms but also a set of codes for a moral and political order.

There is a great deal more to be said about the significations of Constructivist design in both two and three dimensions, and about the degree to which Constructivism paralleled and yet also distanced itself from the full implications of the state programmes for industrialisation and modernisation. As already noted, the somewhat primitive mechanical techniques available to Constructivist designers had the effect of confining their most striking work to two dimensions and the theatre, some notable works of architecture notwithstanding. But this too was a brief phenomenon, and was soon to suffer under a barrage of critical attack.

For example, criticisms that Constructivist theatre had ceased being utilitarian and was merely a new aesthetic in disguise were by no means unfamiliar. Ivan Aksyonov, for example, alleged that 'stage Constructivism . . . has now degenerated almost to a decorative decree, albeit in a new style.'[12] This may be one reason why the design for *The Earth in Turmoil* of February 1923 contained a variety of real objects – cars, lorries, motorcyles, an aeroplane and a mobile kitchen – in addition to a huge wooden gantry and the regular Constructivist screens, ladders, platforms and a crane (Figure 47). *The Earth in Turmoil* was in fact a version of Marcel Martinet's *The Night*, very heavily adapted by Meyerhold and Sergey Tretyakov.[13] Popova was once again the designer. In one sense it was clearly a close relative of

10.   Meyerhold, 'Kak byl postavlen velikodushny rogonosets', *Novy zritel*, Moscow, 1926, no 39, p 6; Braun (ed), *Meyerhold on Theatre*, p 205.

11.   Popova, 'Vstuplenie k diskussii INKhUKa o 'Velikodushnom rogonostse', p 1; Bowlt, 'From Surface to Space: The Art of Lyubov Popova', *Structurist*, 15/16, 1975/6, p 87; Lodder, *Russian Constructivism*, p 173.

12.   A. Aksyonov, in *Zrelishcha*, Moscow, 1923, no 21, p 8; Braun, *Meyerhold on Theatre*, p 188.

13.   Trotsky had written enthusiastically about *La Nuit* in 'A drama of the French Working Class: Marcel Martinet's *La Nuit*'; *Izvestiya*, 16 May 1922.

the mass revolutionary spectacles already mentioned. Here is one eyewitness description of the performance:

> A military signal announces the start of the performance. At once some motor-cars rush diagonally through the auditorium and over a connecting bridge onto the stage. They are followed by a company of cyclists in uniform. With this somewhat sensational opening the piece begins. The play . . . is to reproduce the rise of the Revolution 'in its full dynamics'. Soon the last phase of the World War is unrolled on the stage: a Russian guard comes on, represented as a human butcher dripping with blood; you see the poor soldiers, harmless peasants and proletarians hounded to death. It is not long before the German general staff is captured: it consists of a horde of fierce bloodhounds and absurd caricatures. Soon shooting begins, cannons and machine-guns are brought up and aeroplanes come into action. Over the bridge . . . motors and cycles rush continually; the field-kitchen steams, wounded are carried past. The fury of war rages unfettered on the stage, through the auditorium, through the foyer right out onto the street . . . [14]

14. Fülöp-Miller, *Mind and Face of Bolshevism*, pp 126–7.

At this point everything becomes quiet and the simple stage constructions, perhaps a few feet high and made of metal and wood, are

> transformed into platforms from which soldiers and peasants make speeches. The cannons and other war material are piled up to form barricades, the Revolution is proclaimed in flaming words, and Kerensky appears and is mocked as a phrase-maker and a seducer of the people. The first communist 'Party cells' are formed among the soldiers and workers, a new Civil War blazes up . . . Cannons and machine-guns appear again, aeroplanes and dressing-stations take their places, again the motors and bicycles rush furiously through the auditorium. Finally, the first red flag is hoisted and is soon followed by countless others. The 'construction', the platforms, the auditorium, and the foyer are captured by red troops. The communist Revolution is triumphant. Fiery speeches are delivered, the public strikes up the 'Internationale'.[15]

15. Ibid., p 127.

Figure 47
Meyerhold Theatre, *The Earth in Turmoil*, 1923, Act 1 (photo: *SCR* London)

But all is not over. The various and diverse members of the audience – a 'Nep-Lady', a barefooted boy of twelve, a Chinaman, a man from Kirghis, and others – all rise 'in military fashion' and join in the singing. 'The public marches out singing, while cannons, aeroplanes and field-kitchens again lie quietly in their place waiting for the next performance.'[16]

It is possible that in this return to the use of real objects from the real environment lay the beginnings of a retreat from the purely abstract and utilitarian ideals of Constructivism on the stage. As one critic pointed out, the production 'contained a whole series of compromises with the old theatre'.[17] But there were other attempts to use Constructivist methods in the theatre, such as in Alexandr Vesnin's set for Chesterton's *The Man Who Was Thursday*, directed by Tairov at the Kamerny Theatre in 1923, which helped to influence the buildings Vesnin designed in its wake.

Another sign of the persistence of technicist ambition in the theatre, right into 1923 and 1924, can be gleaned from the work of a different group within the VKhUTEMAS. Solomon Nikritin and several other students had a strong interest in the theatre and wished to explore the extent to which theatre and the visual arts might combine and overlap. One member of this group was Sergey Luchishkin, who while a student at the VKhUTEMAS had taken a course at the Institute of Declamation, and later at the Institute of Speech under V. Serezhnikov. A small theatrical troupe seemed the best way of putting their ideas to the test, and to this end Nikritin and Luchishkin joined the actress A. Amchanitskaya, from the Meyerhold Theatre, the actors A. Bogatirev and A. Svobodin, and the artists Pyotr Vilyams and L. Reznik to form the Projectionists' Theatre Company. The actors V.N. Yachontov and E.A. Tyapkina were also close to the troupe.[18]

In accordance with the Projectionists' interests in the conceptual organisation of materials – light, colour and form – they presented at the Press Club in 1923 a drama called *The Tragedy of A. O. U.*, which was a quasi-Futurist amalgam of abstract movements and vowel-sounds; hence the 'a', 'o' and 'u'. A stage machine by Tatlin's pupil Nikolay Tryaskin had a dynamic, abstract character. (It was also exhibited in model form to some critical acclaim.) The production was, in the words of one Soviet historian, 'one of the first attempts in the history of the theatre to create an abstract spectacle',[19] and must have been much more purely cerebral and experimental than Meyerhold's *The Earth in Turmoil*, which was staged at about the same time.

An interesting incident occurred in 1924 during the Projectionists' Theatre Company's production of A.B. Marienhof's tragedy *Fool's Conspiracy*, which was also treated in an abstract way, that is, with the substance of the plot and story subdued. Here, Tryaskin built a dynamic stage machine in the centre of a hall in which there were no chairs, so that the audience, standing, watched from all sides. Although the performance was reckoned to be a flop, Alexey Gastev, who was in the audience, suggested that the Projectionists' Company contribute to the work of the Central Institute of Labour, where the principles of abstract stage movement were being and could be used

16.   Fülöp-Miller, *Mind and Face of Bolshevism*, p 127.

17.   S. Mokulsky, 'Gastroli teatra Meyerkholda', *Zhizn iskusstva*, no 23, 1924, pp 12–13; Lodder, *Russian Constructivism*, p 178. See also E. Beskin, 'Teatralnyi LEF', *Sovetskoe iskusstvo*, no 6, 1925, p 53.

18.   See V. Kostin, *OST*, Moscow, 1976, p 18.

19.   Ibid., p 18.

to illuminate the problems of the scientific organisation of labour.[20]
Coordinated by Luchishkin, the Projectionists developed a form of
'production gymnastics' for Gastev, to demonstrate the beauty of
organised, rhythmical work. Under various names the Projectionists'
Theatre Company survived until 1932, and pursued important par-
allels to its members' work in the field of visual art – of which more
later.

But the heyday of Constructivism in the theatre was probably over
by 1923. Enamoured of Western European and American ideals of
'scientific management' (both of the material world and of the human
body), Constructivism became, for a time, an expression of Romantic
yearning for a utopian society that it could not possess, and at the
same time a real attempt to conclude a set of new relationships
between men, materials and machines. Constructivism was for a time
active in graphic design, photomontage, posters and other two-
dimensional design, but it cannot be said to have fulfilled its programme of transforming the three-dimensional environment or of
influencing to any real extent the production processes of industry.
Its turn away from these ideals in and after 1923 was part and parcel,
however, of a much wider cultural process of revision and review.

The tendency to mechanised, impersonal form in the labour process also found its reflection in the literary arts, which deserve men-
tioning briefly here. Literature above all the arts was to become a
battleground of conflicting themes and formulations in the 1920s, and
was perhaps more prone to instruction and exhortation by the Party
throughout this period for reason of its proximity to the tasks of
education and 'enlightenment' in the new state. Russian literature
had risen to world heights in the latter part of the nineteenth century,
which made it all the more important that it should successfully adapt
to the new circumstances. Gastev and Mayakovsky had already set
the standards for an authorless, monumental revolutionary poetry in
the early years after 1917. Gastev's proscription on the use of lengthy
words and expressions now recommended itself for poetic and literary use. In his book *A Sheaf of Orders* he used only 'hyperlaconic and
hypertelegraphic' expressions; indeed he went some way towards
the invention of a new language. It is said that some poets followed
Gastev in writing only in compressed and truncated syllables, believing that a revolutionary new Russian language would emerge from
such a tense and energised style. Gastev's own exhortations in the
field of scientific management had the enthusiastic tone of his own
early revolutionary verse, thus:

> Youth! Join the ranks of training!
> Look to the machine, the tool!
> Create the machine, organisation!
> First of all the most concentrated attention!
> Then action!
> First of all the most concentrated attention! [21]

Yet mechanism was by no means the only revolutionary literary
method. At the beginning of the NEP period there existed a variety
of different writers' groups, some wedded to unwavering support for

20. V. Kostin, *OST*, Moscow, 1976, p 19.

21. Fülöp-Miller, *Mind and Face of Bolshevism*, p 210.

'proletarian culture' in its pure form, and some sympathetic to pre-Revolutionary, foreign or non-political writing in any of its many varieties and versions; these too must be described.

In the generally non-propagandistic category we may mention first the Serapion Brotherhood, founded in 1921 by Evgeny Zamyatin and including Lev Lunts, Mikhail Zoshchenko, Konstantin Fedin, Nikolay Tikhonov, Nikolai Nikitin, Vsevelod Ivanov and Vladimir Pozner, and attracting the support of Viktor Shklovsky. Their programme was based on notional allegiance to the hermit Serapion (a character from E. T. A. Hoffmann), which meant non-affiliation with any particular political group and a desire to preserve individuality, as well as an orientation towards Western literature.[22] Zamyatin's satirical novel *We* is concerned precisely with the clash between the life and mind of the individual and the dictatorship of the proletariat under the leadership of the Party. It could not be published in the Soviet Union when it was written in 1920, and subsequently became widely admired in the West as an early science-fiction fantasy (it concerns a love affair between a rocket builder, D-503, and a girl, E-330) with social implications. Boris Pilnyak's early post-Revolutionary writing too is concerned to measure the effects of Revolutionary organisation upon consciousness, but from a distanced, always sceptical standpoint. Likewise the Acmeists such as Akhmatova and Mandelstam continued to believe in the purity and integrity of the word, and attempted to maintain a strict barrier between themselves and political events. So did the various remaining Symbolists from pre-Revolutionary days, still led in a somewhat rearguard manner by Sologub.

But it is with writing from the early NEP period that attempted to establish a mutual, supportive relationship with the Communist Party that we must be primarily concerned. An important initiative by the Party was the founding of the journal *Krasnaya nov* (Red Virgin Soil) in 1921, under the editorship of Alexandr Voronsky. Voronsky's brief (as well, apparently, as his conviction) was the publication of a wide spectrum of writings concerned to uphold high literary standards as well as to reflect the qualities of the Russian and European heritage – in effect Lenin's own policy. Though Voronsky himself had impeccable Revolutionary and Party credentials, his editorial platform was not a narrow class interpretation: following Belinsky and Plekhanov, he always insisted that 'art is a special means for the cognition of life', in whatever literary form this might be embodied.[23] On the other hand writers like Dmitry Furmanov (Figure 48) had developed a documentary, story-telling approach to contemporary events that issued in such works as his very popular novel *Chapaev*, written in 1922, which portrays in vivid narrative form the tribulations of a Red Army commander in the Civil War in the southern Ural steppes. Closer still to the Bolshevik Party was Alexandr Serafimovich, a colleague of Gorky and a Party member whose novel *The Iron Flood*, written after 1921, is widely regarded as another 'classic' of communist narrative, once again placed in the desperate fighting of the Civil War but in which the Soviet government, in effect, becomes the central character. Kozhukh, the leader of a victorious detachment, reflects at the end of the book:

22. See W. Edgerton, 'The Serapian Brothers: An Early Soviet Controversy', *American Slavic and East European Review*, Vol VIII, no 1, Feb 1949.

23. Voronsky, 'Iskusstvo kak poznanie zhizni i sovremennost, *Krasnaya nov*, no 5, 15 August 1923, p 362; E. Braun, *The Proletarian Episode in Russian Literature, 1928–1932*, Columbia University Press, New York, 1953, p 26. A complete study of *Krasnaya nov* is R. A. Maguire, *Red Virgin Soil: Soviet Literature in the 1920s*, Princeton University Press, Princeton, New Jersey, 1968.

Figure 48
S. Malyutin, *Portrait of Dmitry Furmanov*, 1922, Tretyakov Gallery, Moscow (photo: *Tretyakov Gallery*)

I've got no father or mother, no wife and no brothers, I've got no family, no relatives at all . . . All I have is these people whom I've saved from death and led to safety. Yes, I've led them, I myself have done it. But there are millions more like them, all with a noose around their necks, and I shall go on fighting for them . . .

while Serafimovitch adds to this reverie that Kozhukh's troops

still felt that, cut off as they were from the north by limitless steppes, impossible mountains and great, dense, forests, they too were helping to create – albeit to a much lesser degree – the thing that was being created on a world scale far away to the north, in the heart of Russia. And they felt that half-naked, barefoot and starving though they were, they were creating it here, all by themselves, without any assistance whatsoever.[24]

24. A. Serafimovich, *The Iron Flood* (1924), in the edition by N. Luker, *From Furmanov to Sholokov: An Anthology of the Classics of Socialist Realism*, Ann Arbor, Michigan, 1988, p 197.

Far closer to the work of artists, film-makers and composers who had explicit Bolshevik sympathies were the writers of the LEF circle, whose work we shall look at shortly. But we are concerned above all with literary groups who wished to radicalise literature in the name of the proletariat and its specific mode of consciousness. The first of these groups was called Kuznitsa or The Smithy. The founder members of the Smithy were a group of poets who in February 1920 had resigned in dissatisfaction from the Moscow Proletkult to form their own proletarian writers' organisation within the literary division of Narkompros.[25] These men, among them Mikhail Gerasimov, Vasily Kazin, Vladimir Kirillov, Vasily Alexandrovsky and Semyon Rodov, launched a magazine entitled *Kuznitsa* in May 1920. In the same month they convened a conference in Moscow to draw together various other proletarian literary groups, and this led in turn to the setting up of All-Russian Association of Proletarian Writers (Vserossiiskaya assotsiatsiya proletarskikh pisatelei or VAPP) later in the year. This was officially endorsed in the first months of NEP by the People's Commissariat for Education, and until its decline in 1922 the leaders of the original Smithy group held most of the key organisational posts within it.[26]

25. See their letter of protest against the Proletkult, 'Pismo v redaktsiyu', *Pravda*, 5 February 1920.

26. I am indebted here to H. Ermolaev, *Soviet Literary Theories, 1917–1934 : The Genesis of Socialist Realism*, University of California Press, Berkeley, California, 1963, pp 19–26.

The aim of the Smithy group after May 1920 was to organise and develop the practice of proletarian literature by establishing their own 'Smithy of art' as part of the great 'social proletarian Smithy'. Smithy workers were expected to be thoroughly imbued with Marxist concepts of reality from the point of view of the working class, and to address themselves to themes which had been specifically thrown up by the Revolution, and, further, to create new proletarian poetry by the highest standards of craftsmanship, to thus 'forge thoughts and sensations into original poetic forms'.[27] This at least was the theory. These forms were to be monumental in character and embody the concepts of heroic labour and the struggle for communism, in direct negation of bourgeois literary experiments such as Futurism, Symbolism and Imaginism. Some measure of respect for great works of past literature was allowed and indeed actively encouraged. From the beginning, the Smithy writers, strongly supported by Bogdanov, insisted on independence from the Party and its current 'line', and argued against a narrowly propagandistic function for writing, such

27. 'Redaktsiya "Kuznitsa"', *Kuznitsa*, no. 1, May 1920, p 2.

136 The Crisis of Renewal 1917–1924

as might have been imputed to Serafimovich. Yet clearly their support from Narkompros stood the risk of vitiating this independence; all the more so because Narkompros made it clear that 'god-building' tendencies on the part of Smithy poets and novelists would not be welcomed.[28]

So far as state control was concerned, the Smithy were satisfied to be neither controlled by, nor completely autonomous from, the agencies of the Party and the state as embodied in Narkompros. Yet on the whole they remained suspicious of such control, even though the Eleventh Party Congress of March 1922 passed resolutions warning of a restoration of the bourgeoisie, and emphasised 'the extraordinary importance of creating a literature for worker and peasant youth in order to counter the influence on them of 'boulevard' literature, and to further the communist education of the masses of the youth'.[29] Indeed in the early months of NEP a group within the Smithy gave prominence to their grave misgivings about what they saw as a partial restoration of capitalism under the new economic arrangements, and several – Gerasimov and Kirillov among them – left both the Smithy and the Party, and from about 1923 until its eventual dissolution in 1932 the fortunes of the Smithy declined.

In its early years however the themes of heroic labour and the cult of the machine were particularly important to the Smithy, as its name might be taken to imply. The machine was not to be worshipped *per se* since it was felt to be capable of robotising the individual; yet its functions were felt capable of being admired in so far as they showed the way to liberating the human race from drudgery and physical toil. Metals too, were greatly admired by the Smithy. Iron in particular was thought to possess an almost esoteric character because over and above its constructional qualities it suggested a source of strength from which, metaphorically, the proletariat could derive succour.[30] The spirit of collectivism, too, was zealously recommended within the Smithy, such that the 'I' of individual feeling and expression was felt to be thoroughly subsumable within the group, the factory, the city, or even the world, in whose character it would then find itself once again.

The Smithy's main period of literary production, from 1920 to 1923, was characterised by some uneven and occasionally remote and fantastic work. Its best-known prose writers were Nikolay Lyashko, Georgy Nikiforov, and Fyodor Gladkov, whose novel *Cement*, written between 1922 and 1924, won him wide recognition. In poetry, particularly, the Smithy engaged in extreme proletarian romanticism which heroised the labour process and the forward march of the proletariat in a manner that at times bordered on that very mysticism that they were trying to avoid. As Herman Ermolaev summarises it, the hero of this proletarian romanticism

often ascends into interplanetary space, or at times digs deeply into the centre of the earth. The hero is an iron proletarian Messiah, a collective image of the proletariat, devoid of individual traits. A peculiar proletarian mysticism is expressed in celestial and religious images derived from Russian Symbolism, from Christianity, and from the scientist Konstantin Tsiolkovsky's visions of space travel.[31]

28. See V. Zavalishin, Early Soviet Writers, Atlantic Books, New York, 1958, p 157.

29. Cited by C. V. James, *Soviet Socialist Realism: Origins and Theory*, Macmillan, London and Basingstoke, 1973, p 53.

30. N. Lyshako, 'Osnovaye otlichitel-nye priznaki proletarskoe literatury', *Kuznitsa*, October 1922; quoted by Ermolaev, *Soviet Literary Theories*, p 20.

31. Ermolaev, *Soviet Literary Theories*, p 24. For examples of Smithy writing in English see V. Zavalishin, *Early Soviet Writers*, pp 145–78, and G. Z. Patrick, *Popular Poetry in Soviet Russia*, University of California Press, Berkeley, California, 1929, pp 78–285.

By 1923 or 1924 such a literature could obviously be attacked from numerous points of view. Trotsky, easily the most articulate voice on literary matters within the Party leadership, was caustic about the Smithy's poetry and prose. Another difficulty was that international-ism was beginning to decline in popularity among other Party leaders as prospects for world revolution began to recede and domestic issues took over the centre of attention: collectivism was progress-ively replaced by a return to individualism, initially in the economic sphere but also in culture. Images of iron Messiahs or marching proletarian armies gave way to less fantastic flights of fancy. But clearly this change could take either of two forms: either literature could veer even further away from the spirit of the Revolution into 'bourgeois' novel-writing replete with identifiable heroes and enter-taining adventures, or it could devote itself to the task of sober reconstruction and a return, in literature and the other arts, to a measure of naturalism, even of 'realism', under the guidance of politicians both inside and outside the Party.

The latter was the line of reasoning which brought the more overtly political October Group into being at the end of 1922. The Smithy, so the October Group now alleged in *Pravda*, had become an obstacle to the development of 'true' proletarian literature and art.[32] The fifteen signatories to this statement included Rodov from the Smithy, the poets Alexandr Bezymensky and Alexandr Zharov, and the prose writers Artem Vesely and Alexey Sokolov, among others, as well as the Party historian Grigory Lelevich and the critic and politician Ilich Vardin. Also part of October were the young novelist Yury Libedin-sky and the teenage editor of the Komsomol magazine *Young Guard*, Leopold Averbakh. October was far more militant and implacably Party-minded than the Smithy had ever been. All its members be-longed to the Party or the Komsomol. Most October writers were too young to have had Revolutionary experience, and many contributed to two magazines, *Na postu* (On Guard) from 1923 to 1925, and *Oktyabr* (October), from 1924 onwards.

In the first issue of *Na postu* the October writers (sometimes known as 'Onguardists') launched a vitriolic attack on the neo-bourgeoisie of the NEP dispensation, claiming that the proletariat was now con-fronted with the task of 'building its own class culture and, conse-quently, its own imaginative literature as a powerful means of profoundly influencing the emotional receptiveness of the masses'.[33] Although the October platform showed no appetite for images of factories, labouring heroes or metal machines, it shared with the Smithy a dislike of 'bourgeois' literary schools such as Futurism and sought to replace them with a thoroughgoing political analysis of the goals and circumstances of the working class. But the romanticism of the Smithy had gone. As Rodov said in the first issue of *Na postu*, 'We shall stand indefatigably on guard over a clear and firm Communist ideology in proletarian literature', and 'we shall also stand on guard over the organisational structure of VAPP and fight for its unification and consolidation.'[34] Indeed *Na postu* became identified with VAPP as soon as the Smithy declined.

Both the military terminology but also the style advocated by the

32. See 'Pismo v redaktsiyu', *Pravda*, 12 December 1922.

33. *Na postu*, no 1, June 1923.

34. Rodov, 'Nuzhna liniya', *Na postu*, no 1, June 1923.

October writers, namely 'realism', can be directly compared to the heavily supported AKhRR formation in painting and sculpture, founded in 1922, which we shall be examining shortly. The themes specifically advocated for 'realistic' treatment by October were such things as the participation of the working class in the economic life of the country, in factory building and in scientific expeditions and discoveries; the political life of the proletariat at home and abroad, including its role in the October Revolution and the Civil War; the life of the Red Army and the Cheka, as well as, to begin with, the prospects for revolution in Germany and the United States. A third group of suitable themes comprised family relations, the place of women in the new society, the building of new social centres such as factory clubs, and the impact of NEP on the Soviet village.[35]

35. Ermolaev, *Soviet Literary Theories*, pp 31–2.

Thus laid out, the literary programme of the October group was to be adhered to by its members on pain of severe critical reprimand or excommunication. October not only asked of its members strict discipline in the interpretation and execution of its platform, but claimed that it and it alone represented the true literature of the proletarian dictatorship and that it deserved the full sponsorship and support of the Party. October writers regarded NEP as a temporary and regrettable expedient which would be abandoned as soon as the country returned to 'correct' Marxist principles. The best known and most popular poets of October in its earlier years were Alexandr Bezymensky, who composed optimistic, stirring verses on the Red Army, the Komsomol, and the everyday lives of factory workers and peasants; and Demyan Bedny, whom Trotsky admired. As Bezymensky wrote in an early declamatory verse:

> First of all
> I'm a Party member
> And only afterwards a rhymster[36]

36. A. Bezymensky, 'Prelude' (1923) in *Order na mir*, Moscow 1926, p 83; Zavalishin, *Early Soviet Writers*, p 238.

Libedinsky's novels *A Week* (1922) and *Tomorrow* (1923) also gave unstinting support to the Party; the latter work openly supporting Trotsky's controversial thesis of 'permanent revolution'. These writers can accurately be said to have attracted the attention of Party and military leaders for their sympathetic portrayal of deeply-felt Revolutionary situations and for their unshaking adherence to the overriding principle of Party leadership. Though Trotsky himself was more cautious, Kamenev, Radek and Emelyan Yaroslavsky were all fervent supporters of the proletarian writers' groups within the orbit of VAPP, and they endorsed thoroughly and repeatedly the VAPP 'line' against fellow-travelling and bourgeois writers such as were being published by Voronsky and *Krasnaya nov*, as well as VAPP's anathema on other left-wing groups such as the Smithy and LEF. As the editorial group of *Na postu* expressed it,

> In view of the revival, since the beginning of NEP, of the activity of bourgeois literary groups, all ideological doubts are absolutely inadmissible, and we shall make a point of bringing them to light.

> We shall fight those Manilovs [Gogol's complacent hero from *Dead Souls*]

who distort and slander our Revolution by the attention they pay to the rotten fabric of the fellow-travellers' literary work, in their attempt to build an aesthetic bridge between the past and the present.[37]

In case there might be any doubt about the extent of October's support from the Party, let us notice the wording of the Resolution passed at the 12th Congress of the Party in April 1923 entitled 'On the Questions of Propaganda, the Press and Agitation'. This was mainly concerned with the organisation and unification of all activities understood to lie within the meaning of the term 'Communist enlightenment'; that is, with ensuring that the level of political literacy and participation was improved across all sections of the population, including the peasantry and the non-Russian nationals. To this end a system of clubs and reading rooms right across the country was envisaged, each one under the guidance of a local Party Committee, while at the upper end would lie the Communist Universities and various Party Schools. Journals and elementary political agitation were deemed fundamental, particularly in rural areas:

> We must complete the foundation of a publishing house for special mass literature for distribution among the peasantry [the Resolution said] illuminating a series of questions of interest to the rural reader in a form accessible to him, beginning with political education and ending with *belles-lettres* and practical questions of peasant economy . . .[38]

But the attitude of the Resolution towards the arts is instructive in a more general sense. For despite being concerned with propaganda, the press and agitation, certain passages make direct reference to artistic literature, to theatre, to cinema and by implication to all the other arts which could be said to have a press and propaganda function. 'Since during the past two years artistic literature . . . has grown into a great social force', the Resolution states, 'spreading influence above all on the masses of worker and peasant youth, it is essential that the Party place the supervision of this form of social influence on the agenda of its practical work.'[39] The reference to '*belles-lettres*' in the programme of peasant education is another sign of the Party's desire to control and direct these activities. The theatre, also, could and should be used 'for the systematic mass propagandising of the ideas of Communism'. Here, specific subjects were offered: heroic episodes in the struggles of the working class; and anti-religious propaganda. The cinema, too, must break out of its bourgeois and foreign moulds and be developed into a specifically Soviet cinema based on Soviet finance.

But the Party did not go as far as to suggest exact themes or styles either for writing or for art. Indeed the degree of its actual supervision over the work of writers' or theatrical workshops was probably less than the wording of the Resolution suggests. Further, the Party's continuing support for 'fellow-traveller' literature and the broad gamut of *Krasnaya nov* was not seriously in doubt. Therefore such a resolution could be looked at in either of two ways; as supporting the Party's increasing supervision and control over the arts, or as lying outside the scope of the major arts in its central concern for education

37. 'Editorial Manifesto of the On Guard Group', in G. Reavey and M. Slonim, *Soviet Literature: an Anthology*, 1934, p 405; E. J. Brown, *The Proletarian Episode in Russian Literature, 1928–1932*, Columbia University Press, New York, 1953, p 20.

38. 'Resolyutsiya po voprosam propagandy, pechati i agitatsiya', Clause 40 to the XII Party Congress, 1923; C. V. James, *Soviet Socialist Realism*, p 55.

39. 'Resolyutsiya', Clause 24; C. V. James, *Soviet Socialist Realism*, p 54.

and propaganda alone. This radical ambiguity in the Party's attitude to the arts vis-à-vis propaganda, foreshadowed already in the events of the Civil War period, was to remain at the centre of artistic and literary disputes throughout the decade and beyond.

Dada, Expressionism and Montage

The development of montage in photography, theatre and film is one of the Soviet Union's great contributions to twentieth-century art. Photomontage was invented in 1919 by Gustav Klutsis, apparently independently of its slightly earlier uses in German Dada. In 1922 and 1923 the technique of photomontage assumed other functions, in illustration, propaganda and advertising, and came to be used in a particularly significant way in the theatre and cinema from 1923. Some idea of the efficiency and flexibility of this device must be given briefly here.

The use of photographs in art had first occurred in Cubo-Futurism before the Revolution. Malevich, in a departure from French Cubist practice, had incorporated a photograph in his painting 'Women at a Poster Column' of 1913–14. Klutsis, who in 1918 was Malevich's pupil, must have known this – as indeed he must have known examples of American and foreign advertising in which combinations of photographs and other material occurred. Klutsis had studied first with Ilya Mashkov before enrolling at the Second State Free Art Studio with Malevich; then, around the time of Malevich's departure to form the Affirmers of New Art or UNOVIS group in Vitebsk in 1919, he made a photomontage which he called 'The Dynamic City'. It shows a series of interpenetrating planes and facades arranged on a circular disk, with workers positioned at the end of the planes as if stationed on a mobile, revolving microcosm; this was clearly a metaphor for the Soviet Union in the young days of its Revolutionary struggle. In the same year and the next Rodchenko made several small collages out of various printed materials that extended his constructive work with wood and metal units to the two-dimensional plane (Figure 49).

It was Klutsis who first exploited the possibilities of montage. At the time of Lenin's Plan for Electrification in 1920 he made a poster in the montage method entitled 'The Electrification of the Entire Country' (Figure 50) which shows Lenin striding forward with an electricity pylon in his arms, attached to which is a cluster of modernist buildings. Here, Lenin steps into, or onto, the microcosmic circle that must be the Soviet Union in its world role. This work marks Klutsis' joining of the Communist Party and his move away from abstract and Suprematist art into agitational work, and it is this orientation that explains the form of Klutsis' photomontage and its enduring significance throughout the 1920s. The fact that it contains both abstract and 'realistic' elements is probably less significant than the graphic, easily legible quality of the whole image. Given that agitational art calls for immediacy, graphic simplicity and reproducibility irrespective of aesthetic 'laws' such as perspective or the

Figure 49 (opposite)
A. Rodchenko,
*Photomontage, c.*1919–20 (photo: Christie's, Manson and Woods Ltd)

Figure 50
G. Klutsis, design for a poster
The Electrification of the Entire Country, 1920

'rational' arrangement of forms, photomontage satisfied all these requirements cheaply and effectively. Further, those elements in 'The Electrification of the Entire Country' which are out of consonance with 'actual' reality – such as Lenin carrying the electricity pylon – introduce a 'shock effect' into the image which is both humorous and surprising. The 'shock effect' also may derive from the 'alogism' of Malevich's earlier writings and paintings and from the idea frequently heard among Futurists and Formalists that a 'displacement' of the image can give it a new and added resonance. Viktor Shklovsky's concept of *ostranenie* or 'estrangement' may well be significant here.[1]

But if Klutsis was the first to exploit the possibilities of photomontage, Rodchenko was the first to extend them. After the '5x5=25' exhibition in September 1921 Rodchenko and the other Constructivists in the group turned away from 'art' and began to test the possibilities of working in design. In 1922 Rodchenko joined the staff of Alexey Gan's magazine *Kino-Fot*, and made several cover designs in which photographs are used as graphic elements within a total graphic image. It was in 1923 however that Rodchenko's photomontage style really emerged, with the illustrations to Mayakovsky's poem 'Pro eto' (About This). By this time Rodchenko had seen the work of John Heartfield and George Grosz, which Mayakovsky had brought back from his visit to the Berlin exhibition in 1922, and he may have come to know the work of Raoul Hausmann, Hanna Höch and Max Ernst. 'Pro eto' concerns Mayakovsky's unrequited love for Osip Brik's wife Lily and is written in a parodic, almost self-pitying manner, to which Rodchenko's photomontages (the photographs used were taken by the young photographer A. Shterenberg) add elements of personal fantasy with glimpses of modern NEP reality in a wistful, poetic way, in one case referring to memories of Mayakovsky's childhood (Figure 51). In any event they are very far from the aggressive, iconoclastic images produced by the German Dadaists. Much of Rodchenko's virtuosity as a designer was expressed in a collaboration with Mayakovsky between 1923 and 1925 in which they produced advertising graphics for Mosselprom, Rezinotrest, Gosizdat and other government agencies (Figure 52).[2] In many cases however these do not incorporate photographs and stand to one side of both the agitational and poetic uses of photomontage.

Perhaps the most significant application of the early montage technique appeared not in design but in the theatre; and for this we have to remember the Russian tradition of clowning and the circus. Constructivist theatre and the traditional theatre by no means exhausted the entertainment field. In 1920 a young director Sergey Radlov founded a small theatre in Petrograd known as the 'Popular Comedy', based largely on a concept of 'improvisation' that Radlov had learned in pre-Revolutionary days under Meyerhold, for whom, in turn, the 'Commedia dell'Arte' had been important. The concept of improvised gesture became, for Radlov, the concept of improvised speech, to which he added a rumbustious, clowning emphasis. Radlov's method was to suggest the bare outline of a situation to his actors, and let them improvise the rest, giving much encouragement

1. For an exposition of *ostranenie* see V. Markov, *Russian Futurism: A History*, University of California Press, Berkeley, California, 1968; MacGibbon and Kee, London, 1969, and the various essays by Shklovsky in S. Bann and J. Bowlt (eds), *Russian Formalism*, Scottish Academic Press, London and Edinburgh, 1973.

2. These agencies were for agricultural goods, rubber goods and state publishing respectively. Many of the designs are reproduced in colour in M. Anikst (ed) *Soviet Commercial Design of the Twenties*, Thames and Hudson, London 1987.

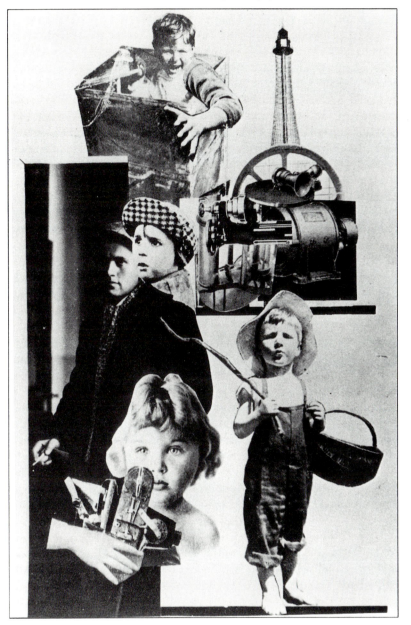

Figure 51
A. Rodchenko, photomontage for
Mayakovsky's *Pro eto*, 1923 (coll:
the Rodchenko estate, photo:
Museum of Modern Art, Oxford)

Figure 52
A. Rodchenko and V. Mayakovsky,
a Rezinotrest poster aimed at popu-
lations in the south-east: 'People of
the East! Buy! The camel is bringing you better galoshes'.
Moscow 1924

to accidents, farcical upsets, unplanned banter and a general atmosphere of buffoonery.

The circus was in many ways the model for Radlov's Popular
Comedy. Jokes about current events, impromptu dialogue with the
audience, unexpected outbursts and general hilarity were the company's stock-in-trade. To Radlov the idea of a 'fixed text' was anathema. It was vital to 'destroy that pernicious being, the armchair
literary man who writes words for the theatre in the tranquillity of
his flat', he said.[3] Jugglers and circus clowns were invited into the
troupe, as were acrobats and artistes of every variety. Radlov felt
alienated from the intelligentsia of his time, and happily encouraged

3. S. Radlov, *Zhizn iskusstva*, 15 January
1920; Rudnitsky, *Russian and Soviet
Theatre: Tradition and the Avant-Garde*,
Thames and Hudson, London, 1988,
p 57.

a widening of the chasm between his own brand of naivety and the officially sanctioned theatre. Radlov himself wrote many of the sketches, in one of which, *The Foster Child*, a gymnast, Sergey, plays a thief who escapes from his pursuers by jumping over barrels, climbing up a rope and swinging over the audience's heads, to general approval.

In the years of the Civil War it quickly became apparent that such merriment was out of tune with the times; Radlov's sketches, though entertaining, were felt to be too far removed from the problems of sustaining a revolutionary atmosphere and defeating the White armies. Critics accused him of ignoring the internal affairs of the country, and Radlov felt obliged to change his manner of approach. He accepted a script by Gorky entitled *The Hardworking Slovotekov*, concerned with poking fun at a nervous bureaucrat who could never take responsibility for his actions but resorted instead to muttering slogans about 'collective discussion', 'coordination' and 'organisation', while doing nothing ('Slovetekov' means 'word-flow' or 'word-babble'). The smallest problem proves too difficult for him, and in his confusion the ceiling falls in upon him followed by dirty water and chunks of plaster, his chattering continuing all the while. But it appears that the clown Georges Delvari, who played the role of Slovotekov, transformed Gorky's lampoon into a farce, and the enterprise was reckoned a failure.[4] Radlov resorted to staging classics, and by 1922 the concept of the Popular Comedy seemed to be over and finished.

But the idea of circus buffoonery in the theatre was far from dead. In 1921 the gymnast Sergey, the Japanese juggler Tokashima, and the young directors Grigory Kozintsev and Leonid Trauberg set up a studio in Petrograd which they called Factory of the Eccentric Actor (Fabrika ekstsentricheskogo aktera or FEKS). Here, Kozintsev and Trauberg quite consciously attempted to achieve the 'Americanisation of theatre', with Charlie Chaplin and Mack Sennett as their idols and with jazz, cinema acting, Kabuki circus and boxing as their models: they proclaimed an art that was 'exaggeratedly crude, which jolts and batters the nerves, is openly utilitarian, mechanically precise, instant, and fast'. The method was to be one of highly self-conscious artifice, aimed 'not at movement, but at affectation, not at mime but at grimace, not at speaking but at shouting'. It was to be a 'conglomeration of stunts aimed at "the rhythmical battering of the nerves"'.[5]

The lifetime of FEKS was sweet but short. In September 1922 they staged a version of Gogol's *The Marriage*, though Gogol's text and stage directions would have been difficult to recognise. In the FEKS production, Gogol appears at the end of the play to express indignation of what he had seen. Mechanical characters were used: a Steam Bridegroom, an Electric Bridegroom, and a Radioactive Bridegroom, not to mention robots who entered on roller skates. In the words of a recent account,

> the chaotic action was accompanied by numerous lights and sound effects. Garlands of multi-coloured electric lights could be seen through the fabric of Kozintsev's scenery, flashing on and off to the sounds of the

4. See Rudnitsky, *Russian and Soviet Theatre*, pp 58–9.

5. G. Kozintsev, *Sobranie sochineniya*, Leningrad, 1982–6; vol 3, pp 73–4; Rudnitsky, *Russian and Soviet Theatre*, p 94.

two-step and Ragtime, while in the meantime hooters, rattles, bells and whistles 'assisted' the pianist. Sergey's somersaults and tumbling, executed against a large portrait of Chaplin, gave way to the Can-Can, the Can-Can in turn to cheeky satirical couplets with topical allusions.[6]

6. K. Rudnitsky, *Russian and Soviet Theatre*, pp 94–5.

The production also included a short film. In fact FEKS was destined to close after only its second production, *Foreign Trade on the Eiffel Tower*, in June 1923.

In November 1922 Meyerhold too adapted his Constructivist theatrical manner to stage a play in the 'eccentric' manner of FEKS. This was for a version of *Tarelkin's Death* by Sukhovo-Kobylin. This 'comedy-jest' had been written in 1869 as a satire on Tsarist police methods, and had been staged by Meyerhold in October 1917 in a phantasmagorical, Hoffmanesque style, to great popular appeal. Now Meyerhold repeated the knockabout comedy style of the earlier production, with the help of Stepanova's acting-machine which took the form of a series of wooden cages, painted white, through which actors were deposited or thrown. There was collapsing furniture, trap doors and 'trick' circus-like effects, now rendered clean and functional and having a somewhat mechanical air (Figure 53). Stepanova

Figure 53
V. Stepanova, stage machine for Meyerhold's production of *Tarelkin's Death* by Sukhovo-Kobylin, 1922

also designed costumes that resembled those of convicts or clowns. Pistol-shots announced the intervals, the characters were cast wrongly on purpose, and the whole thing was presented as a burlesque – quite the opposite of what Sukhovo-Kobylin had intended.

The emphasis on circus and buffoonery in the Popular Comedy and the FEKS Company were but two examples of the extreme diversity of Soviet theatre in the early period of the New Economic Policy. Expressionist drama also became attractive to Soviet producers, but for different reasons. Plays such as *Hoppla, wir leben!* by Ernst Toller and *Gas* by Georg Kaiser clearly referred to the social turmoil which accompanied the revival of class antagonism under NEP, and portrayed the baleful effects of unrestrained big business in particular. In them, the alienating or suffocating consequences of industrial society were vividly depicted. Furthermore their action was frequently episodic, strident and highly agitated, and hence provided at least one kind of answer to the call for a 'new' Soviet theatre that was in some sort of harmony with the times.

What did not prove appealing to Soviet producers and audiences however was the emphasis found in European Expressionist drama on the lonely individual pitted against his fate, his tendency to derangement and his frequent despair. Furthermore, Soviet directors were by and large enamoured of the image of technology rather than opposed to it, and tended to view the machine as a saviour rather than as an enemy. To this extent Expressionist plays from Western Europe needed radical adaptation. Frequently, scripts were changed to depict the isolated individual as backward and uncomprehending rather than as heroically estranged; to include crowd scenes representing the masses; and to inject images of technology as redemptive rather than imprisoning forces.

The Theatre of the Revolution in Moscow and the Bolshoi Dramatic Theatre became the companies which attempted Expressionist drama most regularly. Meyerhold was chief director of the Theatre of the Revolution from 1922 until 1924, and staged, among other things, Ernst Toller's *Masse Mensch*, with designs by Viktor Shestakov. Rudnitsky cites a contemporary critic who gave a sympathetic account of the action. Toller's play is an urban propaganda spectacle, complete with bankers in top hats and coats, share prices flashing up on a screen, can-can girls, speculators and profiteers, in short all the darker aspects of post-war German society. In Meyerhold's version the action was suddenly halted while attention was focused upon an isolated woman who began a dialogue with the masses about the ethics of what was taking place (Figure 54). The critic wrote that

> The theatre ironically presents Toller's naive yet profound arguments and the pretentious tragic pose of the philosophising, divided intellectual that so patently shows through all these earnest dialogues . . . the class nature of the woman's 'lofty' humanitarian morality is unmasked for the audience through her sing-song declamatory reading, her prayerful movements and gestures. In the production, this hypocritical morality is contrasted with the sober morality of the masses, who are not the faceless, doctrinaire crowd of the author's text and scenario, but masses whose movements are filled with action, urgency and anger, deployed by the director as a conscious, rational force that moves events. The masses take the platforms and bastions of the construction by storm, spreading over the stairs, splitting into separate groups, then again gathering together into a whole, emphasising through their movements the meaning and character of the individual episodes in the social conflict that is being enacted . . . [7]

7. B. V. Alpers, *Teatr Revolutsii*, Moscow, 1928, pp 49–50; cited by Rudnitsky, *Russian and Soviet Theatre*, p 101.

Figure 54 (opposite)
E. Toller, *Masse Mensch*, 1922
(photo: *SCR* London)

It is clear too from the description of the rhythm of the play – as in Meyerhold's version of Alexey Faiko's *Lake Lyul* – that many of the effects were almost cinematic, such as the abrupt cutting of the action, the light effects and the crowd scenes.

But it was in the work of the young Sergey Eisenstein that this connection between the dynamically interrupted theatre (more strictly the music-hall) and later cinematic innovations can be seen most vividly. Eisenstein was a regular visitor to the FEKS theatre in Petrograd during its brief existence in 1922 and 1923, and was clearly attracted by the choppy, burlesque style of the action, its capacity for contravening rational connections between episodes and above all by its accelerated, staccato rhythm. Eisenstein had also been a student of Meyerhold during the period of *Tarelkin's Death*. His theatrical debut had been *The Mexican* in 1921, adapted by Proletkult leader Valerian Pletnev from a story by Jack London, which he directed in partnership with Valentin Smyshlyaev at the First Workers' Theatre of the Proletkult.

The Mexican had not been overtly 'circus-ised' – though Eisenstein had included a boxing match in the play, which the film-maker Sergey Yutkevich later compared to Picasso and Braque's introduction of 'bits of coloured paper or newspaper fragments into their pictures'.[8] However Eisenstein's next production, following a period studying Commedia dell'Arte with Forreger and the spell with Meyerhold, was *The Wise Man*, adapted from Ostrovsky's *Enough Stupidity in Every Wise Man*, staged at the First Workers' Theatre of the Proletkult in April 1923. Here, he inaugurated the device by which he was to become justly famous later, the so-called 'montage of attractions', though a montage-like device had already been attempted in the cinema by Lev Kuleshov and D. W. Griffith.[9] The phrase appeared on the posters advertising the première of the play, which was staged in an ornate nineteenth-century mansion built by the art collector Morozov on Prospekt Kalinina in Moscow.[10] In Eisenstein's adaptation Ostrovsky's play was only adhered to in a few sections, with First

8. S. Yutkevich, 'Teenage Artists of the Revolution' in L. and J. Schnitzer and M. Martin, *Cinema in Revolution, the Heroic Era of the Soviet Film*, Secker and Warburg, London, 1973, p 18.

9. On the origins of the cinematic montage see L. Kuleshov, 'The Origins of Montage' in L. and J. Schnitzer, *Cinema in Revolution*, pp 67–76.

10. This is now Friendship House and is at 16, Prospekt Kalinina in Moscow.

World War generals, for example, replacing the original military characters. The whole production was conducted as a political satire, with clowning and gymnastics being the favourite mode of performance. The characters walked a tightrope, climbed a pole, did circus 'dives' and acrobatics, and performed satirical songs at the expense of emigrés and Whites. The stage itself was replaced by a circus ring and, at the end of the performance, a short film by Eisenstein (the first he ever shot) was projected above the stage. This was entitled *Glumov's Diary* – Glumov being the hero of Ostrovsky's play, acted by Grigory Alexandrov – and showed yet more acrobatic stunts, together with a chase and the theft of Glumov's diary.

The presence of the film at the end of the play itself constituted a montage of sorts. But the occasion was significant because it marked the bridge from theatre (more properly the circus) to film in a manner that was to have wide and critical implications for the concept of 'realism' in art, particularly in Germany and other Western countries in the 1930s and beyond.

Eisenstein now came to the belief that montage was the only possible direction for theatre in the new era. He is recounted as addressing a meeting at the House of the Press in these terms:

> What do the masses and the Revolution want from the theatre? Only what goes back to the sources of traditional forms of popular spectacle: circus, fairground attractions. The new theatre must be a sort of 'montage of attractions', that is to say of shock elements that strike and dazzle.[11]

11. Recounted by Evgeny Gabrilovich, cited in Daniel Gerould, 'Eisenstein's *The Wise Man*', in I. Christie and D. Elliott (eds), *Eisenstein at Ninety* (exhibition catalogue) Oxford, Museum of Modern Art, 1988, p 92.

The idea was elaborated in print in the journal *LEF*, for May 1923. In an article called 'Montage of Attractions' he made the seminal observation that: 'it is not in a "revelation" of the playwright's purpose, nor in the "correct interpretation of an author", nor in "the true reflection of the epoch" that a [theatrical] production can base itself.' This is because, as he puts it, 'the basic materials of the theatre arise from the spectator himself – and from our guiding of the spectator in the desired direction . . . which is the main task of every functional theatre (agit, poster, . . . etc)'.[12] For such a functional theatre psychological attractions are insufficient: these, says Eisenstein, 'exist and operate *beneath* the action, in spite of the fact that the theme may be an extremely urgent one'. The mistake made by most agit-theatres is in being satisfied with those attractions that already exist in the script.

12. This and following quotations from 'Montage of Attraction' are from the version of the essay reprinted in S. M. Eisenstein, *The Film Sense*, trans and ed by Jay Leyda, London, 1943, pp 166–8.

A truly functional theatre must put its attractions in montage form, Eisenstein urges. An attraction is an 'aggressive moment' that produces certain emotional shocks, and makes a 'final ideological conclusion visible' – similar to the horrors one might experience in the Theatre Guignole, but having nothing in common with the circus trick, which is completed on the plane of pure craftsmanship only. Such attractions must succeed each other not merely in a logical or literary way. They must form themselves into a system, in which, as Eisenstein says elsewhere, it is the relation between them that gives added meaning to their association. 'This is fully analogous', he says in the *LEF* article, 'with the "pictorial storehouse" employed by George Grosz, or the elements of photographic illustration (photomontage) employed by Rodchenko.' The problem of the theatre is to get away from illusory pictures into a montage of 'real things', while at the same time 'weaving into the montage full pieces of representation which are tied to the plot and the development of the subject, not as self-enforced and all-determining, but as consciously contributing to the whole production and selected for their pure strength as active attractions' (that is rather than as mere representations). It is in the experience of the spectator that these elements will collide and produce fresh meaning.

An example from Eisenstein's *The Wise Man* illustrates the early use of this montage technique. Eisenstein stages two scenes simultaneously which in Ostrovsky were consecutive, one in which Glumov receives instruction on how to woo his aunt, the other in which he puts the advice into practice. 'Instead of a smooth change of scene', Eisenstein observed,

> Glumov races from one to the other and back again. He carries on a segment of dialogue with one in such a way as, having broken it off, to continue the segment already started with the other. The final remark of one series of segments, colliding with the beginning of the second, acquires new meaning, sometimes a punning play on words. The jumps themselves create something like caesuras between the ensemble play of separate moments. The presence of a third person, not taking part in the conversation and as if absent, gives additional effect of illustrative cutting to this or that remark in the dialogue of the two others.[13]

13. Cited in D. Gerould, 'Eisenstein's *The Wise Man*', p 99.

For Eisenstein the origin of the montage device lay in circus and music-hall which he had followed since childhood, as much as in Chaplin, in jazz, and in the early dance rhythms of the 1920s. The circus had already appealed to artists like Picasso, becoming a sign of an illicit, joyous, carnival element in entertainment that spoke of a 'refusal' of 'naturalistic' drama and of passively experienced bourgeois theatre. Performed by social nomads such as acrobats and strolling players, the circus also embodied marvellous physical alertness, cunning and energy. For Eisenstein these were perceived as being precisely the qualities most urgently needed by Revolutionary theatre during the period of its first *embourgeoisement*, the period of early NEP. It may also be significant that Eisenstein introduced montage into the theatrical and cinematic arts in the context of the Proletkult rather than in the traditional theatre. The Proletkult called its theatre in the Prospekt Kalinina the Central Arena, viewing it as a site of physical and emotional contest, similar in some respects to the bullfight, which Eisenstein also admired.

In fact his two other theatrical productions after the acclaim which greeted *The Wise Man* were also staged under the auspices of the Proletkult. The first was *Listen Moscow!* of 1923, an 'agit-Guignole' by Proletkult theoretician Sergey Tretyakov, which was held at the Proletkult Theatre, and the second was *Gas Masks*, of 1924, also by Tretyakov, which was staged in the Moscow Gas Factory.

After 1924 Eisenstein worked principally in film, which is outside the scope of this book. Evidently his early montage work in the photographic and theatrical arts must be seen partly against the background of the Russian tradition of circus and music-hall, partly against the background of the intense national involvement in 'theatricalisation' which burst to life after 1917, and partly in the more immediate context of an atmosphere of experimentation in the arts which brought materials into new and striking conjunctions – whether in sculptural corner reliefs such as those by Tatlin, or in Constructivist sculpture by, for instance, Medunetsky or Stenberg. In wider European terms the use of montage belongs to Dada and Surrealism. In the Soviet Union it is accurate to say that montage techniques were used in several art forms after 1919 and 1920: writing, graphics, theatre, and to a lesser extent, visual art. They did not, however, prosper unheeded, since other artistic ideologies were at the same time seeking to establish links with older artistic forms such as easel painting and representational sculpture. And competition between the various factions was to become very intense indeed.

The Debate around Easel Painting 1922–1924

To read some accounts of Soviet art one would have to believe that Constructivism was the only art form being energetically pursued in the climate of the early NEP years.[1] This is of course not the case. The position was that easel painting of many different kinds was resumed soon after the privations of war communism were over – not that it had ever really ceased – and that a debate raged freely in the many artists' groups and societies, as in the art schools, as to the merits and claims of the various approaches.

We noted already that Constructivism, with its tendency to austere, economical forms and its dependence on nothing more exotic than a few spars of wood and some lengths of wire, was in many ways an ideal expression of the desperate conditions of the late part of the Civil War. At a time when materials were virtually unobtainable, even by scavenging, artists had a specific justification for maintaining that 'decoration' in any shape or form was almost obscene. But this is largely a Constructivist view-point. Following the free (in some cases undirected) atmosphere of the SVOMAS between 1918 and 1920, where easel painting had flourished, artists of several persuasions had continued to produce work with canvas and paints, and much of this existed in a state of rivalry with Constructivist work from the very beginning – as Brik's comments on the origins of Productivism imply. But after 1920 the position began to shift. The first months after the Civil War saw a tentative improvement in the Soviet Union's virtually subsistence economy. Very gradually matters improved, and by the middle of 1921 paint and canvas and other materials became more easily obtainable, and multifarious aesthetic questions relating to this medium came to the surface for debate once more.

And what of the art market, which had after all been almost eradicated by the harsh conditions of the winter of 1919–20 and which, except for black market exchanges, still met with official disapproval for the remainder of 1920? It is a significant historical fact that under the régime of the New Economic Policy the private market

1.   I mention here David Elliott, *New Worlds, Russian Art and Society 1900–1937* (1986); R. Hughes, *The Shock of the New: Art and the Century of Change* (1980), N. Lynton, *The Story of Modern Art* (1980), and similar survey accounts, that accord the briefest of mentions (Elliott) or none at all (Hughes, Lynton) to work outside the Constructivist camp.

for the production and sale of works of art took an upturn – 'flourished' would be an exaggeration. To foreigners the development of
the market in all commodities was generally a welcome change. But
this was not how things were always seen at home. The Menshevik
leader F.I. Dan, who was exiled from Russia in 1922, wrote in his diary
with considerable misgivings about how the new trade

> dealt mainly with the luxuries of the 'new rich', shamelessly standing out
> against a background of general impoverishment and appalling
> hunger . . . Theatres and concerts were packed, women were again flaunt-
> ing luxurious apparel, furs and diamonds. A speculator who was yester-
> day threatened with execution and quietly stayed to the side trying to
> avoid notice, today considers himself important and proudly shows off
> his wealth and luxury. This is evident in every little custom. Again after
> a number of years one can hear from the mouths of cab drivers, waiters,
> and porters at stations the senile expression, which had completely dis-
> appeared from us – 'your honour'.[2]

Advertising with all the vigour of the capitalist countries now reap-
peared, an expedient in which Futurists such as Mayakovsky and
Rodchenko took a leading role.[3] Yet ideologists everywhere were
thrown into confusion about the merits and drawbacks of the new
scheme. In effect, the NEP experiment split the Party into two, or
perhaps three. Lenin's tactical support for the experiment was now
matched by the bitter disappointment of young Bolsheviks who felt
'as though the Revolution had been betrayed . . . If money was
reappearing [it was now said], wouldn't rich people reappear too?'[4]
Trotsky was an opponent of NEP along with Preobrazhensky and
Pyatakov. Yet others such as Bukharin, whose support for strong
Party discipline we already observed, now believed Bolshevism to be
fully consistent with a reformist, gradual approach to socialism.
There is little doubt that this modification of, or retreat from, Revolutionary Bolshevik doctrine was accompanied by a more tolerant
attitude both to the artistic forms of the past as well as to the concept
of a purchasable, collectable artistic object that could adorn a domestic interior in the manner of the pre-Revolutionary bourgeoisie.

In the art schools particularly it became possible after 1921 to
practise easel painting on a serious level once more, and the position
of the Constructivists became less and less secure. The situation was
nevertheless complex, and was further exacerbated by the determination by several of the Constructivists to 'go into production' and
abandon the traditional field of art altogether. The position of the
VKhUTEMAS in the first years of NEP perhaps exemplifies this
tendency. At the very start of this period the painting and sculpture faculty had been partly sympathetic to abstraction and the
'avant-garde', and had included such figures as Klyun, Popova and
Rodchenko among its staff. Then, with the establishment of the First
Working Group of Constructivists within INKhUK at the beginning
of 1921 there occurred the beginnings of a split between production
art (or design) on the one hand and various forms of easel painting
on the other, with 'purists' such as Malevich and Popova (at least in
her painting) being left somewhat on one side. Indeed this reaction

2. F. I. Dan, *Dva goda skitanii*, Berlin 1922; see A. Ball, 'Lenin and the Question of Private Trade in Soviet Russia', *Slavic Review*, Fall 1984, pp 399–412.

3. See above, pp 142–3.

4. A. Barmin, *One Who Survived: The Life Story of a Russian under the Soviets*, G. P. Putnam and Sons, New York, 1945, p 125; Ball, 'Lenin & Private Trade', p 400.

against 'pure' painting around 1921 and 1922 led to many students of the leading experimentalists, Tatlin, Exter and Malevich, for example, losing confidence in the 'purist' programme and beginning to reformulate a position which was more sympathetic to figurative, naturalistic art. Inside the VKhUTEMAS the change of mood was considerable. As already stated, the 'avant-garde' painters gradually left their posts, and figurative and 'realist' artists took up teaching roles with very different platforms. Their number included the Peredivzhniki 'realist' A. Arkhipov, the Cézannists Falk, Mashkov and Konchalovsky, the Cubist-inclined Shevchenko, Udaltsova and Drevin, who had fled from INKhUK when it had adopted a Constructivist platform in 1921, David Shterenberg, who was fundamentally a figurative artist, the (at this time) Cézannists Sergey Gerasimov and Pavel Kuznetsov, and Alexandr Osmerkin and Konstantin Istomin, the latter of whom was an enthusiast of Matisse. The sculpture workshop, though initially having practised a kind of monumental Cubism under Boris Korolev and Anton Lavinsky, by 1923 had moved towards a less modernistic form of monumentality under the guidance of sculptors such as Konenkov, Chaikov and Efimov,[5] whose students Motovilov and Plastov were to become celebrated later. The rectorship of the VKhUTEMAS changed in 1923 to Vladimir Favorsky, who also taught graphic design. The influence of the Constructivists and Productivists at INKhUK was confined to the VKhUTEMAS' Basic Course and the woodwork and metalworking faculties, and consequently exerted most influence on design.

It is instructive to have some detail on the various easel painting groups and the theories that supported them that sprang up either in or near to the VKhUTEMAS in the early years of NEP. In the atmosphere that then prevailed it was entirely possible for them to function independently of, and beyond the range of, Constructivist and Futurist influence. In fact in numerical terms these groups may even have had more supporters. Yet their works have been less frequently seen, and the weight of 'modernist' advocacy in the West has often excluded them altogether.

An important group that belongs to the early and middle years of NEP was Bytie, variously translated as 'Being', 'Life', or 'Objective Reality'. Founded in 1921, members of this group were convinced that Constructivism had foundered on the rocks of extremism; yet they believed in the idea of a contemporaneous, social art that could provide an image of 'life' or of the 'objective reality' of the times. They were opposed to the kind of self-reflexive formalism that they believed had overtaken abstract art, and stylistically followed the 'Cézannist' methods of the former Jack of Diamonds group, particularly those of Konchalovsky. Hence their statement that 'only by rejecting the use of painterly techniques as an end in themselves is it possible for Russian painting once again to become social.'[6] Now emphasising the 'content or the subject matter of art', the members of Bytie included L. Bunatyan, Sergey Sakharov, Grigory Sretensky, Alexandr Taldykin and A. Lebedev.[7]

Another group, known as Makovets, was founded in May 1922 by

5.   Lodder, *Russian Constructivism*, p 116.

6.   *Katalog vystavki kartin obshchestva khudozhnikov 'Bytie'*, Moscow, 1927; I. Matsa (ed), *Sovetskoe iskusstvo za 15 let, Materialy i dokumentatsiya*, Moscow–Leningrad, 1933, p 313; Lodder, *Russian Constructivism*, p 185.

7.   Lobanov, *Khudozhestvennye gruppirovki za poslednie 15 let*, Moscow, 1930, p 11; Lodder, *Russian Constructivism*, p 295, fn 20.

Vasily Chekrygin, when he and 17 others had the first of a series of exhibitions that would continue until 1925. The society was named after the hill on which the Troitse-Sergiyeva Lavra (now the Zagorsk monastery and museum complex) was built in the fourteenth century, in order to signal its members' sympathy for spiritual qualities in art and perhaps also for a concept of Russian national art. Characteristic of this group were lyrical and quasi-religious subjects, painted in an intense, sometimes expressionistic mood (Figure 55). Members of Makovets included Nikolay Grigoriev, Tatyana Alexandrova, Favorsky, L. Shegin, Vera Pestel, Pavel Fonvisin, Nikolay Chernishov, Alexandr Shevchenko, Sergey Gerasimov, Konstantin Istomin and Vadim Rondin. By no means all Makovets work was 'spiritual', however. Much of it was down-to-earth and almost documentary. In the first issue of the journal *Makovets* in 1922 a statement read

Figure 55
V. Chekrygin, *Fate*, 1922

> We presume that art can be revived only if the continuity with the artists of the past is strictly maintained and the sources of what is vital and eternal are resurrected without exception. We are not in contention with anyone; we are not the creators of the latest 'ism' . . .[8]

In some quarters the reaction against Constructivism was intense. A group known as the New Society of Painters (Novoe obshchestvo zhivopistsev or NOZh) consisted of Production artists who had been students of Exter, Malevich and Tatlin but who now rapidly changed their perception of the path that art should follow. NOZh was formed in 1920–21. At its first and only exhibition in November 1922, it issued a declaration which stated that

> we, former leftists in art, were the first to feel the utter rootlessness of further analytical and scholarly aberrations . . . we have not taken the road tramped by the theory of Constructivism, for Constructivism, in proclaiming the death of art, conceives man as an automaton . . . we want to create realistic works of art.[9]

The founding artists of this group were Samuil Adlivankin, Alexandr Gluskin, Amshey Nyurenberg, Mikhail Perutsky, Georgy Ryazhsky and Nikolay Popov.[10] The aim of this new 'realism' was to assert that 'the means and properties [of art] are still able to systematise the feelings of a revolutionary environment'. They believed that

> the future will bring a new form of painting, corresponding to the tempo of modernity and contemporary psychology. We regard realism not as an impersonal and literary representation of life, but its creative reappraisal, a profoundly personal attitude. We have not started from an artistic or sociological theory; emotions have led us here. Artistic feeling lies at the core of our work . . .[11]

Another strand of the NOZh platform was to turn back to 'primitive' art-forms which included the Russian *lubok* and to other early twentieth-century artists who had found sympathy with 'artless' approaches and styles. Adlivankin, to take a notable example, followed

8. 'Our Prologue', *Makovets*, Moscow, no 1, 1922, p 4 in M. Guerman, *Soviet Art, 1920s–1930s, Russian Museum, Leningrad*, Sovietsky khudozhnik, Moscow and Harry N. Abrams, New York, 1988, p 88.

9. Bowlt, *Russian Art of the Avant-Garde: Theory and Criticism, 1902–1934*, The Viking Press, New York, 1976, p xxix; Matsa, *Sovetskoe iskusstvo*, p 310.

10. Lobanov, *Khudozhestvennye gruppirovki*, p 106; Lodder, *Russian Constructivism*, p 295, n 17.

11. Matsa, *Sovetskoe iskusstvo*, p 311; Lodder, *Russian Constructivism*, p 185.

the Douanier Rousseau in his treatment of space, form and colour, and in so doing he no doubt idealised and simplified the complex circumstances of Soviet life in the early NEP years. His painting 'Tram B', for example, shows a tram-load of shoppers and commuters such as might be found in any Western European capital (Figure 56). Yet in the Soviet context the presence of this specifically new urban public had its own significance in 1922.

Figure 56
S. Adlivankin, *Tram B*, 1922

12. See above, pp 132–3.

13. Tugenkhold, 'Exhibition in the House of Artistic Culture', *Izvestiya*, 10 January 1923. See Kostin, *OST*, pp 19 ff, to whom I am much indebted here.

A fourth group that did particularly interesting work in this period was organised by Solomon Nikritin and Sergey Luchishkin under the name of the Projectionists. The work of the Projectionists' theatre troupe, which constituted part of their work, has been mentioned already.[12] In art, the other principal members were Alexandr Labas, Z. Komissarenko, Mikhail Plaskin, Kliment Redko, Nikolay Tryaskin and Alexandr Tyshler.[13] Highly conceptual in character, the work of the Projectionists was allied to the conviction that artists were not producers of industrial goods, but creators principally of psychological entities such as intentions, plans, conceptions and designs for experiments. The manufacture of actual objects, they urged, was the business of engineers and manufacturing experts – an objection clearly aimed at the Productivists.

The Projectionists, like some recent Western conceptualists, still made objects for display, even though those objects stood at one remove from straightforward representation in the tradition of the old 'realists', as well as standing to the side of the abstract easel painting programmes of artists like Popova and Malevich.

The precise circumstances of the Projectionists' main exhibitions are bound up with the story of the Museum for Artistic Culture in Moscow which had been set up in 1919 under Kandinsky and

Rodchenko as a mass-educational facility in modern and contemporary art. In June 1921 the Museum had been closed for lack of funds and its holdings returned to Narkompros for storage. Then, in the autumn of 1922 it reopened at 52 Povarskaya Street, the present home of the Writers' Union of the USSR, under the directorship of an energetic VKhUTEMAS student, Pyotr Vilyams, and it was under his auspices that the Projectionists' first major exhibition was held there later in the year.

The Museum for Artistic Culture was instrumental in the fortunes of the Projectionists in more ways than one. In 1922 and 1923 it formed a focus for debate in the controversies which were animating the various cliques within VKhUTEMAS, as well as providing exhibiting space. Tyshler, Labas and Nikritin joined the council of the Museum, and their group came to form a majority. Exhibitions were staged of the work of Malevich, Miturich and Popova, and the large survey show 'Fifteen Years of "Leftist" Russian Art', as well as, subsequently, the work of a new group called the Society of Easel Painters (Obshchestvo khudozhnikov-stankovistov or OST). Lectures were given by the leading lights of the different theories, such as Malevich (on Suprematism), Nikritin (on Projectionism), and Shimanovich (on Miturich and Khlebnikov). The basic aim of the Museum at this stage was to evolve and strengthen new methods in art, and it did so without partisan adherence to particular tendencies, though traditional 'realists' like Abram Arkhipov were not included. The atmosphere of frenetic and mostly good-natured debate is suggested by a recent Soviet history of the period:

> Young artists . . . would gather in Vilyams' room to argue and to discuss not only their practical domestic problems but also the problems of art. These meetings would carry on in the Museum's galleries, against the background of the pictures collected there, giving rise to endless arguments.[14]

14. Kostin, *OST*, p 21.

Intellectual debate was often exchanged for physical sparring. As Luchishkin, who was present, reminisces,

> Tired of waging a war of words, we often got the boxing gloves out of the cupboard. In a moment, the gallery turned into a ring, where a three-round fight took place according to all the rules, with referee and seconds. Deineka (light-heavyweight) fought with Vilyams (middle-weight). Another pair succeeded them – Pimenov against Vyalov, etc. And then the whole assembly went to a debate with the Polytechnic Museum, or to the serial 'Hateful Homes' at the cinema in Little Dimitrovka Street.[15]

15. Cited by ibid., p 21.

In due course the work of the Projectionists came to official notice. OBMOKhU member Nikolay Denisofsky, who was at that time secretary to Shterenberg at Narkompros, used to come to VKhUTEMAS to convey reports on artistic policy, international links, and events in different parts of the Republic. Instructed by Shterenberg to relay to the VKhUTEMAS faculty the plans for the large exhibition in Berlin, Denisofsky asked to see what the VKhUTEMAS students were doing. The Projectionists' exhibition at the Museum for Artistic Culture was formed partly in response to this request. It was reviewed in *Izvestiya* in January 1923 by the influential Y.A. Tugenkhold, who treated it as a symptom of the debate then raging between the Productivists' denial of easel painting on the one hand and the many attempts being made to resume and modernise it on the other. 'The reaction against aestheticism', Tugenkhold maintained, 'against the picture in the gold frame which decorates the bourgeois drawing-room, has led to an opposite extreme . . . the denial of painting in general.' However the working class would hardly be satisfied only with industrial art, Tugenkhold maintained, and 'will scarcely agree that painting is a "purposeless" activity'. What was needed now was a 'holiday for the eyes', by which he meant 'the joys of colour, pictures and frescoes in public buildings, colours of great emotional strength . . . '. Thus in view of the 'menacing boycott of painting', if for no better reason, he 'welcomed . . . the effort [of the Projectionists] to return to an investigation of the function of colour'. Although these were only experimental works by young artists, nevertheless he felt they had already made 'a small step beyond the four walls of the laboratory, to meet the flesh and blood of the living world – a step forward, beyond the one-dimensional, purely beautifying Suprematism of Malevich or the colourless constructions of Tatlin'.[16] One consequence of the exhibition was that almost the entire body of work was included in the Berlin show. This acted as official encouragement to the group, and largely accounted for their increase in confidence during 1923 which led, in 1924, to many of them regrouping, under a different programme, within the major formation known as OST.

Although in 1922 and 1923 the Projectionists were still occupied by abstract and analytical questions, even at this time the most prominent members of the group were exploring a range of themes and ideas which, as Tugenkhold's review suggests, had no place in Constructivism, let alone in Productivism or Suprematism. Some artists within the group were developing a passionate interest in urban, technical and industrial themes, which they believed constituted more than anything else the substance of the new society. Some tackled apparently unrepresentable themes such as electricity or magnetism. Redko spent some two years attempting to elaborate a system known as 'Electro-Organism' (Figure 57), which gave priority to the important role electricity would play in restructuring society – presumably inspired by Lenin's famous slogan 'Communism equals the Soviets plus the electrification of the country'. Labas was interested in reproducing the sensations of a man flying in an aeroplane. This in turn extended to other hypothetical achievements of science, such as the conquest of space and the attainment of hitherto unheard-of speeds. Kudryashev, for example, though not a Projectionist, became fascinated by Tsiolkovsky's models for rocket flight, and turned his hand to the representation of the energies that could overcome gravity. 'Painting', he wrote in his *Declaration*,

> in that form it has assumed in my work, ceases to be an abstract colour-formal construction, and becomes a realistic expression of contemporary understanding of space . . . Space, volume, density and light – and

16. Kostin, *OST*, p 19.

material reality – here is the new essence, which spatial painting is establishing today.[17]

17. Cited by Kostin, *OST*, p 25.

Radio and telephone were other topics tackled by artists such as Vladimir Lyushin (Figure 58). It is hardly to be wondered at that the fetish of technology, manifest in its most extreme form at the Gastev institute, was also rampant in easel painting at a time when new scientific discoveries were being reported almost daily, not only from the laboratories of Soviet scientists but from all over the world.

The rapid and virtually complete re-orientation of the painting and sculpture faculties of the VKhUTEMAS during 1922 and 1923 met with an alarmed response from the INKhUK Constructivists. Writing in the fourth issue of the magazine *LEF* in 1923, a group which included Brik, Rodchenko, Stepanova, Popova and the Stenberg brothers complained that the 'ideological and organisational breakdown of VKhUTEMAS is an accomplished fact'. What they evidently meant was that the 'production' side of the institution, which they supported, had dwindled to an insignificant fraction of the whole and seemed to be receiving less support with each day that passed. In line with the generally strident tone of the *LEF* editorship, the article probably exaggerates when it says that 'the production faculties are empty' and that 'the machines are being sold off'.[18] The authors say that the Basic Division, where the preliminary training of artists and designers was given, 'is completely in the hands of the "purists", easel painters from the Wanderers to the Cézannists'. This, they allege, has had the result of cutting the work of the VKhUTEMAS off from ideological and practical tasks, 'and from the future of proletarian culture'. Individual painting and sculpture studios

18. This and the following quotations are from O. Brik and others, 'Razval VKhUTEMASa. Dokladnaya zapiska o polozhenii vyshikh khudozhestvenno-tekhnicheskikh masterskikh', *LEF*, no 4, 1923, p 27; Lodder, *Russian Constructivism*, p 121.

for second and third rate artists and easel painters are blossoming luxuriously . . . there is no talk about production. There is no whiff of any kind of social task. No posters, social satire, or grotesque depictions of everyday life – only timeless, spaceless, Party-less, 'sacred' painting and sculpture, with landscapes, still lives and naked models.

Figure 57
K. Redko, *The Factory*, 1922

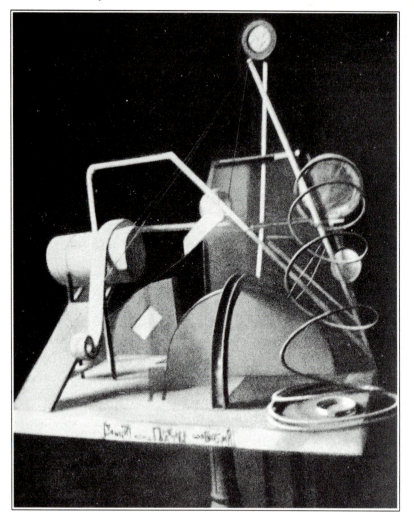

Figure 58
V. Lyushin, *Station for interplanetary communication*, 1922 (photo: V. Kostin, *OST*, 1976)

A series of recommendations follows for 'abolishing mysticism and handicraft', 'expanding the production side', 'establishing the teaching of the social forms of Fine Art', and 'linking the VKhUTEMAS with centres of the state economy and political education' – this last clause intended to bring official Party patronage to the Productivist viewpoint. The name 'engineer-artist' would be reserved for graduates in production.

Yet it is by no means clear that the Party were in a position to listen to these demands in 1923, even if they had wanted to. Lenin was now in poor health, and was unlikely to intervene. Trotsky was unsympathetic to Constructivism – as his *Literature and Revolution* of that summer was to show – and made no particular bid to support production art, even though he regarded the economic recovery of the country as being of paramount importance. I know of no statements by other Party leaders that give any kind of credence to the programme then being pursued by the VKhUTEMAS Productivists.

At the same time there are no statements that overtly condemn the Productivist viewpoint. It is probably safer to assume that the

VKhUTEMAS was to a significant degree left to its own devices in 1922 and the beginning of 1923, on the understanding that it would hold its debates in its own manner. There must have been, and were, literally dozens of hastily-formed allegiances, dignified by a name and a 'platform', which disappeared almost as quickly as they had arisen. In all likelihood there was grudging acceptance by the government that art and design required freedom of invention, exhibition and publication. At least, one is aware of no decrees on the arts during these years that specifically guided artistic activity, beyond the ambiguous resolution 'On Questions of Propaganda, the Press and Agitation' that has already been mentioned. The Party was unlikely to give support for overt mysticism in art at a time when it was waging war against religion; but beyond that there were few enough directions to follow. At least the 'gradualist' members of the leadership must have thought so. Had the Party not itself set up the SVOMAS in 1918 to give free rein to different contending groups? Had they not encouraged individuals to choose their own path and to determine what they were to be taught, and by whom? Was not this policy part and parcel of the struggle against archaic, Tsarist institutions with their rigid regulations and their hierarchic structures, not to mention their irrelevant themes and subjects and their fawning regard for the life of the aristocracy and the Court? And was not Lenin still very much amongst them – in spite of his now faltering health – the Lenin who had always pressed for a robust, communist culture that was nevertheless free of communist boasting, and free of exaggerated claims that a single stylistic direction could win a place as the 'true' or 'only' communist art? Of course, this 'freedom' should never be equated with that bourgeois freedom which allowed anything to be art if the artist called it so. At the very least, art had to reflect and consolidate the achievement of the Proletariat in its victory of October. And the spirit of October must remain the motive force of all cultural work. But beyond this it was difficult and probably inadvisable to say.

Yet there is no escaping the fact that – as the revival of 'realist' easel painting after 1922 was already demonstrating – simultaneously there were other opinions gaining currency within the Party to the effect that 'left' art could no longer command universal support, whether it was taking leave of the studio in favour of the shop floor or not. Here too Lenin's example was capable of being used. Had he not inveighed against those who would forsake the forms of the past, as well as against the 'infantile leftists' who indulged in pretentious formulations and wilful experimentation for its own sake? (These proscriptions, at least, could be read into his incursions against Mayakovsky's verse.) Did his support for the 'bourgeois specialists' not in effect suggest a different solution to the country's need for better design and more efficient technology – one that would to a significant extent marginalise the efforts of the Productivists? Could not his example be used in support of a traditionalist, representational art?

Inside the VKhUTEMAS itself the position quickly developed into one of confrontation between opposing interests rather than disinterested academic and theoretical debate. Following the acrimonious exchanges between the LEF group, who represented the anti-painting faction, and the painters, whose increasing confidence was visible for all to see, there arose towards the end of 1923 an idea to hold a 'discussional' exhibition which would display examples of the work of the rival groups and hence promote discussion by deed as much as by word. The nature and consequences of this exhibition will be discussed in the context of the quickly changing atmosphere of the post-1924 period, in Volume Two.

The Founding of AKhRR

But first, we must go back one step. Several factors contributed to the revival, or continuation, of easel painting around 1922. One was that by the end of 1921 and the beginning of 1922 the 'left' groups within VKhUTEMAS and INKhUK, and especially the Constructivist formation within INKhUK, had taken up a defiant position to the effect that 'art' as previously understood was irrelevant to the needs of the new state and should be peremptorily abandoned. This 'revolutionary' position was also applied to the materials of art. Thus paint and canvas were said to have belonged to the bourgeois past, whereas metal, wire and steel were to be treated as materials of the present. In splitting themselves off from all types of easel painting, therefore, supporters of the Productivist tendency within Constructivism in effect left the field relatively free for their opponents. They did not foresee, or else ignored, the fact that easel painters and sculptors would continue to work in a variety of traditional and modern ways.[1]

Another factor was that many people could not see the relevance of Futurist and 'avant-garde' approaches to art in a society that was not only struggling to survive economically and materially, but was trying to consolidate some far-reaching and very recently conceived social and economic changes, with all the disruption and unfamiliarity that this would cause. Lenin's and Lunacharsky's views on the prospects of the 'avant-garde' have already been noted. Another important factor at the end of 1920 and throughout the first months of 1921 was the mood of war-weariness which was still sweeping the country. These were widely considered to be months of reconstruction rather than frantic advance; a time of sober reassessment rather than of continued revolutionary zeal and turbulent overthrowing of the existing order. Further, doubts about the impracticality of 'Futurist' art had been expressed by young men, not exclusively by older artists already set in their ways: the reaction against 'left' art was thus by no means exclusively a generational reaction by fathers against their sons. And we should remember too the wider European context of reaction to experimental art in the early 1920s. This was not a uniquely Soviet phenomenon, but one with far wider causation and origins.

The circumstances of the Soviet reaction are still, in part, unique. For example, it must be borne in mind that an older generation of artists could still remember the revolutionary ideals of the populist

1. As Brik recognised in his paper 'What are Artists to do?' of April 1922, 'the grouping of artists is now such that right and left are being strengthened, the middle is collapsing . . .'; quoted in Lodder, *Russian Constructivism*, p 100.

movement of the 1860s and 1870s. Indeed many members of this generation were still painting, albeit no longer with the same attachment to populist ideals as before. Like millions of others, the surviving artists of the Peredvizhniki had not initially responded to the Revolution of 1917, and in many cases had gone into hiding; yet they continued to work and to look for patronage. They exhibited in some of the mixed exhibitions sponsored by Narkompros, and despite their official disfavour managed to retain enough organising ability to plan a few of their own exhibitions. However, it was the 47th Exhibition, in the early months of 1922 – the first Peredvizhniki group showing since 1917 – that was to provide the spark for a veritable burgeoning of 'realistic' easel art.

Fifty-four artists took part in this exhibition, which opened on 20 February 1922 and ran until the beginning of March. As presented by its catalogue, the programme of the exhibition was not revolutionary but populist. It reminded its readers that the Association of Travelling Art Exhibitions had begun its work 'under the spontaneous influence of the ideas of the populist movement, [and that] the first task of the Association was to give the people a living, intelligible art which faithfully reflected their life'.[2] It proceeded to remind its readers that 'in this work, the Association not infrequently suffered persecution at the hands of the old power'. (This was true in its early days, but hardly at all after 1890.) Now, as well as hoping to endear itself to a new revolutionary constituency, the Association claimed that the 47th Exhibition 'coincides with the final consolidation of worker-peasant power'; that the Association 'now considers it necessary to hoist its banner in order to come closer to fulfilling the precepts of its founders', which was 'to reflect with documentary accuracy, in genre, portrait and landscape, the life of contemporary Russia, and to depict the whole working life in its multi-faceted national character'.[3] The Association remained adamant that it would continue to strive to have its shows transported 'to the deepest corners of Russia'; and ended by appealing to 'all the forces of youth who are sympathetic' to 'realism' to come and support the continuation and development of its programme. It would, it added, be sure to attain a definite place among the 'diverse currents' of contemporary painting.[4]

For their exhibition, the artists of the Association of Travelling Art Exhibitions evidently attempted to bring their 'realism' up to date by giving to it themes of revolutionary life, both from 1905 and 1917. But many of the paintings gave merely anecdotal accounts of striking workers, hungry families, and revolutionary deeds. By all accounts the show suffered critically from its backward-looking appearance. Although even an ardent Futurist like Nikolay Punin had admitted that Peredvizhniki-style 'realism' had tremendous popular appeal despite its 'coarse, naive' qualities,[5] the show was not even a success with those who waited for the demise of Futurism. 'This is not the realism we were waiting for after the liquidation of Futurism,' wrote D. Melnikov in *Tvorchestvo*.[6] The poet Sergey Gorodetsky, writing in *Izvestiya*, confessed that the Peredvizhniki had undergone a massive decline since the 1890s, having fallen under the influence of various fashionable intellectual tendencies and having made countless

2. *Katalog 47-oi vystavki kartin v tsentralnom dome prosveshcheniya i iskusstvo*, Moscow, 1922; reprinted as 'Association of Travelling Exhibitions, declaration of 20 February 1922', V. N. Perelman (ed), *Borba za realizm: v izobrazitelnom iskusstve 20kh godov: Materiali, dokumenti, vospominaniya*, Moscow, 1962 (hereafter *Borba za realizm*), p 103.

3. Katalog, *Borba za realizm*, p 103.

4. Ibid., p 103.

5. N. Punin, 'Proletarskoe iskusstvo', *Iskusstvo kommuny*, no 19, 13 April 1919, p 1; Valkenier, *Russian Realist Art: The Peredvizhniki and their Tradition*, Ardis, Ann Arbor, Michigan, 1977, p 146.

6. D. Melnikov, '47-ya Peredvizhnaya vystavka', *Tvorchestvo*, no 1–4, 1922, pp 70–2; Valkenier, *Russian Realist Art*, 149.

concessions to 'petty-bourgeois taste'. Equally, its best artists such as Repin 'had suffered from a tendency to mysticism'. The majority had even shown sympathy for the feelings of the disappearing landed class: 'There appeared in Peredvizhniki art a sickly sweetness in its depiction of the countryside', which in turn reflected the decay of populism. Only 'a few artists such as Kasatkin' had continued to depict working life.[7] If the present-day Peredvizhniki wanted to dispel the suspicions aroused by their new declaration, said Gorodetsky, they would have 'first of all to work on themselves, to liberate themselves from the heavy ballast they have been burdened with for the last decade of the old order, and which persists today'. The works of Baksheev, Bakhtin, Kelin, Korin, Korytin, Maksench, Milorado-vich, Makovsky and Savitsky are a reflection only of the past, and the distant past at that. 'It's all 1890s,' moaned Gorodetsky, 'and in Makovsky's case the 1880s. It's all Turgenevism, the weeping of the ruined estates.' The perspective adopted (for example in Medvedev) was 'that of the landowner, watching the workers from his porch'. Only in Kasatkin and Pavel Radimov were these deficiencies over-come:

> The painter of the miners and of the 1905 revolution, Kasatkin, in his severe, spartan manner gives us truthful pictures of working life. Radi-mov, who is not entirely free of the old feeling, in several studies of hunger and of the Kazan tartars, does achieve greater power. This method of realism, at a time of a rising tide in the forces of youth, and on condition of technical improvement, may lead the Association of Travelling Art Exhibitions to great and useful work . . . but a condition of this is a persistent study of the life and existence of our working and peasant class.[8]

A significant point made by Gorodetsky was that the Revolution, until now, had gone largely undepicted in art – which was essentially true. The new Republic cannot afford to ignore such artists, he suggested, particularly if they can show themselves capable of scientific (as opposed to sentimental) landscape, the empirical study, the accurate portrait. Such distinctions would have to be drawn. The Peredvizhniki, who, at least to judge from their catalogue declaration appeared to have begun to feel the demands of the present,

> can now take up the necessary work. Those among them who prove the strongest will perhaps be the initiators of an authentic revival of the Travelling Art Exhibition idea, no more on the soil of populism, however, but based on the scientific world-view of the working class.[9]

Gorodetsky's words, in one sense, were already coming true. The week before the publication of his report, on 4 March 1922, a critical discussion of the Peredvizhniki's 47th Exhibition had been held, following which a new society had been established under the leader-ship of the poet and artist Pavel Radimov, entitled the Association of Artists Studying Revolutionary Life, which declared its intention to distance itself from the remnants of the older Peredvizhniki. This Association contained, besides Radimov himself, Kasatkin, Arkhi-pov, Malyutin (Figure 59) and Yuon from the older generation; with Grigoriev, Katsman and a group of younger artists such as Nikolai

7. S. Gorodetsky, '47-ya Peredvizhnaya vystavka' (47th Exhibition of the Travel-ling Art Association), *Izvestiya*, no 58, 1497, 12 March 1922, *Borba za realizm*, p 104.

8. Ibid., p 104.

9. Ibid., p 104.

Figure 59
S. V. Malyutin, *The Agitator*, 1923

Kotov, Vasily Zhuralev, Pyotr Shukhmin, Boris Yakovlev and Pyotr Kiselis, altogether totalling 25 members. The group changed its name to Society of Artists of Revolutionary Russia, and changed it again (on 13 May 1922) to become the Association of Artists of Revolutionary Russia (Assotsiatsiya khudozhnikov revolyutsionnoi Rossii or AKhRR). By this time the exhibition which is normally reckoned to be AKhRR's first, namely the 'Exhibition by Artists of the Realist Direction in Aid of the Starving People of the Volga Region', had opened in Moscow on 1 May 1922.[10] Throughout the remainder of the 1920s AKhRR was to become the largest and most influential society devoting itself to easel painting and sculpture in a 'realist' style, and the extent and nature of its political support was to have an impact upon the fortunes of every other artistic group bar none.

The aims of AKhRR were formally declared in the catalogue to its second Moscow Exhibition of June–July 1922, 'Exhibition of Studies, Sketches, Drawings and Graphics from the Life and Customs of the Workers' and Peasants' Red Army'. The exhibition contained 166 works by 40 artists, and apart from the Fifth Exhibition of 1923 was the smallest of all AKhRR's Moscow shows. Its brief 'Declaration' however contains the beginnings of a revised and updated vocabulary for 'realist' art. The relationship of AKhRR to tradition was complex; certainly it was not quite the 'copy' of nineteenth-century art that its detractors have made out. In fact the Peredvizhniki are not even mentioned in the Declaration's claim that AKhRR now represented, 'artistically and documentarily, the revolutionary impulse of this great movement of history', that is the October Revolution and its aftermath.[11] The Revolution, it said, 'in liberating the forces of the people, has aroused the consciousness of the masses and of artists – the spokesmen of the people's spiritual life'. The old art groups existing before the Revolution 'have lost their meaning . . . and continue to exist merely as circles of people linked together by personal connections, devoid of any ideological basis or content' – presumably a reference to the Peredvizhniki. Nevertheless AKhRR's 'Declaration' took over one aspect of the Peredvizhniki's original programme when it described the task ahead as not merely an artistic one, nor necessarily a revolutionary one, but as 'a civic duty'. But in other respects its appeal was to a fundamentally new constituency. It committed itself wholeheartedly to 'the life of the Red Army, the workers, the peasants, the revolutionaries, the heroes of labour' whose activities it would now attempt to represent. This in itself is significant, because the Red Army was already becoming one of AKhRR's major patrons and supporters. And finally it introduced the concept of 'heroism' in both art and life: the Revolution, it declared, was a moment, a day, of heroism; 'and now we must reveal our artistic experiences in the monumental forms of the style of heroic realism'. This style, it suggested, was to be the foundation of 'the universal building of the art of the future, the art of a classless society', and would go far beyond those 'abstract concoctions which discredit our Revolution in the face of the international proletariat'.[12]

Much of the work in the exhibition was directly concerned with military events and personnel, painted in the same sober, 'documen-

10. Little appears to be known about this first exhibition. Although it is recorded in I. Gronsky and V. Perelman (eds), *Assotsiatsiya khudozhnikov revolyutsionnoi Rossii. Sbornik, vospominanii, statei, dokumentov*, Moscow, 1973 (hereafter *Assotsiatsiya khudozhnikov*, 1973), p 333 and elsewhere, its works are not listed in the exhaustive documentation which follows on pp 334–419. Whether or not this is because AKhRR had not yet been officially formed is unclear.

11. 'Deklaratsiya Assotsiatsii khudozhnikov revolyutsionnoi Rossii', June 1922; reprinted in Bowlt, *Russian Art of the Avant-Garde*, p 266.

12. 'Deklaratsiya', Bowlt, *Russian Art of the Avant-Garde*, pp 266–7.

tary' fashion that the Declaration had called for. Of those who exhibited more than one work were Yakov Bashilov, Alexandr Grigoriev, Matvey Zaitsev, Boris Vladimirsky and Evgeny Katsman (the latter showed only military portraits); Pyotr Kiselis (a total of 23 works including portraits of George Lansbury, the British Communist, and the German Spartacist leader Eugen Levine); Vladimir Krinsky ('Meeting', 'Red Guard', 'First of May' and others); E. Lvov ('Red Guard', 'By the Camp Fire', etc.); Konstantin Maksimov (military portraits); the president Pavel Radimov (15 paintings including 'In the Barracks, Reading', 'Red Guard' and 'Signal'); Nikolay Terpsikhorov, Pyotr Shukhmin, and Boris Yakovlev ('Buildings of the Staff College' and other works). Several of these artists were to become mainstays of AKhRR throughout the 1920s, although it is a curious fact that not all of the founding artists exhibited at all of the shows – Yuon, for example, did not show with any regularity until 1925.[13]

Predictably enough the critics were again divided. Supportive voices from N. Shcheketov, V. Lobanov and F. Roginskaya were drowned out by the complaints of the 'centre' and 'left', to the effect that AKhRR had revived a merely passive naturalism which had little or no 'heroism' in it; certainly not of the monumental sort. 'Belated Narodniki' was one charge levelled at them by the less friendly voices.

Other critics were torn between the laudable aims of AKhRR and what they saw as the inferior quality of its work. A. Nyurenberg, for example, wrote a review in *Pravda* in which he stated that the October Revolution was changing the entire life of the Soviet Union and had therefore to be reflected in culture. Painting, he said, was moving ahead of the other arts in its understanding of contemporary issues – something which the remnants of the bourgeois intelligentsia obviously could not do. This is why the work of AKhRR was to be welcomed: it was attempting to present 'a real picture of events and not an abstract fabrication'.[14] We are fully agreed, says Nyurenberg, that a 'style of heroic realism in monumental forms' – he quotes from AKhRR's own 'Declaration' – must be created now. But unfortunately the exhibition does not achieve this goal. There is not one seriously developed canvas, he complains. The portraits are for the most part painted carelessly. The difficult and heroic life of the Red Army is only occasionally captured by the AKhRR painters – in Malyavin's portrait of Lunacharsky,[15] in Yakovlev's and Katsman's drawings – but was otherwise all but missing. The canvasses of Bashilov and Radimov, he contends, 'are utterly undeveloped; this is raw material'.[16] What was wanted was more than just an ability to control 'emotional' qualities such as colour effects and vigorous handling; something comparable to the art of the French Revolution was called for, in which the idea of 'art for art's sake' was harmoniously merged with the spirit of 'revolutionary art'; in which the artist was nourished with the same spiritual food as political activists. This could still be sensed today in front of ancient canvasses in the Louvre, claimed Nyurenberg. Would Soviet Revolutionary art affect the public of the future in anything like the same way?

13. This information is continued in *Assotsiatsiya khudozhnikov*, 1973, pp 334–419. Yuon exhibited a single work in the first of two 1923 exhibitions: 'Red Army Parade'.

14. A. Nyurenberg, 'Vystavka "Zhizn i byt Krasnoi Armii"', *Pravda*, 2 July 1922; *Borba za realizm*, pp 123–4.

15. This was the only work shown by Malyavin; and apart from a single work shown in the third exhibition he does not figure in the AKhRR listings at all.

16. Nyurenberg, 'Vystavka', p 123.

But there were other factors which attended the Second Exhibition of AKhRR which indicated a new set of relationships between 'realist' and 'heroic' painting and the machinery of the Soviet state. The very decision to mount an exhibition on the life and customs of the Red Army, for example, by itself signified a new level of involvement in art by the military forces – an involvement which was to last for many decades.[17]

It is said that Kliment Voroshilov (Figure 60), himself an amateur artist, took an interest in the affairs of AKhRR from the very beginning, as did other military leaders. Radimov's own memoirs are helpful here. He tells us that 1922 was his first year in Moscow.

> I had a lot of plans, but a complete absence of cash ... In 1922, at the Fourth Congress of the Comintern, [November–December 1922] I made the acquaintance of K. E. Voroshilov and one day went to see him in his small room at the National Hotel to talk about the proposed Red Army Exhibition. I did a sketch painting of Voroshilov, and also of Budyonny, who was there at the same time. Comrade Budyonny jokingly commented that it was much easier to take part in a battle than to pose for a painting. On looking at the study I had done he became carried away, and, seizing the brush, corrected his portrait a little. I left the National Hotel inspired by the comradely conversation·I had had.[18]

The exhibition mentioned here is in fact AKhRR's Fourth, of 1923, also on the Red Army. But the anecdote is symptomatic nevertheless. Radimov relates how, in preparing for the Second Moscow Exhibition, he wrote to the Revolutionary Military Council asking for material assistance, which was given in the form of glass and canvas. The support of active military leaders who were also Party men must have seemed essential; despite Lunacharsky's evolving sympathy for their work AKhRR could not count upon the support of Narkompros, and patronage during the first years of NEP was not forthcoming from the private sector in any quantity. Beyond this, it is still unclear whether AKhRR itself or the military leaders initiated the relationship.

It has been customary in the West to spurn both the work of AKhRR and their military connections; yet such an attitude shows little understanding of the role played by the Red Army and Navy in early Soviet life and in the national consciousness. Back in the days of the October Revolution Lenin had urged the proletariat and the peasantry to arm themselves; had stressed, emphatically, that the Revolution would not succeed without such action. The Central Executive Committee VTsIK had proclaimed in 1918 that 'the Russian Soviet Republic must have a mighty army under the protection of which the reorganisation of society on a communistic basis can take place'.[19] Trotsky, as Commissar for War, had assembled a massive and efficient fighting force during the years of civil war, which had now emerged from battle victorious but exhausted; and with some justification these men and women regarded themselves, and were regarded by others, as heroes of the Soviet nation. Furthermore the language of militarisation had assumed an increasingly important function in the definition of many national tasks after 1918, and not

Figure 60
K. Voroshilov (photo: *David King*)

17. For a recent example see the large retrospective exhibition 'Guarding the Achievements of Socialism: A Commemoration of the 70th Anniversary of the Soviet Army', Manezh, Moscow, February/March 1988; reported by B. Taylor in 'Two Soviet Exhibitions', *Art Monthly*, April 1988, no 115, pp 8–9.

18. P. A. Radimov, 'Pervyi god AKhRR' (1964), in *Assotsiatsiya khudozhnikov*, p 101.

19. J. Bunyan, *Intervention, Civil War, and Communism in Russia: April–December 1918, Documents and Materials*, Johns Hopkins Press, Baltimore, Maryland, 1936, p 266.

only in regard to Trotsky's thesis of labour-militarisation. Discipline and strict allegiance to a work programme, or to the Party, were regarded as transferable qualities which, though embodied in the achievements of the Red Army, were applicable elsewhere. These might even be the terms on which the energies of the exhausted proletariat and peasantry could be revived.

Secondly, it should be remembered that the literary and artistic education of most Soviet citizens in 1922 was still alarmingly low, in very many cases virtually non-existent. Peasants still accounted for well over 80 per cent of the population and even the proletariat was largely taken from peasant stock. The gap between the sophistication of cosmopolitan intellectuals (among them the Futurists, Constructivists and so-called 'left' artists) and the mass of the population could scarcely have been wider.

Thirdly, it is important to realise that above the peasants and the proletariat a new class of officials and military men was being formed which was beginning to exercise a new kind of influence over artistic affairs, as well as over national life generally. How to describe this new class is very controversial. According to a sceptical analysis, the October Revolution had not in fact been won by workers and peasants, but by a closed group of professional revolutionaries who were intellectuals, former members of the bourgeoisie, and highly educated members of an international élite who had little in common with the mass of workers and peasants;[20] and it is at least arguable that this gap between the Party leadership and the broad mass of the public had helped generate an administrative stratum that was not internationally educated, whose habitat was the trade unions and the military organisations, and whose power in those quarters was considerable.

The very existence of this administrative class, military or otherwise, is not in serious doubt. Lenin himself placed great emphasis on administrative ability: 'We need people who are masters of administrative technique, who have political and economic experience, for the administration and construction of the state'.[21] And it is a fact that young communists came forward in considerable numbers after 1920 and 1921 gradually to take over administrative functions from the old guard of the Bolshevik Party. Inevitably they brought with them their aesthetic and cultural preferences. Inevitably too this organisational class had little sympathy for internationally-inspired 'avant-garde' art and tended to fall back upon a concept of simple, accessible 'realism' that had a Revolutionary or 'thematic' content. This relatively uneducated 'new' class also tended to look upon itself as the true heir to the Revolution, in contradistinction to the cosmopolitan Bolshevik old guard whose real allegiances were said to rest elsewhere – in European ideas and in European political philosophy. Certainly the aesthetic and cultural preferences of this new stratum cannot be separated from the cultural history of the period up to 1932. They were as much a part of Soviet reality as, say, Malevich or Tatlin believed themselves to be. And it is a fact of some importance that the naturalism of the AKhRR style, even if not of peasant origin, did much

20.   This is argued for example by M. Voslensky, *Nomenklatura: Anatomy of the Soviet Ruling Class*, Bodley Head, London, 1980, Chapters 1 and 2.

21.   Lenin, *Polnoe sobranie sochinenii*, Vol 40, p 222, Voslensky, *Nomenklatura*, p 42.

to rekindle interest in both culture and national life across a very wide constituency indeed.

The military authorities were so flattered and impressed by the results of the Second AKhRR Exhibition that, despite the critical voices raised against it by the intelligentsia, they commissioned AKhRR to organise a more ambitious show for the fifth anniversary of the Red Army which was to take place in the following year.

Before that, however, a third AKhRR exhibition was staged in the autumn of 1922 entitled 'Life of the Workers', which was planned to coincide with the opening of the Fifth Congress of Trade Unions. With 208 works by 43 artists, it was particularly rich in portraits. There were also works by artists such as Boris Vladimirsky ('Dinner in the Leather Factory', 'Games in a Children's Holiday Camp', 'The Bogatir Factory'), Alexandr Grigoriev (portraits of cultural workers), Grigory Medvedev, Dmitry Melnikov, P. Pokarzhevsky and P. Radimov (portraits of trade union personnel). The most prolific exhibitors were the Peredvizhniki realist Nikolay Kasatkin, with 17 paintings, including 'Revolutionary with a Revolver in his Hands, defending Burning Documents', 'Unknown Victim of the Struggle for Freedom', 'The Spy's Last Journey', 35 studies of miners from the Donbass, 'The Poor Looking for Shelter in a Disused Mine', and others; and P. Radimov, with 24 works including 'Session of the VTsSPS' and 24 caricatures and cartoons.[22]

22. See *Assotsiatsiya khudozhnikov*, pp 334–419.

Once again the exhibition had to face the criticism that good intentions were more in evidence than successful works. In an article caustically entitled 'The Exhibition of Good Intentions', published in the magazine *Trud* (Labour), Y. Topolev quotes approvingly from the exhibition's catalogue to the effect that 'the civic duty of AKhRR was to capture in a documentary spirit the greatest moment in history . . .'; that 'the revolutionary day, the revolutionary moment, is a heroic day, a heroic moment, and [that] we must reveal in the documentary forms of the style of heroic realism our artistic experience of this day and moment'. And yet 'very slight and disappointingly paltry are the works by the authors of those intentions', Topolev says. He complains that instead of 'heroic realism' we in fact see a very humble naturalism, sometimes amounting to little more than conscientious sketching from nature. The portraits of the leading figures of VTsSPS (the All-Union Central Council of Trade Unions) are commendable in their way. But where, asks Topolev, is the working life of the proletariat in its refashioned form? Some things have changed, he says, whereas other things have stayed the same:

> Today's miner in the mines is using the same methods as before the revolution. So are the metalworker, the typesetter and the store-man. The new life and the revolutionary creativity that goes with it has not had any effect on the forms and machinery of work, only on the form of leadership, on socio-cultural life, and on the psychology of work, and this the Association [of Artists of Revolutionary Russia] has not touched on at all. They have sketched a row of workers at work, factory workshops, and labour in its various manifestations. But they have failed to show a single characteristic of the new revolutionary life of the workers; not a single workers' meeting or factory committee, not a single workers' school or

revolutionary holiday, etc. There is not a single work on which it would be possible to put the date 1922 . . . [23]

Nevertheless, he finishes, one must welcome such an exhibition, even if only for its good intentions.

A less discriminating and more militant report appeared under the signature of 'Baratov' in the journal *Bednota* (The Poor), which as well as championing the work of the AKhRR artists at the same time took the opportunity to ridicule modernist paintings for their distortions and 'inaccuracies'. Some modernists, Baratov wrote, are trying to flatter; but their paintings

> show a Red Army man with squinting eyes and a triangular nose, while a peasant is shown as almost some kind of monster . . . in a word it is an absurdity. The beauty, the grandeur of the worker-peasant cause, its newness in the history of mankind, goes completely unreflected in the concoctions of these scribblers and daubers.[24]

However the Revolution could not but awaken the creativity of the working masses in the field of fine arts, Baratov avers. Numerous great, truly proletarian and peasant verses have already been made. Now, the tasks of strengthening the artistic expression of the Revolution and its workers is coming to the boil, indeed 'must be stepped up'.[25] We must imprint in our paintings and in the artistic word all that has been undergone and all that will be done in the future, he says; we must 'depict life without the slightest element of fantasy or adornment', since

> neither the worker-revolutionary nor the peasant who has unthinkingly tilled the virgin soil of his fields for centuries on end, nor the Red Army man in his sandals and grey overcoat, has any need of embellishment. Quite simply, one must know and understand in order to depict.

Here, the Association of Artists of Revolutionary Russia were achieving significant work. They are depicting factory life of the past and present, Baratov says; they are sketching the workers and peasants in different work situations; and the spirit of unification signified by the very existence of the new Association is evidence of how 'the forces of youth are rising up, and even the old masters such as Kasatkin are joining them, masters who had worked for the Revolution but who before that were banned'. It is good, says Baratov, to see these once forbidden works on show.[26]

In view of this impressive upsurge in 'realistic' proletarian art, Baratov continues, it is nevertheless regrettable that there are scarcely any artistic materials to work with; no paint, no brushes, no canvas. And the same goes for money. Yet Baratov was able to report that the Soviet authorities had promised their support, and that, increasingly, artists who might otherwise have gone abroad were now able to work in their own country. Evidently Baratov and other guests had been taken round the exhibition by Alexandr Grigoriev, the Association's President, who had lamented the shortage of materials but had revealed that the Party had just appointed him to the Ministry of

23. I. Topolev, 'Vistavka blagikh namerenii', *Trud*, 21 October 1922; in *Assotsiatsiya khudozhnikov*, pp 196–8.

24. I have been unable to identify what Baratov is referring to here, or whether, as may be the case, he is creating merely imaginary descriptions of typical 'Futurist' art-works.

25. Baratov, 'Iskusstvo revolyutsii', *Bednota*, 1 October 1922; reprinted in *Assotsiatsiya khudozhnikov*, pp 194–6.

26. Baratov, 'Iskusstvo revolyutsii', p 195.

Foreign Trade 'in order to catch speculators'; and thus felt optimistic about the future. Most important, says Baratov, the Association's call for unification has already met with a 'warm response from all corners of the Republic'. In artistic terms, the central thing was that real life was being depicted – nothing more was being asked. On the question of quality Baratov suggests that 'if occasionally real life has been depicted unskillfully, then this is just a matter of time; the comrades are working and . . . their success is apparent'[27]; but even this caveat was not strictly necessary in view of the fine works by comrades Arzhennikov, Bashilov, Bogatov, Vladimirsky, Kostyanitsin, Lvov, Malyutin, Malyshko, Melkov, Meshkov, Perelman, Pokarzhevsky, Sviridov, Freshkov and others. These painters had succeeded in depicting different aspects of work in various factories. Even Kozlov, the typesetter of *Bednota*, was pictured at his machine. Portraits of figures in the trade union movement and the like, were also finely executed. 'Here', says Baratov, 'you see your real self and your life . . . we must wish the comrades of the Association every success.'

It is clear at any rate that the issue between Topolev and Baratov was decided not by the press but by the organisers of the exhibition. Group tours were provided for the delegates to the Trades Unions Congress, which proved so popular that the Congress bought the entire exhibition with its own funds and used the paintings and sculptures to set up a Museum of Labour, to which AKhRR artists were then invited to add new works. With patrons in both the Army and the Trade Unions, AKhRR now seemed destined to an existence substantially free of material and financial difficulties.

It must probably be admitted in retrospect that for many people – artists and spectators alike – the simple, unassuming style of the paintings of the early AKhRR exhibitions provided an attractive way out of the uncertainties of the 'avant-garde', while at the same time meeting an identifiable need for an easily intelligible style, comprehensible even to the peasantry in far-flung districts. An experience recorded by the ardent AKhRR member A. A. Volter is perhaps instructive in this context. Volter explains in his reminiscences how, having suffered exile and imprisonment under the Tsars followed by military action in the Civil War, he was able to return to painting only towards the end of the war. Sent to Moscow by the Glavkusstprom section of VSNKh in May 1920 to investigate the possibilities of exporting works of art abroad, he recalls finding the debates in the Narkompros journals *Izobrazitelnoe isskustvo* and *Iskusstvo kommuny* dominated by the cries of 'formalists' to do away with easel painting and develop an art of 'pure form'. Not only the Peredivzhniki but also Impressionist art were being roundly decried. Volter says he was 'surprised and alarmed' at the extent to which these voices had taken over.[28]

But Volter also tells us how AKhRR organised help for folk artists in the countryside. The icon painters of Palech, Msteri and Kholui were known to be in severe difficulties because, as he puts it, 'the Soviet people no longer needed their work'.[29] The leaders of the local village soviet regarded these people as 'aiders and abetters of a

27. In this instance Baratov refers to the exhibition as 'the second one' held by the comrades, which suggests that the May 1922 exhibition in aid of the starving people of the Volga region was not included by some authorities, even in 1922, as an AKhRR exhibition. See fn 10 above.

28. A. A. Volter, 'Kak i pachemu ya vstupil v AKhRR' (1965), *Assotsiatsiya khudozhnikov*, p 120.

29. Volter, 'Kak i pachemu ya vstupil v AKhRR', p 122.

religious cult, helping to spread obscurantism', and were sending them out into the fields to do heavy agricultural work. Volter himself arranged to receive some of the Palech artists at the Cottage Industry Museum in Moscow and was 'dazzled' by their technique. He told them that if they could forget their religious subject-matter and paint Russian fairy-tales and folk epics, they would be supported. Apparently to begin with they turned in yet more scenes of the Creation, of Adam in Paradise, etc., but slowly came round to Soviet and Revolutionary subject-matter. Kalinin took a hand in their support. They exhibited to enormous popular approval at the 'Workshop of Ancient Painting' at the 1923 'All-Union Agricultural Exhibition' in Moscow, began to exhibit their products at foreign exhibitions, and were soon released from their agricultural work. Palech products subsequently became known throughout the world.

Following its three initial exhibitions in Moscow in 1922, AKhRR's pattern of activity was continued throughout 1923, with the anniversary exhibition for the Red Army and a smaller show later in the year entitled 'Lenin's Corner' in which paintings were hung next to documents, photographs, newspapers and leaflets related to the history of the Revolution.[30]

The 'Red Army 1918–1923' exhibition was once again a tribute to the military achievements of the recent past, and relied upon the same cohort of artists as the previous year (Figures 48, 61 and 62), although with some new names such as B. Efimov, Boris Ioganson, Alexey

30. See H. Gassner and E. Gillen, *Zwischen Revolutionskunst und Sozialitischem Realismus*, p 268.

Figure 61
P. M. Shukhmin, *Showing the way*, 1923

Figure 62
V. N. Yakovlev, *Newspaper at the front*, 1923 (the headline says 'To arms!').

Kravchenko, Evgeny Lanceray, Boris Kustodiev, Vladimir Kuznet-sov, Isaak Mendelevich, Dmitry Moor, Nikolay Nikonov, Vasily Pshchenitsnikov and Konstantin Yuon, all of whom were to exhibit regularly from this date on. Once again, military commanders were shown round the exhibition, and on their recommendation the entire show was purchased by the Revolutionary Military Council to become the nucleus of the Museum of the Revolution in Moscow.[31]

By this time AKhRR had established itself decisively enough. Volter tells us of how the organisational base of AKhRR was quickly expanded after 1922. In 1923 he met the painter Pyotr Kiselis, and asked whether he could join AKhRR, by that time in its second year. At this stage AKhRR was based in temporary premises in the Bogoy-avlensky Monastery, and was still very short of cash. Volter was accepted by Radimov and Grigoriev, and was appointed to a special Party cell within AKhRR, of which he, Volter, immediately became the leader. This cell consisted of Grigoriev, Friedrich Lecht, Evgeny Lvov, N. N. Maslennikov, Georgy Ryazhsky and Y. Malotsislennost. They in turn were instrumental in raising the organisational and financial level of the organisation by forming a Publishing Group (under Perelman), a Production Bureau for manufacturing prints of works of art (under Volter), and eventually an Exhibition Bureau (1923) and an Information Bureau (1925).

The question of AKhRR's significance in its early years is obviously still controversial. It is probably not adequate to dismiss these artists

31. For this information see Valkenier, *Russian Realist Art*, p 215 n 51.

as 'conservatives' who were ranged against the better-known experimenters of the 'left'. By 1922 and 1923 the 'left' had abandoned representation and were in the process of abandoning painting; there was a vacuum to fill. The Party too was generally sympathetic towards a link with the past, which meant that, for better or worse, an 'official' aesthetic was in the process of being formed which at the same time could make some claim to being based in 'popular' opinion.

For AKhRR this 'link with the past' became the crucial complexity. For though Radimov and his group had declared themselves in opposition to the Peredvizhniki manner, it soon became clear that the Peredvizhniki would supply the model on which most official rhetoric on the visual arts would be based. The official view of this relationship is well illustrated by the honours accorded to Kasatkin. He had been instrumental in organising the Museum of Trade Unions at the time of the Third AKhRR Exhibition, and his studies of miners and Revolutionary agitators were widely considered to set a standard to which the new Association should aspire (Figure 63).[32] Therefore

32. See P. Radimov, 'Pervyi god AKhRR' (1964), *Assotsiatsiya khudozhnikov*, p 102.

Figure 63
N. A. Kasatkin, *Miners Changing Shift*, 1923

the Association appealed to VTsIK to have Kasatkin made a People's Artist of the Republic. (At 64 he was a 'senior' figure among artists of that milieu.) The request was granted, and Lunacharsky made a lengthy speech at the ceremony on 9 May 1923 in which he covered a wide range of theoretical issues.

The speech represents, in fact, an important step in Lunacharsky's gradual departure from the even-handed support he had previously given to different groups, towards a new measure of support for 'realism' of a certain kind. Lunacharsky allows, of course, that the artist-fabricator working in industry, no less than the architect manipulating new forms, is engaged in a 'profoundly social art', one that will have dramatic effects on the environment as a whole – he says that the state 'cannot be indifferent to this'. The work of Soviet folk-artists, too, could prove valuable by 'exerting a certain influence on our balance of trade', says Lunacharsky, notwithstanding the fact that enthusiasm for the art industry 'must have its boundaries'.[33]

But Lunacharsky reserves his real energies for demarcating the line of difference between the modernists and the 'realists' such as Kasatkin and his colleagues. He is now scathing about the modernists as never before. Artists may have the theoretical right to solve formal problems, he concedes; yet standing immediately behind the Formalists there existed a class who are thinking 'not about restructuring life, but merely about observing it'. This is a 'bourgeois attitude', he says, and has a deleterious effect upon young minds. Cubism is an example:

> The basic idea of Cubism is to construct the data of nature in the manner of a crystal, to give it logicality, order and principle. Hence the leaning towards geometricization. Here, human orderliness is set over against the order of nature . . . In this there is only a sign of the recently intensified instinct of the bourgeoisie to plan and to organise its preconceptions. Yet such a metaphysical art cannot alter the appearance of the world.

Cubism is merely a 'fricassee of actuality and metaphor which cannot change nature', Lunacharsky maintains; and in any case is handled in a chancy, arbitrary manner by the Cubists themselves. Bourgeois art, he says, having lost its way, 'now takes a stone for bread'.[34]

One begins to sense Lunacharsky's real excitement at AKhRR's proximity to the Peredvizhniki when we hear him openly extol the virtues of 'themes', 'ideas', even tendentiousness in art. Yet his argument is that the most powerfully tendentious art will rise above tendentiousness. At the highest level the artist may subscribe to the cause of Marxism as it were subconsciously, and may imbue his work with Marxist ideas by semi-conscious creative work. The essence of the matter is that the proletariat cannot remain indifferent to art, any more than they can remain indifferent to the social transformation which is taking place throughout the world. 'What grandeur there is here!' says Lunacharsky,

> what opportunities to influence the flow of events by means of the elements of art . . . acting specifically upon the emotions and will of the people. *This* is the sort of art that I call agitational. And I would like artists coming up from the working class to have an effect upon present and future society . . . such an artist must be a realist.[35]

Still, Lunacharsky chooses his words carefully. He proposes, for example, that although art must take its language 'from the depths of reality', it must go further, breaking if necessary with what exists outside of us, for, he implies, *merely* providing a mirror of that reality is not enough. Naturally the modernist idea of a painting as a 'world

33. Lunacharsky, 'Iskusstvo i rabochii klass', 3 May 1923. *Assotsiatsiya khudozhnikov*, pp 255–9, from which these quotations are taken.

34. Lunacharsky, 'Iskusstvo i rabochii klass', p 258.

35. Ibid., p 257.

in itself' is of no value. 'The main thing', says Lunacharsky, 'is to overcome a revulsion to themes and subjects in art.' And here it is the idea that counts; it must be such as to 'organise a whole series of previously determined moments of experience of the spectator' and in this way 'ignite the soul of every person who sees it . . . As the old Beethoven said about music: we wrote ideological things'.

This emphasis on 'ideas' in art leads Lunacharsky to the Peredivzhniki, and finally to Kasatkin. The Peredvizhniki achieved a high point in art by laying down a counterbalance to power and capital, Lunacharsky says. Kasatkin, for his part, like Demyan Bedny, 'knows what to say to the worker, to the peasant, and to the Red Army soldier . . . from him [Kasatkin] we must learn a stern, heroic, realism'. He was perhaps the first, suggests Lunacharsky, to pay special attention to the proletariat: 'this artist is close to the working class'. Finally, Lunacharsky appeals to the assembled company with these words: 'whether you have the same language as Kasatkin had, and what you say with it, thus will be judged your proximity to the front ranks of humanity'. The will of the working class places the greatest hope in artists who bear three things principally in mind: 'a maximally intelligible language, the presence of deep, living experience, and an attempt to penetrate the inner world of the people, not in its backward layers, but in its front ranks, in its Communist Party'.[36]

36. Lunacharsky, 'Iskusstvo i rabochii klass', p 259.

The speech is worth quoting at length because it indicates the availability of new arguments for 'realism' at a relatively early date. A striking departure from the Proletkult emphasis on agitation is found in Lunacharsky's repeated insistence upon the emotional function of art, its origins in 'deep, living, experience' and its organising effect upon the will and the intellect of the people. There is the idea too that 'realism' must function on the level of ideas rather than as 'imitation' or 'reflection'. There is the explicit association of modernism with the bourgeoisie. And then there is a new (for Lunacharsky) insistence on a link between art and the Party, the proletariat's leading cadre. 'The inner consonance between the working people and the Party', says Lunacharsky, 'in spite of many sufferings and trials', is what will 'stand as guarantee that an art which answers to the Party will answer to the working people as well.'

And what of NEP, in Lunacharsky's eyes? He admits that NEP creates an external, extrinsic dependence on the much reviled NEP-man, the speculators and the profiteers. He admits too that it offers a small element of support to artistic conservatism. But it cannot divert real artists, says Lunacharsky, who know that ultimately the master is not the NEP-people but the working class.

Such distinctions are finely judged, and represent Lunacharsky at perhaps his theoretical best; conversant with the ideological dilemmas of the day yet capable nevertheless of laying down support for a specific artist and a specific group with considerable conviction. It is impossible to say with certainty whether Lunacharsky was being led in 1923 by the already nascent AKhRR ideology, by the military chiefs who stood behind it, or by a section of the Party in its artistic leanings – or whether he was leading them. In giving some weight to the former possibility we do not necessarily call into question

Lunacharsky's probity or his judgement on art. In supporting AKhRR
he was wrestling with a dilemma which no one could apparently
solve. His brief for 'realism' was not after all a simple one; and he
clearly believed that the best of AKhRR's artists were coming close to
fulfilling its terms. In this, he remained remarkably consistent for
most of the rest of the decade.

He also appears to have been trying to consolidate the platform on
which he and Lenin seemed agreed: that art should be anchored in
the past, while it should organise the experience of the masses for the
future. Thus by the end of 1922 AKhRR had become something of a
touchstone for 'official' revolutionary opinion and a guiding light for
a whole generation of younger communists, in a context where
'conservative' and 'avant-garde' were terms that were quickly losing
their established connotations. In any case, in 1923 there was precious
little remaining of 'leftist' art, and what there was was out of harmony
with the times. AKhRR, on the other hand, by dint of organising
exhibitions, publishing brochures, catalogues, reproductions and
placards, and aided by an influential Party cell, was growing rapidly
from a fledgling art group to becoming the central artistic and exhibition society of the decade. Some version of 'realism' would be the
artistic signature tune of the Soviet Communist Party for many years
to come.

LEF and the Vision of Utopia

Some of the above may help to set into perspective the aspirations
and achievements of 'left' artists and theorists in the years after the
end of the Civil War. The split within the Constructivist group at
INKhUK which resulted in the departure of Kandinsky at the beginning of 1921, the ousting of the other easel painters by the autumn of
1921, and the decision to turn to a Productivist programme which
attempted to link art with industry and design, had meant, ironically,
that the 'left' had become isolated, and that the very easel artists
whom the 'left' had decried were able to stage a comeback and make
at least a credible claim to represent the artistic policy of the new state.

However, if the intensification of 'left' positions in art had led to a
fragmentation of the ideological spectrum, it was still considered
imperative by the theoretical writers of the 'avant-garde' to expound
and consolidate their own positions as firmly and convincingly as
possible. The 'left' thesis that easel painting was finished, that art
must merge with work, and that creation must merge with production, was still supported from a number of viewpoints after 1922.
Journals like *Krasnaya nov* (Red Virgin Soil), *Pechat i revolyutsiya* (Press
and Revolution), *Zhizn iskusstva* (Life of Art) and *Gorn* (Furnace), as
well as *Pravda* and eventually *LEF*, carried repeated denunciations of
bourgeois aesthetic attitudes as the 'left' perceived them, and issued
clarion calls for a new art of utility, modernity and practical efficiency.

Nikolay Tarabukin, in his important book *From the Easel to the
Machine*, published in 1923, defended a form of 'realism' which was
intentionally very different from the programme adopted by AKhRR.

The progress of art since Impressionism had been one of gradual purification of means from the ideological 'content' of painting, said Tarabukin. Technique had separated itself from subject-matter and had become important in itself. It stood for material reality, for construction. 'Realism' in the new sense, Tarabukin wrote, is to be distinguished from naturalism, which is 'one of the forms of realism, the most primitive and naive in its expression'. He continues:

> Modern aesthetic understanding of realism has moved from the subject to the form of the work. The copying of reality is no longer the motive of realistic striving, but, on the contrary, reality has ceased to bear any relationship to the stimulus of creativity

1. N. Tarabukin, *Ot molberta k mashine* (From the Easel to the Machine), Moscow, 1923 (French edition, *Le Dernier Tableau*, Paris 1972), pp 7, 9; Lodder, *Russian Constructivism*, p 103–4.

by which he implied that the artist 'does not reproduce reality but presents an object as an end in itself'.[1] The argument here must be distinguished from that of later Western formalists who argued that the progress of art consisted in its self-purification, since Tarabukin was proposing that Cubism, Futurism and other modern easel painting movements had in effect come up against the limits of painting, not that they were its twentieth-century apogee. Since painting was basically a figurative art, it had no function under the total separation of subject-matter from technique. Rather than revert to figurative painting on the easel, Tarabukin advocated a leap into three dimensions and the presentation of real materials in real space as the new art of the Soviet era.

The Constructivists themselves had only reached a partial solution to this problem, Tarabukin argued. Although they adhered to the basic idea of three-dimensional construction, they did not really have the skill or the technical knowledge to build useful, functional things. Instead, they idealised the engineering profession, but ended up only copying or mimicking its typical structures. For all their sound criticisms of bourgeois art and especially paint and canvas, they remained, for all that, aesthetes and champions of 'pure' art. Their work in this respect was comparable to the absurdities of the Suprematists.[2]

2. N. Tarabukin, *Dernier Tableau*, p 11.

In contrast, Tarabukin believed Constructivism could only be of benefit if it forged a real liaison with industry and with production. Artists would therefore need a technical training to help them out of their dilletantism – but the pity was that this seemed foreign to their nature, and in any case there was no time. In any case artists should not delude themselves that they could bring about a transformation of production without a corresponding (and probably independent) revival of industrial culture and the culture of the machine, Tarabukin asserted.

The irony is that Tarabukin's criticisms of the Constructivist programme were close to those that would have been, and occasionally were, expressed by the Bolshevik Party leadership. For the Party, the revival of industry was paramount; yet by 1922 and 1923 it was clear that Constructivism was having little impact on anything beyond graphics and the theatre. Lenin himself, though by now in failing health, was impatient with experimentation which did not result in

immediate and tangible improvements. Lunacharsky, too, was scathing about the Constructivists' flirtation with industry. Brik and his
colleagues (he said) believed

> that all functions of human society will be reduced to mechanical produc-
> tion, to the production of mechanically, at best physiologically helpful
> objects or even (it seems he doesn't say this but in actual fact this idea
> dominates the Constructivists in everything) in the mimicry of the ma-
> chine . . . Tatlin mimics the machine, but this is a machine on which it is
> impossible to work. This is peculiarly ape-like technicism.

The Constructivists were naive: 'They play at being engineers', Lunacharsky alleged, 'but they don't know as much of the essence of
machinery as a savage.'[3]

3. Lunacharsky 'Vstupitelnaya statya', in G. Kaizer, *Dramy*, Moscow–Lening-rad 1923; and 'Teatra RSFSR', *Pechat i revolyutsiya*, no 7, 1922; Lodder, *Russian Constructivism*, p 283 n 165.

A new journal, *LEF*, on the other hand, attempted to defend, after
1923, the Constructivist ideal of art in production, as well as present
a consolidated 'left front' in all the arts, against what must have
seemed like a tide of hostile opinion. In 1922 Mayakovsky had re-
quested permission of the Agit Section of the Central Committee to
publish a new journal. To his request he had appended a statement
of editorial aims: 'The extreme revolutionary movements in art', he
had said, 'do not yet have their own journal, particularly since official
organs like *Krasnaya nov* are not exclusively concerned with art and
devote little space to it', and had added 'we cannot obtain private
capital for the organisation of our journal since we are ideologically
a communist group.'[4] Mayakovsky's request was duly accepted and
forwarded to the state publishing house Gosizdat for implementation.

4. This quotation is from the rough draft of Mayakovsky's letter which ap-peard in O. Brik, 'Mayakovsky and the Literary Movements of 1917–30', *Screen*, Autumn 1974, Vol 15, no 3, p 70.

Founded in 1923, *LEF*'s editorial board consisted of Osip Brik and
Boris Kushner, late of *Art of the Commune*, Mayakovsky, Nikolay
Aseev, Nikolay Chuzhak and Sergey Tretyakov, as well as Boris
Arvatov, the theorist of Constructivism. Mayakovsky had stated that
the aims of *LEF* were to be

> (a) to find a communist direction for all forms of art, (b) to review the
> ideology and practice of so-called left art, rejecting its individualist dis-
> tortions and developing its valuable, communist aspects, (c) to carry out
> vigorous agit-work within production art . . . (d) to bring in the most
> revolutionary movements in art and serve as an *avant-garde* for both
> Russian and world art, (e) to familiarise the Russian workers' audience
> with the achievements of European art as represented not by its canonised
> and official figures, but by the young writers and artists who, while
> rejected by the European bourgeoisie, in themselves represent the begin-
> nings of a new proletarian culture . . . (g) to give examples of literary and
> artistic works not in order to indulge aesthetic tastes, but to indicate
> devices for the creation of effective agit works, and (h) to fight against
> decadence, against aesthetic mysticism, self-satisfied formalism and un-
> committed naturalism, for the affirmation of a partisan realism based on
> the use of the technical devices of all revolutionary schools of art.[5]

5. Mayakovsky's letter in Brik, 'Mayakovsky and the Literary Move-ments of 1917–30', *Screen*, Autumn 1974, p 70.

In its short incarnation from 1923 to 1925 *LEF* issued seven numbers,
and included writings of a broad-based and experimental character.
The Formalist Viktor Shklovsky contributed essays on Babel and
Pilnyak, and a theoretical article on the novel. The linguists

Figure 64
A. Rodchenko, cover to *LEF*, no. 1,
1923

6. These and following quotations are
from 'What is LEF Fighting For?' *Form*,
10, Cambridge, October 1969, pp 31–2.

7. 'What is LEF Fighting For?', p 32.

Tynyanov, Eikhenbaum and Tomashevsky published analyses of language and linguistic forms; Grigory Vinokur contributed a study of Futurism and language. Rodchenko and Mayakovsky designed some of the covers in the photo-montage manner (Figure 64).

The first issue of *LEF* in March 1923 contained a declamatory piece 'What is LEF fighting for?', written by the editorial board, in which they followed the familiar 'left' practice of giving a swift summary of the whole development of art in the immediately preceding period. For them the starting point was 1905. After 1905, they believed, reaction had set in, creating art in its own image – the Symbolists, the Mystics, 'the petty bourgeois and the Philistines'.[6] Futurism on the other hand had opposed the war and had created a new art, and after the victory of 1917 had come to embrace both 'production-Futurists' and Constructivists; they had opposed Proletkult ('these writers . . . remained complete reactionaries') and had created the paper *Art of the Commune* and consolidated this in the Tvorchestvo (Creation) group in the Far East and in Siberia. Then 'academicians' had begun to influence Narkompros, and there had begun 'the baiting of left art' which had resulted in the closing of *Art of the Commune*. Now, after war and hunger, *LEF* was able to 'demonstrate the panorama of art of the RSFSR, to set perspectives and to occupy our rightful place'. The editors summarised the position as they saw it as of 1 February 1923: 'prolet-art' had degenerated into trite writers expert only in bureaucratic prose and the ABC of politics, or, on the other hand, academicism. The 'latest' literature, such as Pilnyak and the Serapion Brotherhood, had diluted 'our devices' and larded them with Symbolism, fit for the new NEP audience. Minor figures like Alexey Tolstoy were 'already polishing up the white horse of his collected works ready for his triumphant entry into Moscow'. Finally, and in various corners, were the 'individual 'lefts', INKhUK and VKhUTEMAS, GITIS, Meyerhold, OPOYAZ. These and other people will

> sever the shackles of antiquarianism . . . LEF must reject the superfluous past, and unite behind a front for the explosive detonation of antiquity, for the fight for a new culture . . . we shall find things out by competition. We believe that by the strength of the things we make, we shall prove that we are on the correct road to the future.[7]

It seems clear from the language used even in the first issue of *LEF* that its authors regarded themselves not merely as contributing to the new art of production and utility, but as carrying out an embattled rear-guard action against declining morale as well as against powerful and unwelcome counter-arguments. 'Futurists!' the article suddenly urged;

> your services to art are great; but don't dream of living on the dividend of yesterday's revolutionary spirit. Show by your work that your outburst is not the wailing of a wounded intelligentsia, but a struggle, labouring shoulder-to-shoulder with all those working for the victory of the commune. Constructivists! Be on guard against becoming just another aesthetic school . . . Production-artists! Be on your guard against becoming applied-artist handicraftsman. In teaching the worker, learn from the

worker . . . Your school is the factory floor . . . Masters and students of LEF! The question of our very existence is being decided. The very greatest idea will perish if we do not mould it skilfully . . . LEF is on guard. LEF will throw out all the old fuddy-duddies, all the ultra-aesthetes, all the copiers.[8]

8. 'What is LEF Fighting For?', p 32.

In particular, the question of Constructivism and production art was hotly debated within LEF. In an article about Rodchenko, Brik concedes that 'at the moment things are hard for the Constructivist-production-artist. Artists turn their back on him. Industrialists wave him away in annoyance. The man in the street goggles and fearfully whispers "Futurist!"'. Added to this, even those within Constructivism have lapsed into empty formulae. They defend the slogans of Constructivism, but 'they are all still doing the same old thing: little pictures, landscapes, portraits'. There are those who talk about 'construction' but 'still come out with the very same, age-old ornamental and applied types of art, little cockerels and flowers, or circles and dashes'. And there are the mystics, who do not paint pictures but gaze about, purporting to '"creatively apprehend" the "eternal laws" of colour'.[9] This was serious enough criticism. However, Rodchenko, Brik says, is none of these things. For him, the artist is one who has 'the practical ability to resolve any task involving the shaping of a concrete object'. Rodchenko 'takes art into production'. He does not embellish an object. He shapes it; he considers only the purpose of the object which defines the organisation of the colour and form. Moreover Brik alleges that there is a new consumer who does not want embellishment, 'who does not need pictures and ornaments, and who is not afraid of iron and steel'. He claims that Rodchenko 'cannot go astray . . . he will break through and prove to the industrialists that only the Productivist-constructive approach gives the highest proficiency to production'. Everything at the moment, however, is concentrated on quantity rather than on quality. Therefore the victory of Rodchenko's method will not happen quickly, Brik says; but he is 'revolutionising taste, clearing the ground for the future non-aesthetic, expedient and yet material culture'.[10]

9. O. Brik, 'From LEF: Into Production'; *Form*, 10, Cambridge, October 1969, p 33.

10. O. Brik, 'From LEF: Into Production', p 33.

Perhaps some comment is in order here on the language of such statements; for like the corresponding pleas on behalf of AKhRR, its stated intentions soar high above what was actually achieved, or could be achieved. In both cases it seems as if the sheer practicalities of art could be lost sight of altogether amidst the effusions of a particular programme or style. In the case of *LEF*, particularly, such declamations may seem inspiring, full of the fervour of the Revolution. But equally they can seem histrionic and utopian. They were also not always self-consistent. For example, *LEF* made full use of the idea of the 'individual artist creator' to which other parts of communist ideology were vehemently opposed. But both sides were guilty of hyperbole. AKhRR resorted to crude rhetoric with the help of fighting phrases such as 'militant proletariat' and 'revolutionary struggle'. *LEF* too employed an aggressive and frequently libellous vocabulary, a stirring and visionary tone. AKhRR was by turns indignant and patronising, as if it possessed 'rights' to art which other groups did not have. Throughout, language as a practice and as an institution lies at the centre of Soviet politics and art. If its flourishes could be unfixed from the 'process' of revolution and looked at sociologically, as behaviour, this might reveal its rhetorical and symbolic nature, its distance (very often) from events.

To the theorists of *LEF* the idea of utopia did sometimes at least begin to interact with the realities of practice. For example, in its early issues *LEF* continued a debate that had taken place in architectural circles in 1919 and 1920 about the character of the ideal city. The argument here is interesting because it constitutes another attempt to define the artist's role in relation to that of the engineer. Boris Arvatov, who agreed with Tarabukin that production art was the art of the new proletariat and that easel painting of any kind – particularly with its individualist bias – belonged to the bourgeois era, defended a utopian scheme by Anton Lavinsky for a circular city, on springs, made of glass and asbestos and which was raised above the earth in order to release the space underneath. To build such a structure a new form of alliance with engineers would be needed, Arvatov quite reasonably pointed out. Engineers build straightforwardly and with modern techniques, he said, so long as they restrict themselves to bridges, cranes and platforms. (Significantly these are all devices of the Constructivist stage.) But when larger-scale construction is called for, 'the familiar old face of the aesthetic peers out from beneath the engineer's mask' and his work falls into the sweet embrace of aestheticism, a narrowing of the task, and of social conservatism.[11] Lavinsky's project, Arvatov claims – and here he seems to depart from what was strictly practicable – 'using engineering in its future dynamics, engineering as a universal method, engineering released from beneath the moulds of art and subordinated only to the law of sociotechnical expediency, strikes at both the artist and the engineer' (Figure 65). To the artist, it says: 'Hands off the business of life, you have remained on Parnassus.' The engineer it summons to 'revolutionary boldness and to a break with traditional aesthetising, towards the organisation of life in all its parts'.[12]

Arvatov does concede that the matter is not straightforward. Utopian plans in themselves are not to be decried – think of Fourier, he says, who inspired Marx. Lavinsky's project, he writes, is openly romantic, a leap across the abyss from the idea on the one side to production on the other. (He remarks that in Germany, where ideal cities have been begun, they nevertheless enjoy a bad heredity: 'With an old architect for a father and an expressionist painting for a mother, you won't get far beyond aestheticism!'[13]) But we have to face the question of practicality, Arvatov confesses. Are such schemes technically possible? 'I do not know,' he admits; 'I am ready to assume the worst – that the literal realisation of the plan in all its details is unthinkable either with today's or with any other level of technique.'[14] But pioneers 'sometimes hold torn banners without ceasing to be pioneers'. Lavinsky is 'making suggestions', to use Mayakovsky's phrase; 'let the engineers now say what is possible and what is not possible . . . that would not be useless work'.[15]

In a slightly later issue, Arvatov answered the accusation that his

11. B. Arvatov, 'From LEF: Materialised Utopia', *LEF* no 1; *Form*, 10, Cambridge, October 1969, p 34.

12. Arvatov, 'Materialised Utopia', p 34.

13. Ibid., p 35.

14. Ibid., p 35.

15. Ibid., p 35.

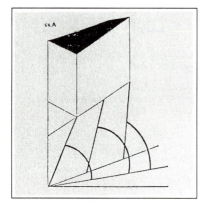

Figure 65
A. Lavinsky, Plan of a housing block (from *LEF*)

programme was utopian by resorting to the paradigm of science. In
'Utopia or Science?', published in *LEF* no. 4, he defended the Productivist programme as being in tune with Taylorist attitudes to labour
and to the complete industrialisation of life. But he is careful to specify
the field. Speaking of the theatre, Arvatov says that 'leftists' must be
opposed to the traditional stage:

> The 'leftists' demand production methods, a production consciousness, a
> production-attitude and approach to every sphere of art without excep-
> tion. We must not sanctify industrial, collective life with the 'beauties' of
> easel-art theatre, but totally subordinate the theatre to the constructive
> methods and problems of collectivised industrial life.[16]

16. B. Arvatov, 'Utopia or Science?'
LEF, no 4, pp 16–21, in *Screen*, Winter
1971/2, Vol 12, no 4, p 47.

This, he implies, would constitute at least a *partial* realisation of the
programme of production art.

Yet the same comment suggests that the Productivist vision of a
completely redesigned material environment has now significantly
receded. Productivism can at least be applied in certain fields, Arvatov says, such as 'furniture, clothing production, etc.', and so applied
would constitute a blow to the 'debauched applied art which has
flourished in proletarian art (witness the uniform of the Red Army,
the equipment of the Agricultural Exhibition, etc.) . . . ' .[17] But he
remains doubtful about its applicability elsewhere. He rounds off the
argument with an attack upon easel painting and a defence of its
replacement by 'the placard, the illustration, the advertisement,
photo- and cine-montage, i.e. for those types of *utilitarian*-repre-
sentational art which could be art for the masses, put into effect by
means of machine techniques and closely tied to the material life of
the urban industrial workers'. The easel painting he still regards as
synonymous with the drawing room and the museum, since it 'fosters
passive admiration of illusion and diverges from life'. It was for this
reason 'not suited to become an efficient weapon in the hands of the
proletariat'.[18]

17. B. Arvatov, 'Utopia or Science?',
p 46.

18. Ibid., p 47.

In *LEF*'s second issue, dated April-May 1923, there is a short
declaration concerned with all the arts including painting and sculpture, which once again attempts to divide artists into 'left' and 'right',
and to pour scorn on all but the former. This piece, entitled 'Comrades, Organisers of life!' begins by proclaiming 'five years of victory . . . five years of slogans renewed and realised daily',[19] but also
complains of 'five years of monotonous designs for celebrations, five
years of languishing art'.[20] It asks stage-managers 'how long will you
and other rats continue to gnaw at [this] theatrical sham?' and in-
quires of poets 'when will you throw away your sickly lyrics?' Artists,
it says, must 'stop making patches of colour upon moth-eaten canvases, stop decorating the easy life of the bourgeoisie . . . [and] exercise your artistic strength to encircle cities until you are able to take
part in the whole global reconstruction'. It urges artists to

19. LEF Declaration, 'Comrades, Organisers of Life!'; Bowlt, *Russian Art of
the Avant-Garde*, p 199.

20. 'Comrades, Organisers of Life!',
Bowlt, p 200.

> give the world new colours and outlines . . . break down the barriers of
> 'beauty for beauty's sake' . . . break down the barriers of those nice
> little artistic schools. Add your strength to the united energy of the

collective . . . Split leftist art from rightists everywhere! With leftist art prepare the European Revolution! Strengthen it in the USSR! [21]

21. 'Comrades, Organisers of Life!', Bowlt, p 201.

These brief excerpts will suffice to give at least a partial idea of the attitudes of the 'left' in general and of *LEF* in particular in 1923. Relatively unspecific programmes and a plethora of utopian designs seemed appropriate for a group that was knowledgeable about and in occasional communication with the Western European 'avant-garde', with which it shared much, particularly in the field of design. 'Left' artists and critics still clearly believed that they had inherited the Revolutionary flame and still possessed the momentum to transform its light and heat into art. Yet it must be said that there is a defensiveness in these statements too. At the very least, they suggest that in 1923 the Revolution was regarded by the 'avant-garde' as far from complete; that bourgeois attitudes were still considered rife, and that, above all, 'left' artists were feeling encircled and therefore in need of solidarity under the banner of Futurist, Productivist, Constructivist and Formalist techniques, however vaguely these were defined.

There are numerous explanations for this embattled, while still declamatory tone. Perhaps *LEF* felt itself to be out-manoeuvred by the easel painting groups, or anyway outnumbered by them. At the least, *LEF* appears to have felt that identifying specific targets such as AKhRR would bring with it the opprobrium of Party leaders. A third consideration is that the streamlined, hyperlaconic phraseology used by the *LEF* writers – in conformity with the Constructivist ideal – militated against discursive argumentation, indeed robbed it of the use of paragraphs of more than one or two sentences long. The *LEF* exhortations were short on argument but strong on appropriately symbolic 'Futuristic' utterences that sought to reimagine the world over and against the pull of the present and the persistent appeal of the past.

And cracks were already beginning to show in *LEF*'s appeal to be the most 'radical' of the 'left' journals. One problem was that the original Futurist poets, Khlebnikov, Kruchonykh and Kamensky, who had experimented with 'trans-sense' or nonsense poems before the Revolution, were now giving *LEF*'s opponents a justified reason to complain. Certainly the production artists inside *LEF* considered that this type of Futurism should be consigned to the rubbish-heap or the dustbin. Secondly, though *LEF* became influential abroad at a much later date, it was never widely circulated within Soviet Russia – a fact which was later used by other 'left' literary organisations against it. Furthermore it was using up paper and printing facilities. Its cry against imitation, against tendentious 'realism', against easel painting in any illusionistic form, against any form of decoration and against the concept of 'the aesthetic' – these were anathema to a large body of artists who had come to working maturity since the Revolution and who believed in the need for uncomplicated, direct representations in art, having a wide appeal as well as a revolutionary significance. For better or worse, the highly experimental and iconoclastic work of Futurism, as well as its utilitarian off-shoots in

Constructivism and production art, were by the end of 1923 and the beginning of 1924 coming to an end. Increasingly, *LEF*'s audience was simply not there. *LEF*'s circulation dwindled throughout 1924 and in 1925 it ceased publication through lack of demand.

Lenin, Trotsky and Stalin in 1923

The views of the Party leadership in artistic matters in the early part of the NEP period are of the greatest importance, for it remains true that even in the relatively 'free' cultural atmosphere then prevailing, many literary and artistic groups openly courted the support and even the patronage of state organs, all of which were ultimately answerable to the Party. We have seen how some writers and artists wished either for independence from the Party, or for freedom to range freely over styles and subjects that had little ostensible connection with revolutionary life. Yet for all artists and literary groups, whether or not they were seeking to attract state patronage, the disposition of Party leaders on questions of culture were necessarily germane, even if those dispositions were sometimes only dimly visible amidst the pressure of events outside the cultural field.

To begin to appreciate the complexity of policy positions within the Party in 1923 it is instructive to look to that moment, shortly before the death of Lenin, when a mood of crisis was beginning to overtake the Party and when Lenin's own grip on the Party was beginning to loosen. We saw earlier how the resolution 'On Questions of Propaganda, the Press and Agitation', passed at the Twelfth Party Congress in April 1923, was a sign that the Party was prepared to take a hand in art and literature, particularly where this overlapped with the function of education and the improvement of political literacy.

But it must be emphasised that the Party had no all-embracing view. It combined staunch vigilance in the area of education and propaganda with some tolerance for the idea of building on the achievements of bourgeois and foreign literature and art – this, more or less, was Lenin's counsel. Yet the price to be paid for such freedom of operation was a higher supervisory control of the so-called 'independent' cultural organisations. In September 1922, for example, there had occurred another incident in which Lenin had shown himself to be hostile to Proletkult. Valerian Pletnev had written an article entitled 'On the Ideological Front' in *Pravda*,[1] to which Lenin's attention had been drawn and to which he reacted with great vehemence. The article by Pletnev had appeared on 27 September 1922 and had reiterated once more the aims and the programme of the Proletkult movement. The incident might have passed unnoticed, but for the fact that Lenin, in his copy of the article, underlined several passages and wrote derisive comments in the margin, the text of which has survived as a unique record of Lenin's views on the Proletkult at a crucial stage in the early history of Soviet life and letters.

To Pletnev's assertion that 'the creation of a new proletarian class culture is the basic aim of the Proletkult', Lenin scribbled the words

1. V. Pletnev, 'On the Ideological Front', *Pravda*, 27 September 1922.

'Ha! Ha!' in the margin. To some of Pletnev's statements Lenin obviously agreed; for example to the passage 'Thesis: bourgeois class culture. Antithesis: the class culture of the proletariat, and only beyond class society, in socialism, is the synthesis'. But the Party leader characteristically added emphasis to Pletnev's question 'What are the *concrete* forms of struggle in the field of culture?', adding the letters 'NB' three times underlined, as if in complete support. In a further discussion of the role of bourgeois artists within Proletkult, Lenin asks in the margin 'but the peasants?' And when Pletnev points out that collective existence is so far alien to the peasant, that the Revolution is being nourished by the construction of locomotives by the working class in a spirit of unity, Lenin asks 'but are peasants building locomotives?' And when Pletnev argues that everything in the life of the Proletariat is becoming 'clear and mathematically precise,' Lenin asks: 'but the religion of the workers and peasants?' In short, Lenin persistently opposes that part of Pletnev's argument which draws a contrast between the peasants and the urban work-force, and which assumes that only the latter, exclusively, can forge a new art in the image of the industrial process, with a view that seeks to assimilate the life-style of the workers and peasants. To Pletnev's idea that the entire struggle for Soviet culture is to take place 'under the banner of the proletarian culture and in no other way' Lenin writes – 'Ouf!'

Pletnev's allegation of the supremacy of 'intellectuals, artists and engineers' within the proletariat Lenin ridicules as 'arch-fiction'. This comment is important because it suggests the Party leader's scepticism about the idea of the artist-engineer that was so central to the Productivists. Indeed to a further remark by Pletnev in which he calls for the creation of 'a new type of intellectual, a social engineer, an engineer-organiser . . . a technologist and an economist at the same time', Lenin adds two prominent question-marks in the margin as if the concept was disagreeable. And he seemed to dislike the idea that the artist should, in Pletnev's phrase, 'think monistically' – Bogdanov's concept of his 1920 lectures – as if this was overly metaphysical and not appropriate to the cultural level of the country as a whole. More general statements, to the effect that bourgeois power had been conquered, that the task of the proletariat was to bring the content of science into correspondence with socialist industry, and others, Lenin merely underlined without comment. [2]

To reply to Pletnev in detail, Lenin instructed Y. Yakovlev, then assistant director of the Propaganda Section of the Central Committee, to draft an alternative argument for publication in *Pravda*. Editor Bukharin took this as an attack upon himself, and threatened to respond 'with all severity' if Lenin insisted on publishing Yakovlev's piece in full. According to Bukharin's later testimony, Lenin revised the article fully before publication.[3] Appearing in *Pravda* on 24 and 25 October 1922 under the title 'On Proletarian Culture and the Proletkult', the article urged once more that the way to create a proletarian culture was not to relegate bourgeois culture to complete darkness,

2. V. Pletnev, 'On the Ideological Front', 27 September 1922; I have used the version printed with Lenin's comments in *Borba za realizm*, pp 65–76.

3. According to Bukharin in 'Proletariat i voprossy khudozhestvennoy politiki', *Krasnaya nov*, May 1925, no 4, p 265.

but to come to terms with it, to criticise it and put it to use. 'To Comrade Pletnev', Yakovlev said sarcastically,

> proletarian culture is a sort of chemical reaction which can be produced in the Proletkult retort with the aid of a group of specially selected people. He seems to see the elements of the new proletarian culture emerging from the Proletkult studio like an ancient goddess appearing ready-made out of the foaming sea . . . [4]

4. Y. A. Yakovlev, 'On Proletarian Culture and the Proletkult', *Pravda*, 24/25 October, 1922.

Yakovlev also inveighed against Pletnev for ignoring the low level of peasant literacy, the need of the peasants to fight for hygiene and agriculture, and the necessity of abolishing bureaucratism and bribery. The very idea that the proletariat could create its own culture he described as absurd: witness the fact that they, too, were semi-literate, and that many came from peasant families and possessed all the backward psychology (including religion) of ancient Russian stock. But they were arguments that Lenin had published before.

Other elements within the leadership must be referred to. Lunacharsky did not always take the uniformly 'liberal' attitude with which he is usually ascribed. At the beginning of the NEP period he too believed that the press, propaganda and agitation should be strictly supervised so as to castrate the prospects of counter-revolutionary groups. In a speech to university professors in June 1921 he said, perhaps with some sadness,

> . . . we cannot allow full freedom in science and teaching. It is a hard time; chains have to be borne, and for the time being we are bearing our chains. Youth is our future, and we cannot allow counter-revolutionary propaganda among our youth. The smallest weight might tip the scales against us, and therefore with a heavy hand we take on the role of censor . . . [5]

5. Fitzpatrick, *Commissariat*, p 233.

As we saw too from Lunacharsky's involvement with AKhRR in its formative phase, he supported 'realism' as a method in the arts and denounced the pretensions of unrestrained experimentalism and so-called 'left' activity. But this was in 1923. Before this date it is difficult to judge how far the conflict between Lunacharsky's *idea* of support for different ideological groups and his *instinct* for traditional art was in practice reconciled.

We must come now to Trotsky (Figure 66). Whether it was wise or desirable for Trotsky to take time away from his political duties in the early NEP period to indulge in art and literary criticism will be forever open to dispute. Late in 1922 Lenin's health had gone into decline and the question of a successor had come suddenly to occupy the minds of the Politburo. A bloc of three – the so-called triumvirate, namely Zinoviev, Kamenev and Stalin – was forming inside the Politburo and was threatening to exert hegemony over the policies of the Party and the apparatus of the state. Evidently this threatened implications for Soviet culture in its widest sense. Yet Trotsky had left Moscow for a holiday in mid-1922, the majority of which he had devoted to literary criticism. He had planned to write, among other things, a preface for a collection of his pre-Revolutionary essays on literature which the State Publishing House Gosizdat was making ready for publication.

Figure 66
Leon Trotsky, *c*.1923 (photo: *David King*)

6. For these items see P. N. Siegel (ed), *Leon Trotsky on Literature and Art*, New York, 1970, pp 127–42, 142–7,148–61.

7. Many of these are contained in L. Trotsky, *Problems of Everyday Life*, Monad Press, New York, 1973.

8. Trotsky, *Pravda*, 16 May 1923; *Sochineniya*, Vol XXI, pp 26–31; in *Problems of Everyday Life*, also in Rosenberg (ed), *Bolshevik Visions*, pp 185, 188; this quotation p 185.

9. Trotsky, 'Struggle for Cultured Speech', Rosenberg (ed), *Bolshevik Visions*, p 186.

His intention had been to compose a preface on Russian literature and letters since the Revolution; however this grew in size and the work was only finished the following summer, 1923, when it bore the title of an independent work, *Literature and Revolution*. By this time Trotsky had reacted in a lukewarm manner to Lenin's efforts to move against Stalin for his rudeness and ineptitude; he had also rejected Lenin's offer to make him, Trotsky, Vice-Premier. Indeed Trotsky had conciliated with the triumvirs in a manner that suggested a drastic lack of awareness of their animosity towards him. Yet these were the months during which one of the greatest works of Bolshevik and Marxist art criticism was written.

Apart from his early critical writings, Trotsky had already written about Tolstoy and about Marcel Martinet's *La Nuit*.[6] It should be noted that Trotsky's writings on culture were never confined to novels, poems, and plays, but covered all uses of language from that of the press to the argot of every day. They extended too to the family and the church, to the habit of vodka, to the cinema, and to customs of speech within the Red Army.[7] In the summer of 1923 for instance Trotsky published in *Pravda* an article on 'The Struggle for Cultured Speech' in which he pointed out that peasant swearing was that of the desperate, the embittered and the hopeless, whereas that of the upper classes before the Revolution had been that of 'class rule, slave-owner's pride, and unshakeable power . . .'.[8] But what effect had the Revolution, which is 'primarily the awakening of the human personality in the masses', had on these habits, asked Trotsky? How could one create a life based on self-respect, equality and care 'in an atmosphere poisoned with the roaring, rolling, ringing and resounding swearing of masters and slaves . . .'?[9] The struggle against 'foul language', Trotsky pleaded, was as essential a condition of mental hygiene as the struggle against filth and vermin was a condition of physical hygiene.

Such passages provide a sense of the delicacy and connectedness with which Trotsky approached all cultural matters, of how he wished where possible to dismantle the striking contrasts and violently opposed polarities by which Soviet life and culture was still characterised. In general Trotsky was able to perceive profound connections between the culture of everyday life and that of the whole nation in both politics and art – a perception he shared only with Bukharin and with Lenin himself. Above all he was concerned to combat the frame of mind which handed out cultural orders 'from above' as if they represented the necessary truth for all time. The workers' government was a stern government, Trotsky here insisted. The workers' state has 'the right and the duty to apply compulsion'. But it had no business to issue instructions in the cultural field, and still less to flatter the working class with theories about 'proletarian culture': 'In the education of the working class this "here-is-truth-down-on-your-knees" method . . . contradicts the very essence of Marxism.'[10]

It is in this spirit that the central argument of *Literature and Revolution* turned to Bogdanov's programme for proletarian culture. It was senseless of the Proletkult to cut itself off from works of art of the past, as if nothing could be learnt from these, Trotsky maintained. The communist approach to the art of the past must on the contrary be critical, and selective. Even works of the feudal and bourgeois eras, insofar as they enabled men and women to surmount the limitations of their immediate existence, could strike resonating chords in a period of proletarian revolution. This is why it is

> fundamentally wrong to oppose proletarian to bourgeois culture and art. Proletarian culture and art will never exist. The proletarian regime is temporary and transitory. Our revolution derives its historic significance and moral greatness from the fact that it lays the foundation for a classless society and for the first truly universal culture.[11]

Trotsky's argument here is that the dictatorship of the proletariat came into being precisely to oppose class differences, including the differences between itself and other groups. Therefore even though the proletarian dictatorship may last years or even decades, it would not last longer; yet its savage struggle to eliminate classes would leave little room for the growth of a distinctive and organically produced culture of its own. In any case, the main advocates of 'proletarian culture' were intellectuals and Party men, with little experience of the working class.

But Trotsky's case against Proletkult was by no means one in favour of Futurism, Formalism, or any other existing group. At the beginning of *Literature and Revolution* Trotsky castigates emigré writers – Russian writers who had gone abroad – for having written nothing significant: writers like Vetlugin, Alexey Tolstoy and Aldanov 'have nothing to say'. Trotsky argues that since art can be revived 'only from the point of view of October . . . he who is outside the October perspective is utterly and hopelessly reduced to nothing . . . For this and for no other reason, emigré literature does not exist. And what is not, cannot be judged.'[12] This is also his verdict upon the

10. Trotsky, address of June 1924; *Sochineniya*, xxi, p 163; Deutscher, *Prophet Armed*, p 170.

11. Trotsky, *Literature and Revolution* (Moscow, 1923) International Publishers, New York, 1925 (Preface).

12. Ibid., p 25.

13. Trotsky, *Literature and Revolution* (Moscow, 1923) International Publishers, New York, 1925, p 29.

so-called internal emigrés, writers like Hippius, Odoevtzeva and even Zamyatin and Andrey Bely, whose works Trotsky says are about as useful to the 'modern post-October man' as 'a glass bead to a soldier on a battlefield'.[13] The Moscow Art Theatre writers are unfortunately still living in the mood of *Uncle Vanya* and *The Cherry Orchard*, he thinks; while the Poets Guild, though refined, are nevertheless rooted in the past, and in European culture: 'they are not the creators of life, they do not participate in the creation of its sentiments and moods, they are only tardy skimmers, left-overs of a culture created by the blood of others.'[14]

14. Ibid., p 33.

Equally disappointing are what Trotsky calls the *ralliés*, meaning those who have accepted the reality of October but without assuming any responsibility. They are silent when it suits them, he says, but take part sometimes, as much as they are able. They are 'pacified philistines of art, its ordinary civil servants. They are not ungifted, and indeed we find them everywhere': they

> paint 'Soviet' portraits and sometimes great artists do the painting. They have experience, technique, everything . . . Yet somehow the portraits are not good likenesses. Why? Because the artist has no inner interest in his subjects, no spiritual kinship, and he paints a Russian or a German Bolshevik as he used to paint a carafe or a turnip for the Academy, and even more neutrally, perhaps. I do not name names, because they form a whole class . . .

Is Trotsky talking here about the fledgling AKhRR artists including the older Peredvizhniki men? He probably is. And yet Trotsky acknowledges that 'although these *ralliés* will not snatch the Polar Star from the heavens, nor invent smokeless powder, nevertheless they are useful and necessary, and will be the manure for the new culture. And that is not so little'.[15]

15. Ibid., p 37.

16. Ibid., p 47.

Trotsky is more flattering here by far than he is about Bely, of whom he accuses that he was 'most loudly destroyed by October'.[16] Both Bely and Blok – though Trotsky reserves some time for Blok's 'The Twelve' – are 'people of another epoch, of another world, of a past epoch, of an unreturnable world'. In Bely

> one feels how deep is buried the old Russia, the landlord and official Russia, or at best the Russia of Turgenev and Goncharov. How astronomically remote this is from us, how good it is that it is remote, and what a jump through the ages from this to October!

Bely is a

> spiritual conservative who has lost the ground under his feet and is in despair . . . Torn from the pivot of custom and individualism, Bely wishes to replace the whole world with himself, to build everything with himself and through himself, to discover everything anew in himself . . . [but] this servile preoccupation with oneself, this apotheosis of the ordinary facts of one's personal and spiritual routine, became so unbearable in our age where mass and speed are really making a new world.[17]

17. Ibid., p 54.

His 'stagnant thinking' and 'terrible prose' contain nothing of value, Trotsky says, and his infatuation with Rudolf Steiner ('I have never read Steiner and don't intend to', Trotsky commented) does him even greater harm.

Trotsky's accusations are at once savage and acute. He strenuously opposes mysticism and aestheticism wherever it occurs, proposing to insert in their place 'a new art, a new point of view, a new union of feelings, a new striving for the word . . .'.[18] A group who failed to achieve this, says Trotsky, were the 'fellow-travellers', writers such as Pilnyak, Ivanov, Tikhonov, Yesenin and the Serapion Brotherhood. They 'subsist between non-October and October'. These young writers have no revolutionary past and though they form 'a very important division of Russian literature at present, and have accepted the fact of the Revolution', they possess no real dynamism, no real historical awareness or insight. Pilnyak is 'an excellent observer with fresh eyes and a good ear';[19] Marietta Shaginyan has a sympathetic attitude, and Yesenin has absorbed some of the consciousness of the peasant; but none has sufficiently and uncompromisingly identified with the October viewpoint, with 'the idea which underlies our epoch'. Blok, who is not a fellow-traveller but a pre-Revolutionary bourgeois intellectual with some capacity for change, stopped writing after the publication of 'The Twelve', because he was at heart a romantic and a mystic and could not surpass those 'formless lyrics . . . that hang like a cloud-patch' that he wrote before 1918.[20]

Of the Futurists in general Trotsky said that 'Futurism has not mastered the Revolution, but it has an internal striving which, in a certain sense, is parallel to it'. Futurism Trotsky characterised as being of bourgeois origin, as being violently oppositional in its pre-Revolutionary phase, as being internationalist, infatuated with technology, but also capable – as in Italy – of consorting with the spirit of Fascism. The workers' Revolution in Russia 'broke loose before Futurism had time to free itself from its childish habits, from its yellow blouses, from its excessive excitement . . .'.[21] Its wish to break the bonds of the past, to smash tradition, to burn museums, to throw Pushkin overboard, only has meaning within the closed-in circle of the intelligentsia.

> It has a meaning only insofar as the Futurists are busy cutting the cord which binds them to the priests of bourgeois literary tradition. But the meaninglessness of this call becomes evident as soon as it is addressed to the proletariat [since] the working class cannot break with such a tradition because it is not in the grip of such a tradition.[22]

To believe otherwise is pure Bohemian nihilism, Trotsky says. To reject art as a means of picturing and imagining knowledge because of one's opposition to the contemplative and impressionistic bourgeois art of the last few decades is to strike from the hands of the class which is building a new society its most important weapon. 'To us, on the contrary, the Revolution appeared as the embodiment of a familiar tradition, internally digested . . . we entered a world which was already familiar to us, as a tradition and a vision.'[23] The trouble with Futurism was not principally that it denied the traditions of the intelligentsia, serious though that was; but 'that it does not feel itself

18. Trotsky, *Literature and Revolution*, p 54

19. Ibid., p 76.

20. Ibid., p 112.

21. Ibid., p 129.

22. Ibid., p 130.

23. Ibid., p 131–2.

to be part of the revolutionary tradition. We stepped into the Revolution, while Futurism fell into it'.[24]

24. Trotsky, *Literature and Revolution*, p 132.

About the LEF artists and writers, Trotsky acknowledges that their problems were undeniably important: their link between art and life, their need to renew language, their interest in production. But (and he names Mayakovsky and Meyerhold) they 'have no bridge to the future because they have abandoned that which the future will need'. When Meyerhold 'produces on the stage the few semi-rhythmic movements he has taught those actors who are weak in movement, and calls this bio-mechanics, the result is – abortive . . . an impression of provincial dilettantism'.[25] Mayakovsky 'promises to write verse in mathematical formulas, but', says Trotsky, 'we have mathematicians for that purpose'.[26] All this smacks of trying to deduce from the nature of the proletariat – its collectivism, its activism, its atheism – a new style of pure idealism. In architecture, for example, the sleeping cars, staircases and subway stations, the metal bridges, elevators, cranes and skyscrapers are undoubtedly elements of a new style. But 'beyond a practical problem and the steady work of solving this problem, one cannot create a new architectural style . . . and will give nothing but an ingenious expression of one's ego, an arbitrary allegorism, and the same old provincial dilettantism'.[27] LEF is utopian, Trotsky alleges, and spends more time in seeking than in finding. That is one reason – beyond the general view that the Party cannot have preformed opinions in matters of art – why the Party cannot and should not canonise LEF as the definitive 'communist art'. Their works resemble musical exercises which are not yet ready to be played in public: 'It is as impossible to canonise seekings as it is impossible to arm an army with an unrealised invention'.[28] But towards LEF's intentions to produce a socialist art, guided by a Marxist criterion, Trotsky is entirely sympathetic.

25. Ibid., p 135.

26. Ibid., p 134.

27. Ibid., pp 135–6.

28. Ibid., p 139.

Tatlin's tower is an example of architectural utopianism which, though laudable in its general concepts, Trotsky finds completely out of step with its time. 'At present we are beginning to repair the pavements a little', Trotsky says, 'to re-lay the sewage pipes, to finish the unfinished houses left to us as a heritage . . .'. But from this it followed that large-scale visionary projects would have to be put off. When a period of surplus arrives, 'when the most urgent and acute needs of life are covered, the Soviet state will take up the problem of gigantic construction that will suitably express the monumental spirit of our epoch', he writes. But the delay would do no harm; it would give Tatlin time for 'more thought, for revision, and for radical re-examination'.[29]

29. Ibid., p 246.

Tatlin is right to discard national styles, allegorical sculpture, 'monograms, flourishes and tails', says Trotsky. He is right to subordinate the design to a constructive use of materials. But 'he still has to prove that he is right in what seems to be his own personal invention, a rotating cube, a pyramid and a cylinder of glass'. The props and the piles which are to support this cylinder and pyramid Trotsky describes as ' . . . so cumbersome and heavy that they look like unremoved scaffolding'. One cannot think what those props and piles are for, he complains. 'They say: they are there to support the rotating cylinder in which the meetings will take place. But one answers: meetings are not necessarily held in a cylinder and the cylinder does not necessarily have to rotate.' Then Trotsky proposes an analogy:

> I remember seeing once as a child, a wooden temple built in a beer bottle. This fired my imagination, but I did not ask myself at that time what it was for. Tatlin proceeds by a reverse method; he wants to construct a beer bottle for the World Council of People's Commissars which would sit in a spiral concrete temple. But for the moment, I cannot refrain from the question: what is it for? To be more exact; we would probably accept the cylinder and its rotating, if it were combined with a simplicity and a lightness of construction, that is, if the arrangements for its rotating did not depress the aim . . .

For good or bad, Trotsky concludes, 'circumstances are going to give Tatlin plenty of time to find arguments for his side'.[30]

But Trotsky concedes that one cannot but help recognise and value the progressive and creative work of Futurism in the field of rhythm and rhyme. Against mysticism and the passive deification of nature, it stands 'for technique, for scientific organisation, for the machine, for planfulness, for will-power, for courage, for speed, for precision, and for the new man, who is armed with all these things'.[31] And here Mayakovsky proves to be an enormous talent. He has imbibed the spirit of the Revolution, and has emerged from it a 'bold master' who

> handles words and the dictionary . . . according to his own laws, regardless of whether his artisanship pleases or not . . . He gathers into his own circle war and revolution, heaven and hell . . . [but] he does not claim to be the priest of art; on the contrary, he is entirely ready to place his art at the service of the Revolution. [32]

Nevertheless Trotsky is alert to the dangers of such a dynamic, thunderous style. There is frequently individualistic, bohemian arrogance in Mayakovsky's work, he points out, in which the poet is consequently sometimes too much in evidence. Sometimes the events and facts of the Revolution, and the mass character of its deeds and experience, are drowned out by the gigantic ego of the poet and his ability to perform athletic feats with words. Thus '150,000,000', 'War and Peace' and *Mystery Bouffe* turn out to be among Mayakovsky's weakest works, not his greatest, of which Trotsky calls 'A Cloud in Trousers' a special case. But Mayakovsky may yet overcome this momentary decline, and refashion the Futurism which has already had an inestimable influence on ranks of other poets. However, Trotsky argues, Futurism generally must stand on its own feet 'without any attempt to have itself decreed official by the government, as happened in the beginning of the Revolution'. Although much in Futurism will serve to revive and elevate art, the new forms

> must find for themselves, and independently, an access into the consciousness of the advanced elements of the working class as the latter develop culturally. Art cannot live and cannot develop without a flexible atmosphere of sympathy around it. On this road, and on no other, does the process of complex inter-relation lie ahead. The cultural growth of the

30. Trotsky, *Literature and Revolution*, pp 246–7.

31. Ibid., p 145.

32. Ibid., pp 147–8.

working class will help and influence those innovators who really had something in their bosom. The mannerisms which inevitably come out in all small groups will fall away, and from the vital sprouts will come fresh forms for the solution of new artistic tasks.[33]

33. Trotsky, *Literature and Revolution*, p 161.

Such was the position from which Trotsky was to launch his vigorous critique of proletarian art. Will the proletariat have enough time to create a 'proletarian culture'? he asks. The difficulty is that in the transition to socialism, which may take decades, years or centuries, rather than months, the energy of the proletariat will be spent 'mainly in conquering power, in retaining and strengthening it and in applying it to the most urgent needs of existence and of further struggle'. Furthermore, as this process evolves and as the conditions for cultural creation improve, the proletariat 'will be more and more dissolved into a socialist community and will free itself from its class characteristics and will thus cease to be a proletariat'.[34] In other words, proletarian culture, in beginning to exist, will have created the conditions for its own disappearance. Yet at present, the dictatorship of the proletariat is in a primitive, changing state; it is 'not an organisation for the production of culture of a new society, but a revolutionary and military system struggling for it. One must not forget this'.[35] At present, Trotsky says, the masses are unprepared. They are still mastering the elements of reading, writing and arithmetic – itself a cultural achievement of a high order. But in terms of real artistic culture they are thus far immature, and lack acquaintance even with the bourgeois culture of the past.

34. Ibid., p 185.

35. Ibid., p 190.

36. Ibid., p 212.

37. Ibid., pp 212–3.

38. Ibid., p 213.

Within the ranks of proletarian writers and artists Trotsky makes a striking exception for Demyan Bedny (Figure 67). Bedny, whom advocates of proletarian poetry usually pass by, is nevertheless one who, 'more than anyone else, has the right to be called the poet of revolutionary Russia'.[36] No complex critical methods are needed to determine his tendencies or his social bases, Trotsky says; he is not merely a poet who has approached the Revolution and has accepted it. 'He is a Bolshevik whose weapon is poetry . . . for him the Revolution is not merely material for creation, but the highest authority, which has placed him at his post.'[37] Bedny grew up in the Party, he lived through the various phases in its development, he learned to 'think and feel with his class from day to day and to reproduce this world of thoughts and feelings in the language of verses which have the shrewdness of fable, the sadness of songs, the boldness of couplets, as well as indignation and appeal'. Let all the supporters of proletarian poetry find another who by his verses has 'influenced so directly and actively the masses, the working and peasant masses, the Red Army masses, the many-millioned masses, during this greatest of all epochs'.[38]

And yet Bedny does not feverishly seek for new forms, like the Futurists: the old forms are resurrected and reborn in his work as an invaluable mechanism for the transmission of Bolshevist ideas. If one could free oneself from a metaphysical concept of proletarian culture, says Trotsky, and approach the question from the point of view of what the proletariat reads, what it needs, what absorbs it, what

Figure 67
Demyan Bedny (photo: *Novosti*)

impells it to action, what elevates its cultural level and so prepares the ground for a new art, 'then the work of Demyan Bedny would appear as proletarian and popular literature, that is, as literature vitally needed by an awakened people. If this is not 'true' poetry, it is something more than that'.[39] Bedny is the only artist in *Literature and Revolution* about whom Trotsky has almost nothing critical to say.

When he turns finally to the requirements of present and future art, Trotsky repeats his previous injunctions against Futurism, yet reminds his readers that Pilnyak and Ivanov, though uneven, have shown things about the Revolution – particularly the life of the peasant in the provinces – immeasurably more clearly and more tangibly than others. If we eliminate them, Trotsky asks – not to mention Mayakovsky and Yesenin – will there be anything left 'but a few unpaid promissory notes of a future proletarian literature?'[40]

But does partial acceptance of a few poets and writers mean that the Party occupies a purely eclectic position in the field of art? In the first place, Trotsky makes it clear that in his conception 'the domain of art is not one in which the Party is called upon to command'.[41] Art must make its own way by its own methods. Thus the role of the Party is to *support* various groups which are attempting a revolutionary art, but cannot take sides among competing factions of equal worth. On the other hand it will 'repel the clearly poisonous, disintegrating tendencies of art and will guide itself by its political standards' in its role of guardian of the historic role of the working class. Here Trotsky urges that 'we ought to have a watchful revolutionary censorship, and a broad and flexible policy in the field of art, free from petty partisan maliciousness'. Yet at the same time the Party's standard must be 'political, imperative and intolerant'.[42] Such was the balance of guidance and control that Trotsky finally advocated.

Obviously, he conceded, the problems were stupendous. The peasants were behind the proletariat in their cultural level. And here Trotsky draws a compelling analogy with electricity. He points out that although the antagonism between industry and agriculture could be eliminated by means of the provision of electricity throughout the countryside, the fact remains that the electric stations and power lines do not yet exist. Similarly, *proletarian art does not yet exist*, and so is not in a position to lead the peasants in their search for revolutionary Soviet culture. 'Proletarian art . . . is about as near to artistically gratifying the needs of the city and the village as . . . Soviet industry is near to solving the problems of universal economics.'[43]

However this does not prevent Trotsky from imagining a future in which all material problems have been overcome and where classes have ceased to exist.

> In a society which will have thrown off the pinching and stultifying worry about one's daily bread, in which community restaurants will prepare good, wholesome and tasteful food for all to choose, in which communal laundries will wash clean everyone's good linen, in which children, all the children, will be well fed and strong and gay, and in which they will absorb the fundamental elements of science and art as they absorb albumen and air and the warmth of the sun, in a society in which electricity

39. Trotsky, *Literature and Revolution*, p 214.

40. Ibid., p 217.

41. Ibid., p 218.

42. Ibid., pp 220–1.

43. Ibid., p 224.

and the radio will not be the crafts they are today, but will come from inexhaustible sources of super-power at the call of a control button, in which the liberated egotism of man – a mighty force! – will be directed wholly towards the understanding, the transformation and the betterment of the universe,[44]

44. Trotsky, *Literature and Revolution*, p 189.

In such a society the dynamic development of culture will be incomparable with anything that went on in the past. In such a society, says Trotsky, the powerful force of competition, which in bourgeois society degenerates into market competition, will assume a more fertile form, one in which 'there will be struggle for one's opinion, for one's project, for one's taste'. Art will be 'mature and tempered', and become the instrument of the progressive building of life in every field. This is the vision – utopian or not – that Trotsky holds up before his readers.

Yet he makes it clear that before reaching that society we will have to distinguish between socialist art – for which no basis has as yet been made and which lies almost wholly in the future – and revolutionary art, of which there is still very little but which is hinted at and attempted by a few artists and groups. The main characteristic of revolutionary art, he says, is that it will be transitional, that it will 'inevitably reflect all the contradictions of a revolutionary social system'. Most important, there is the gradual rise of revolutionary man, 'who is forming the new generation in his own image and who is more and more in need of this art'.[45] And what will this new art be like? Above all, it will be an art of 'realism'. Trotsky then attempts to define this 'realism'. It will possess 'a definite and important feeling for the world. It [realism] consists in a feeling for life as it is, in an artistic acceptance of reality, and not a shrinking from it'. It will have no preordained formal or literary definition, but will be created by 'an active world-attitude and an active life-attitude'. Its feeling will be

45. Ibid., p 229.

> a striving either to picture life as it is or to idealise it, either to justify or condemn it, either to photograph it or generalise and symbolise it. But it is always a preoccupation with our life of three dimensions as a sufficient and invaluable theme for art.[46]

46. Ibid., pp 235–6.

It is striking, perhaps, how impervious Trotsky is to fashion and how attentive he is to the production and reception of art at a human and emotional level. The *sine qua non* of both, for Trotsky, is the thoroughly committed grounding of artist and spectator in the mood and consciousness of revolutionary Marxism. But he always adds to this that the concern of art is with the tangible and with the here and now. He gives an example from the theatre. In the theatre, he argues, what we are most immediately in need of is a new repertory – whatever one may say about bio-mechanics. Above all we need a 'new Soviet comedy of manners, one of laughter and indignation'[47] with which to mirror the new stupidities and vanities which the Revolution has brought in its wake. Bio-mechanics will have to 'wait for the future'. And between the past on which the theatre feeds, and the very distant future, there is the present in which we live: 'Between *passéism* and

47. Ibid., p 238.

Futurism, it would be well to give 'Presentism' a chance behind the footlights,' Trotsky argues. 'Let us vote for such a tendency!'[48]

The unique interest of *Literature and Revolution* arises partly from the fact that a high-ranking revolutionary politician had shown himself to be both involved and competent in the affairs of art. No subsequent Commissar for War would play such a part off the field of battle. This is perhaps what lends to the book its universalising, visionary range. Indeed towards the end of *Literature and Revolution* Trotsky's prose achieves an inspirational, almost apocalyptic tone. In its generality art will have a utilitarian, purposeful quality, Trotsky says. Art will absorb industry, and industry art. The barrier between both, and nature, will also fall. The changes that man has already made to nature are insignificant compared with what is to come. Technology is actually capable of cutting down mountains and moving them, but

> in the future this will be done on an immeasurably larger scale, according to a general industrial and artistic plan. Man will occupy himself with re-registering mountains and rivers, and will earnestly and repeatedly make improvements in nature. In the end, he will have rebuilt the earth, if not in his own image, then at least according to his own taste . . . he will change the course of the rivers, and he will lay down rules for the oceans.[49]

The passive enjoyment of nature will disappear from art, Trotsky says, and the village with all its aesthetic traditions will disappear as an archaic form. Man will learn how to build people's palaces on the peaks of Mont Blanc and at the bottom of the Atlantic, and to his own life this will

> add richness, brilliancy and intensity, but also a dynamic quality of the highest degree. The shell of life will hardly have time to form before it will burst open again under the pressure of new technical and cultural inventions and achievements. Life in the future will not be monotonous.[50]

But more than that, Trotsky asserts, man will

> at last begin to harmonise himself in earnest. The movement of his limbs will be purposeful and precise. Both his work and his play will be economic, and hence beautiful. He will even learn to subordinate his bodily processes to the control of reason and will. Man's elemental subconscious will be investigated creatively, and hence made into a force for emancipation in which his instincts will be raised to the height of consciousness.[51]

These twin processes – of psycho-physical self-education and social reconstruction – will combine in the future to become but two aspects of the same process and, says Trotsky, literature, art, drama, painting, music and architecture will 'lend this process beautiful form'. More particularly, he supposes,

> the shell in which the cultural construction and self-education of communist man will be enclosed, will develop all the vital elements of contemporary art to the highest point. Man will become immeasurably stronger, wiser and subtler; his body will become more harmonised, his

48. Trotsky, *Literature and Revolution*, p 240.

49. Ibid., p 252.

50. Ibid., p 254.

51. It is evident from this and other passages that Trotsky was an eager and sympathetic reader of Freud. There is an echo here of Freud's formula 'where id was, there shall ego be'.

52. Trotsky, *Literature and Revolution*, p 256.

movements more rhythmic, his voice more musical. The forms of life will become dynamically dramatic. The average human type will rise to the heights of an Aristotle, a Goethe, or a Marx. And above this ridge new peaks will rise.[52]

It would perhaps be unprofitable to attempt to reduce to summary formulae such a stern, complex, yet ultimately optimistic view of art. No doubt, too, such a programme would be difficult to carry out. Trotsky's view of the artistic process was so loaded with requirements and criteria – each of them stemming in the most dialectical fashion from the events and spirit of October – that no poet, writer or artist was likely to be able to satisfy them for more than a few lines or a few creations before some transgression was made. The demand in Trotsky's writings is constantly for art which is critical of the past yet sensible of its faults, imbued with the meaning of the Revolution yet capable of comprehending the dangers which came with it. It is always dialectically full of contraries: it is conducive to personal emancipation yet not individualistic; in tune with the works of the present and the future yet also capable of speaking to and of the uneducated artisan or agricultural worker; rhythmical, lively, dynamic, and yet somehow aware of the paradoxes that 'there is no revolutionary art as yet',[53] that 'proletarian culture will never exist'.[54] Yet *Literature and Revolution* remains among the seminal art-critical texts of modernity, one which brilliantly expresses the multiple contradictions in which the art and literature of his day were so movingly caught.

53. Ibid., p 229.

54. Ibid., p 14.

It is therefore not surprising that the subtleties of the book were lost upon the majority of artistic partisans in 1923, not least because, in it, most of them suffered to some degree the lashes of Trotsky's tongue. In particular the desire of the Party to supervise artistic life that was becoming evident in 1923 could gain little guidance from Trotsky's difficult recommendations. Yet the experimental writers and artists on the 'left' must have felt betrayed as well: he gave them no final or unconditional support. And his strictures against proletarian art were perceived as being disloyal, as well as unrealistic. The time-scale allowed by Trotsky for the dictatorship of the proletariat was far too short. (This was to be Bukharin's argument in 1925.) And Trotsky's sympathies for Freud were inimical to some.

For these and other reasons Trotsky's views on culture became part and parcel of an attempt to progressively discredit him politically after 1924 – an attempt whose roots lay in the personality clashes of 1919 and 1920 and in the ambiguous and much-abused policy mechanisms created by the Revolution which had never been brought up to date. An anti-Trotskyist 'front' sprang up in the cultural field which coincided with and gave life to an anti-Trotskyist front in politics.

There is an interesting passage in the middle of *Literature and Revolution* which helps to clarify Trotsky's attitude to the conservatives and revivalists who wanted Soviet culture to remain rooted in the Russian past, and who were some of the same people who later sought to discredit him politically. The point at issue was the 'neo-

Classicism' of the early NEP years, of which the return to the model
of nineteenth-century 'realism' and the exhibitions of AKhRR in
particular are the examples that Trotsky presumably had in mind.
Against the claim – that of Anna Akhmatova, Leonard Grossman and
Abram Efros – that Classicism is 'the child of the Revolution', Trotsky
counterposed the question whether the Classical revival was not a
child of a Revolution 'in the same sense in which NEP is?'[55] The
question was highly appropriate, he thinks. The neo-Classicists appear to want to strengthen and order the achievements of the Revolution under the banner of 'revolutionary conservatism'. He himself
was prepared to accept the argument that if Futurism was attracted
'towards the chaotic dynamics of the Revolution . . . then neo-Classi-
cism expresses the need for peace, for stable forms, and for correct
punctuation'.[56] But he points out that the neo-Classicists think 'that
what ought to be preserved is this state of rest after the disorder of
movement has finally stopped'.[57] 'We' (Bolsheviks) on the other hand
consider that NEP is 'only a brief stop at the station for the purpose
of taking on water and getting up steam'. Applied to 'classicising' and
'conservative' artistic tendencies in 1923, the argument is highly
revealing. Trotsky could not have realised how long the influence of
the preservationists was to last, or how firmly they would eventually
gain the upper hand.

Such, at least, were the artistic concerns of the Party leaders who
expressed themselves on the subject in 1923. But it is important to
understand the political tensions that were growing in the Party in
1923 which were also, fundamentally, cultural tensions as well. During the interval between the Eleventh Party Congress in March 1922
and the Twelfth, in April 1923, matters in the Party had changed
crucially and decisively. The dangers inherent in the unchecked rise
of the bureaucracy Lenin now perceived to be paramount. He dis-
tinctly saw the dangers for Soviet Russia presented by 'the onslaught
of that really Russian man, the Great-Russian chauvinist, in substance
a rascal and a tyrant, such as the typical Russian bureaucrat is . . .'.
'There is no doubt', Lenin continued, 'that the infinitesimal percent-
age of sovietised workers will drown in the tide of chauvinistic
Great-Russian riffraff like a fly in milk.'[58] The great internal danger is
the bureaucrat, he notes elsewhere – 'the communist who occupies a
responsible (or not responsible) Soviet post and enjoys universal
respect as a conscientious man'.[59] But now we have bureaucrats
everywhere, he complained during the early months of his illness
(Figure 68). The Party was now 'suffering from the general conditions
of our truly Russian (even though Soviet) bureaucratic ways'.[60]

Lenin's comment about 'that really Russian man, the Great-
Russian chauvinist' was written in description of Stalin towards the
end of 1922, when Lenin's apprehensions about the reliability of his
Commissar for National Minorities were growing apace. Stalin had
already shown himself to be fundamentally a Russian nationalist at
heart, with little sympathy for the self-development of minority
groups within a Federation of equal members, as Lenin wanted. Stalin
had also expressed doubt over the proposition – still dear to Lenin
and the leadership in 1920–22 – that Germany, Poland, Hungary and

55. Trotsky, *Literature and Revolution*,
p 111.

56. Ibid., p 113.

57. Ibid., p 112.

58. Lenin, *Collected Works*, Vol 36,
p 606; Voslensky, *Nomenklatura*, p 43.

59. Lenin, *Collected Works*, Vol 33, p 225.

60. Ibid., p 229.

Figure 68
Lenin in August 1922 (photo: *SCR*)

possibly Finland would soon undergo revolutionary upheaval and wish to join such a Federation. Now Stalin attempted, along with his ally and colleague Ordzhonikidze, to carry out a purge of the Central Committee of the Georgian Bolshevik Party when they showed resistance to the imposition of colonial relations with the Russian Federation. The leadership in Moscow realised that something abnormal was afoot, and Lenin carried out a personal investigation to determine the cause of the trouble. (He ignored Dzerzhinsky's official report on the affair, which largely exonerated the chauvinists.) He concluded that Stalin had been hasty, imperious and bad-mannered, and had misused his power in an effort to get the Georgian committee to succumb quickly. This was important evidence that Stalin was administratively crude as well as ambitious, and that his increasing power should be watched.

Yet circumstances now played their part. Lenin had had a minor stroke in May 1922. In the middle of the Georgian crisis late in the same year he had another, which curtailed his active opposition to the Stalin faction on the Georgian question. Yet this was not before he dictated the notes that became known as his 'testament', in December 1922. In them, Lenin warned not only of a dangerous 'split' that might open up between the proletariat and the peasantry, but also of a deterioration in the 'split' between Stalin and Trotsky which, though brewing for several years, now appeared capable of dividing the Party irrevocably. He also dictated a memoir on the matter of his succession, particularly the rivalry between 'the two outstanding leaders of the present Central Committee', Stalin and Trotsky. Stalin, he noted, had concentrated 'boundless power' in his hands, and yet may not prove capable of using this power with sufficient caution.[61] Trotsky was distinguished by his exceptional capabilities and was 'personally perhaps the most able man in the present Central Committee'; yet his abilities were marred by his 'too far-reaching self-confidence and excessive absorption in the purely administrative side of things'. Lenin spoke well of the younger men Bukharin and Pyatakov, particularly the former, whom he thought was 'not only the most valuable and biggest theoretician of the Party but is rightly considered the favourite of the whole Party'. The decisive passage however was dictated on 4 January 1923 as a postscript, which recommended Stalin's removal from the post of General Secretary.

> Stalin is too rude, and this fault, fully tolerable in our midst and in the relations among us Communists, becomes intolerable in the office of General Secretary. Therefore I propose to the comrades that they devise a way of shifting Stalin from this position and appointing to it another man who in all other respects falls on the other side of the scale from Comrade Stalin, namely more tolerant, more loyal, more polite and more considerate of comrades, less capricious, etc. This circumstance may seem an insignificant trifle. But I think that from the point of view of preventing a split, and from the point of view of what I have written above about the relation between Stalin and Trotsky, this is no trifle, or it is a trifle that may take on decisive significance.

Then came Lenin's final and incapacitating stroke, on 9 March 1923.

61. Lenin, Vol 45, pp 343–8. In this and following quotations from the testament I am relying upon the version reproduced in R. C. Tucker, *Stalin as Revolutionary 1879–1929*, Chatto & Windus, London, 1974, pp 270–1.

He was unable to attend the Twelfth Congress of the Party, and hence to speak against Stalin on the Georgian question. He was also unable to publish his advice to the Party that 'Comrade Stalin be removed from the office' of General Secretary; and from that day until several weeks after his death some ten months later, the note which contained the advice remained in its envelope, unopened and unread.

Precisely why the testament and its postscript remained unread and unpublished is still a matter of urgent historical controversy.[62] But the fact is that by a mixture of circumstance and a failure to plan such matters prudently, no adequate mechanisms for changes in the Bolshevik leadership were worked out in 1923, and the succession was effectively left to the politics of factional dispute, in which the main contenders were all immensely capable and ruthless. The proletariat, by this stage, had lost most of its organic contact with the Party hierachy, and the peasants, who had been so central to Lenin's concern, had not yet been adequately brought within its fold to enable them to participate. By a steady process of attrition, the 'culture' of Bolshevism was changing fast. No doubt, too, was the climate in which it would survive. The effects of these rapid changes on the arts will be examined in Volume Two.

62. One may refer here to the standard accounts of Soviet political history such as Tucker, *Stalin as Revolutionary*, Chapter 7; Carr, *The Russian Revolution from Lenin to Stalin 1917–1929*, Macmillan, London and Basingstoke, 1979, pp 61–3, 71–3 ; and Schapiro, *The Communist Party of the Soviet Union* (first edition), Methuen, London, 1963, Chapter 4.

Glossary of Abbreviations

Agitprop   *Agitation and Propaganda* (Agitatsiya i propaganda)

AKhRR   *Association of Artists of Revolutionary Russia* (Assotsiatsiya khudozhnikov revolyutsionnoi Rossii)

Bytie   *Life (or Being)*

Cheka   *Extraordinary Commission for Combating Counter-Revolution and Sabotage* (Vserossiskaya chrezvychainaya kommissiya po borbe s kontrrevolyutsiey i sabatazhem)

FEKS   *Factory of the Eccentric Actor* (Fabrika ekstsentricheskogo aktera)

GITIS   *State Institute for Theatrical Art* (Gosudarstvennyi institut teatralnogo iskusstva)

GIZ   *State Publishing House*

Glavlit   *Central Literary Office* (Glavnoe upravlenie literaturnikh izdatelstv)

Glavpolit-prosvet   *Central Political Education Committee of Narkompros* (Glavnyi politiko-prosvetitelnyi komitet Narkomprosa)

INKhUK   *Institute of Artistic Culture* (Institut khudozhestvennoi kultury)

IZO   *Art Department* (Otdel izobrazitelnykh iskusstv)

KOMFUT   *Communist Futurists*

Komintern   *Communist International* (Kommunistichesky internatsional)

Komsomol   *Communist Youth Organisation* (Kommunistichesky soyuz molodezhi)

LEF   *Left Front of the Arts* (Levyi front iskusstv)

Metfak   *Metalwork Faculty of the VKhUTEMAS* (Metalloobrabatyvayushchii fakultet)

MUZO   *Musical Department of Narkompros* (Muzeinoe otdelenie)

Narkompros   *People's Commissariat of Enlightenment* (Narodnyi komissariat prosveshcheniya)

Narkomzem   *People's Commissariat of Agriculture* (Narodnyi komissariat zemledeliya)

NEP   *New Economic Policy* (Novaya ekonomicheskaya politika)

NOT   *The Scientific Organisation of Labour* (Nauchnaya organizatsiya truda)

NOZh   *New Society of Painters* (Novoe obshchestvo zhivopistsev)

OBMOKhU   *Society of Young Artists* (Obshchestvo molodykh khudozhnikov)

OPOYAZ   *Society for the Study of Poetic Languages* (Obshchestvo po izucheniyu poeticheskogo yazyka)

OST   *Society of Easel Painters* (Obshchestvo khudozhnikov-stankovistov)

Peredvizhniki   *Association for Travelling Art Exhibitions*

Pereval   *The Pass or Crossing*

Proletkult   *Proletarian Culture* (Proletarskaya kultura)

Rabkor   *Worker Correspondent* (Rabochii korrespondent)

RAPM   *Russian Association of Proletarian Musicians* (Rossiiskaya assotsiatsiya proletarskikh muzykantov)

ROSTA   *Russian Telegraph Agency* (Rossiiskoe telegrafnoe agentsvo)

RSFSR   *Russian Soviet Socialist Federal Republic* (Rossiiskaya sovetskaya federativnaya sotsialisticheskaya respublika)

Sinskulptarch   *Collective for Sculptural and Architectural Synthesis* (Kollektiv skulpturno-arkhitekturnyi sintez)

Sovnarkom   *Council of People's Commissars* (Sovet narodnykh komissarov)

SRs   *Social-Revolutionaries*

SVOMAS   *State Free Art Studios* (Svobodniye khudozhestvennye gosudarstvennye masterskie)

TEO   *Theatre Department of Narkompros* (Teatralnoe otdelenie)

TsIT   *Central Institute of Labour* (Tsentralnyi institut truda)

UNOVIS   *Affirmers of New Art* (Utverditeli
            novogo iskusstvo)
VAPP   *All-Russian Association of Proletarian
            Writers* (Vserossiiskaya assotsiatsiya
            proletarskikh pisatelei)
VKhUTEMAS   *Higher State Artistic & Technical
            Workshops* (Vysshie
            gosudarstvennye khudozhestvenno-
            tekhnicheskie masterskie)
VKP(b)   *All-Russian Communist Party
            (Bolsheviks)* (Vserossiskaya
            kommunisticheskaya partiya
            [Bolshevikov]).

VSNKh   *Supreme Council of the National
            Economy* (Vysshyi sovet narodnogo
            khozyaistva)
VTsIK   *All-Russian Central Executive
            Committee* (Vserossiiskii
            tsentralnyi ispolnitelnyi komitet)
VTsSPS   *All Union Central Council of Trade
            Unions* (Vsesoyuznii tsentralnyi
            sovet professionalnikh soyuzov)
Zhivskulp- *Collective for the Synthesis of Painting,
tarkh   Sculpture and Architecture* (Kollectiv
            zhivopisno-skulpturno-arkhitektur-
            nogo sintez)

Bibliography

M. Adams, '"Red Star": Another Look at Alexander Bogdanov', *Slavic Review*, Spring 1989, pp 1–15.

D. Ades, *Photomontage*, Thames and Hudson, London 1976.

AKhR (exhibition catalogue), Cologne 1929.

V. Alexandrova, *A History of Soviet Literature, 1917–1964: from Gorky to Solzhenitsyn*, translated by Mirra Ginzburg, Doubleday & Co., New York 1964.

T. Ali, *The Stalinist Legacy*, Penguin, Harmondsworth 1984; Boulder, Colorado 1985.

V. Allen, *The Russians are Coming: The Politics of Anti-Sovietism*, The Moor Press, Shipley 1987.

B. V. Alpers, *Teatr Revolyutsii*, Moscow 1928.

T. Andersen, *Moderne Russisk Kunst 1910–1930*, Borgen, Copenhagen, 1967.

M. Anikst (ed), *Soviet Commercial Design of the Twenties*, Thames and Hudson, London 1987.

Y. Annenkov, 'Soviet Art and Socialist Realism', *Studies in the Soviet Union* (Munich), Vol 7, no 2, November 1967, pp 152–7.

Art and Revolution: Soviet Art and Design since 1917 (exhibition catalogue), Arts Council of Great Britain, Hayward Gallery, London 1971.

Art and Revolution, Russian and Soviet Art, 1910–1932/Kunst und Revolution, Russische und Sowjetische Kunst 1910–1932 (exhibition catalogue), Osterreichischen Museum für Angewandte Kunst, Vienna 1988.

Art et Poesie Russes, 1900–1932, Textes Choisis (exhibition catalogue), Centre Georges Pompidou, Paris 1979.

Art in the Soviet Union from 1917 to the 1970s, Aurora, Leningrad 1977.

Art into Production: Soviet Textiles, Fashion and Ceramics, 1917–1935 (exhibition catalogue), Museum of Modern Art, Oxford and Crafts Council, London 1984.

Artists Write to W. Grohmann (ed. K. Gutbrod), Verlag M. Dumont Schauberg, Cologne 1968.

W. W. Austin, *Music in the Twentieth Century from Debussy through Stravinsky*, J. M. Dent and Sons Ltd, London 1966.

L. Averbakh, *Za proletarskaya literaturnu*, Leningrad 1925.

V. Azarkovich et al (eds) *Vystavki sovetskogo izobrazitelnogo iskusstva Vol 1 (1917–1932)*, Moscow, 1965.

K. Bailes, 'Lenin and Bogdanov: the End of an Alliance', in A. Cordier (ed), *Columbia Essays in International Affairs*, Vol 2, New York 1967.

K. Bailes, 'Alexei Gastev and the Soviet Controversy over Taylorism, 1918–1924', *Soviet Studies*, Vol XXIX, no 3, July 1977, pp 373–94.

K. Bailes, *Technology and Society under Lenin and Stalin*, Princeton University Press, Princeton, New Jersey 1978.

A. Ball, 'Lenin and the Question of Private Trade in Soviet Russia', *Slavic Review*, Fall 1984.

S. Bann and J. Bowlt (eds), *Russian Formalism*, Scottish Academic Press, London and Edinburgh 1973.

S. Bann (ed), *The Tradition of Constructivism*, Thames and Hudson, London 1974.

N. Barabanova, *Yury Pimenov*, Leningrad 1972.

J. Barber, 'Stalin's Letter to the Editor of *Proletarskaya revolyutsia*', *Soviet Studies*, January 1976, pp 21–41.

A. Barmin, *Memoirs of a Soviet Diplomat: Twenty Years in the Service of the USSR*, Lovat Dickson, London 1938.

A. Barmin, *One Who Survived: The Life Story of a Russian under the Soviets*, G. P. Putnam and Sons, New York 1945.

S. Baron, *The Russian Jew under the Tsars and Soviets*, Macmillan Co., New York, Collier Macmillan, London 1964.

V. Barooshian, *Russian Cubo-Futurism 1910–1930: A Study in Avant-Gardism*, Mouton 1974, The Hague, Paris 1974.

V. Barooshian, 'The Avant-Garde and the Russian Revolution', *Russian Literature Triquarterly*, Fall 1972, pp 347–60.

A. Barr, *Cubism and Abstract Art*, Museum of Modern Art, New York 1936.

A. Barr, 'Russian Diary 1927–28', *October*, Vol 7, Winter 1978, pp 7–56.

S. Barron and M. Tuchman (eds), *The Avant-Garde in Russia, 1910–30; New Perspectives*, MIT Press, Cambridge, Massachusetts, London, Los Angeles 1980.

R. Bauer, *The New Man in Soviet Psychology*, Harvard University Press, Cambridge, Massachusetts 1952.

L. Baxandall and S. Morawski (eds), *Marx and Engels on Literature and Art*, International General, New York 1974.

F. Belov, *The History of a Soviet Collective Farm*, Frederick A. Praeger for the Research Programme on the USSR, New York 1955; also Routledge and Kegan Paul, London 1956.

W. Benjamin, *Moscow Diary* (ed. G. Smith), Harvard University Press, Cambridge, Massachusetts, and London 1986.

W. Benjamin, 'Disputation bei Meyerhold', *Gesammelte Schrifte*, IV, pp 481–3.

A. Berkman, *The Bolshevik Myth (Diary 1920–1922)*, Pluto Press, London 1989.

A. Berkman, *The Anti-Climax. The Concluding Chapter, My Russian Diary 'The Bolshevik Myth'*, Pluto Press, London 1989.

A. C. Birnholz, 'On the Meaning of Malevich's "White on White"', *Art International*, XXXI/I, 1972.

B. Biro, 'Bukharin and Socialist Realism', *Marxist Studies*, Vol 2, no 1, London 1970.

P. Blake and M. Hayward (eds), *Dissonant Voices in Soviet Literature*, George Allen and Unwin, London 1964.

A. Blok, *The Twelve and other poems* (translated by J. Stallworthy and P. France), Journeyman Press, London 1982.

A. Blunt, 'Art under Socialism and Capitalism', in C. Day Lewis (ed), *The Mind in Chains*, Frederick Muller, 1937.

A. Bogdanov, 'Die Kunst und das Proletariat', *Der Kentaur*, Leipzig 1919.

A. Bogdanov, *O proletarskoi kulture, 1904–1924*, Moscow 1925.

A. D. Borovsky, *V. Malagis*, Leningrad 1987.

J. E. Bowlt, 'The Failed Utopia: Russian Art 1917–32', *Art in America*, Vol 59, no 4, July/Aug 1971, pp 40–51.

J. E. Bowlt, 'The Virtues of Soviet Realism', *Art in America*, Vol 60, no 6, November 1972, pp 100–7.

J. E. Bowlt, 'Russian Formalism in the Visual Arts', *20th Century Studies*, no 7/8, December 1972, pp 131–46.

J. E. Bowlt, 'Pavel Filonov', *Studio International*, July/Aug 1973, pp 30–5.

J. E. Bowlt, 'Pavel Filonov: An Alternative Tradition?' *Art Journal*, XXIV, Spring 1975, pp 208–16.

J. E. Bowlt, 'Early Soviet Art', *Art and Artists*, November 1975, pp 34–43.

J. E. Bowlt, 'From Surface to Space: The Art of Lyubov Popova', *Structurist*, 15/16, 1975/6.

J. E. Bowlt, *Russian Art 1875–1975. A Collection of Essays*, MSS Information Corporation, New York 1976.

J. E. Bowlt, 'The Blue Rose: Russian Symbolism in Art', *Burlington Magazine*, August 1976, pp 566–75.

J. E. Bowlt, 'Rodchenko and Chaikov', *Art and Artists*, London, October 1976.

J. E. Bowlt, *Russian Art of the Avant-Garde: Theory and Criticism, 1902–1934*, the Viking Press, New York 1976.

J. E. Bowlt, 'The Union of Youth', in G. Gibson and H. Tjalsma (eds), *Russian Modernism: Culture & the Avant-Garde*, Cornell University Press, Ithaca, New York 1976, pp 165–87.

J. E. Bowlt, 'Russian Sculpture and Lenin's Plan of Monumental Propaganda', in H. A. Millon and L. Nochlin (eds), *Art and Architecture in the Service of Politics*, MIT Press, London and Cambridge, Massachusetts 1978.

J. E. Bowlt, 'Afterword', *October*, Winter 1978, p 52.

H. N. Brailsford, 'The Russian Communist Party', *Contemporary Review*, January 1921.

H. N. Brailsford, 'Education & Art in Russia', *The Nation*, 24 December 1920, 15 January 1921.

E. Braun (ed), *Meyerhold on Theatre*, Methuen and Co., London and New York 1969.

B. Brewster (ed and intro), 'Documents from NOVY LEF', *Screen*, XV, no 3, 1974.

B. Brewster, 'The Soviet State, The Communist Party and the Arts', *Red Letters*, no 3, London 1976.

B. Brewster, 'From Shklovsky to Brecht: A Reply', *Screen*, XV, no 2, 1974, pp 82–102.

O. Brik, *Iskusstvo v proizvodstve*, Moscow 1921.

O. Brik, 'Selected Writings', *Screen*, XV, no 3, 1974.

O. Brik, 'Mayakovsky and the Literary Movements of 1917–30', *Screen*, Autumn 1974, XV, no 3.

A. Broderson, *The Soviet Worker, Labour and Government in Soviet Society*, Random House, New York 1966.

N. Brodsky, V. Lvov-Rogachevski and N. Sidorov, *Literaturnye Manifesty*, Moscow 1929.

A. Brodsky, *Isaak Izrailevits Brodsky*, Moscow 1973.

R. Browder and A. Kerensky (eds), *Provisional Government of 1917: Documents*, Princeton University Press, 1961.

E. J. Brown, *The Proletarian Episode in Russian Literature, 1928–1932*, Columbia University Press, New York 1953.

E. J. Brown (ed), *Major Soviet Writers: Essays in Criticism*, Oxford University Press, Oxford and London 1973.

E. J. Brown, *Russian Literature since the Revolution*, Collier Books, New York, Collier Macmillan, London 1963 (revised edition, Harvard University Press, Cambridge, Massachusetts, and London 1982).

A. S. Bubnov, *VKP (b)*, Moscow 1931.

B. Buchloh, S. Guilbaut and D. Solkin (eds), *Modernism and Modernity: the Vancouver Conference Papers*, Nova Scotia College of Art and Design 1983.

N. Bukharin, *Historical Materialism: a system of society*, New York International Publishers, 1925.

N. Bukharin, *Culture in Two Worlds: the crisis of capitalist cultures and the problem of culture in the USSR*, New York International Pamphlets no 42, 1934.

N. Bukharin and E. Preobrazhensky, *The ABC of Communism*, trans E. and C. Paul, Communist Party of Great Britain, London 1922.

M. M. Bullitt, 'Towards a Marxist Theory of Aesthetics: The Development of Socialist Realism in the Soviet Union', *Russian Review*, January 1976, pp 53–76.

C. Bunt, *Russian Art From Scyths to Soviets*, The Studio, London and New York 1946.

J. Bunyan, *Intervention, Civil War, and Communism in Russia: April–December 1918, Documents and Materials*, Johns Hopkins Press, Baltimore 1936.

J. Bunyan and H. Fisher, *The Bolshevik Revolution, 1917–18*, Stanford University Press, Stanford, California, 1934.

J. Burbank, *Intelligentsia and Revolution: Russian Views of Bolshevism, 1917–1922*, Oxford University Press, Oxford and New York 1986.

E. H. Carr, *The Twenty Years' Crisis, 1919–39, An Introduction to the Study of International Relations*, Macmillan, London and Basingstoke 1946, 1981.

E. H. Carr, *The Bolshevik Revolution, 1917–1923* (3 Vols), Penguin, Harmondsworth, 1950; London 1966.

E. H. Carr, 'A Historical Turning Point: Marx, Lenin, Stalin', in R. Piper (ed) *Revolutionary Russia*, Harvard University Press, Cambridge, Massachusetts 1968.

E. H. Carr, *Socialism in One Country, 1924–26*, Vol 1, Harmondsworth, Penguin, London 1970.

E. H. Carr, *The Russian Revolution from Lenin to Stalin, 1917–1929*, Macmillan, London and Basingstoke, 1979.

E. H. Carter, *The New Theatre and the Cinema of Soviet Russia*, Chapman & Dodd, London 1924.

E. H. Carter, 'Russian Art Movements Since 1917', *Drawing and Design* (London), Vol 4, February 1928, pp 37–42.

M. Chagall, *My Life*, Owen, London 1985.

M. Chamot, *Russian Painting and Sculpture*, Tate Gallery, London 1963.

L. Chasanowitsch and L. Motzkin (eds), *Die Judenfrage der Gegenwart: Dokumenten sammlung*, Stockholm 1919.

S. Chase, R. Dunn, R. Tugwell (eds), *Soviet Russia in the Second Decade*, US Department of Trade, New York 1928.

W. Chase, 'Voluntarism, Mobilisation and Coercion: *Subbotniki*, 1919–1921', *Soviet Studies*, Vol XLI, no 1, January 1989, pp 111–28.

V. E. Chazanova, *Iz istorii sovetskoy arkhitectury, 1926–32*, Moscow 1970.

I. Christie and D. Elliott (eds), *Eisenstein at Ninety* (exhibition catalogue), Museum of Modern Art, Oxford 1988.

I. Christie and J. Gillet (eds), *Futurism, Formalism, Feks, Eccentrism and Soviet Cinema, 1918–1936*, British Film Institute, London 1978.

T. Clark, 'Constructivism and Soviet Cultural Policies', unpublished PhD thesis, University of Sussex, 1989.

J. L. Cohen, *Le Corbusier et La Mystique de L'URSS: Theories et Projects pour Moscou, 1928–1936*, Brussels 1987.

S. Cohen, *Bukharin and the Bolshevik Revolution: A Political Biography 1888–1938*, London 1971 and Wildwood House, New York 1974.

Communist Morality (essays by Marx, Engels, Lenin, Dzerzhinsky, Krupskaya, et al), Moscow, n.d.

S. Compton, 'Malevich's Suprematism: The Higher Intuition', *Burlington Magazine*, no 881, August 1926, pp 576–85.

S. Compton, 'Malevich and the Fourth Dimension', *Studio International*, Vol 187, no 965, April 1974, pp 190–5.

S. Compton, *The World Backwards: Russian Futurist Books, 1912–16*, British Library, London 1978.

S. Compton, *Chagall*, Royal Academy of Arts with Weidenfeld & Nicolson, London 1985.

B. Comrie and G. Stope, *The Russian Language since the Revolution*, Clarendon Press, Oxford 1978.

R. Conquest (ed), *The Politics of Ideas in the USSR*, Bodley Head, London 1967.

R. Conquest, *The Great Terror*, Macmillan & Co., London, Melbourne 1968.

C. Cooke, *The Town of Socialism: from Reformers and Constructivists to a Systems View of the Soviet City*, Academy Editions, London 1986.

C. Cooke, 'Russian Responses to the Garden City Idea', *Architectural Review*, June 1978, pp 353–63.

A. Cordier (ed), *Columbia Essays in International Affairs*, Vol 2, Columbia University Press, New York 1967.

G. S. Counts, *The Soviet Challenge to America*, The Stratford Company, Boston, Mass 1930.

J. Cournos, 4 articles on Russian Proletkult in *The New Europe*, 30 October – 20 November, 1919.

M. Cullerne Brown, *Art Under Stalin*, Phaidon, Oxford 1991.

M. Damus, *Sozialistischer Realismus und Kunst im National-Sozialismus*, Fischer Taschenbuch, Frankfurt 1981.

T. Dan, *The Origin of Bolshevism* (1946) Secker and Warburg, London 1964.

I. Davies, 'Aspects of Art and Theory in Russia from 1905 to 1924 in their Relationship to the Development of Avant-Garde Ideas in the West', unpublished PhD Thesis, University of Edinburgh, 1974.

I. Davies, 'Primitivism in the First Wave of the Twentieth Century Avant-Garde in Russia,' *Studio International*, Vol 186, no 958, September 1973, pp 80–4.

C. Day Lewis, *The Mind in Chains*, Fredrick Muller, London 1937.

F. Deak, 'The Influence of Italian Futurism in Russia', *The Drama Review*, Vol 19, no 4, December 1975, pp 88–94.

A. Deineka, *Zhizn, Iskusstvo, Vremiya*, Leningrad 1974.

L. Denisov, *Sergei Vasilievich Gerasimov*, Moscow 1972.

I. Deutscher, *Stalin: A Political Biography*, Oxford University Press, Oxford and London 1949.

I. Deutscher, *The Prophet Armed; Trotsky 1879–1921*, Oxford University Press, London and Oxford 1954.

I. Deutscher, *The Prophet Unarmed; Trotsky 1921–1929*, Oxford University Press, Oxford and London 1959.

I. Deutscher, *The Prophet Outcast: Trotsky 1928–1941*, Oxford University Press, London and Oxford 1963.

I. Deutscher, *Lenin's Childhood*, Oxford University Press, London and Oxford 1970.

I. Deutscher, *Marxism in Our Time* (ed T. Deutscher), Berkeley, Ramparts Press, London 1971.

I. Deutscher, 'The Roots of Bureaucracy', *Canadian Slavic Studies*, Fall 1969; in I. Deutscher, *Marxism in Our Time*, London 1971.

M. Djilas, *The New Class*, Thames and Hudson, London and New York 1957.

W. Duranty, *I Write as I Please*, Thames and Hudson, London and New York 1935.

M. Eastman, *Education and Art in Soviet Russia in the Light of Official Decrees and Documents*, Socialist Publication Society, New York 1919.

M. Eastman, *Leon Trotsky: The Portrait of a Youth*, Faber and Gwyer, London 1926.

M. Eastman, *Artists in Uniform: A Study of Literature and Bureaucratism*, G. Allen and Unwin, London 1934.

W. Edgerton, 'The Serapion Brothers: An Early Soviet Controversy', *American, Slavic and East European Review*, Vol VIII, no 1, February 1949.
N. Edmunds, 'The Politics of Music: The Development of Soviet Music, 1917–1939', unpublished MA dissertation, University of Sussex, 1988.
B. Efimov, *Karikatury*, Moscow 1924.
Ezhegodnik literatury i iskusstva, Moscow 1929.
I. Ehrenberg, *A Street in Moscow* (trans. S. Volochova), Grayson and Grayson, London 1933.
I. Ehrenberg, *People & Life: Memoirs of 1891–1917*, MacGibbon and Kee, London 1961.
I. Ehrenberg, *The First Years of the Revolution, 1918–1921*, MacGibbon and Kee, London 1962.
S. Eisenstein, *Film Sense* (ed and trans. J. Leyda), London 1943.
J. Elderfield, 'The Line of Free Men; Tatlin's Tower and the Age of Invention', *Studio International*, Vol 178, no 916, November 1969, pp 162–7.
J. Elderfield, 'Constructivism and the Objective World: An Essay on Production Art and Proletarian Culture', *Studio International*, Vol 180, no 923, Sept 1970, pp 73–80.
D. Elliott (ed), *Alexander Rodchenko*, Oxford, Museum of Modern Art, 1979.
D. Elliott, *New Worlds, Russian Art and Society 1900–1937*, Thames and Hudson, London 1986.
C. Emsley (ed), *Conflict and Stability in Europe*, Croom Helm, for the Open University Press, London 1979.
M. Enzensberger, 'Osip Brik, LEF and Formalism', *Screen*, XV, no 3, Autumn 1974.
V. Erlich, 'Social and Aesthetic Criteria in Soviet Russian Criticism', in E. J. Simmons (ed), *Continuity and Change in Russian and Soviet Thought*, Harvard University Press, Cambridge, Massachusetts 1955.
V. Erlich, *Russian Formalism: History, Doctrine*, Mouton & Co, s'Gravenhage 1955.
V. Erlich, 'Russian Formalism', *Journal of the History of Ideas*, XXXIV, 4, 1973.
H. Ermolaev, *Soviet Literary Theories, 1917–34: The Genesis of Socialist Realism*, University of California Press, Berkeley, California 1963.
Erste Russische Kunstausstellung (exhibition catalogue), Van Diemen Gallery, Berlin, 1922.
S. Esenin, *Confessions of a Hooligan: Fifty Collected Poems by S. Esenin*, trans & intro by G. Thurley, Carcanet Press, Cheadle 1973.
Etapi bolshogo pyti: Ekspozitsiya proizvedenii sovetskogo izobrazitelnogo iskusstva, posvashennaya XXVI sezdy KPCC, iz sovremennoi gosudarstvennoi tretyakovskoi galerei gosudarstvennoi kartinnoi galerei SSSR, Moscow 1986.
M. Etkind, *Natan Altman*, Moscow 1971.
Exhibition of Contemporary Art of Soviet Russia, Painting, Graphic, Sculpture (foreword by Christian Brinton, introduction by P. Novitsky), Grand Central Palace, New York, February 1929.
Exhibition of Soviet Art, 1927–33 (exhibition catalogue), Akademie der Künste, Berlin 1977.
Exposition Internationale des Arts Decoratifs et Industriels Modernes. Union de Republic Sovietistes Socialistes (catalogue), Paris 1925.

M. Fainsod, *How Russia is Ruled*, Harvard University Press, Cambridge, Massachusetts 1953.
S. Fitzpatrick, 'The Emergence of Glaviskusstvo: Class War on the Cultural Front, Moscow 1928–9', *Soviet Studies*, October 1971, pp 236–7.
S. Fitzpatrick, 'The "Soft" Line on Culture and its Enemies: Soviet Cultural Policy, 1922–1927', *Slavic Review*, no 2, 1974, pp 267–87.
S. Fitzpatrick, *The Commissariat of Enlightenment: Soviet Organisation of the Arts under Lunacharsky*, Cambridge University Press, 1970.
S. Fitzpatrick, 'Cultural Revolution in Russia, 1928–32', *Journal of Contemporary History*, January 1974, pp 33–5.
S. Fitzpatrick (ed), *Cultural Revolution in Russia, 1928–1931*, Indiana University Press, Bloomington, Indiana 1978.
S. Fitzpatrick, 'Cultural Revolution as Class War', in S. Fitzpatrick (ed), *Cultural Revolution in Russia*, 1978.
S. Fitzpatrick, 'Stalin and the Making of a New Elite, 1928–1939', *Slavic Review*, Vol XXXVIII, 1979, pp 377–402.
J. Fizer, 'The Problem of the Unconscious in the Creative Process as Treated by Soviet Aesthetics', *Journal of Aesthetics and Art Criticism*, Vol XXI, no 4, Summer 1963, pp 399–406.
K. Frampton, 'Notes on Soviet Urbanism', *Architects' Year Book 12*, London 1977.
J. Freeman, J. Kunitz and L. Lozowick, *Voices of October, Art and Literature in Soviet Russia*, Vanguard Press, New York 1930.
R. Fülöp-Miller, *The Mind and Face of Bolshevism: An Examination of Cultural Life in Soviet Russia*, G. P. Putnam and Sons: London and New York, 1927.

N. Gabo, 'The 1922 Soviet Exhibition', *Studio International*, Vol 182/3, no 938, p 171.
H. Gassner and E. Gillen, *Zwischen Revolutionskunst und Sozialistischem Realismus: Dokumente und Kommentare: Kunstdebatten in der Sowjetunion von 1917 bis 1934*, DuMont Verlag, Cologne 1979.
A. Gastev, *Poeziya rabochego udara*, Moscow 1971.
J. Arch Getty, *The Origin of the Great Purges; The Soviet Communist Party Reconsidered, 1933–1938*, Cambridge University Press, Cambridge 1985.
G. Gibian (ed and trans), *Russia's Lost Literature of the Absurd: Selected Works of Daniil Kharms and Alexander Vvedensky*, Cornell University Press, Ithaca 1971.
G. Gibian and H. Tjalsma (eds), *Russian Modernism: Culture and the Avant-Garde, 1900–1930*, Cornell University Press, Ithaca & London 1976.
Z. Gifelman, 'The Communist Party and Soviet Jewry', in R. H. Marshall (ed) *Aspects of Religion in the Soviet Union, 1917–1967*, University of Chicago Press, Chicago and London 1971.
G. Gill, *The Rules of the Communist Party of the Soviet Union*, Macmillan, Basingstoke 1988.
E.S. Ginzburg, *Within the Whirlwind*, Collins & Harvill, London 1981.
M. Ginzburg, *Style and Epoch* (1924), trans & intro by A. Senkevitch Jr, MIT Press, Cambridge, Massachusetts and London, England, 1982.

A. Gleason, P. Kenez, R. Stites (eds) *Bolshevik Culture; Experiment and Order in the Russian Revolution*, Indiana University Press, Bloomington, Indiana 1985.

A. Gleizes and J. Metzinger, *Du Cubisme*, Paris 1912.

M. V. Glenny (ed), *Three Soviet Plays*, Penguin Books, Harmondsworth 1966.

M. V. Glenny (ed and intro), *Novy Mir: A Selection, 1925–1967*, Jonathan Cape, London 1972.

4 Goda AKhRR, 1922–1926 Sbornik (ed A. V. Grigoriev and others), Moscow 1926.

E. Goldman, *My Disillusionment in Russia*, William Heinemann, London 1923.

D. Goldstein, 'Zabolotskii and Filonov: the Science of Composition', *Slavic Review*, Winter 1989, pp 578–91.

N. Goncharenko, 'Notes on Soviet Aesthetics', *British Journal of Aesthetics*, V, 1965, pp 191–6.

D. Gorbov, *Poiski Galatei*, Moscow 1929.

M. Gorby, *Days with Lenin*, Martin Lawrence, London and New York 1932.

N. Gorchakov, *Stanislavsky Directs*, Limelight Editions, New York 1985.

M. Gordon, 'Meyerhold's Biomechanics', *The Drama Review*, Vol 18, no 3, September 1974.

M. Gordon, 'Radlov's Theatre of Popular Comedy', *The Drama Review*, Vol 19, no 4, December 1975, pp 113–16.

G. Gorzka, *A. Bogdanov und der russische Proletkult: Theorie und Praxis einer sozialistischen Kulturrevolution*, Frankfurt am Main, 1980.

F. de Graaff, *Sergei Esenin: A Biographical Sketch*, Mouton & Co, London, The Hague, Paris 1966.

I. Grabar, et al (eds), *Istoriya russkogo iskusstva*, Akademia Nauk SSR, Moscow 1957.

L. R. Graham, *The Soviet Academy of Sciences and the Communist Party, 1927–1932*, Princeton University Press 1967.

C. Gray, 'The Genesis of Socialist Realist Painting: Futurism – Suprematism – Constructivism', *Soviet Survey*, no 27, Jan/March 1959, pp 32–9.

C. Gray, *The Great Experiment: Russian Art 1863–1922*, Thames and Hudson, London 1962.

A. Grechaninov, *My Life*, Coleman-Ross, New York 1952.

D. Grille, *Lenin's Rivale: Bogdanov und seine Philosophie*, Abhandlungen des Bundesinstituts fur ostwissenschaftliche and internationale Studien, Cologne 1986.

W. Grohmann, *Wassily Kandinsky, Life and Work*, Thames and Hudson, London, Cologne and New York 1958.

I. Gronsky and V. Perelman (eds), *Assotsiatsiya khudozhnikov revolyutsionnoi Rossii: sbornik, vospominanii, statei, dokumentov*, Moscow 1973.

J. Grossman, 'Alexander Bogdanov and the Ideology of Proletarian Culture', Master's essay, Columbia University 1965.

M. Guerman (ed), *Art of the October Revolution*, Aurora Art Publishers, Leningrad, 1979.

M. Guerman (intro), *Soviet Art, 1920s–1930s, Russian Museum, Leningrad*, Sovietsky Khudozhnik, Moscow and Harry N. Abrams, New York 1988.

K. Gutbrot (ed), *Artists Write to W. Grohmann*, Cologne 1968.

M. Haraszti, *The Velvet Prison: Artists under State Socialism*, Taurus, London 1988.

N. Harding, *Lenin's Political Thought*, Macmillan, London and Basingstoke, 1977.

M. Hayward, *Writers in Russia, 1917–1978*, Harvill, London 1983.

M. Heller and A. Nekrich, *Utopia in Power*, Hutchinson, London 1986.

S. Hendel, *The Soviet Crucible*, Van Nostrand, Princeton 1959.

A. Higgens, 'Art and Politics in the Russian Revolution', *Studio International*, Vol 180, no 927, November 1970, pp 164–7; no 929, December 1970, pp 224–7.

A. Higgens, 'The Development of the Theory of Socialist Realism in Russia, 1917 to 1932', *Studio International*, Vol 181, no 932, April 1971, pp 155–9.

J. Holl, *La Jeune Peinture Contemporaine*, Paris 1912.

C. Holme (ed), *Art in the USSR*, Studio Special, London 1935.

M. Holquist, 'The Mayakovsky Problem', in J. Ehrmann (ed), *Literature and Revolution* (Yale French Studies), Boston 1970.

J. Howard, 'Nikolai Kulbin and the Union of Youth: A History of the St. Petersburg Avant-Garde, 1908–1914', unpublished PhD Thesis, University of St Andrews, 1990.

R. Hughes, *The Shock of the New: Art and the Century of Change*, BBC Publications, London 1980.

E. W. Hullinger, *The Reforging of Russia*, H. F. & G. Witherby, London and New York 1925.

R. Hunt, 'For Factography!' *Studio International*, Vol 191, no 980, March/April 1976, pp 96–9.

M. Hyde, *Stalin, the History of a Dictator*, Rupert Hart-Davis, London 1971.

In Search for New Horizons (intro V. Riabov), Leningrad, 1986.

Institut Khudozhvestennoi Kultury v Moskve (INKhUK) pri otdele IZO NKP. Sktematicheskaya programma V.V. Kandinskogo, Moscow 1920.

L. Ivanova et al, *Kulturnaya zhizn v SSSR, 1917–1927*, Moscow 1975.

Iz istorii khudozhestvennoi zhizn SSSR: Internatsionalnye svyazi v oblasti izobrazitelnogo iskusstva, 1917–1940: materiali i dokumenti (L. S. Aleshina and N. V. Yavorskaya, eds), Moscow 1987.

R. Jackson, 'The Generation that Squandered its Poets', in J. Ehrmann (ed), *Literature and Revolution* (Yale French Studies), Boston 1970.

R. Jackson, 'On Realism in Art', in L. Matejka and K. Pomorska (eds), *Readings in Russian Poetics*, MIT Press, Cambridge, Massachusetts and London 1971.

C. V. James, *Soviet Socialist Realism, Origins and Theory*, Macmillan, London and Basingstoke 1973.

F. Jameson, *The Prison-House of Language: A Critical Account of Structuralism and Russian Formalism*, Princeton University Press, Princeton, New Jersey 1972.

K. Jowitt, *Revolutionary Breakthroughs and National Development*, University of California Press, Berkeley and Los Angeles, 1971.

L. Kaganovich, *Socialist Reconstruction of Moscow & Other Cities in the USSR*, New York, n.d.

G. Kaizer, *Dramy*, Moscow–Leningrad 1923.

W. Kandinsky, *Concerning the Spiritual in Art*, 1912; in K. Lindsay and P. Vergo (eds), *Kandinsky's Complete Writings*, 2 Vols, Faber and Faber, London 1982.

F. I. Kaplan, 'The Origins and Functions of Subbotniks and Vokresniks', *Tahrbucher für Gesohrchte Osteuropas*, 13, no 1, 1965, pp 30–9.

G. Karginov, *Rodchenko*, Budapest 1975; Thames and Hudson, London 1979.

A. Karlgren, *Bolshevist Russia* (trans A. Barwell), George Allen and Unwin, London 1927.

Katalog vystavki proizvedenii Gustava Klyutsisa, Riga 1970.

A. Kaun, *Soviet Poets and Poetry*, University of California Press, Berkeley and Los Angeles, Berkeley 1943.

B. W. Kean, *All the Empty Palaces: the Merchant Patrons of Modern Art in Pre-Revolutionary Russia*, Barrie and Jenkins, London 1983.

P. Kerzhentsev, *Tvorcheskii teatr*, Moscow 1919.

P. Kerzhentsev, *Printsipy organizatsii*, Moscow 1924.

S. O. Khan-Magomedov, 'Creative Trends, 1917–1932 in Russia', *Architectural Design*, no 40, February 1970, pp 71–6.

S. O. Khan-Magomedov, *Rodchenko: The Complete Work*, Thames and Hudson, London 1986.

S. O. Khan-Magomedov, *Pioneers of Soviet Architecture, The Search for New Solutions in the 1920s and 1930s*, Thames and Hudson, London 1987.

N. I. Khardzhiyev, *Istorii russkogo avantgarda*, Stockholm 1976.

N. Khrushchev, *Khrushchev Remembers* (intro E. Crankshaw), André Deutsch, London 1971.

Khudozhniki gruppi 'Trinadtsat': Iz istorii khudozhestvennoi zhizni 1920–1930 godov, Moscow 1986.

V. Kirschon, *Bread* (trans S. Volochova) in E. Lyons (ed), *Six Soviet Plays*, 1934.

V. Kniazeva, *AKhRR: Assotsiatsiya Khudozhnikov Revolyutsionnoi Rossii*, Leningrad 1967.

W. Kolarz, *How Russia is Ruled*, Batchworth Press, London 1953.

V. Konashevits, Moscow 1988.

A. Kopp, *Town and Revolution, Soviet Architecture and City Planning, 1917–1935*, Thames and Hudson, London and New York 1970.

A. Kopp, *Constructivist Architecture in the USSR*, Academy Editions, London and St Martins Press, New York 1985.

V. Kostin, *K. S. Petrov-Vodkin*, Moscow 1966.

V. Kostin, *OST*, Moscow 1976.

G. Kozintsev, G. Kryzhitsky, L. Tranberg and S. Yutkevich, 'Eccentrism', *The Drama Review*, Vol 19, no 4, December 1975, pp 95–109.

G. Kozintsev, *Sobranie sochinenie*, Leningrad 1982–6, 3 Vols.

V. Kravchenko, *I Chose Freedom: the personal and political life of a Soviet official*, Hale, London 1947.

S. Krebs, *Soviet Composers and the Development of Soviet Music*, George Allen and Unwin, London 1970.

N. Kruchonykh, *Victory Over the Sun*, 1913 (trans E. Bartos and V. Kirby), *The Drama Review*, Fall 1971, pp 107–25.

N. Krupskaya, *Memories of Lenin* (Moscow 1930), London, n.d.

G. Kucherenko, *Estafeta traditsii: Grekovtsy*, Moscow 1975.

'Kunst in die Production!' Sowjetische Kunst wahrend der Phase der Kollektivierung und Industrialisierung, 1927–33 (exhibition catalogue), Neue Gesellschaft für Bildende Kunst, Berlin 1977.

A. Kurella, *The Five Year Plan and the Cultural Revolution*, Modern Books, London 1930.

L. Labedz (ed), *Revisionism: Essays on the History of Marxist Ideas*, Praeger, New York 1962.

Asja Lacis, *Revolutionär im Beruf*, Rogner & Bernard, Munich 1971.

D. Laing, *The Marxist Theory of Art*, Harvester Press, Sussex 1978.

G. Lansbury, *What I Saw in Russia*, Leonard Press, London 1920.

A. Law, 'Interview with Vladimir Stenberg', *Art Journal*, Fall 1982.

A. Lebedev (ed), *Soviet Painting in the Treyyakov Gallery*, Leningrad 1976.

LEF, 1923–25 (reprint edition), Mouton, The Hague 1970.

H. Lehmann-Haupt, *Art Under a Dictatorship*, Oxford University Press, New York 1954.

L. T. Lemon and M. J. Reis (eds), *Russian Formalist Criticism: Four Essays*, University of Nebraska, Nebraska 1965.

V. I. Lenin, *Polnoe sobranie sochineniya*, 55 Vols, Izdatelstvo Politicheskoi Literatury, Moscow 1967.

V. I. Lenin, 'On Cooperation', *Pravda*, no 115, 26 May 1923, and no 116, 27 May 1923; *Soviet Weekly*, 23 April 1988, p 9.

V. I. Lenin, *Collected Works*, 45 Vols, Lawrence & Wishart, London 1960–70.

V.I. Lenin, *'Left Wing' Communism, an Infantile Disorder*, Collected Works, Vol 31.

V. I. Lenin i A. V. Lunacharsky, Perepiska, doklady, dokumenty, Izdatelstvo Nauka, Moscow 1971.

Lenin on Culture and Cultural Revolution, Progress Publishers, Moscow 1966.

Lenin on Literature and Art, Progress Publishers, Moscow 1967.

M. Lentulova, *Khudozhnik Aristarkh Lentulov*, Moscow 1969.

I. D. Levin, 'The Collision of Meanings: the Poetic Language of Daniel Kharms and Alexander Vvedenski', PhD thesis, University of Texas, 1986.

I. D. Levin, 'The Fifth Meaning of the Motor-Car: Malevich and the Oberiuty', *Soviet Union/Union Sovietique*, 5, Pt 2, 1978, pp 286–300.

M. Lewin, *Russian Peasants and Soviet Power: A Study in Collectivisation*, George Allen and Unwin, London 1968.

M. Lewin, *Lenin's Last Struggle*, Faber & Faber, New York and London 1968.

J. Leyda, *Kino: A History of Russian and Soviet Film*, George Allen and Unwin, London and New York 1960.

A. Lezhrev, *Vosprosy Literatury i Kritiki*, Moscow-Leningrad 1926.

A. Lezhnev and D. Gorbov, *Literatura Revolyutsionnogo desyatiletiya 1917–1927*, Moscow 1929.

I. Libedinsky, *A Week* (intro A. Ransome), Huebsch, New York 1929.

S. Lieberstein, 'Technology, Work and Sociology in the USSR: the NOT Movement', *Technology and Culture*, January 1975, pp 61–4.

M. Lifshitz, *The Philosophy of Art of Karl Marx* (trans R. B. Winn), New York 1938.

K. Lindsay and R. Vergo (eds), *Kandinsky's Complete Writings*, 2 Vols, Faber and Faber, London 1982.

E. Lissitsky, *Russia: An Architecture for World Revolution* (1930), Lund Humphries, London 1979 (trans E. Dluhosch).

V. Lobanov, *Khudozhestvennye gruppirovki za poslednie 25 let*, Moscow 1930.

C. Lodder, *Russian Constructivism*, Yale University Press, New Haven and London 1983.

C. Lodder, 'Lenin's Plan of Monumental Propaganda', *Sbornik: nos 6–7; Study Group on the Russian Revolution*, Leeds 1981, pp 67–84.

K. London, *The Seven Soviet Arts*, Faber and Faber, London 1937.

R. Lorenz (ed), *Proletarische Kulturrevolution in Sowjetrussland, 1917–1921 Dokumente des 'Proletkult'*, Deutscher Taschenbuch Verlag, Munich 1969.

G. K. Loukowski, *History of Modern Russian Painting, 1840–1940*, London 1945.

L. Lozowick, *Modern Russian Art*, Société Anonyme, New York 1925.

N. Luker (ed & intro), *From Furmanov to Sholokhov: An Anthology of the Classics of Socialist Realism*, Ardis Books, Ann Arbor, Michigan 1988.

A. V. Lunacharsky, 'Working-Class Culture', *Plebs Magazine*, October/November 1920.

A. V. Lunacharsky, *O teatre i dramaturgy*, Moscow 1958.

A. V. Lunacharsky, *Revolutionary Silhouettes* (1923) (trans Michael Glenny), Allen Lane, The Penguin Press, London 1967.

A. V. Lunacharsky, 'Gogol-Meyerhold's *The Inspector General*', *Novy Mir*, no 2, 1927; *October*, 7, Winter 1978, pp 57–70.

A. V. Lunacharsky, *On Literature and Art*, Progress Publishers, Moscow 1965.

N. Lynton, *The Story of Modern Art*, Phaidon Press, Oxford 1980.

E. Lyons (ed), *Six Soviet Plays*, Boston 1934.

M. McCaulay, *Stalin and Stalinism*, Longman, London 1983.

F. A. Mackenzie, *Russia before Dawn*, T. Fisher Unwin, London 1923.

R. Maguire, *Red Virgin Soil: Soviet Literature in the 1920s*, Princeton University Press, Princeton, New Jersey 1968.

H. Mclean Jr, 'Voronsky and VAPP', *American Slavic and East European Review*, VIII, no 3, October 1949, pp 185–200.

J. McClelland, 'Utopian versus Revolutionary Heroism in Bolshevik Policy: The Proletarian Culture Debate', *Slavic Review*, no 3, Sept 1980.

C. S. Maier, 'Between Taylorism and Technology: European Ideologies and the Vision of Industrial Productivity in the 1920s', *Journal of Contemporary History*, no 5, 1970, pp 27–61.

K. S. Malevich, 'From 1/42, Notes', in T. Anderson (ed), *Writings*, Vol II, 1966.

K. S. Malevich, *Essays on Art, 1915–1928* Vols I–III (ed. T. Andersen), Rapp and Whiting/André Deutsch 1967–9.

K. S. Malevich, *The Artist, Infinity and Suprematism: Unpublished Writings 1913–1933*, Vol IV (ed. T. Andersen), Borgen Forlag, Copenhagen 1978.

K. Malevich, 'Autobiography', *October*, 34, Fall 1985, pp 25–44.

Malevich, compiled by T. Anderson, Stedelijk Museum, Amsterdam 1970.

N. Mandelstam, *Hope against Hope*, Collins and Harvill Press, London 1971.

N. Mandelstam, *Hope Abandoned*, Collins and Harvill Press, London 1974.

V. Markov, *Russian Futurism, A History*, University of California Press, Berkeley, California 1968; MacGibbon and Kee, London 1969.

V. Markov and M. Sparks (eds), *Modern Russian Poetry: An Anthology with Verse Translations*, MacGibbon and Kee, London 1966.

H. Marshall, *Mayakovsky and his Poetry*, Pilot Press, London 1945.

K. Marx and F. Engels, *The Communist Manifesto, 1848*, Penguin Books, Harmondsworth 1967.

K. Marx and F. Engels, *Selected Correspondence*, Moscow 1965.

L. Matejka and K. Pomorska (eds), *Readings in Russian Poetics*, MIT Press, Cambridge, Massachusetts and London 1971.

R. W. Mathewson, *The Positive Hero in Russian Literature*, Columbia University Press, New York 1958.

I. Matsa (ed), *Sovetskoe iskusstvo za 15 let. materialy i dokumentatsiya*, Moscow–Leningrad 1933.

V. V. Mayakovsky, *The Bed Bug* (trans M. Hayward, intro P. Blake), in M. V. Glenny, *Three Soviet Plays*, Penguin Books, Harmondsworth 1966.

V. Mayakovsky, *Plays, Articles, Essays*, Vol 3 of *Selected Works in Three Volumes*, Raduga Publishers, Moscow 1987.

T. Maynard, *Before October*, Victor Gollancz, London 1941.

T. Maynard, *The Russian Peasant and Other Studies*, Victor Gollancz 1943.

M. Mead, *Soviet Attitudes to Authority*, McGraw-Hill Book Co, New York 1951.

R. Medvedev, *All Stalin's Men*, Basil Blackwell, Oxford 1983.

F. Meyer, *Marc Chagall*, Thames and Hudson, London 1974.

P. Miliukov, *Outlines of Russian Culture, II: Literature in Russia* (trans V. Ughel and E. Davis, ed M. Karpovich), University of Philadelphia Press, Philadelphia 1942.

N. Miliutin, *Sotsgorod: the Construction of Socialist Cities*, MIT Press, Cambridge, Massachusetts 1975.

H. Millon and L. Nochlin (eds), *Art and Architecture in the Service of Politics*, MIT Press, Cambridge, Massachusetts and London 1978.

J. Milner, *Russian Revolutionary Art*, Yale University Press, New Haven and London 1979.

R. Milner-Gulland, 'Left Art in Leningrad: the OBERIU Declaration', *Oxford Slavonic Papers*, new series, Oxford 1970, Vol 3, pp 65–75.

R. Milner-Gulland, 'Tower and Dome: Two Revolutionary Buildings', *Slavic Review*, Spring 1988, pp 39–50.

N. Misler and J. Bowlt, *Pavel Filonov: A Hero and His Fate*, Silvergirl, Austin 1983.

S. Mitchell, 'From Shklovsky to Brecht, Some preliminary remarks towards a history of the politicisation of Russian Formalism', *Screen*, Vol XV, no 2, Summer 1944, pp 74–81.

S. Morawski, 'Lenin as a Literary Theorist', *Science & Society*, XXIX, Winter 1965, pp 1–25.

E. Murina, *Aristakh Lentulov – 1882–1943*, Sovietski Khudozhnik, Moscow 1988 (catalogue to the Venice Biennale, Soviet Pavilion, 1988).

A. B. Nakov, 'Dada Russland', *Tendenzen der Zwanzige Yahre*, Berlin 1977, Section 3, pp 96–9.

A. B. Nakov, 'Rodchenko's "The Line"', *Arts Magazine*, Vol 47, no 7, 1973, pp 50–2.

S. Nearmy, *Education in Soviet Russia*, International Publishers, New York 1926.

M. Neiman, *Petr Konchalovsky*, Moscow 1967.

J. P. Nettl, *The Soviet Achievement*, Thames and Hudson, London 1967.

E. Neuman, 'Russia's Leftist Art in Berlin, 1922', *Art Journal*, Vol 27, no 1, 1967.

N. A. Nilsson (ed), *Art, Society, Revolution: Russia 1917–1921*, Stockholm 1979.

A. Nove, 'Was Stalin Really Necessary?', *Encounter*, April 1962.

A. Nove, *An Economic History of the USSR*, Allen Lane, the Penguin Press, London 1969.

Novy LEF, 1927–28 (reprint edition), Mouton, The Hague 1970.

L. Oginskaya, *Gustav Klutsis*, Moscow 1981.

I. Olesha, *Envy*, 1927 (trans P. Ross), Westhouse, London 1947.

C. Osman (ed), 'Rodchenko: Aesthetic, Autobiographical and Ideological Writings', *Camera International Yearbook*, London 1978.

Paris–Moscow 1900–1930 (catalogue), Centre Georges Pompidou, Paris 1979.

G. Z. Patrick, *Popular Poetry in Soviet Russia*, University of California Press, Berkeley 1929.

E. and C. Paul, *Proletkult* (no publisher stated) New Era Series Vol 12, London 1921.

V. N. Perelman (ed), *Borba za realizm: v izobrazitelnom iskusstve 20kh godov: materiali, dokumenti, vospominaniya*, Moscow 1962.

K. Petrov-Vodkin, *Khilinovsk*, Leningrad 1930.

K. Petrov-Vodkin, *Prostranstvo Evklida*, Leningrad 1970.

E. Piscator, *Political Theatre 1920–1966*, exhibition catalogue, London 1971.

Plastyka radziecka sztuka okresu pierwszych pieciolatek 1930–41 (Soviet art of the early Five-Year Plans) (exhibition catalogue), Warsaw 1983.

G. V. Plekhanov, *Art and Social Life*, Lawrence and Wishart, London 1912.

M. Pleynet, 'The Left Front of the Arts', *Screen*, I, XIII, 1972.

O. Podobedova, *Igor Emmaniulovich Grabar*, Moscow 1965.

G. Poppoff, *The Tcheka: The Red Inquisition*, A. M. Philpot Ltd, London 1925.

Y. Prokushev, *Sergei Esenin: the Man, the Verse, the Age*, Moscow 1979.

Protokoly pervoi vserrossiiskoi konferentsii proletarskikh kulturno-prosvetitelnykh organizatsii, 15–20 Sept, 1918, Moscow 1918.

N. Punin, *Pervyi tsikl lektsii*, Petrograd 1920.

S. Radlov, *Futurism*, Petersburg 1923.

S. Radlov, 'On the Pure Elements of the Actor's Art', *The Drama Review*, Vol 19, no 4, December 1975, pp 117–23.

A. Ransom, *Six Weeks in Russia 1919*, G. Allen and Vernon, London 1919.

G. Reavey (ed), *Modern Soviet Short Stories*, Grosset and Dunlop, New York 1961.

G. Reavey and M. Slonim (eds), *Soviet Literature: An Anthology*, Wishart and Co, London 1933.

I. Repin, *Dalekoe Blizkoe*, Moscow 1937.

The Russian Art Exhibition (intro I. Grabar), New York 1924.

T. H. Rigby, 'Staffing Incorporated: The Origins of the Nomenklatura System', *Soviet Studies*, Vol XL, no 4, October 1988, pp 523–37.

T. H. Rigby, *Lenin's Government: Sovnarkorn, 1917–22*, Cambridge University Press, Cambridge 1979.

T. Riha (ed), *Readings in Russian Civilisation*, University of Chicago Press, Chicago and London 1964.

L. Robel (trans), *Manifestes Futuristes Russes*, Les Editeurs Français Reunis, Paris 1972.

S. Rodov, *V Literaturnykh Boyakh: Stati, Zametki, Dokumenty, 1922–25*, Moscow 1926.

P. Romanov, *Three Pairs of Silk Stockings: a Novel of the Life of the Educated Class under the Soviet* (trans L. Zarine, ed S. Graham), Ernest Benn, London 1931.

W. Rosenberg (ed), *Bolshevik Visions, First Phase of the Cultural Revolution in Soviet Russia*, Ardis, Ann Arbor, Michigan 1984.

A. Rosmer, *Moscou sous Lenine* (translated as *Lenin's Moscow*), Bookmarks, London, Chicago and Melbourne 1971).

R. A. Rothstein, 'The Quiet Rehabilitation of the Brick Factory: Early Soviet Popular Music and its Critics', *Slavic Review*, no 3, September 1980.

M. Rowell and A. Z. Rudenstine, *Art of the Avant-Garde in Russia: Selections from the George Costakis Collection*, Solomon R. Guggenheim Museum, New York 1981.

K. Rudnitsky, *Russian and Soviet Theatre: Tradition and the Avant-Garde* (trans R. Permar), Thames and Hudson, London 1988.

K. Rudnitsky, *Meyerhold, The Director* (trans G. Petrov, ed S. Schultze), Ardis, Ann Arbor, Michigan 1981.

Y. Rusakov, *Petrov-Vodkin*, Moscow 1975.

Russian and Soviet Painting (trans and intro by J. E. Bowlt), Metropolitan Museum of Art, New York 1977.

Russian Avant-Garde Art: The George Costakis Collection (ed A. Rudenstine), Thames and Hudson, London 1971.

Russian Constructivism Revisited (exhibition catalogue), the Hatton Gallery, Newcastle upon Tyne 1974.

H. Salisbury, *Russia in Revolution, 1900–1930*, Deutsch, London and New York 1978.

A. Salmon, *Art Russe Moderne*, Paris 1928.

D. Sarabianov, *Russian Painters of the Early Twentieth Century, New Trends*, Aurora Art Publishers, Leningrad 1973.

D. Sarabianov, *Robert Falk*, Dresden 1974.

L. Schapiro, *The Communist Party of the Soviet Union*, Methuen, London 1963 (first edition).

L. Schapiro, 'Trotsky, wie er eigentlich gewesen', *Government and Opposition*, Vol 17, no 3, 1982, pp 259–67.

L. and J. Schnitzer and M. Martin, *Cinema in Revolution. The Heroic Era of Soviet Film*, Secker and Warburg, London 1973.

B. Schwarz, *Music and Musical Life in Soviet Russia, 1917–1970*, W. W. Norton and Co, New York 1972.

J. Scott, *Behind the Urals*, Cambridge, Massachusetts 1942, Indiana University Press, Bloomington and London 1973.

J. Scott, 'A Day in Magnitogorsk', in T. Riha (ed), *Readings in Russian Civilisation*, Chicago and London 1964, pp 574–92.

A. Senkevich, *Soviet Architecture, 1917–62: a bibliographical guide to source material*, University Press of Virginia, Charlottesville 1974.

R. Serdel, 4 articles on Proletkult in *Volksbuhne*, no 3, vol 1, 1920–1.

V. Serge, *Memoirs of a Revolutionary, 1901–1941*, Oxford University Press, London 1963.

V. Serge, 'Is a Proletarian Literature Possible?' (1925), in J. Ehrmann (ed), *Literature and Revolution*, Yale French Studies, Boston 1970.

R. Sherwood, 'Introduction to *LEF*: Journal of the Left Front of the Arts', *Form*, Cambridge, October 1969.

R. Sherwood (trans and intro) 'Documents from LEF', *Screen* 4, Vol XII, Winter 1971/2, pp 25–100.

V. Shklovsky, *A Sentimental Journey. Memoirs, 1917–1922* (trans R. Sheldon), Cornell University Press, Ithaca and London 1970.

V. Shklovsky, *Mayakovsky and His Circle* (trans and ed L. Feiler), Pluto Press, London 1974.

M. Sholokhov, *Virgin Soil Upturned*, Moscow, n.d.

D. Shub, *Lenin*, 1948 (Penguin Books, Harmondsworth, 1966 edition).

G. Shudakov, O. Suslova, L. U. Khtomskaya, *Pioneers of Soviet Photography*, Thames and Hudson, London 1983.

O. Shvidkovsky, et al, *Building in the USSR, 1917–1932*, Studio Vista, London 1971.

P. N. Siegel (ed), *Leon Trotsky on Literature and Art*, Pathfinder Press, New York, 1970.

K. Silver, 'Straightening Up After the War', *Artforum* 1977.

W. S. Simmons, 'The Step Beyond: Malevich and the KA'. *Soviet Union/Union Sovietique*, 5, pt 2, 1978, pp 149–70.

K. A. Sitnik, *Nikolai Alekseyevich Kasatakin: his life and work*, Moscow 1955.

M. Skolee, 'Homeless children in the USSR: 1917–1957', *Soviet Studies*, January 1988, pp 64–83.

M. Slonim, *Soviet Russian Literature, Writers and Problems, 1917–1967*, Oxford University Press, New York 1964.

N. Slonimsky, 'Soviet Music and Musicians', *The Slavonic and East European Review*, Vol 22, Dec 1944, pp 1–19.

A. Solzhenitsyn, *Lenin in Zurich*, Bodley Head, London 1976 (also Farrar Strauss and Giroux, New York 1976).

B. Souvarine, *Stalin, A Critical History of Bolshevism*, Secker and Warburg, London, n.d.

Sovetskoe iskusstvo 20-30-kh godov, Iskusstvo, Leningrad 1988.

J. Stalin, *Problems of Leninism*, Moscow 1947.

J. Stalin, *Works*, 13 Vols, Foreign Languages Publishing House, Moscow 1950.

J. Stalin, *Sochineniya*, 13 Vols, Gosudarstvennoe izatelstvo politicheskoi literatury, Moscow, 1946–51.

K. Stanislavksy, *Sobranie sochinenii*, Moscow 1954–61.

H. Stephan, '*Lef* and the Left Front of the Arts', Verlag Otto Sagner, Munich 1981.

G. Struve, *Soviet Russian Literature 1917–50*, University of Oklahoma Press, Norman, Oklahoma 1951.

J. Tagg, 'The idea of the avant-garde' in B. Taylor (ed), *Art and Politics*, Winchester School of Art Press, Winchester 1979, pp 88–100.

N. Tarabukin, *Ot molberta k mashine*, Moscow 1923 (French edition, *Le Dernier Tableau*, Paris 1972).

V. Tatlin and S. Dymshits-Tolstaya, 'Memorandum from the Visual Arts Section of the People's Commissariat for Enlightenment to the Soviet of People's Commissars: Project for the Organisation of Competitions for Monuments to Distinguished Persons' (*Izvestiya VTsIK*, no 155, 24 July 1918, Moscow), translated and introduced by J. E. Bowlt, *Design Issues*, Vol 1, no 2, Fall 1984, pp 70–4.

B. Taylor (ed), *Art and Politics*, Winchester School of Art, Winchester 1979.

B. Taylor, 'Two Soviet Exhibitions', *Art Monthly*, no 115, April 1988, pp 8–9.

B. Taylor, 'Russians on the Road', *Art in America*, October 1988, pp 32–47.

R. Taylor, 'A Medium for the Masses: Agitation in the Soviet Civil War', *Soviet Studies*, 22, 4, April 1971, pp 62–75.

R. Taylor (ed), *Eisenstein Writing, 1922–1934*, BFI, London 1987.

A. Tertz (A. D. Sinyavsky), *On Socialist Realism* (trans G. Dennis), Pantheon, New York 1960.

A. Tertz (A. D. Sinyavsky) *The Trial Begins* (trans M. Hayward), Collins and Harvill, London 1960.

B. Thomson, *The Premature Revolution: Russian Literature & Study, 1917–46*, Weidenfeld and Nicolson, London 1972.

B. Thomson, *Lot's Wife and the Venus of Milo: Attitudes to the Cultural Heritage in Modern Russia*, Cambridge University Press, Cambridge 1978.

Tradition and Revolution in Russian Art (catalogue), Cornerhouse Publications, Manchester 1990.

L. Trotsky, *My Life; An Attempt at Autobiography*, Scribner, New York 1930.

L. Trotsky, *The Revolution Betrayed* (trans M. Eastman), Doubleday, Doran & Co, Garden City 1937.

L. Trotsky, *Stalin: An Appraisal of the Man & his Influence* (trans C. Malamuth), Hollis and Carter Ltd, London 1947.

L. Trotsky, *Literature and Revolution* (Moscow 1923), Ann Arbor, Michigan 1966.

L. Trotsky, *The History of the Russian Revolution* (trans M. Eastman), Sphere Books, London 1967.

L. Trotsky, *Writings of Leon Trotsky, 1929–40*, 12 Vols, Pathfinder Press, New York 1969–72.

L. Trotsky, *On Literature and Art* (ed and intro P. Siegel), Pathfinder Press, New York 1970.

L. Trotsky, *On Lenin: Notes Towards a Biography* (1924), George Harrap & Co, London 1971.

L. Trotsky, *Problems of Everyday Life: and Other Writings on Culture and Science*, Monad Press, New York 1973.

L. Trotsky, *The Class Nature of the Soviet State: The Workers' State and the Question of Thermidor and Bonapartism*, New Park Publishers, London 1973.

R. Tucker, *Stalin As Revolutionary, 1879–1929, A Study in History and Personality*, Chatto and Windus, London 1974.

R. Tucker (ed), *Stalinism: Essays in Historical Interpretation*, W. W. Norton and Co, New York 1977.

K. Umansky, *Neue Kunst in Russland*, Potsdam, Munich 1920.

P. Unger, 'Party and State in Soviet Russia and Nazi Germany', in C. Emsley (ed), *Conflict and Stability in Europe*, London 1979.

S. V. Utechin, 'Bolsheviks and their Allies after 1917: The Ideological Pattern', *Soviet Studies*, 10, no 2, October 1958, pp 113–35.

S. V. Utechin, 'Philosophy and Society: Alexander Bogdanov', in L. Labedz (ed), *Revisionism: Essays on the History of Marxist Ideas*, 1962, pp 117–25.

Utopies et réalités en URSS, 1917–1934: Agit Prop, Design, Architecture (catalogue), Centre Georges Pompidou, Paris 1980.

A. Vaksberg, 'Vyshinsky', *The Literary Gazette*, Moscow, Vol 1, no 1, 3 June 1988, pp 37–8, 40–1.

N. Valentinov (N. N. Volsky), *Encounters with Lenin*, Oxford University Press, London 1968.

E. Valkenier, *Russian Realist Art: The Peredvizhniki and their Tradition*, Ardis, Ann Arbor, Michigan 1977.

I. Vardin, *Kvoprosu o politike RKP(b) v khudozhestvennoi i literature*, Moscow 1924.

Vasilii Chekrygin (exhibition catalogue), Pushkin Museum, Moscow 1969.

A. Voronsky, *Proletariat and Literature*, Foreign Languages Publishing House, Moscow 1927.

K. Voroshilov, *Stalin and the Red Army*, Moscow 1941.

M. Voslensky, *Nomenklatura: Anatomy of the Soviet Ruling Class*, Bodley Head, London 1980.

Vystavki sovetskogo izobrazitelnogo iskusstvo, spravochnik, Vol I, Moscow 1965.

G. Weisberg (ed), *The European Realist Tradition*, Indiana University Press, Indiana 1982.

H. G. Wells, *Russia in the Shadows*, Hodder and Stoughton, London 1920.

J. Willett, *The New Sobriety, Art and Politics in the Weimar Republic, 1917–1933*, Thames and Hudson, London 1978.

R. C. Williams, *Artists in Revolution, Portraits of the Russian Avant Garde, 1905–1925*, Scolar Press, London 1977.

R. C. Williams, 'Collective Immortality: The Syndicalist Origins of Proletarian Culture, 1905–1910', *Slavic Review*, no 3, September 1980, pp 389–402.

R. C. Williams, *Russian Art & American Money, 1900–1940*, MIT Press, Cambridge, Massachusetts, and London 1980.

P. Wollen, 'Art in Revolution: Russian Art in the Twenties', *Studio International*, Vol 181, no 932, April 1971, pp 149–54.

N. Worrall, *Modernism to Realism on the Soviet Stage: Tairov, Vakhtangov, Okhlopkov*, Cambridge University Press, Cambridge 1989.

A. Yarmolinsky, *Two Centuries of Russian Verse: An Anthology from Lomonosov to Voznesensky*, Random House, New York 1966.

Y. Zamyatin, *The Dragon & Other Stories*, Penguin Books, Harmondsworth 1972.

Y. Zamyatin, *We* (1924); trans B. Guerney, Penguin Books, Harmondsworth 1983.

V. Zavalishin, *Early Soviet Writers*, Atlantic Books, New York 1958.

L. Zhadova, *Malevich*, Thames and Hudson, London 1982.

Index